Communications
in Computer and Information Science   937

Commenced Publication in 2007
Founding and Former Series Editors:
Phoebe Chen, Alfredo Cuzzocrea, Xiaoyong Du, Orhun Kara, Ting Liu,
Dominik Ślęzak, and Xiaokang Yang

More information about this series at http://www.springer.com/series/7899

Bee Wah Yap · Azlinah Hj Mohamed
Michael W. Berry (Eds.)

Soft Computing in Data Science

4th International Conference, SCDS 2018
Bangkok, Thailand, August 15–16, 2018
Proceedings

 Springer

Editors
Bee Wah Yap
Faculty of Computer and Mathematical
Sciences
Universiti Teknologi MARA
Shah Alam, Selangor, Malaysia

Michael W. Berry
Department of Electrical Engineering
and Computer Science
University of Tennessee at Knoxville
Knoxville, TN, USA

Azlinah Hj Mohamed
Faculty of Computer and Mathematical
Sciences
Universiti Teknologi MARA
Shah Alam, Selangor, Malaysia

ISSN 1865-0929   ISSN 1865-0937 (electronic)
Communications in Computer and Information Science
ISBN 978-981-13-3440-5   ISBN 978-981-13-3441-2 (eBook)
https://doi.org/10.1007/978-981-13-3441-2

Library of Congress Control Number: 2018962152

This Springer imprint is published by the registered company Springer Nature Singapore Pte Ltd.
The registered company address is: 152 Beach Road, #21-01/04 Gateway East, Singapore 189721, Singapore

Preface

We are pleased to present the proceeding of the 4th International Conference on Soft Computing in Data Science 2018 (SCDS 2018). SCDS 2018 was held in Chulalongkorn University, in Bangkok, Thailand, during August 15–16, 2018. The theme of the conference was "Science in Analytics: Harnessing Data and Simplifying Solutions." SCDS 2018 aimed to provide a platform for highlighting the challenges faced by organizations to harness their enormous data, and for putting forward the availability of advanced technologies and techniques for big data analytics (BDA).

SCDS 2018 provided a platform for discussions on innovative methods and also addressed challenges, problems, and issues in harnessing data to provide useful insights, which results in more impactful decisions and solutions. The role of data science and analytics is significantly increasing in every field from engineering to life sciences, and with advanced computer algorithms, solutions for complex real-life problems can be simplified. For the advancement of society in the twenty-first century, there is a need to transfer knowledge and technology to industrial applications to solve real-world problems that benefit the global community. Research collaborations between academia and industry can lead to the advancement of useful analytics and computing applications to facilitate real-time insights and solutions.

We were delighted to collaborate with the esteemed Chulalongkorn University this year, and this increased the submissions from a diverse group of national and international researchers. We received 75 paper submissions, among which 30 were accepted. SCDS 2018 utilized a double-blind review procedure. All accepted submissions were assigned to at least three independent reviewers (at least one international reviewer) in order to ensure a rigorous, thorough, and convincing evaluation process. A total of 36 international and 65 local reviewers were involved in the review process. The conference proceeding volume editors and Springer's CCIS Editorial Board made the final decisions on acceptance with 30 of the 75 submisssions (40%) published in the conference proceedings. Machine learning using LDA (Latent Dirichlet Allocation) was used on the abstracts to define the track sessions.

We would like to thank the authors who submitted manuscripts to SCDS 2018. We thank the reviewers for voluntarily spending time to review the papers. We thank all conference committee members for their tremendous time, ideas, and efforts in ensuring the success of SCDS 2018. We also wish to thank the Springer CCIS Editorial Board and the various organizations and sponsors for their continuous support. We sincerely hope that SCDS 2018 provided a venue for knowledge sharing, publication of good research findings, and new research collaborations. Last but not least, we hope everyone benefited from the keynote and parallel sessions, and had an enjoyable and memorable experience at SCDS 2018 in Bangkok, Thailand.

August 2018   Bee Wah Yap
                                                                        Azlinah Hj. Mohamed
                                                                        Michael W. Berry

Organization

Patron

Hassan Said   Universiti Teknologi MARA, Malaysia
  (Vice-chancellor)

Honorary Chairs

Azlinah Mohamed   Universiti Teknologi MARA, Malaysia
Kritsana Neammanee   Chulalongkorn University, Thailand
Michael W. Berry   University of Tennessee, USA
Yasmin Mahmood   Malaysia Digital Economy Corporation, Malaysia
Fazel Famili   University of Ottawa, Canada
Mario Koppen   Kyushu Institute of Technology, Japan

Conference Chairs

Yap Bee Wah   Universiti Teknologi MARA, Malaysia
Chidchanok Lursinsap   Chulalongkorn University, Thailand

Secretary

Siti Shaliza Mohd Khairy   Universiti Teknologi MARA, Malaysia

Secretariat

Shahrul Aina Abu Bakar   Universiti Teknologi MARA, Malaysia
Amirahudin Jamaludin   Universiti Teknologi MARA, Malaysia
Norkhalidah Mohd Aini   Universiti Teknologi MARA, Malaysia

Finance Committee

Sharifah Aliman (Chair)   Universiti Teknologi MARA, Malaysia
Nur Huda Nabihan Shaari   Universiti Teknologi MARA, Malaysia
Azizah Samsudin   Universiti Teknologi MARA, Malaysia

Technical Program Committee

Dhiya Al-Jumeily   Liverpool John Moores University, UK
Marina Yusoff (Chair)   Universiti Teknologi MARA, Malaysia
Muthukkaruppan   Universiti Teknologi MARA, Malaysia
  Annamalai

| Peraphon Sophatsathit | Chulalongkorn University, Thailand |
| Maryam Khanian | Universiti Teknologi MARA, Malaysia |

Registration Committee

Monnat Pongpanich (Chair)	Chulalongkorn University, Thailand
Somjai Boonsiri	Chulalongkorn University, Thailand
Athipat Thamrongthanyalak	Chulalongkorn University, Thailand
Darunee Sawangdee	Chulalongkorn University, Thailand
Azlin Ahmad	Universiti Teknologi MARA, Malaysia
Ezzatul Akmal Kamaru Zaman	Universiti Teknologi MARA, Malaysia
Nur Aziean Mohd Idris	Universiti Teknologi MARA, Malaysia

Sponsorship Committee

Nuru'l-'Izzah Othman (Chair)	Universiti Teknologi MARA, Malaysia
Haryani Haron	Universiti Teknologi MARA, Malaysia
Norhayati Shuja'	Jabatan Perangkaan Malaysia
Saiful Farik Mat Yatin	Universiti Teknologi MARA, Malaysia
Vasana Sukkrasanti	Chulalongkorn University, Thailand
Sasipa Panthuwadeethorn	Chulalongkorn University, Thailand

Publication Committee (Program Book)

Nur Atiqah Sia Abdullah (Chair)	Universiti Teknologi MARA, Malaysia
Marshima Mohd Rosli	Universiti Teknologi MARA, Malaysia
Zainura Idrus	Universiti Teknologi MARA, Malaysia
Muhamad Khairil Rosli	Universiti Teknologi MARA, Malaysia
Thap Panitanarak	Chulalongkorn University, Thailand
Dittaya Wanvarie	Chulalongkorn University, Thailand

Website Committee

| Mohamad Asyraf Abdul Latif | Universiti Teknologi MARA, Malaysia |
| Muhamad Ridwan Mansor | Universiti Teknologi MARA, Malaysia |

Publicity and Corporate Committee

Azlin Ahmad (Chair)	Universiti Teknologi MARA, Malaysia
Ezzatul Akmal Kamaru Zaman	Universiti Teknologi MARA, Malaysia
Nur Aziean Mohd Idris	Universiti Teknologi MARA, Malaysia

Chew XinYing	Universiti Sains Malaysia
Saranya Maneeroj	Chulalongkorn University, Thailand
Suphakant Phimoltares	Chulalongkorn University, Thailand
Jaruloj Chongstitvatana	Chulalongkorn University, Thailand
Arthorn Luangsodsai	Chulalongkorn University, Thailand
Pakawan Pugsee	Chulalongkorn University, Thailand

Media/Photography/Montage Committee

Marina Ismail (Chair)	Universiti Teknologi MARA, Malaysia
Norizan Mat Diah	Universiti Teknologi MARA, Malaysia
Sahifulhamri Sahdi	Universiti Teknologi MARA, Malaysia
Nagul Cooharojananone	Chulalongkorn University, Thailand
Boonyarit Intiyot	Chulalongkorn University, Thailand
Chatchawit Aporntewan	Chulalongkorn University, Thailand

Logistics Committee

Hamdan Abdul Maad (Chair)	Universiti Teknologi MARA, Malaysia
Abdul Jamal Mat Nasir	Universiti Teknologi MARA, Malaysia
Ratinan Boonklurb	Chulalongkorn University, Thailand
Monnat Pongpanich	Chulalongkorn University, Thailand
Sajee Pianskool	Chulalongkorn University, Thailand
Arporntip Sombatboriboon	Chulalongkorn University, Thailand

Conference Workshop Committee

Norhaslinda Kamaruddin (Chair)	Universiti Teknologi MARA, Malaysia
Saidatul Rahah Hamidi	Universiti Teknologi MARA, Malaysia
Sayang Mohd Deni	Universiti Teknologi MARA, Malaysia
Norshahida Shaadan	Universiti Teknologi MARA, Malaysia
Khairul Anuar Mohd Isa	Universiti Teknologi MARA, Malaysia
Richard Millham	Durban University of Technology, South Africa
Simon Fong	University of Macau, SAR China
Jaruloj Chongstitvatana	Chulalongkorn University, Thailand
Chatchawit Aporntewan	Chulalongkorn University, Thailand

International Scientific Committee

Adel Al-Jumaily	University of Technology Sydney, Australia
Chidchanok Lursinsap	Chulalongkorn University, Thailand
Rajalida Lipikorn	Chulalongkorn University, Thailand
Siti Zaleha Zainal Abidin	Universiti Teknologi MARA, Malaysia
Agus Harjoko	Universitas Gadjah Mada, Indonesia

Sri Hartati	Universitas Gadjah Mada, Indonesia
Jasni Mohamad Zain	Universiti Teknologi MARA, Malaysia
Min Chen	Oxford University, UK
Simon Fong	University of Macau, SAR China
Mohammed Bennamoun	University of Western Australia, Australia
Yasue Mitsukura	Keio University, Japan
Dhiya Al-Jumeily	Liverpool John Moores University, UK
Dariusz Krol	Wroclaw University, Poland
Richard Weber	University of Chile, Santiago, Chile
Jose Maria Pena	Technical University of Madrid, Spain
Yusuke Nojima	Osaka Prefecture University, Japan
Siddhivinayak Kulkarni	University of Ballarat, Australia
Tahir Ahmad	Universiti Teknologi Malaysia, Malaysia
Daud Mohamed	Universiti Teknologi MARA, Malaysia
Mazani Manaf	Universiti Teknologi MARA, Malaysia
Sumanta Guha	Asian Institute of Technology, Thailand
Nordin Abu Bakar	Universiti Teknologi MARA, Malaysia
Suhartono	Insititut Teknologi Sepuluh Nopember, Indonesia
Wahyu Wibowo	Insititut Teknologi Sepuluh Nopember, Indonesia
Edi Winarko	Universitas Gadjah Mada, Indonesia
Retantyo Wardoyo	Universitas Gadjah Mada, Indonesia
Soo-Fen Fam	Universiti Teknikal Malaysia Melaka, Malaysia

International Reviewers

Albert Guvenis	Bogazici University, Turkey
Ali Qusay Al-Faris	University of the People, USA
Dariusz Krol	Wroclaw University of Science and Technology, Poland
Dedy Dwi Prastyo	Institut Teknologi Sepuluh Nopember, Indonesia
Deepti Prakash Theng	G. H. Raisoni College of Engineering and RTMNU, India
Dhiya Al-Jumeily	Liverpool John Moores University, UK
Dittaya Wanvarie	Chulalongkorn University, Thailand
Edi Winarko	Universitas Gadjah Mada, Indonesia
Ensar Gul	Istanbul Sehir University, Turkey
Harihar Kalia	Seemanta Engineering College, India
Eng Harish Kumar	King Khalid University, Saudi Arabia
Indika Perera	University of Moratuwa, Sri Lanka
J. Vimala Jayakumar	Alagappa University and Karaikudi, India
Jaruloj Chongstitvatana	Chulalongkorn University, Thailand
Karim Hashim Al-Saedi	University of Mustansiriyah, Iraq
Khairul Anam	University of Jember, Indonesia
Mario Köppen	Kyushu Institute of Technology, Japan
Michael Berry	University of Tennessee, USA
Moulay A. Akhloufi	University of Moncton and Laval University, Canada

Nagul Cooharojananone	Chulalongkorn University, Thailand
Nikisha B Jariwala	Veer Narmad South Gujarat University, India
Noriko Etani	Kyoto University, Japan
Pakawan Pugsee	Chulalongkorn University, Thailand
Retantyo Wardoyo	Universitas Gajah Mada, Indonesia
Richard C. Millham	Durban University of Technology, South Africa
Rodrigo Campos Bortoletto	São Paulo Federal Institute of Education, Brazil
Rohit Gupta	Thapar University, India
Siddhivinayak Kulkarni	Griffith University, Australia
Siripurapu Sridhar	LENDI Institute of Engineering and Technology, India
Sri Hartati	Gadjah Mada University, Indonesia
Suhartono	Institut Teknologi Sepuluh Nopember, Indonesia
Sumanta Guha	Asian Institute of Technology, Thailand
Suphakant Phimoltares	Chulalongkorn University, Thailand
Tri K. Priyambodo	Gadjah Mada University, Indonesia
Wahyu Wibowo	Institut Teknologi Sepuluh Nopember, Indonesia
Widhyakorn Asdornwised	Chulalongkorn University, Thailand

Local Reviewers

Aida Mustapha	Universiti Tun Hussein Onn Malaysia, Malaysia
Angela Siew-Hoong Lee	Sunway University, Malaysia
Asmala Ahmad	Universiti Teknikal Malaysia, Malaysia
Azizi Abdullah	Universiti Kebangsaan Malaysia, Malaysia
Azlan Iqbal	Universiti Tenaga Nasional, Malaysia
Azlin Ahmad	Universiti Teknologi MARA, Malaysia
Azman Taa	Universiti Utara Malaysia, Malaysia
Azree Shahrel Ahmad Nazri	Universiti Putra Malaysia, Malaysia
Bhagwan Das	Universiti Tun Hussein Onn Malaysia, Malaysia
Bong Chih How	Universiti Malaysia Sarawak, Malaysia
Choong-Yeun Liong	Universiti Kebangsaan Malaysia, Malaysia
Ely Salwana	Universiti Kebangsaan Malaysia, Malaysia
Fakariah Hani Hj Mohd Ali	Universiti Teknologi MARA, Malaysia
Hamidah Jantan	Universiti Teknologi MARA, Malaysia
Hamzah Abdul Hamid	Universiti Malaysia Perlis, Malaysia
Izzatdin Abdul Aziz	Universiti Teknologi PETRONAS, Malaysia
Jafreezal Jaafar	Universiti Teknologi PETRONAS, Malaysia
Jasni Mohamad Zain	Universiti Teknologi MARA, Malaysia
Khairil Anuar Md Isa	Universiti Teknologi MARA, Malaysia
Kok-Haur Ng	University of Malaya, Malaysia
Maheran Mohd Jaffar	Universiti Teknologi MARA, Malaysia
Marina Yusoff	Universiti Teknologi MARA, Malaysia
Maryam Khanian	Universiti Teknologi MARA, Malaysia
Mas Rina Mustaffa	Universiti Putra Malaysia, Malaysia
Mashitoh Hashim	Universiti Pendidikan Sultan Idris, Malaysia
Masrah Azrifah	Universiti Putra Malaysia, Malaysia

Mazani Manaf	Universiti Teknologi MARA, Malaysia
Michael Loong Peng Tan	Universiti Teknologi Malaysia, Malaysia
Mohamed Imran Mohamed Ariff	Universiti Teknologi MARA, Malaysia
Mohd Fadzil Hassan	Universiti Teknologi PETRONAS, Malaysia
Mohd Hilmi Hasan	Universiti Teknologi PETRONAS, Malaysia
Mohd Zaki Zakaria	Universiti Teknologi MARA, Malaysia
Mumtaz Mustafa	University of Malaya, Malaysia
Muthukkaruppan Annamalai	Universiti Teknologi MARA, Malaysia
Natrah Abdullah Dolah	Universiti Teknologi MARA, Malaysia
Noor Azilah Muda	Universiti Teknikal Malaysia, Malaysia
Noor Elaiza Abd Khalid	Universiti Teknologi MARA, Malaysia
Nor Fazlida Mohd Sani	Universiti Putra Malaysia, Malaysia
Norshita Mat Nayan	Universiti Kebangsaan Malaysia, Malaysia
Norshuhani Zamin	Universiti Sains Komputer and Kejuruteraan Malaysia, Malaysia
Nur Atiqah Sia Abdullah	Universiti Teknologi MARA, Malaysia
Nursuriati Jamil	Universiti Teknologi MARA, Malaysia
Nuru'l-'Izzah Othman	Universiti Teknologi MARA, Malaysia
Puteri Nor Ellyza Nohuddin	Universiti Kebangsaan Malaysia, Malaysia
Rizauddin Saian	Universiti Teknologi MARA, Malaysia
Roselina Sallehuddin	Universiti Teknologi Malaysia, Malaysia
Roslina Othman	International Islamic Universiti Malaysia, Malaysia
Rusli Abdullah	Universiti Putra Malaysia, Malaysia
Saidah Saad	Universiti Kebangsaan Malaysia, Malaysia
Salama Mostafa	Universiti Tun Hussein Onn Malaysia, Malaysia
Seng Huat Ong	Universiti Malaya, Malaysia
Sharifah Aliman	Universiti Teknologi MARA, Malaysia
Shuzlina Abdul-Rahman	Universiti Teknologi MARA, Malaysia
Siow Hoo Leong	Universiti Teknologi MARA, Malaysia
Siti Meriam Zahari	Universiti Teknologi MARA, Malaysia
Siti Rahmah Atie Awang	Universiti Teknologi Malaysia, Malaysia
Soo-Fen Fam	Universiti Teknikal Malaysia, Malaysia
Suraya Masrom	Universiti Teknologi MARA, Malaysia
Syazreen Niza Shair	Universiti Teknologi MARA, Malaysia
Tengku Siti Meriam Tengku Wook	Universiti Kebangsaan Malaysia, Malaysia
Waidah Ismail	Universiti Sains Islam Malaysia, Malaysia
XinYing Chew	Universiti Sains Malaysia, Malaysia
Yap Bee Wah	Universiti Teknologi MARA, Malaysia
Zaidah Ibrahim	Universiti Teknologi MARA, Malaysia
Zainura Idrus	Universiti Teknologi MARA, Malaysia

Organized by

Hosted by

Technical Co-sponsor

In Co-operation with

Supported by

Contents

Machine and Deep Learning

Image Processing

Financial and Fuzzy Mathematics

Optimization Algorithms

Data and Text Analytics

Data Visualization

Machine and Deep Learning

A Hybrid Singular Spectrum Analysis and Neural Networks for Forecasting Inflow and Outflow Currency of Bank Indonesia

Suhartono[1(✉)], Endah Setyowati[1], Novi Ajeng Salehah[1],
Muhammad Hisyam Lee[2], Santi Puteri Rahayu[1],
and Brodjol Sutijo Suprih Ulama[1]

[1] Department of Statistics, Institut Teknologi Sepuluh Nopember,
Kampus ITS Sukolilo, Surabaya 60111, Indonesia
suhartono@statistika.its.ac.id
[2] Department of Mathematical Science, Universiti Teknologi Malaysia (UTM),
81310 Skudai, Johor, Malaysia

Abstract. This study proposes hybrid methods by combining Singular Spectrum Analysis and Neural Network (SSA-NN) to forecast the currency circulation in the community, i.e. inflow and outflow. The SSA technique is applied to decompose and reconstruct the time series factors which including trend, cyclic, and seasonal into several additive components, i.e. trend, oscillation and noise. This method will be combined with Neural Network as nonlinear forecasting method due to inflow and outflow data have non-linear pattern. This study also focuses on the effect of Eid ul-Fitr as calendar variation factor which allegedly affect inflow and outflow. Thus, the proposed hybrid SSA-NN is evaluated for forecasting time series that consist of trend, seasonal, and calendar variation patterns, by using two schemes of forecasting process, i.e. aggregate and individual forecasting. Two types of data are used in this study, i.e. simulation and real data about the monthly inflow and outflow of 12 currency denominations. The forecast accuracy of the proposed method is compared to ARIMAX model. The results of the simulation study showed that the hybrid SSA-NN with aggregate forecasting yielded more accurate forecast than individual forecasting. Moreover, the results at real data showed that the hybrid SSA-NN yielded as good as ARIMAX model for forecasting of 12 inflow and outflow denominations. It indicated that the hybrid SSA-NN could not successfully handle calendar variation pattern in all series. In general, these results in line with M3 competition conclusion, i.e. more complex methods do not always yield better forecast than the simpler one.

Keywords: Singular spectrum analysis · Neural network · Hybrid method
Inflow · Outflow

1 Introduction

The currency has a very important role for the Indonesian economy. Although non-cash payment system has grown rapidly, currency or cash payment is still more efficient for individual payment for small nominal value. Forecasting inflow and outflow can be an

© Springer Nature Singapore Pte Ltd. 2019
B. W. Yap et al. (Eds.): SCDS 2018, CCIS 937, pp. 3–18, 2019.
https://doi.org/10.1007/978-981-13-3441-2_1

option to maintain the stability of currency. The prediction of the amount of currency demand in Indonesia is often referred as the autonomous liquidity factor, so in predicting the demand for currency by society will be difficult [1]. The development of inflow and outflow of currency both nationally and regionally has certain movement patterns influenced by several factors, such as government money policy. Moreover, it is also influenced by trend, seasonal and calendar variation effect caused by Eid ul-Fitr that usually occurred at different date in each year [2]. Decomposition of time series data into sub patterns can ease the process of time series analysis [3]. Hence, a forecasting method that could capture and reconstruct each component pattern in the data was needed.

This study proposes a forecasting method that combining Singular Spectrum Analysis as decomposition method and Neural Network (known as SSA-NN) for forecasting inflow and outflow data in both scheme, i.e. individual and aggregate forecasting. The SSA method was applied to decompose and reconstruct the time series patterns in inflow and outflow data which including trend, cyclic, and seasonal into several additive components, while the NN method is used to handling non-linear pattern which contained in inflow and outflow data. In addition, this study also focuses to learn whether the SSA-NN could handle calendar variation effect in time series, particularly the effect of Eid ul-Fitr to inflow and outflow data.

As widely known, SSA is a forecasting technique that combines elements of classical time series analysis, multivariate statistics, multivariate geometry, dynamic systems, and signal processes [4]. SSA can decompose common patterns in time series data, trend, cycle, and seasonal factors into some additive components separated by trend, oscillatory, and noise components. SSA was first introduced by Broomhead and King [5] and followed by many studies that applied this method [6, 7]. SSA has a good ability in characterizing and prediction of time series [8]. Furthermore, it is also known that SSA method can be used for analyzing and forecasting short time series data with various types of non-stationary and produce more accurate forecast [9, 10].

In the past decades, many researchers have increasingly developed SSA by combining this method with other forecasting methods. Hybrid SSA model tends to be more significant and provides better performance than other methods [12]. A combination of SSA and NN could forecast more accurately and it could effectively reconstruct the data [13, 14]. A comparative study was done by Barba and Rodriguez [15] also showed that SSA-NN produced better accuracy for multi-step ahead forecasting of traffic accident data. The rapid research development about the combinations of SSA showed that this method can improve forecasting performance and could be a potential and competitive method for time series forecasting [16–18].

In this study, two types of data are used, i.e. simulation and real data about the monthly inflow and outflow data of 12 banknotes denomination from January 2003 to December 2016. These data are secondary data obtained from Bank Indonesia. The data are divided into two parts, i.e. training data (from January 2003 to December 2014) and testing data (from January 2015 to December 2016). The forecast accuracy of the proposed method is compared to ARIMAX model by using RMSE, MAE and MAPE criteria. The results of the simulation study showed that the hybrid SSA-NN with aggregate forecasting scheme yielded more accurate forecast than individual forecasting scheme. Moreover, the results at real data showed that the hybrid SSA-NN yielded as good as ARIMAX model for forecasting of 12 inflow and outflow denominations. It indicated that the hybrid SSA-NN could not handle calendar variation pattern in all data series. Generally, these results in line with M3 competition results which concluded that more complex methods do not always yield better forecast than the simpler one.

The rest of paper is organized as follows: Sect. 2 reviews the methodology, i.e. ARIMAX, Singular Spectrum Analysis, and Neural Networks as forecasting method; Sect. 3 presents the results and analysis; and Sect. 4 presents the conclusion from this study.

2 Materials and Methods

2.1 ARIMAX

The ARIMAX is an ARIMA model with the addition of exogenous variables. This model has a similar form with linear regression that has additional variables such as trend, seasonal, and calendar variation factors, or other explanatory variables. The ARIMAX model which consists of linear trend (represented by t variable), additive seasonal (represented by $M_{i,t}$ variables), and calendar variation pattern (represented by $V_{j,t}$ variables) is written as follows:

$$Y_t = \beta_0 + \beta_1 t + \sum_{i=1}^{I} \gamma_i M_{i,t} + \sum_{j=1}^{J} \delta_j V_{j,t} + N_t \tag{1}$$

where $M_{i,t}$ is dummy variables for I seasonal effects, $V_{j,t}$ is dummy variables for J calendar variation effects, and N_t is noise variable that follows ARMA model. The identification of calendar variation effect, particularly about the duration effect, can be done graphically by using time series plot [19].

2.2 Singular Spectrum Analysis (SSA)

SSA is a forecasting method that combines elements of classical forecasting, multivariate statistics, multivariate geometry, dynamic systems, and signal processing. SSA method does not require the fulfillment of statistical assumptions such as stationary, and ergodicity. The main objective of the SSA method is to decompose the original time series into several additive components, such as trend, oscillatory, and noise components [4]. In general, SSA has two main stages as follows:

a. Decomposition (Embedding and Singular Value Decomposition)
The procedure in embedding is to map the original time series data into a multidimensional sequence of lagged vector. Let's assume L is an integer number represents window length with $1 < L < n$, the formation of lagged vectors where $K = n - L + 1$ is

$$Y_i = (f_i, f_{i+1}, \ldots, f_{i+L-1})^T, 1 \leq i \leq K \tag{2}$$

which has a dimension of L. If the dimensions of Y_i are emphasized, then Y_i is referred as L-lagged vectors. The path matrix of the F series is illustrated as follows:

$$\mathbf{Y} = [Y_i : \ldots : Y_K] = \begin{bmatrix} f_1 & f_2 & f_3 & \cdots & f_K \\ f_2 & f_3 & f_4 & \cdots & f_{K+1} \\ f_3 & f_4 & f_5 & \cdots & f_{K+2} \\ \vdots & \vdots & \vdots & \ddots & \vdots \\ f_L & f_{L+1} & f_{L+2} & \cdots & f_n \end{bmatrix} \tag{3}$$

Let $\mathbf{S} = \mathbf{YY}^T$ and $\lambda_1, \lambda_2, \ldots, \lambda_L$ be the eigenvalues of the matrix $\mathbf{S}$ Where $\lambda_1 \geq \lambda_2 \geq \ldots \geq \lambda_L \geq 0$ and $U_1, U_2, \ldots, U_L$ are eigenvectors of the matrix $\mathbf{S}$ corresponding to the eigenvalues. Note that $d = \max\{i\}$ so that $\lambda_i > 0$ is the rank of the matrix $\mathbf{Y}$. If $\mathbf{S} = V_i = \mathbf{Y}^T U_i / \sqrt{\lambda_i}$ for $i = 1, 2, \ldots, d$, then SVD of the path matrix $\mathbf{Y}$ can be written as

$$\mathbf{Y} = \mathbf{Y}_1 + \mathbf{Y}_2 + \ldots + \mathbf{Y}_d \tag{4}$$

where $\mathbf{Y}_i = \sqrt{\lambda_i} U_i V_i^T$. Matrix $\mathbf{Y}_i$ has rank 1 and often called as an elementary matrix. The set $\left(\sqrt{\lambda_i}, U_i, V_i \right)$ is called i-th eigentriple to SVD.

b. Reconstruction (Grouping and Diagonal Averaging)

After SVD equation is obtained, the grouping procedure will partition the set of indices $\{1, 2, \ldots, d\}$ into m subsets of mutually independent, $I_1, I_2, \ldots, I_m$. Let $I = \{i_1, i_2, \ldots, i_p\}$, the resulting $\mathbf{Y}_i$ matrix corresponds to group I defined as a matrix with $\mathbf{Y}_I = \mathbf{Y}_{i_1} + \mathbf{Y}_{i_2} + \ldots + \mathbf{Y}_{i_p}$. This matrix is calculated for groups $I = I_1, I_2, \ldots, I_m$ and this step will lead to decomposition form as follows:

$$\mathbf{Y} = \mathbf{Y}_{I_1} + \mathbf{Y}_{I_2} + \ldots + \mathbf{Y}_{I_m}. \tag{5}$$

Set m selection procedures, $I_1, I_2, \ldots, I_m$ are called eigentriple groupings. If $m = d$ and $I_j = \{j\}$, $j = 1, 2, \ldots, d$, then the corresponding grouping is called elementary.

Let $\mathbf{Z}$ be $L \times K$ matrix with element z_{ij}, $1 \leq i \leq L$, $1 \leq j \leq K$ for $L \leq K$. Let's assume the values of $L^* = \min\{L, K\}$, $K^* = \max\{L, K\}$ and $n = L - K - 1$. If $L < K$ then $z_{ij}^* = z_{ij}$, and if $L > K$ then $z_{ij}^* = z_{ji}$. Diagonal averaging moves the $\mathbf{Z}$ matrix to the series $g_1, g_2, \ldots, g_n$ by following formula:

$$g_k = \begin{cases} \frac{1}{k} \sum_{m=1}^{k} z_{m,k-m+1}^* & \text{for } 1 \leq k < L^* \\ \frac{1}{L^*} \sum_{m=1}^{L^*} z_{m,k-m+1}^* & \text{for } L^* \leq k < K^* \\ \frac{1}{n-k+1} \sum_{m=k-K^*+1}^{n-K^*+1} z_{m,k-m+1}^* & \text{for } K^* \leq k < n \end{cases} \tag{6}$$

This equation corresponds to the average matrix element over the 'antidiagonals' $i + j = k + 1$. If the averaging diagonal is applied to the matrix $\mathbf{Y}_{I_k}$, then this process will obtain a reconstructed series $F^{(k)} = \left(f_1^{(k)}, f_1^{(k)}, \ldots, f_1^{(k)} \right)$. Therefore, the initial series $f_1, f_2, \ldots, f_n$ are decomposed into a sum of the m reconstructed series, i.e.

$$f_j = \sum_{k=1}^{m} f_j^{(k)}, j = 1, 2, \ldots, n \qquad (7)$$

2.3 Neural Networks

The most commonly used form of neural network architecture (NN) is Feedforward Neural Networks (FFNN). In statistical modeling, FFNN can be viewed as a flexible class of nonlinear functions. NNs has several unique characteristics features such as its adaptability, nonlinearity, arbitrary function mapping ability – make this method quite suitable and useful for forecasting tasks [20]. In general, this model works by accepting a vector from input x and then compute a response or output $\hat{y}(x)$ by processing (propagating) x through interrelated process elements. In each layer, the inputs are transformed into layers using a nonlinear form, and it will be processed forward to the next layer. Finally, the output values $\hat{y}$, which can be either scalar or vector values, are calculated on the output layer [21]. FFNN architecture with a hidden layer consisting of q unit neurons and output layer consisting only of one unit of neuron is shown as Fig. 1.

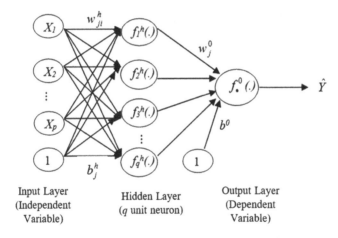

Fig. 1. FFNN architecture with one layer hidden, p input unit, q unit of neuron in hidden layer, and one output neuron unit

The response or output $\hat{y}$ values are calculated by:

$$\hat{y}_{(k)} = f^0 \left[\sum_{j=1}^{q} \left[w_j^0 f_j^h \left(\sum_{i=1}^{p} w_{ji}^h x_{i(k)} + b_j^h \right) + b^0 \right] \right]. \qquad (1)$$

where f_j^h is activation function in the j-th neuron in the hidden layer, and f^0 is the activation function of the neuron in the output layer.

2.4   Hybrid Singular Spectrum Analysis and Neural Network

In general, SSA method is able to decompose a data series into trend, seasonal, and noise patterns. From the decomposition of data patterns, the forecasting will be done using NN with inputs are the lags of component or known as Autoregressive Neural Networks (ARNN). Forecasting can be used either individual or aggregate scheme. Individual forecasting is done by forecasting every major component formed without combining as a trend and seasonal. Specifically, the noise components will be always modelled in aggregate scheme.

Aggregate forecasting is done by summing the components that have same pattern. Thus, the forecast value is calculated from three main patterns, i.e. trend, seasonal, and noise. Then, the results of forecasting with ARNN on individual patterns will be summed to get the forecast of main series (forecast aggregation). These procedure stages are shown in Figs. 2 and 3 for individual and aggregate scheme, respectively.

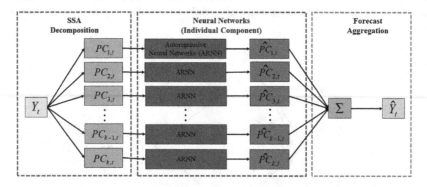

Fig. 2. SSA-NN forecasting using individual forecasting

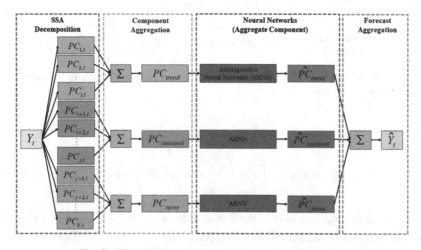

Fig. 3. SSA-NN forecasting using aggregate forecasting

The algorithm of SSA-NN has several steps as follows:

a. Data series decomposition with SSA
    i. Embedding
    ii. Singular Value Decompotition (SVD)
    iii. Grouping
    iv. Diagonal Averaging
b. Modeling the decomposition results using the NN method.
    i. Determine the input variables in NN based on the significant lags of the Partial Autocorrelation Function or PACF of stationary data [22].
    ii. Conduct a nonlinearity test using Terasvirta test.
    iii. Determine the number of units on hidden layer using cross validation method.
    iv. Estimate parameters/weights of NN by using backpropagation algorithm.
    v. Forecast the testing data.
c. Summarize the results of the forecast at each component to get the forecast of testing data.
d. Calculate the level of forecasting errors for testing data.
e. Forecast data by using the corresponding NN model for each data component.

2.5 Model Evaluation

Cross-validation is used for model evaluation, which focusing only on the forecast results for out-sample or testing data [23]. The model evaluation will be done based on the accuracy of the forecast by using RMSE, MAE and MAPE which shown in following equation [24], where C is the forecast period:

$$RMSE = \sqrt{\frac{1}{C}\sum_{c=1}^{C}(Y_{n+c} - \hat{Y}_n(c))^2} \tag{2}$$

$$MAE = \frac{1}{C}\sum_{c=1}^{C}|Y_{n+c} - \hat{Y}_n(c)| \tag{3}$$

$$MAPE = \frac{1}{C}\sum_{c=1}^{C}\left|\frac{Y_{n+c} - \hat{Y}_n(c)}{Y_{n+c}}\right| \times 100\%. \tag{4}$$

3 Results

3.1 Simulation Study

Inflow and outflow currency data are suspected to contain trend, seasonal patterns and influenced by certain calendar variations. To gain better knowledge and understanding about the proposed SSA-NN method, a simulation study was conducted by assuming the data are observed on the period from January 2001 to December 2016 or have 192 observations. In this simulation study, data were generated for each component of trend, seasonal, calendar variation patterns as well as random and non-random noise (has nonlinear pattern) as follows:

a. Trend, $T_t = 0.2t$
b. Seasonal,

$$M_t = 20M_{1,t} + 23.7M_{2,t} + 25M_{3,t} + 23.7M_{4,t} + 20M_{5,t} + 15M_{6,t} +$$
$$10M_{7,t} + 6.3M_{8,t} + 5M_{9,t} + 6.3M_{10,t} + 10M_{11,t} + 15M_{12,t}$$

c. Calendar Variation,

$$V_t = 65V_{1,t} + 46V_{2,t} + 47V_{3,t} + 18V_{4,t} + 28V_{1,t+1} + 23V_{2,t+1} + 41V_{3,t+1} + 60V_{4,t+1}$$

d. Linear Noise Series (white noise assumption is fulfilled),
   $N_{1,t} = a_t$, where $a_t \sim IIDN(0,1)$
e. Nonlinear Noise Series which follow ESTAR(1) model,
   $N_{2,t} = 6.5N_{2,t-1} \cdot \exp(-0.25N_{t-1}^2) + a_t$, where $a_t \sim IIDN(0,1)$.

There are two scenarios of simulation series that following equation,

$$Y_t = T_t + M_t + V_t + N_t$$

where the scenario 1 consisting of trend, seasonal, calendar variation and noise that fulfill white noise, and the scenario 2 containing of trend, seasonal, calendar variation and noise that follow nonlinear ESTAR model. Both scenarios are used to evaluate the performance of SSA in handling all these patterns, particularly calendar variation effect pattern. The time series plot of simulation data are shown in Fig. 4.

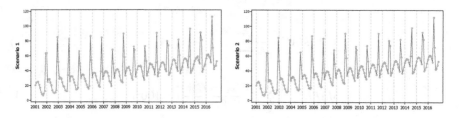

Fig. 4. Time series plot of the scenario 1 and 2 of simulation data

Decomposition results with SSA indicate that the effects of calendar variation could not be decomposed on their own. The results show that the effects of calendar variations on aggregate forecasting are captured into seasonal components and partly as noise components. Furthermore, both individual and aggregate data are modeled by using NN and it will be summed to obtain the forecast of data-testing. The model evaluation of individual and aggregate forecasting is shown in Table 1.

Table 1. Model evaluation using individual and aggregate forecasting in simulation data

Method	Scenario 1			Scenario 2		
	RMSE	MAE	MAPE	RMSE	MAE	MAPE
Aggregate	8.17	6.63	10.5	8.64	7.23	11.8
Individual	8.60	7.18	11.4	8.73	7.52	12.4

Table 1 shows that in this simulation study, an aggregate forecasting has better results than an individual forecasting. It can be seen from the RMSE, MAE and MAPE of aggregate method are smaller than the individual method, both in scenario 1 and 2. Based on Table 1, it could be concluded that SSA-NN method yield better forecast on data containing random noise than data containing nonlinear noise.

3.2 Inflow and Outflow Data

The data that be used as case study are the monthly inflow and outflow data of banknotes per denomination from January 2003 to December 2016. These data are secondary data that be obtained from Bank Indonesia. The data are divided into training data (from January 2003 to December 2014) and testing data (from January 2015 to December 2016). The description of the data is shown at Table 2.

Table 2. Research variable (in billion IDR)

Inflow		Outflow	
Variable	Denomination	Variable	Denomination
$Y_{1,t}$	Rp2.000,00	$Y_{7,t}$	Rp2.000,00
$Y_{2,t}$	Rp5.000,00	$Y_{8,t}$	Rp5.000,00
$Y_{3,t}$	Rp10.000,00	$Y_{9,t}$	Rp10.000,00
$Y_{4,t}$	Rp20.000,00	$Y_{10,t}$	Rp20.000,00
$Y_{5,t}$	Rp50.000,00	$Y_{11,t}$	Rp50.000,00
$Y_{6,t}$	Rp100.000,00	$Y_{12,t}$	Rp100.000,00

The pattern of inflow and outflow of currency at Indonesia (National) from January 2003 until December 2016 shown in Fig. 5. The national inflow and outflow in Indonesia has generally fluctuated, although it declined in 2007 due to the implementation of Bank Indonesia's new policy on deposits and payments to banks. While starting in 2011, the inflow and outflow data increase due to imposition of deposits and withdrawals. In general, the increasing value of national inflow and outflow is high in certain months occurred as the effect of calendar variations, i.e. Eid ul-Fitr. The Eid ul-Fitr is suspected to affect certain months in both inflow and outflow data. In addition, Eid ul-Fitr that occur on different week will also give different impact on the increasing amount of inflow and outflow.

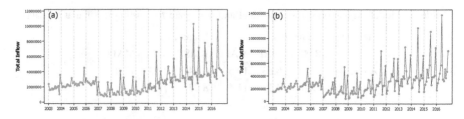

Fig. 5. Inflow (a) and outflow (b) in Indonesia (billion IDR)

The effect of Eid ul-Fitr influences the amount of inflow of Bank Indonesia in the one month after Eid ul-Fitr. This is related to people's habit to save money after carrying out Eid ul-Fitr holiday. In general, Eid ul-Fitr that occurs at the beginning of the month will result in a sharper increase in inflow. Otherwise, Eid ul-Fitr that occurs at the end of the month will yield the highest inflow in one month after this holiday. Additionally, the outflow was also affected by the occurrence of Eid ul-Fitr due to people tend to withdraw money to fulfill their needs during Eid ul-Fitr. In the month of Eid ul-Fitr, the highest outflow will happened when Eid ul-Fitr occurs at the end of the month. As for one month before Eid ul-Fitr, the highest outflow occurs when Eid ul-Fitr occurs at the beginning of the month.

3.3 Forecasting Inflow and Outflow Data Using ARIMAX

Forecasting inflow and outflow with ARIMAX method is using components as exogenous variables, which are trend, seasonal, and calendar variations component effects. These components are represented by the dummy variables as in Eq. (1).

The steps in ARIMAX method is to regress first the effects of trend, seasonal and calendar variation and then applying the ARIMA model on the residuals of this regression if these residuals not fulfill the white noise assumption. Based on model estimation at every denomination, the best ARIMA model for each residual time series regression is shown in Table 3. The ARIMAX equation model is obtained by combining time series regression model and the best ARIMA model from each of the inflow and outflow fractions. For example, the ARIMAX model for inflow Rp100.000,00 data can be written as:

$$
\begin{aligned}
Y_{7,t} = {} & 1.5t + 2956.4M_{1,t} - 1434.4M_{2,t} - 624.8M_{3,t} - 38.2M_{4,t} - 213.4M_{5,t} + \\
& 74.7M_{6,t} - 595.2M_{7,t} + 2941.3M_{8,t} - 3925.5M_{9,t} + 1433.0M_{10,t} - \\
& 11.8M_{11,t} + 428.9M_{12,t} + 5168.9V_{1,t} + 11591.4V_{2,t} + 9110.3V_{3,t} - \\
& 3826.1V_{4,t} - 6576.5V_{1,t+1} - 13521.5V_{2,t+1} - 13059.2V_{3,t+1} + \\
& 3102.7V_{4,t+1} + \frac{(1 - 0.80B)(1 - 0.17B^{12})}{(1 - B)(1 - B^{12})} a_t.
\end{aligned}
$$

Table 3. The best ARIMA model for each series

Data	ARIMA model	Data	ARIMA model
Y_1	ARIMA(0,1, [12])	Y_7	ARIMA(1,1,0)
Y_2	ARIMA(1,1, [1, 12])	Y_8	ARIMA(1,1, [1, 23])(0,1,1)^{12}
Y_3	ARIMA(0,1,1)	Y_9	ARIMA(1,0, [12, 23])
Y_4	ARIMA([12],1, [1, 23])	Y_{10}	ARIMA([1, 11, 12],1, [1, 12, 23])
Y_5	ARIMA(1,1, [12])	Y_{11}	ARIMA([12],0,2)
Y_6	ARIMA(0,1,1)(0,1,1)^{12}	Y_{12}	ARIMA([1, 10, 12],1, [1, 12, 23])

3.4 Forecasting Inflow and Outflow Data Using SSA-NN

In the previous study, it showed that a NN model could not capture the trend and seasonal patterns well [25]. To overcome it, the proposed SSA-NN firstly reconstruct the components of data using SSA. Each fraction of the inflow and outflow is decomposed by determining the L value of half of the data ($L = 84$). The SVD process obtained 50 eigentriples values. The grouping step is done by determining the value of effect grouping (r) to limit the number of eigentriples to grouping the trend and seasonal components. The r value is obtained from the sum of the singular values that have the graph show the noise component. Due to the simulation data show that aggregate forecasting gives better results than individual forecasting, then the forecasting inflow and outflow use aggregate forecasting. To do this, it is necessary to grouping the component pattern, i.e. trend, seasonal, and noise components.

Based on the results of principal component, there are 12 main components in inflow Rp 100.000,00. In Fig. 6, the components that tend to slowly increase or decrease are trend components, while components that follow periodic patterns and have corresponding seasonal periods are grouped into seasonal components, and other components are grouped into noise. Subsequent groupings are made to identify incoming inputs on the NN model. The result of reconstruction of each components of inflow Rp 100.000,00 is shown in Fig. 7.

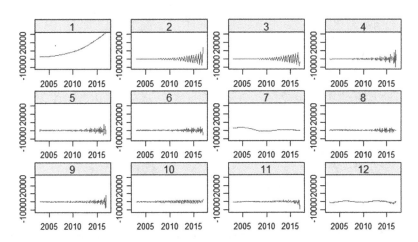

Fig. 6. Principal component plot of inflow Rp 100.000,00

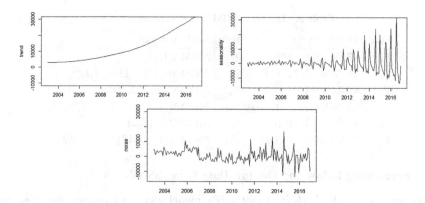

Fig. 7. Grouping trend, seasonal, and noise components of inflow Rp 100.000,00

Then, each component in Fig. 7 are modeled by NN. Based on the best model with the smallest value of goodness of fit criteria, the final NN model for each component can be written as

$$\hat{Y}_{7,t} = \hat{T}_{7,t}^* + \hat{S}_{7,t}^* + \hat{N}_{7,t}^*$$

where $\hat{T}_{7,t}^*$ is standardized value of T_t, $\hat{S}_{7,t}^*$ is standardized value of S_t, and $\hat{N}_{7,t}^*$ is standardized value of N_t. The architecture model of NN for denomination currency of Rp100.000,00 for trend and noise components are shown in Fig. 8.

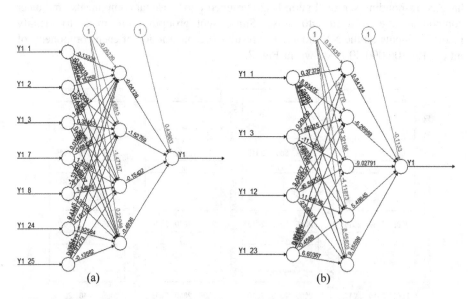

Fig. 8. NN architecture for trend (a) and noise (b) components of inflow Rp100.000,00

The SSA-NN modeling was performed on each denomination of inflow and out-flow. In overall, hybrid SSA-NN model could capture well the pattern of calendar variation present in training data. However, in several denominations, the forecast value of testing data using SSA-NN model could not capture the calendar variation pattern (Fig. 9). The model evaluation using hybrid SSA-NN in each fraction presented in Table 4.

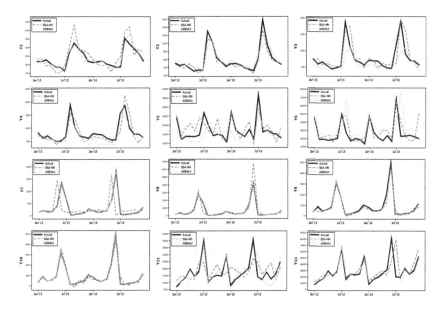

Fig. 9. Comparison of forecast value using SSA-NN and ARIMAX

Table 4. Model evaluation of hybrid SSA-NN model in each denomination

Variable	RMSE	MAE	MAPE	Variable	RMSE	MAE	MAPE
Y_1	84.2	67.9	26.8	Y_7	541.4	289.9	104.5
Y_2	87.3	63.9	11.2	Y_8	600.8	262.7	44.3
Y_3	245.8	154.5	19.3	Y_9	259.2	187.1	37.0
Y_4	254.5	190.3	20.9	Y_{10}	267.9	196.3	50.7
Y_5	4539	3701	23.2	Y_{11}	7591	6147	39.6
Y_6	9766	6368	29.7	Y_{12}	15138	8421	34.7

The forecast accuracy comparison between SSA-NN and ARIMAX methods for each denomination of inflow and outflow are shown in Fig. 9. Moreover, it is also necessary to analyze the reduced forecasting error for SSA-NN method compared to ARIMAX method. The comparison results of these methods are shown at Table 5.

The ratio value less than one indicates that SSA-NN with aggregate forecasting scheme is better and capable for reducing forecast error than ARIMAX based on RMSE criteria. In general, the results show that hybrid SSA-NN method give better results for predicting 6 out of 12 denominations of inflow and outflow. It is indicated by the RMSE ratio value that smaller than 1, which mean SSA-NN produces smaller forecast error than ARIMAX. Moreover, these results in line with M3 competition results, conclusion, and implication, i.e. more complex methods do not necessary yield better forecast than the simpler one [26].

Table 5. RMSE ratio between SSA-NN and ARIMAX methods

Data	RMSE Ratio	Data	RMSE Ratio
Y_1	1.92	Y_7	6.30
Y_2	0.51	Y_8	1.46
Y_3	0.78	Y_9	0.70
Y_4	1.16	Y_{10}	0.67
Y_5	0.93	Y_{11}	1.30
Y_6	0.55	Y_{12}	1.46

4   Conclusion

The results of simulation study showed that the proposed hybrid SSA-NN with aggregate forecasting scheme by grouping trends, seasonal, and noises yielded more accurate forecast than individual forecasting scheme. These results also showed that hybrid SSA-NN gave better performance in modeling series with random noise than nonlinear noise. Furthermore, the empirical study proved that Eid ul-Fitr had significant effect on the amount of inflow and outflow. The results for inflow and outflow data showed that hybrid SSA-NN could capture well the trend and seasonal pattern. Otherwise, this hybrid SSA-NN could not capture well the effects of calendar varia-tions. Hence, it could be concluded that hybrid SSA-NN is a good forecasting method for time series which contain trends and seasonal only. Moreover, the results of forecast value comparison indicated that hybrid SSA-NN model performed as good as ARI-MAX model, i.e. 6 of 12 denominations were better to be forecasted by the hybrid SSA-NN method, and the rests were more accurate to be forecasted by ARIMAX model. These results in line with the M3 competition conclusion, i.e. more complex methods do not necessary yield better forecast than the simpler one [26]. Hence, further research is needed to handle all patterns simultaneously, i.e. trend, seasonal, and cal-endar variation effects, by proposing new hybrid method as combination of SSA-NN and ARIMAX methods.

Acknowledgements. This research was supported by DRPM-DIKTI under scheme of "Penelitian Berbasis Kompetensi", project No. 851/PKS/ITS/2018. The authors thank to the General Director of DIKTI for funding and to anonymous referees for their useful suggestions.

References

1. Sigalingging, H., Setiawan, E., Sihaloho, H.D.: Money Circulation Policy in Indonesia. Bank Indonesia, Jakarta (2004)
2. Apriliadara, M., Suhartono, A., Prastyo, D.D.: VARI-X model for currency inflow and outflow with Eid Fitr effect in Indonesia. In: AIP Conference Proceedings, vol. 1746, p. 020041 (2016)
3. Bowerman, B.L., O'Connell, R.T.: Forecasting and Time Series. Wadsworth Publishing Company, Belmont (1993)
4. Golyandina, N., Nekrutkin, V., Zhigljavsky, A.A.: Analysis of Time Series Structure: SSA and Related Techniques. Chapman & Hall, Florida (2001)
5. Broomhead, D.S., King, G.P.: Extracting qualitative dynamics from experimental data. Physica D **20**, 217–236 (1986)
6. Broomhead, D.S., King, G.P.: On the qualitative analysis of experimental dynamical systems. In: Sarkar S (ed.) Nonlinear Phenomena and Chaos, pp. 113–144. Adam Hilger, Bristol (1986)
7. Broomhead, D.S., Jones, R., King, G.P., Pike, E.R.: Singular Spectrum Analysis with Application to Dynamic Systems, pp. 15–27. IOP Publishing, Bristol (1987)
8. Afshar, K., Bigdeli, N.: Data analysis and short-term load forecasting in Iran electricity market using singular spectral analysis (SSA). Energy **36**(5), 2620–2627 (2011)
9. Hassani, H., Zhigljavsky, A.: Singular spectrum analysis: methodology and application to economic data. J. Syst. Sci. Complex. **22**, 372–394 (2008)
10. Zhigljavsky, A., Hassani, H., Heravi, S.: Forecasting European Industrial Production with Multivariate Singular Spectrum Analysis. Springer (2009)
11. Zhang, Q., Wang, B.D., He, B., Peng, Y.: Singular Spectrum Analysis and ARIMA Hybrid Model for Annual Runoff Forecasting. Springer, China (2011)
12. Li, H., Cui, L., Guo, S.: A hybrid short term power load forecasting model based on the singular spectrum analysis and autoregressive model. Adv. Electr. Eng. Artic. ID **424781**, 1–7 (2014)
13. Lopes, R., Costa, F.F., Lima, A.C.: Singular spectrum analysis and neural network to forecast demand in industry. In: Brazil: The 2nd World Congress on Mechanical, Chemical, and Material Engineering (2016)
14. Sun, M., Li, X., Kim, G.: Precipitation analysis and forecasting using singular spectrum analysis with artificial neural networks. Clust. Comput., 1–8 (2018, in press)
15. Barba, L., Rodriguez, N.: Hybrid models based on singular values and autoregressive methods for multistep ahead forecasting of traffic accidents. Math. Probl. Eng. **2016**, 1–14 (2016)
16. Zhang, X., Wang, J., Zhang, K.: Short-term electric load forecasting based on singular spectrum analysis and support vector machine optimized by cuckoo search algorithm. Electr. Power Syst. Res. **146**, 270–285 (2017)
17. Lahmiri, S.: Minute-ahead stock price forecasting based on singular spectrum analysis and support vector regression. Appl. Math. Comput. **320**, 444–451 (2018)
18. Khan, M.A.R., Poskitt, D.S.: Forecasting stochastic processes using singular spectrum analysis: aspects of the theory and application. Int. J. Forecast. **33**(1), 199–213 (2017)
19. Lee, M.H., Suhartono, A., Hamzah, N.A.: Calendar variation model based on ARIMAX for forecasting sales data with Ramadhan effect. In: Regional Conference on Statistical Sciences, pp. 349–361 (2010)
20. Zhang, P.G., Patuwo, E., Hu, M.Y.: Forecasting with artificial neural networks: the state of the art. Int. J. Forecast. **14**, 35–62 (1998)

21. Suhartono: New procedures for model selection in feedforward neural networks. Jurnal Ilmu Dasar **9**, 104–113 (2008)
22. Crone, S.F., Kourentzes, N.: Input-variable specification for neural networks - an analysis of forecasting low and high time series frequency. In: International Joint Conference on Neural Networks, pp. 14–19 (2009)
23. Anders, U., Korn, O.: Model selection in neural networks. Neural Netw. **12**, 309–323 (1999)
24. Wei, W.W.S.: Time Series Analysis: Univariate and Multivariate Methods, 2nd edn. Pearson Education, Inc., London (2006)
25. Zhang, G.P., Qi, M.: Neural network forecasting for seasonal and trend time series. Eur. J. Oper. Res. **160**(2), 501–514 (2005)
26. Makridakis, S., Hibon, M.: The M3-competition: results, conclusions and implications. Int. J. Forecast. **16**(4), 451–476 (2000)

Scalable Single-Source Shortest Path Algorithms on Distributed Memory Systems

Thap Panitanarak[(⊠)]

Department of Mathematics and Computer Science, Chulalongkorn University,
Patumwan 10330, Bangkok, Thailand
Thap.p@chula.ac.th

Abstract. Single-source shortest path (SSSP) is a well-known graph computation that has been studied for more than half a century. It is one of the most
common graph analytical analysis in many research areas such as networks,
communication, transportation, electronics and so on. In this paper, we propose
scalable SSSP algorithms for distributed memory systems. Our algorithms are
based on a Δ-stepping algorithm with the use of a two dimensional (2D) graph
layout as an underlying graph data structure to reduce communication overhead
and improve load balancing. The detailed evaluation of the algorithms on various large-scale real-world graphs is also included. Our experiments show that
the algorithm with the 2D graph layout delivers up to three times the performance (in TEPS), and uses only one-fifth of the communication time of the
algorithm with a one dimensional layout.

Keywords: SSSP · Parallel SSSP · Parallel algorithm · Graph algorithm

1 Introduction

With the advance of online social networks, World Wide Web, e-commerce and
electronic communication in the last several years, data relating to these areas has
become exponentially larger day by day. This data is usually analyzed in a form of
graphs modeling relations among data entities. However, processing these graphs is
challenging not only from a tremendous size of the graphs that is usually in terms of
billions of edges, but also from graph characteristics such as sparsity, irregularity and
scale-free degree distributions that are difficult to manage.

Large-scale graphs are commonly stored and processed across multiple machines or
in distributed environments due to a limited capability of a single machine. However,
current graph analyzing tools which have been optimized and used on sequential
systems cannot directly be used on these distributed systems without scalability issues.
Thus, novel graph processing and analysis are required, and parallel graph computations are mandatory to be able to handle these large-scale graphs efficiently.

Single-source shortest path (SSSP) is a well-known graph computation that has
been studied for more than half a century. It is one of the most common graph
analytical analysis for many graph applications such as networks, communication,
transportation, electronics and so on. There are many SSSP algorithms that have been
proposed such as a well-known Dijkstra's algorithm [9] and a Bellman-Ford algorithm

© Springer Nature Singapore Pte Ltd. 2019
B. W. Yap et al. (Eds.): SCDS 2018, CCIS 937, pp. 19–33, 2019.
https://doi.org/10.1007/978-981-13-3441-2_2

[3, 10]. However, these algorithms are designed for serial machines, and do not efficiently work on parallel environments. As a result, many researchers have studied and proposed parallel SSSP algorithms or implemented SSSP as parts of their parallel graph frameworks. Some well-known graph frameworks include the Parallel Boost Graph Libray [14], GraphLab [16], PowerGraph [12], Galois [11] and ScaleGraph [8]. More recent frameworks have been proposed based on Hadoop sytems [26] such as Cyclops [6], GraphX [27] and Mizan [15]. For standalone implementations of SSSP, most recent implementations usually are for GPU parallel systems such as [7, 25, 28]. However, high performance GPU architectures are still not widely available and they also require fast CPUs to speed up the overall performance. Some SSSP implementations on shared memory systems include [17, 20, 21].

In this paper, we focus on designing and implementing efficient SSSP algorithms for distributed memory systems. While the architectures are not relatively new, there are few efficient SSSP implementations for this type of architectures. We aware of the recent SSSP study of Chakaravarthy et al. [5] that is proposed for massively parallel systems, IBM Blue Gene/Q (Mira). Their SSSP implementations have applied various optimizations and techniques to achieve very good performance such as direction optimization (or a push-pull approach), pruning, vertex cut and hybridization. However, most techniques are specifically for SSSP algorithms and can only be applied to a limited variety of graph algorithms. In our case of SSSP implementations, most of our techniques are more flexible and can be extended to many graph algorithms, while still achieving good performance. Our main contributions include:

- Novel SSSP algorithms that combine advantages of various well-known SSSP algorithms.
- Utilization of a two dimensional graph layout to reduce communication overhead and improve load balancing of SSSP algorithms.
- Distributed cache-like optimization that filters out unnecessary SSSP updates and communication to further increase the overall performance of the algorithms.
- Detailed evaluation of the SSSP algorithms on various large-scale graphs.

2   Single-Source Shortest Path Algorithms

Let $G = (V, E, w)$ be a weighted, undirected graph with $n = |V|$ vertices, $m = |E|$ edges, and integer weights $w(e) > 0$ for all $e \in E$. Define $s \in V$ called a source vertex, and $d(v)$ to be a tentative distance from s to $v \in V$ (initially set to ∞). The single source shortest path (SSSP) problem is to find $\delta(v) \leq d(v)$ for all $v \in V$. Define $d(s) = 0$, and $d(v) = \infty$ for all v that are not reachable from s.

Relaxation is an operation to update $d(v)$ using in many well-known SSSP algorithms such as Dijkstra's algorithm and Bellman-Ford. The operation updates $d(v)$ using a previously updated $d(u)$ for each $(u, v) \in E$. An edge relaxation of (u, v) is defined as $d(v) = \min\{d(v), d(u) + w(u, v)\}$. A vertex relaxation of u is a set of edge relaxations of all edges of u. Thus, a variation of SSSP algorithms is generally based on the way the relaxation taken place.

The classical Dijkstra's algorithm relaxes vertices in an order starting from a vertex with the lowest tentative distance first (starting with s). After all edges of that vertex are relaxed, the vertex is marked as settled that is the distance to such vertex is the shortest possible. To keep track of a relaxing order of all active vertices v (or vertices that have been updated and wait to be relaxed), the algorithm uses a priority queue that orders active vertices based on their $d(v)$. A vertex is added to the queue only if it is visited for the first time. The algorithm terminates when the queue is empty. Another variant of Dijkstra's algorithm for integer weight graphs that is suited for parallel implementation is called Dial's algorithm. It uses a bucket data structure instead of a priority queue to avoid the overhead from maintaining the queue while still giving the same work performance as Dijkstra's algorithm. Each bucket has a unit size, and holds all active vertices that have the same tentative distance as a bucket number. The algorithm works on buckets in order starting from the lowest to the highest bucket numbers. Any vertex in each bucket has an equal priority, and can be processed simultaneously. Thus, the algorithm concurrency is from the present of these buckets.

Another well-known SSSP algorithm, Bellman-Ford, allows vertices to be relaxed in any order. Thus, there is no guarantee if a vertex is settled after it has been once relaxed. Generally, the algorithm uses a first-in-first-out (FIFO) queue to maintain the vertex relaxation order since there is no actual priority of vertices. A vertex is added to the queue when its tentative distance is updated, and is removed from the queue after it is relaxed. Thus, any vertex can be added to the queue multiple times whenever its tentative distance is updated. The algorithm terminates when the queue is empty. Since the order of relaxation does not affect the correctness of the Bellman-Ford algorithm, it allows the algorithm to provide high concurrency from simultaneous relaxation.

While Dijkstra's algorithm yields the best work efficiency since each vertex is relaxed only once, it has very low algorithm concurrency. Only vertices that have the smallest distance can be relaxed at a time to preserve the algorithm correctness. In contrast, Bellman-Ford requires more works from (possibly) multiple relaxations of each vertex. However, it provides the best algorithm concurrency since any vertex in the queue can be relaxed at the same time. Thus, the algorithm allows simultaneously relaxations while the algorithm's correctness is still preserved.

The Δ-stepping algorithm [18] compromises between these two extremes by introducing an integer parameter $\Delta \geq 1$ to control the trade-off between work efficiency and concurrency. At any iteration $k \geq 0$, the Δ-stepping algorithm relaxes the active vertices that have tentative distances in $[k\Delta, (k+1)\Delta - 1]$. With $1 < \Delta < \infty$, the algorithm yields better concurrency than the Dijkstra's algorithm and lower work redundancy than the Bellman-Ford algorithm. To keep track of active vertices to be relaxed in each iteration, the algorithm uses a bucket data structure that puts vertices with the same distant ranges in the same bucket. The bucket k contains all vertices that have the tentative distance in the range $[k\Delta, (k+1)\Delta - 1]$. To make the algorithm more efficient, two processing phases are introduced in each iteration. When an edge is relaxed, it is possible that the updated distance of an adjacency vertex may fall into the current bucket, and it can cause cascading re-updates as in Bellman-Ford. To minimize these re-updates, edges of vertices in the current bucket with weights less than Δ (also called light edges) are relaxed first. This forces any re-insertion to the current bucket to happen earlier, and, thus, decreasing the number of re-updates. This phase is called a light phase, and it can iterate multiple times until there is no more re-insertion, or the current bucket is empty. After that, all edges of vertices which are previously relaxed in the light phases with weights greater than Δ (also called heavy edges) are then relaxed. This phase is called a heavy phase. It only occurs once at the end of each iteration since, with edge weights greater than Δ, the adjacency vertices from updating tentative distances are guaranteed not to fall into the current bucket. The Δ-stepping algorithm can be viewed as a general case of SSSP algorithms with the relaxation approach. The algorithm with $\Delta = 1$ is equivalent to Dijkstra's algorithm, while the algorithm with $\Delta = \infty$ yields Bellman-Ford.

3 Novel Parallel SSSP Implementations

3.1 General Parallel SSSP for Distributed Memory Systems

We consider SSSP implementations in [19] which are based on a bulk-synchronous Δ-stepping algorithm for distributed memory sysyem. The algorithm composes of three main steps, a local discovery, an all-to-all exchange and a local update for both light and heavy phases. In the local discovery step, each processor looks up to all adjacencies v of its local vertices u in the current bucket, and generates corresponding tentative distances $dtv = d(u) + w(u, v)$ of those adjacencies. Note that, in the light phase, only adjacencies with light edges are considered, while, in the heavy phase, only adjacencies with heavy edges are processed. For each (u, v), a pair (v, dtv) is generated, and stored in a queue called QRequest. The all-to-all exchange step distributes these pairs in QRequest to make them local to processors so that each processor can use these information to update a local tentative distance list in the local update step. An edge relaxation is part of the local update step that invokes updating vertex tentative distances, and adding/removing vertices to/from buckets based on their current distances.

3.2 Parallel SSSP with 2D Graph Layout

A two dimensional (2D) graph layout had been previously studied in [4] for breadth-first search. This approach partitions an adjacency matrix of graph vertices into grid blocks instead of a traditional row partition or as one dimensional (1D) graph layout. The 2D layout reduces communication space and also provides better edge distributions of a distributed graph than the 1D layout as any dense row of the high degree vertices can now be distributed across multiple processors instead of only one processor as in the 1D layout.

To apply the 2D graph layout for the Δ-stepping algorithm, each of the three steps needs to be modified according to the changes in the vertex and edge distributions. While the vertices are distributed in similar manner as in the 1D graph layout, edges are now distributed differently. Previously in the 1D layout, all edges of local vertices are assigned to one processor. However, with the 2D layout, these edges are now

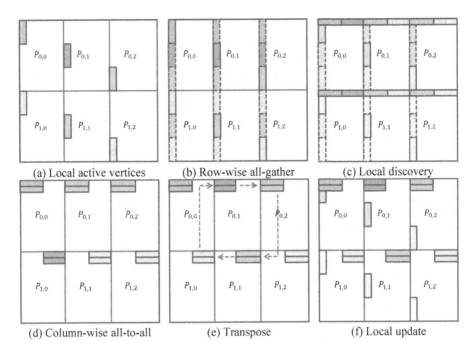

Fig. 1. The main SSSP operations with the 2D layout. (a) Each color bar shows the vertex information for active vertices owned to each processor $P_{i,j}$. (b) The row-wise all-gather communication gathers all information of actives vertices among the same processor rows to all processors in the same row. (c) Each processor uses the information to update the vertex adjacencies. (d,e) The column-wise all-to-all and transpose communications group the information of the updated vertices owned by the same processors and send this information to the owner processors. (f) Each processor uses the received information to update its local vertex information (Color figure online).

distributed among row processors that have the same row number. Figure 1(a) illustrates the partitioning of vertices and edges for the 2D layout.

In the local discovery step, there is no need to modify the actual routine. The only work that needs to be done is merging all current buckets along the processor rows by using a row-wise all-gather communication. The reason is that the edge information (such as edge weights and adjacencies) of local vertices owned by each processor is now distributed among the processor rows. Thus, each processor with the same row number is required to know all the active vertices in the current bucket of their neighbor processor rows before the discovery step can take place. After the current buckets are merged (see Fig. 1(b)), each processor can now simultaneously work on generating pairs (v, dtv) of its local active vertices (see Fig. 1(c)).

In the all-to-all exchange step, the purpose of this step is to distribute the generated pairs (v, dtv) to the processors that are responsible to maintain the information relating to vertices v. In our implementation, we use two sub-communications, a column-wise all-to-all exchange and a send-receive transposition. The column-wise all-to-all communication puts all information pairs of vertices owned by the same owner onto one processor. Figure 1(d) shows a result of this all-to-all exchange. After that, each processor sends and receives these pair lists to the actual owner processors. The latter communication can be viewed as a matrix transposition as shown in Fig. 1(e).

In the local update step, there is no change within the step itself, but only in the data structure of the buckets. Instead of only storing vertices in buckets, the algorithm needs to store both vertices and their current tentative distances so that each processor knows the distance information without initiating any other communication. Figure 1(f) illustrates the local update step. Since all pairs (d, dtv) are local, each processor can update the tentative distances of their local vertices simultaneously.

The complete SSSP algorithm with the 2D graph layout is shown in Algorithm 1. The algorithm initialization shows in the first 10 lines. The algorithm checks for the termination in line 11. The light and heavy phases are shown in lines 12–25 and lines 26-35, respectively. The termination checking for the light phases of a current bucket is in line 12. The local discovery, all-to-all exchange and local update steps of each light phase are shown in lines 13–19, 20 and 22, respectively. Similarly for each heavy phase, its local discovery, all-to-all exchange and local update steps are shown in lines 26–31, 32 and 34, respectively. Algorithm 2 shows the relaxation procedure used in Algorithm 1.

3.3   Other Optimizations

To further improve the algorithm performance, we apply other three optimizations, a cache-like optimization, a heuristic Δ increment and a direction optimization. The detailed explanation is as follows.

Cache-like optimization: We maintain a tentative distance list of every unique adjacency of the local vertices as a local cache. This list holds the recent values of tentative distances of all adjacencies of local vertices. Every time a new tentative distance is generated (during the discovery step), this newly generated distance is compared to the local copy in the list. If the new distance is shorter, it will be processed in the regular manner by adding the generated pair to the QRequest, and the local copy in the list is updated to this value. However, if the new distance is longer, it will be discarded since the remote processors will eventually discard this request during the relaxation anyway. Thus, with a small trade-off of additional data structures and computations, this approach can significantly avoid unnecessary work that involves both communication and computation in the later steps.

Algorithm 1 Distributed SSSP with 2D Graph Layout

1: **for** each u **do**
2:      $d[u] \leftarrow \infty$
3: **end for**
4:      $current \leftarrow 0$
5: **if** $onwer(s) = rank$ **then**
6:      $d[s] \leftarrow 0$
7: **end if**
8: **if** $onwerRow(s) = rankRow$ **then**
9:      $Bucket[current] \leftarrow Bucket[current] \cup (s, 0)$
10: **end if**
11: **while** $Bucket \neq \emptyset$ **do**   //Globally check
12:     **while** $Bucket[current] \neq \emptyset$ **do** //Globally check
13:         **for** each $(u, du) \in Bucket[current]$ **do**
14:             **for** each $(u, v) \in LightEdge$ **do**
15:                 $dtv \leftarrow du + w(u, v)$
16:                 $QRequest \leftarrow QRequest \cup (v, dtv)$
17:             **end for**
18:             $QHeavy \leftarrow QHeavy \cup (u, du)$
19:         **end for**
20:         $Alltoallv(QRequest, row); Transpose(QRequest)$
21:         **for** each $(v, dtv) \in QRequest$ **do**
22:             $Relax(v, dtv)$
23:         **end for**
24:         $Allgatherv(Bucket[current], col)$
25:     **end while**
26:     **for** each $(u, du) \in QHeavy$ **do**
27:         **for** each $(u, v) \in HeavyEdge$ **do**
28:             $dtv \leftarrow du + w(u, v)$
29:             $QRequest \leftarrow QRequest \cup (v, dtv)$
30:         **end for**
31:     **end for**
32:     $Alltoallv(QRequest, row); Transpose(QRequest)$
33:     **for** each $(v, dtv) \in QRequest$ **do**
34:         $Relax(v, dtv)$
35:     **end for**
36:     $current \leftarrow current + 1$ //Move to next bucket
37:     $Allgatherv(Bucket[current], col)$
38: **end while**

Algorithm 2 $Relax(v, dtv)$

1: **if** $d[v] > dtv$ **then**
2:     $old \leftarrow d[v]/\Delta; \ new \leftarrow dtv/\Delta$
3:     $Bucket[old] \leftarrow Bucket[old] - (v, d[v])$
4:     $Bucket[new] \leftarrow Bucket[new] \cup (v, dtv)$
5:     $d[v] \leftarrow dtv$
6: **end if**

Heuristic Δ increment: The idea of this optimization is from the observation of the Δ-stepping algorithm that the algorithm provides a good performance in early iterations when Δ is small since it can avoid most of the redundant work in the light phases. Meanwhile, with a large Δ, the algorithm provides a good performance in later iterations since most of vertices are settled so that the portion of the redundant work is low. Thus, the benefit of the algorithm concurrency outweighs the redundancy. The algorithm with Δ that can be adjusted when needed can provide better performance. From this observation, instead of using a fix Δ value, we implement algorithms that starts with a small Δ until some thresholds are met, then, the Δ is increased (usually to ∞) to speed up the later iterations.

Direction-optimization: This optimization is a heuristic approach first introduced in [2] for breadth-first search (BFS). Conventional BFS usually proceeds in an top-down approach such that, in every iteration, the algorithm checks all adjacencies of each vertex in a frontier whether they are not yet visited, adds them to the frontier, and then marks them as visited. The algorithm terminates whenever there is no vertex in the frontier. We can see that the algorithm performance is highly based on processing vertices in this frontier. The more vertices in the frontier, the more work that needs to be done. From this observation, the bottom-up approach can come to play for efficiently processing of the frontier. The idea is that instead of proceeding BFS only using the top-down approach, it can be done in a reverse direction if the current frontier has more work than the work using the bottom-up approach. With a heuristic determination, the algorithm can alternately switch between top-down and bottom-up approaches to achieve an optimal performance. Since the discovery step in SSSP is done in similar manner as BFS, Chakaravarthy et al. [5] adapts a similar technique called a push-pull heuristic to their SSSP algorithms. The algorithms proceed with a push (similar to the top-down approach) by default during heavy phases. If a forward communication volume of the current bucket is greater than a request communication volume of aggregating of later buckets, the algorithms switch to a pull. This push-pull heuristic considerably improves an overall performance of the algorithm. The main reason of the improvement is because of the lower of the communication volume, thus, the consequent computation also decreases.

3.4   Summary of Implementations

In summary, we implement four SSSP algorithms:

1. **SP1a**: The SSSP algorithm based on Δ-stepping with the cache-like optimization
2. **SP1b**: The SP1a algorithm with the direction optimization
3. **SP2a**: The SP1a algorithm with the 2D graph layout
4. **SP2b**: The SP2a algorithm with the Δ increment heuristic

The main differences of each algorithm are the level of optimizations that additionally increases from SP#a to SP#b that is the SP#b algorithms are the SP#a algorithms with more optimizations, and from SP1x to SP2x that is the SP1x algorithms use the 1D layout while the SP2x algorithms use the 2D layout.

4   Performance Results and Analysis

4.1   Experimental Setup

Our experiments are run on a virtual cluster using StarCluster [24] with the MPICH2 complier version 1.4.1 on top of Amazon Web Service (AWS) Elastic Compute Cloud (EC2) [1]. We use 32 instances of AWS EC2 m3.2xlarge. Each instance consists of 8 cores of high frequency Intel Xeon E5-2670 v2 (Ivy Bridge) processors with 30 GB of memory. The graphs that we use in our experiments are listed in Table 1. The graph500 is a synthetic graph generated from the Graph500 reference implementation [13]. The graph generator is based on the RMAT random graph model with the parameters similar to those use in the default Graph500 benchmark. In this experiment, we use the graph scale of 27 with edge factor of 16 that is the graphs are generated with 2^{27} vertices with an average of 16 degrees for each vertex. The other six graphs are real-world graphs that are obtained from Stanford Large Network Dataset Collection (SNAP) [22], and the University of Florida Sparse Matrix Collection [23]. The edge weights of all graphs are randomly, uniformly generated between 1 and 512.

Table 1. The list of graphs used in the experiments

Graph	Number of vertices (millions)	Number of edges (billions)	Reference
graph500	134	2.1	[13]
it-2004	41	1.1	[23]
sk-2005	50	1.9	[23]
friendster	65	1.8	[22]
orkut	3	0.12	[22]
livejournal	4	0.07	[22]

We fix the value of Δ to 32 for all algorithms. Please note that this value might not be the optimal value in all test cases, but, in our initial experiments on the systems, it gives good performance in most cases. To get the optimal performance in all cases is not practical since Δ needs to be changed accordingly to the systems such as CPU, network bandwidth and latency, and numbers of graph partitions. For more discussion about the Δ value, please see [19].

4.2   Algorithm and Communication Cost Analysis

For SSSP algorithms with the 2D layout, when the number of columns increases, the all-to-all communication overhead also decreases, and the edge distribution is more balanced. Consider processing a graph with n vertices and m edges on $p = r \times c$ processors. The all-to-all and all-gather communication spaces are usually proportional to r and c, respectively. In other words, the maximum number of messages for each all-to-all communication is proportional to m/c while the maximum number of messages for each all-gather communication is proportional to n/r. In each communication phase, processor $P_{i,j}$ requires to interact with processors $P_{k,j}$ for the all-to-all communication where $0 \le k < r$, and with processors $P_{i,l}$ for the all-gather communication

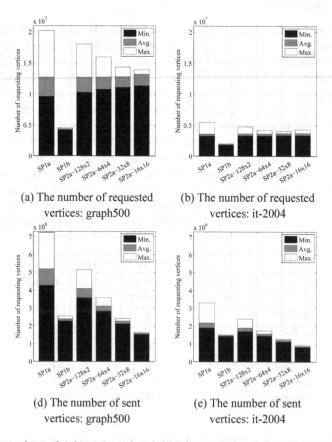

(a) The number of requested vertices: graph500

(b) The number of requested vertices: it-2004

(d) The number of sent vertices: graph500

(e) The number of sent vertices: it-2004

Fig. 2. The numbers of (a,b) requested and (c,d) sent vertices during the highest relaxation phase of the SP2a algorithm on graph500 and it-2004 using different combinations of processor rows and columns on 256 MPI tasks.

where $0 \leq l < c$. For instance, by setting $r = 1$ and $c = p$, the algorithms do not need any all-to-all communication, but the all-gather communication now requires all processors to participate.

During the SSSP process on scale-free graphs, there are usually a few phases of the algorithms that consume most of the computation and communication times due to the present of few vertices with high degrees. The Fig. 2(a,b) and (c,d) show the average, minimum and maximum vertices to be requested and sent, respectively, for relaxations during the phase that consumes the most time of the algorithms SP1a, SP1b and SP2a on graph500 and it-2004 with 256 MPI tasks. Note that we use the abbreviation SP2a-R × C for the SP2a algorithm with R and C processor rows and columns, respectively. For example, SP2a-64 × 4 is the SP2a algorithm with 64 row and 4 column processors (which are 256 processors in total). The improvement of load balancing of the requested vertices for relaxations can easily be seen in Fig. 2(a,b) as the minimum and maximum numbers of the vertices decrease on both graphs from SP1a to SP1b and SP1a to SP2a. The improvement from SP1a to SP1b is significant as the optimization is specifically implemented for reducing the computation and communication overheads during the high-requested phases. On the other hand, SP2a still processes on the same number of vertices, but with lower communication space and better load balancing. Not only the load balancing of the communication improves, but the numbers of (average) messages among inter-processors also reduce as we can see in Fig. 2(c,d). However, there are some limitations of both SP1b and SP2a. For SP1b, the push-pull heuristic

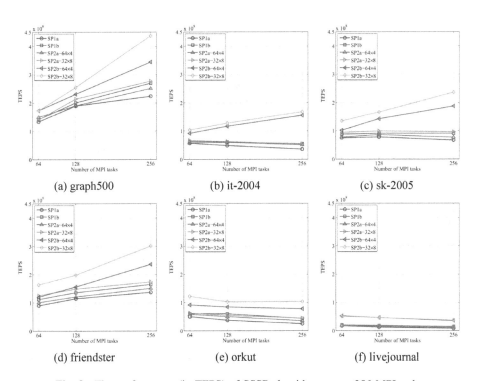

(a) graph500   (b) it-2004   (c) sk-2005

(d) friendster   (e) orkut   (f) livejournal

Fig. 3. The performance (in TEPS) of SSSP algorithms up to 256 MPI tasks

may not trigger in some phases that the costs of push and pull approaches are slightly different. In contrast, for SP2a, although increasing numbers of columns improves load balancing and decreases the all-to-all communication in every phase, it also increases the all-gather communication proportionally. There is no specific number of columns that gives the best performance of the algorithms since it depends on various factors such as the number of processors, the size of the graph and other system specifications.

4.3 Benefits of 2D SSSP Algorithms

Figure 3 shows the algorithm performance in terms of traversed edges per second (TEPS) on Amazon EC2 up to 256 MPI tasks. Although SP1b can significantly reduce computation and communication during the high-requested phases, its overall performance is similar to SP2a. The SP2b algorithm gives the best performance in all cases, and it also gives the best scaling when the number of processors increases. The peak performance of SP2b-32 × 8 is approximately 0.45 GTEPS that can be observed on graph500 with 256 MPI tasks, which is approximately 2x faster than the performance of SP1a on the same setup. The SP2b algorithm also shows good scaling on large graphs such as graph500, it-2004, sk-2005 and friendster.

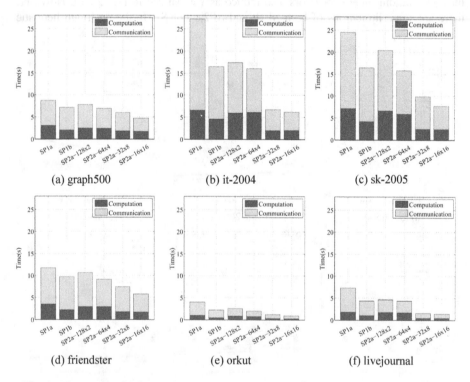

Fig. 4. The communication and computation times of SSSP algorithms on 256 MPI tasks

4.4   Communication Cost Analysis

Figure 4 shows the breakdown execution time of total computation and communication of each algorithm. More than half of the time for all algorithms is spent on communication as the networks of Amazon EC2 is not optimized for high performance computation. The improvement of SP1b over SP1a is from the reduction of computation overhead as the number of processing vertices in some phases are reduced. On the other hand, SP2a provides lower communication overhead over SP1a as the communication space is decreased from the use of the 2D layout. The SP2b algorithm further improves the overall performance by introducing more concurrency in the later phases resulting in lower both communication and communication overhead during the SSSP runs. Figure 5 shows the breakdown communication time of all algorithms. We can see that when the number of processor rows increases, it decreases the all-to-all communication, and slightly increases the all-gather and transpose communications. In all cases, SP2b shows the least communication overhead with up to 10x faster for the all-to-all communication and up to 5x faster for the total communication.

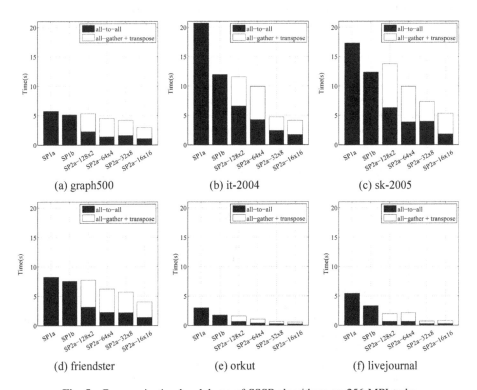

      (a) graph500   (b) it-2004   (c) sk-2005

      (d) friendster   (e) orkut   (f) livejournal

Fig. 5. Communication breakdown of SSSP algorithms on 256 MPI tasks

5 Conclusion and Future Work

We propose scalable SSSP algorithms based on the Δ-stepping algorithm. Our algorithms reduce both communication and computation overhead from the utilization of the 2D graph layout, the cache-like optimization and the Δ increment heuristic. The 2D layout improves the algorithm performance by decreasing the communication space, thus, reducing overall communication overhead. Furthermore, the layout also improves the distributed graph load balancing, especially, on scale-free graphs. The cached-like optimization avoid unnecessary workloads for both communication and communication by filtering out all update requests that are known to be discarded. Finally, by increasing the Δ values during the algorithms progress, we can improve the concurrency of the algorithms in the later iterations.

Currently, our algorithm is based on the bulk-synchronous processing for distributed memory systems. We plan to extend our algorithms to also utilize the shared memory parallel processing that can further reduce the inter-processing communication of the algorithms.

Acknowledgement. The author would like to thank Dr. Kamesh Madduri, an associate professor at Pennsylvania State University, USA, for the inspiration and kind support.

References

1. Amazon Web Services: Amazon Elastic Compute Cloud. http://aws.amazon.com/ec2/. Accessed 15 July 2018
2. Beamer, S., Asanovi´c, K., Patterson, D.: Direction-optimizing breadth-first search. Sci. Prog. **21**(3–4), 137–148 (2013)
3. Bellman, R.: On a routing problem. Q. Appl. Math. **16**, 87–90 (1958)
4. Buluc, A., Madduri, K.: Parallel breadth-first search on distributed memory systems. In: Proceedings of High Performance Computing, Networking, Storage and Analysis (SC) (2011)
5. Chakaravarthy, V.T., Checconi, F., Petrini, F., Sabharwal, Y.: Scalable single source shortest path algorithms for massively parallel systems. In: Proceedings of IEEE 28th International Parallel and Distributed Processing Symposium, pp. 889–901 May 2014
6. Chen, R., Ding, X., Wang, P., Chen, H., Zang, B., Guan, H.: Computation and communication efficient graph processing with distributed immutable view. In: Proceedings of the 23rd International Symposium on High-Performance Parallel and Distributed Computing, pp. 215–226. ACM (2014)
7. Davidson, A.A., Baxter, S., Garland, M., Owens, J.D.: Work-efficient parallel GPU methods for single-source shortest paths. In: International Parallel and Distributed Processing Symposium, vol. 28 (2014)
8. Dayarathna, M., Houngkaew, C., Suzumura, T.: Introducing ScaleGraph: an X10 library for billion scale graph analytics. In: Proceedings of the 2012 ACM SIGPLAN X10 Workshop, p. 6. ACM (2012)
9. Dijkstra, E.W.: A note on two problems in connection with graphs. Numer. Math. **1**(1), 269–271 (1959)
10. Ford, L.A.: Network flow theory. Technical. report P-923, The Rand Corporation (1956)
11. Galois. http://iss.ices.utexas.edu/?p=projects/galois. Accessed 15 July 2018

12. Gonzalez, J.E., Low, Y., Gu, H., Bickson, D., Guestrin, C.: PowerGraph: distributed graph-parallel computation on natural graphs. In: OSDI, vol. 12, p. 2 (2012)
13. The Graph 500. http://www.graph500.org. Accessed 15 July 2018
14. Gregor, D., Lumsdaine, A.: The Parallel BGL: a generic library for distributed graph computations. Parallel Object-Oriented Sci. Comput. (POOSC) **2**, 1–18 (2005)
15. Khayyat, Z., Awara, K., Alonazi, A., Jamjoom, H., Williams, D., Kalnis, P.: Mizan: a system for dynamic load balancing in large-scale graph processing. In: Proceedings of the 8th ACM European Conference on Computer Systems, pp. 169–182. ACM (2013)
16. Low, Y., Bickson, D., Gonzalez, J., Guestrin, C., Kyrola, A., Hellerstein, J.M.: Distributed GraphLab: a framework for machine learning and data mining in the cloud. Proc. VLDB Endow. **5**(8), 716–727 (2012)
17. Madduri, K., Bader, D.A., Berry, J.W., Crobak, J.R.: An experimental study of a parallel shortest path algorithm for solving large-scale graph instances, Chap. 2, pp. 23–35 (2007)
18. Meyer, U., Sanders, P.: Δ-stepping: a parallelizable shortest path algorithm. J. Algorithms **49**(1), 114–152 (2003)
19. Panitanarak, T., Madduri, K.: Performance analysis of single-source shortest path algorithms on distributed-memory systems. In: SIAM Workshop on Combinatorial Scientific Computing (CSC), p. 60. Citeseer (2014)
20. Prabhakaran, V., Wu, M., Weng, X., McSherry, F., Zhou, L., Haridasan, M.: Managing large graphs on multi-cores with graph awareness. In: Proceedings of USENIX Annual Technical Conference (ATC) (2012)
21. Shun, J., Blelloch, G.E.: Ligra: a lightweight graph processing framework for shared memory. In: Proceedings of the 18th ACM SIGPLAN Symposium on Principles and Practice of Parallel Programming, PPoPP 2013 pp. 135–146 (2013)
22. SNAP: Stanford Network Analysis Project. https://snap.stanford.edu/data/. Accessed 15 July 2018
23. The University of Florida Sparse Matrix Collection. https://www.cise.ufl.edu/research/sparse/matrices/. Accessed 15 July 2018
24. StarCluster. http://star.mit.edu/cluster/. Accessed 15 July 2018
25. Wang, Y., Davidson, A., Pan, Y., Wu, Y., Riffel, A. Owens, J.D.: Gunrock: a high-performance graph processing library on the GPU. In: Proceedings of the 20th ACM SIGPLAN Symposium on Principles and Practice of Parallel Programming, pp. 265–266. PPoPP 2015 (2015)
26. White, T.: Hadoop: The Definitive Guide. O'Reilly Media Inc, Sebastopol (2012)
27. Xin, R.S., Gonzalez, J.E., Franklin, M.J. Stoica, I.: Graphx: A resilient distributed graph system on spark. In: First International Workshop on Graph Data Management Experiences and Systems, p. 2. ACM (2013)
28. Zhong, J., He, B.: Medusa: simplified graph processing on GPUs. Parallel Distrib. Syst. IEEE Trans. **25**(6), 1543–1552 (2014)

Simulation Study of Feature Selection on Survival Least Square Support Vector Machines with Application to Health Data

Dedy Dwi Prastyo[1(✉)], Halwa Annisa Khoiri[1],
Santi Wulan Purnami[1], Suhartono[1], and Soo-Fen Fam[2]

[1] Department of Statistics, Institut Teknologi Sepuluh Nopember,
Surabaya 60111, Indonesia
dedy-dp@statistika.its.ac.id
[2] Department of Technopreneurship, Universiti Teknikal Malaysia Melaka,
Melaka, Malaysia

Abstract. One of semi parametric survival model commonly used is Cox Proportional Hazard Model (Cox PHM) that has some conditions must be satisfied, one of them is proportional hazard assumption among the category at each predictor. Unfortunately, the real case cannot always satisfy this assumption. One alternative model that can be employed is non-parametric approach using Survival Least Square-Support Vector Machine (SURLS-SVM). Meanwhile, the SURLS-SVM cannot inform which predictors are significant like the Cox PHM can do. To overcome this issue, the feature selection using backward elimination is employed by means of c-index increment. This paper compares two approaches, i.e. Cox PHM and SURLS-SVM, using c-index criterion applied on simulated and clinical data. The empirical results inform that the c-index of SURLS-SVM is higher than Cox PHM on both datasets. Furthermore, the simulation study is repeated 100 times. The simulation results show that the non-relevant predictors are often included in the model because the effect of confounding. For the application on clinical data (cervical cancer), the feature selection yields nine relevant predictors out of twelve predictors. The three predictors among the nine relevant predictors in SURLS-SVM are the significant predictors in Cox PHM.

Keywords: Survival · Least square SVM · Features selection
Simulation · Cervical cancer

1 Introduction

The parametric approach in survival analysis demands that the prior distribution of survival time. This requirement can be considered as drawback, because in the real applications sometimes it is difficult to be satisfied [1]. To overcome such problem, semi-parametric approaches are introduced, for example Cox Proportional Hazard Model (Cox PHM). However, it demands proportional hazard (PH) assumption and linearity within predictor [2, 3]. In the real case, this requirement is not easy to be satisfied, so that the non-parametric approach can play into role; one of it is Support

© Springer Nature Singapore Pte Ltd. 2019
B. W. Yap et al. (Eds.): SCDS 2018, CCIS 937, pp. 34–45, 2019.
https://doi.org/10.1007/978-981-13-3441-2_3

Vector Machine (SVM) that has global optimum solution [4]. The SVM is initially used for classification problem and then developed for regression [5]. Previous studies [2, 3, 6, 7] employed and extended Support Vector Regression (SVR) for survival data analysis. The SVM and SVR have inequality constrain that require quadratic programming. Least Square-SVM (LS-SVM) is applied on survival data because it has equality constrain [8].

The LS-SVM on survival data so-called Survival LS-SVM (SURLS-SVM) employs prognostic index instead of hazard function. The existing papers about SURLS-SVM do not explain how the effect of each predictor to the performance measures. The effect of each predictor cannot be known directly; therefore, the feature selection can be used to solve this issue. The feature selection that often used on SVM is filter and wrapper. Author [9] applied it on breast cancer data.

In this paper, the SURLS-SVM and Cox PHM are applied on simulated and real data. This work also applies the proposed approach on cervical cancer data obtained from a Hospital in Surabaya, Indonesia [10, 11]. The empirical results show that the SURLS-SVM outperforms the Cox PHM before and after feature selection. This paper is organized as follows. Section 2 explains the theoretical part. Section 3 describes simulation set up, clinical data, and method. Section 4 informs empirical results and discussion. At last, Sect. 5 shows the conclusion.

2 Literature Review

The purpose of classical survival analysis is estimating survival function denoted as probability of failure time greater than time point t as shows in (1):

$$S(t) = P(T > t) = 1 - F(t), \tag{1}$$

with T denotes failure time and $F(t)$ is its cumulative distribution function. The hazard function $h(t)$ shows failure rate instantaneously after objects survive until time t. It has relationship with survival function as in (2).

$$h(t) = \frac{f(t)}{S(t)}, \tag{2}$$

with $f(t)$ is first order derivative of $F(t)$. The popular semi-parametric approach to model $h(t, \mathbf{x})$, where $\mathbf{x}$ is features, is Cox PHM as in (3):

$$h(t, \mathbf{x}) = h_0(t) exp(\boldsymbol{\beta}' \mathbf{x}), \tag{3}$$

with $h_0(t)$ is baseline hazard (time-dependent) and coefficient $\boldsymbol{\beta} = (\beta_1, \beta_2, \ldots, \beta_d)$.

2.1 Least Square SVM for Survival Analysis

The optimization problem of SVM is defined as follows [9]:

$$\min_{w,\xi} \frac{1}{2}\|\mathbf{w}\|^2 + \gamma \sum_{i=1}^{n} \xi_i \tag{4}$$

subject to: $y_i(\mathbf{x}_i' \mathbf{w} + b) \geq 1 - \xi_i$; $\xi_i \geq 0$. Some problems need non-linear classifier that transforms data space to feature space using kernel trick [12]. The SVM is developed into LS-SVM [8] which is more efficient. It can be solved using linear programming with objective function as:

$$\min_{w,\xi} \frac{1}{2}\|\mathbf{w}\|^2 + \frac{1}{2}\gamma \sum_{i=1}^{n} \xi_i^2 \tag{5}$$

subject to: $y_i[\varphi(\mathbf{x}_i)' \mathbf{w} + b] = 1 - \xi_i; i = 1, 2, \ldots, n$.

Moreover, the SVM is developed not only applied on classification problem but also on survival data so called as Survival SVM (SUR-SVM) formulated as follows [6]:

$$\min_{w,\xi} \frac{1}{2}\mathbf{w}'\mathbf{w} + \frac{\gamma}{2}\sum_{i}\sum_{i<j} v_{ij}\xi_{ij}; \gamma \geq 0 \tag{6}$$

subject to: $\mathbf{w}'\varphi(\mathbf{x}_j) - \mathbf{w}'\varphi(\mathbf{x}_i) \geq 1 - \xi_{ij}; \forall i < j$; $\xi_{ij} \geq 0; \forall i < j$. The comparable indicator (v_{ij}) plays role as indication whether two subjects are comparable or not. The definition of v_{ij} will be explained in turn.

The least square version of SUR-SVM is Survival Least Square SVM (SURLS-SVM) which is simpler because it has equality constrains. Instead of employ hazard function as in Cox PHM, the SURLS-SVM uses prognostic index (commonly called health index) [2] to predict the rank of observed survival time given the known features. The prognostic function is defined as follows [6]:

$$u(\mathbf{x}) = \mathbf{w}^T \varphi(\mathbf{x}), \tag{7}$$

with $u : \mathbb{R}^d \rightarrow \mathbb{R}$, $\mathbf{w}$ is weight vector, and $\varphi(\mathbf{x})$ is feature mapping of features. The prognostic function theoretically increases as the failure time increases. Let two samples i, j and the event is deaths that have prognostic index and survival time, respectively, $u(\mathbf{x}_i), u(\mathbf{x}_j), t_i, t_j$. If $t_i < t_j$, then it is expected that $u(\mathbf{x}_i) < u(\mathbf{x}_j)$.

The prediction of survival time is not easy to be obtained. Instead, it can be done by predicting rank of prognostic index that correspond to observed survival time. Because of the large number of characteristics that determine prognostic index, it requires model to predict [13].

The SURLS-SVM model has optimization problem as follows (8) [6]:

$$\min_{w,\xi} \frac{1}{2}\mathbf{w}'\mathbf{w} + \frac{\gamma}{2}\sum_{i}\sum_{i<j} v_{ij}\xi_{ij}^2; \gamma \geq 0 \tag{8}$$

subject to: $\mathbf{w}'\varphi(\mathbf{x}_j) - \mathbf{w}'\varphi(\mathbf{x}_i) = 1 - \xi_{ij}; \forall i < j$, with γ is parameter of regularization, and v_{ij} is indicator variable defined as [6, 7]:

$$v_{ij} = \begin{cases} 1; (\delta_i = 1, t_i < t_j) \text{ or } (\delta_j = 1, t_j < t_i) \\ 0; \text{otherwise} \end{cases} \quad (9)$$

with δ is censored status, $\delta = 1$ when failure time is observed and $\delta = 0$ is censored. The certain ranking should be obtained if $\mathbf{w}'\varphi(\mathbf{x}_j) - \mathbf{w}'\varphi(\mathbf{x}_i) > 0$ is satisfied. In (9), the constraints of the optimization problem are equality. The optimization problem has solution as follows [6]:

$$[\gamma \mathbf{D K D}^T + \mathbf{I}]\boldsymbol{\alpha} = \gamma \mathbf{1}, \quad (10)$$

with $\mathbf{D}$ is matrix containing $\{-1, 0, 1\}$ that has size $n_c \times n$, i.e. n_c is number of comparable objects and n is number observation, $\mathbf{K}$ is kernel matrix with size $n \times n$, with $K_{ij} = \varphi(\mathbf{x}_i)'\varphi(\mathbf{x}_j)$. The $\mathbf{I}$ is identity matrix and 1 is a vector containing ones, both have size equal to comparable objects, and α is Lagrange multiplier. The kernel used in this case is Radial Basis Function (RBF):

$$K(x_i, x_j) = \exp(-||x_i - x_j||_2^2/\sigma^2), \quad (11)$$

with σ^2 denotes tuning parameter of RBF Kernel. Considering (7), prediction of prognostic function $(\hat{\mathbf{u}}^*)$ of SURLS-SVM is defined by (12) [6]:

$$\hat{\mathbf{u}}^* = \hat{\mathbf{w}}^T \varphi(\mathbf{x}^*) = \sum_i \sum_{i<j} \hat{\alpha}_{ij}(\varphi(\mathbf{x}_j) - \varphi(\mathbf{x}_i))^T \varphi(\mathbf{x}^*) = \hat{\alpha}^T \mathbf{D K}_n(\mathbf{x}^*), \quad (12)$$

with $(\hat{\mathbf{u}}^*)$ is vector that has size equal to number of observed objects.

2.2 Performance Measure

The c-index produced from prognostic index [2, 3, 6] is formulates as:

$$c_{ij}(u) = \sum_{i=1}^{n} \sum_{i<j}^{n} v_{ij} I((u(\mathbf{x}_j) - u(\mathbf{x}_i))(t_j - t_i) > 0) / \sum_{i=1}^{n} \sum_{i<j}^{n} v_{ij} \quad (13)$$

Prognostic index of SURLS-SVM is in (12), while for Cox PHM is as (7) where $\mathbf{w}'\varphi(\mathbf{x})$ is replaced by calculating $\boldsymbol{\beta}'\mathbf{x}$. The higher c-index, the better performance.

The performance of model can be improved using feature selection to gain important predictors. There are several feature selection methods such as filter methods, wrapper methods, and embedded methods [13]. In this study, the feature selection applied on two data (clinical and simulated data) is wrapper method, i.e. backward selection, as illustrated in Fig. 1 [13]. The backward elimination is selected because this method can identify suppressor variable, while forward and stepwise elimination cannot. The suppressor features give significant effect when all of them include in the model, otherwise, it cannot be significant individually [14].

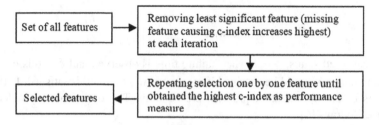

Fig. 1. The algorithm of backward elimination for feature selection in SURLS-SVM

3 Data Description and Methodology

3.1 Data Description

The simulated data is obtained by generating predictors, survival time, and censored status. There are 17 features that each has distribution and some of them has non-linear relation expressed as interaction. The censored status, i.e. 1 for death and 0 for alive, is generated on various percentage (10%, 20%, ..., 90%).

Cancer is one of the health problems that often is studied. The cervical cancer (CC) is one of the cancers deserved concern because it is the second most suffered by woman in the world [15]. In Indonesia, there were 98,692 cases of CC in 2013 and it increases over time. The main cause of cervical cancer is Human Papilloma Virus (HPV) infected from sexual intercourse. In this paper, the cervical cancer is observed from dr. Soetomo Hospital Surabaya in 2014–2016 that contains 412 records. The inclusion criteria in this data as follows: (i) woman patients, (ii) event of interest are death, and (iii) patients have complete medical records used as predictor. The data is right censored. There are 27 (or 7%) patients died and 385 (or 93%) patients survive. The predictors are: Age (P_1), complication status (P_2), anaemia status (P_3), type of treatment (P_4) {chemotherapy, transfusion, chemotherapy and transfusion, others}, stadium (P_5), age of married (P_6), age of first menstruation period (P_7), menstruation cycle (P_8), length of menstruation (P_9), parity (P_{10}), family planning status (P_{11}), and education level (P_{12}) {elementary school, junior high school, senior high school or higher}.

3.2 Methodology

The artificial data that used in this paper is generated using (14) as follows [15].

$$T = \left(-\frac{\log(U)}{\lambda \exp(\boldsymbol{\beta}'\mathbf{x})} \right)^{1/\theta} \tag{14}$$

with T denotes survival time, U is survival probability, $\boldsymbol{\beta}$ is vector of coefficient parameters, $\mathbf{x}$ is predictors, λ and θ are scale and shape parameters, respectively. Equation (14) follows Weibull distribution. The vector of coefficient parameters is defined as follows:

$$\beta = (0.01, -0.015, 0.015, -0.021, -0.05, -0.07, 0.04, -0.08, 0.015, 0.01, -0.03,$$
$$-0.028, 0.05, 0.03, -0.08, 0.04, -0.018, -0.15, -0.08, -0.01, -0.02, -0.075, 0, 0)$$

The simulated data generates 1000 sample size that contains 17 predictors with each predictor is generated from distribution shown in Table 1. Notation Bin(n, size, prob) refers to Binomial distribution with "n" observations, probability of success "prob" in "size" trials. The notation Mult(n, size, prob) refers to Multinomial distribution with probability of success for each category is written in vector "prob". The notation for "n" sample size of Normal distribution is written as N(n, mean, sigma).

Table 1. Distribution of generated predictors.

Feature	Distribution	Feature	Distribution	Feature	Distribution
X_1	Bin (n, 1, 0.5)	X_7	Mult (n, 1, 0.5, 0.1, 0.2, 0.2)	X_{13}	N (n, 20, 3)
X_2	Bin (n, 1, 0.3)	X_8	Mult (n, 1, 0.3, 0.1, 0.6)	X_{14}	N (n, 35, 2)
X_3	Bin (n, 1, 0.7)	X_9	Mult (n, 1, 0.2, 0.4, 0.4)	X_{15}	N (n, 17, 2)
X_4	Bin (n, 3, 0.4)	X_{10}	Mult (n, 1, 0.7, 0.2, 0.1)	X_{16}	N (n, 50, 1.5)
X_5	Bin (n,1, 0.2)	X_{11}	N (n, 40, 3)	X_{17}	N (n, 65, 1)
X_6	Mult (n, 1, 0.2, 0.3, 0.4, 0.1)	X_{12}	N (n, 25, 2)		

Survival time was generated by imposing non-linear pattern within predictor expressed by interaction between two predictors, i.e. (X_1, X_{15}) and (X_1, X_{12}) with corresponding coefficients are -0.0001 and 0.25, respectively. The interactions are only used to generate survival time, but they are not used in model prediction. To show how performance of SURLS-SVM to indicate predictors which give significant effect, then feature selection using backward elimination is employed. The replication 100 times generates 100 datasets with the same scenario. This replication can explain how consistency of the result produced by the SURLS-SVM.

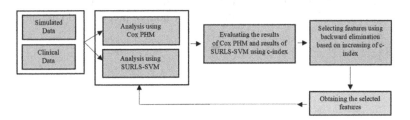

Fig. 2. The steps of analysis (with 100 replications for simulation study).

Analyses in this paper employ SURLS-SVM and Cox PHM on artificial data and CC data. The results of each model are compared by c-index. The tuning parameters used on SURLS-SVM are γ and σ^2. The selection of optimal hyper parameters uses grid search with c-index as criterion. The complete process of analysis is shown on Fig. 2.

4 Empirical Results

4.1 Simulation Study

The objective of this simulation study is to compare the performance of SURLS-SVM with Cox PHM as a benchmark. The feature selection is applied to the SURLS-SVM. The replication was done to know the stability of the performance of proposed approach. Moreover, the effect of confounding is also studied in this simulation study.

Figure 3 shows that the c-index of SURLS-SVM is much higher than Cox PHM; hence the SURLS-SVM is better than Cox PHM in all censored percentage. The lowest c-index is obtained when the data contains 10% of censored data. High censoring percentage data means there are many events happen; hence the probability of mis-ranking increase. The c-index is produced by prognostic index; hence prognostic index of SURLS-SVM is obtained by parameter optimization, while the Cox PHM only use estimate of parameter that certainly has error when it is predicted.

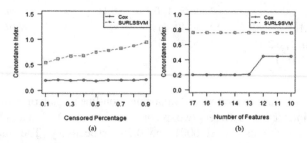

Fig. 3. The c-index obtained from Cox PHM and SURLS-SVM on simulated data based on censored percentage (a) and number of features (b).

Using the same data, backward elimination is applied to obtain predictors which give significantly effect in increasing c-index. The Fig. 3(b) yields increasing of c-index when the feature selection is employed. Based on scenario, the two predictor, i.e. X_{16} and X_{17} has coeeficient zero, then theoritically both of predictors do not include on model.

Fig. 4. The percentage of significance for each predictor after backward elimination.

To see how the SURLS-SVM and backward elimination can detect this condition, the replication was done on simulation. It is replicated 100 times on 10% censored percentage because this censored percentage has the lowest c-index when all predictors include on model. The measure that used as considering to eliminate predictor is c-index. The result of replication is shown by Fig. 4.

The Fig. 4 explains that X_2 has the highest significant percentage (77%). It means that predictor often include on model. Supposedly, X_{16} and X_{17} has the lowest significance percentage than others, meanwhile from Fig. 4 can be known that both predictors have significant percentage up to 50%, then X_{16} and X_{17} the fourth and eighth of lowest percentage. Furthermore, the lowest significant percentage is produced by X_{12} and X_{15}; hence the theory is different with the simulation result. The percentage of increasing c-index in each data is different. Figure 5 describes how increasing of c-index in each data after backward elimination is applied.

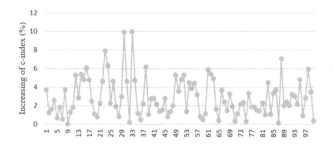

Fig. 5. The c-index increment after feature selection at each replication.

The Fig. 5 describes that increasing of c-index is not more than 10% for all data. The number of predictors gives effect on increasing c-index when feature selection is applied. For example, dataset-9 has the lowest increment then feature selection only eliminate a predictor, in other hand; the feature selection on data which has the highest increasing can eliminate six predictors. Furthermore, two predictors, i.e. X_{16} and X_{17} also give effect on increasing c-index. The data which has it after feature selection is applied has low increasing of c-index.

Based on Figs. 4 and 5, the result explain that SURLS-SVM and backward elimination cannot detect X_{16} and X_{17} appropriately. The statement which can answer this condition is the interaction within predictors, where X_{18} is interaction between $(X_1 * X_{15})$ and X_{19} is interaction between $(X_1 * X_{12})$. The one of predictors to whom has high significant percentage is X_1, it is about 74%. The setting of interaction is known that X_1 is main confounder which interaction with more than a predictor, i.e. X_{12} and X_{15}, moreover it gives effect corresponding with c-index; hence when X_1 is eliminated from final model caused c-index decrease. Furthermore, the predictors which interaction with X_1 are called sub-main confounder, where both of predictors have the high probability to be eliminated from model. This condition already has been explained on Fig. 4; hence the two predictors have the lowest significant percentage. To know how the interaction of predictors give effect on c-index increment, the X_{18} and X_{19} must be include on model.

4.2 Application on Health Data

The second data which used in this paper is cervical cancer data. The two predictors of cervical cancer, i.e. stadium and level of education, are merged because they do not have sufficiency data based on cross tabulation for each predictor. The cross tabulation of stadium after merging are shown in Table 2. The same condition is obtained from level of education as tabulated in Table 3.

Table 2. Cross tabulation after merging stadium category.

	Stadium 1 & 2	Stadium 3 & 4	Total
Alive	189 (45.87%)	196 (45.57%)	385 (93.44%)
Expected	180.4	204.6	385
Death	4 (0.97%)	23 (5.59%)	27 (6.56%)
Expected	12.6	14.4	27
Total	193 (46.84%)	219 (53.16%)	412 (100%)

Table 3. Cross tabulation after merging category of education level.

	0 (Elem.)	1 (Junior HS)	2 (Senior HS and Univ.)	Total
Alive	121 (29.4%)	60 (14.6%)	204 (49.5%)	385 (93.5%)
Expected	117,7	58,9	208,4	385
Death	5 (1.2%)	3 (0.7%)	19 (4.6%)	27 (6.5%)
Expected	8.3	4.1	14.6	27
Total	126 (30.58%)	63 (15.29%)	217 (52.67%)	412 (100%)

The stadium does not satisfy PH assumption based on Table 4. This condition indicates that Cox PHM is not appropriate to analyze this data; hence this analysis requires another model, i.e. SURLS-SVM. Furthermore, the results of estimation parameters and test significant for each predictor yield three significant predictors, i.e. type of treatments (type chemotherapy and transfusion), stadium, and level of education (junior high school).

Table 4. The association test between censored status and categorical predictors (left) and proportional hazard assumption test (right).

	Association test			Proportional hazard test	
Predictors	df	χ^2	p-value	Correlation	p-value
Complication status	1	1.22	0.27	−0.269	0.165
Anemia status	1	5.48	**0.02**	−0.304	0.087
Type of treatment	3	12.23	**0.01**	0.301	0.096
Stadium	1	11.90	**0.00**	−0.444	**0.031**
Family planning status	3	3.03	0.39	−0.087	0.612
Level of education	2	3.11	0.21	−0.157	0.331

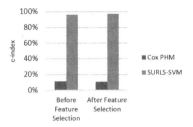

Fig. 6. The c-index of models on cervical cancer data before and after backward elimination.

Table 5. The c-index for each predictor after backward elimination.

Deleted predictor	Before deleted	After deleted	Difference
P_1	97.17%	96.60%	**-0.57**
P_2	97.17%	97.17%	0.00
P_4	97.17%	97.14%	-0.03
P_5	97.17%	97.11%	-0.06
P_6	97.17%	96.65%	-0.52
P_8	97.17%	97.12%	-0.05
P_9	97.17%	97.17%	0.00
P_{10}	97.17%	97.16%	-0.01
P_{12}	97.17%	97.17%	0.00

Figure 6 describes that c-index increase after backward elimination is applied. The first predictor which eliminated is anemia status (P_3), followed by family planning status (P_{11}), and the age of first menstruation period (P_7). The c-index for each that predictor after backward elimination is 97.09%, 97.14%, and 97.17%, respectively, furthermore the c-index for each predictor after backward elimination is appeared on Table 5.

Table 5 describes c-index for each predictor after backward elimination is applied. The difference for each predictor shows that predictors cannot be eliminated, then the predictor that gives the highest effect is age (P_1) because it has highest difference. Therefore, the order of predictors based on effected c-index are age (P_1), age of marriage (P_6), stadium (P_5), menstruation cycle (P_8), type of treatment (P_4), parity (P_{10}), and the last is features which do not have decreasing c-index, i.e. complication status (P_2), length of menstruation (P_9), and level of education (P_{12}).

This study uses c-index instead of significant level; hence the predictors which give the smallest increasing of c-index are eliminated. In other hand, the feature selection can delete redundant predictors from the final model, and then the c-index of final model can be increased. To validate how feature selection works on SURLS-SVM, this paper use replication (on simulated data) with same scenario, furthermore the result of replication shows the irrelevant predictors (predictor which has zero coefficient) is often include in model. It is caused by main-confounder and sub-main confounder features where they have interaction that generates survival time, but they do not include in analysis.

This work can be expanded by considering interaction in the analysis and work on more advance method for feature selection, for example feature selection with regularization approach [16] as part of embedded approach which has simpler step. Model based feature selection [17] may also be considered to give more intuitive reasoning even the proposed method is nonparametric approach.

5   Conclusion

The results of simulation study yield that SURLS-SVM outperforms Cox PHM in all censored percentage data based on c-index criterion. The higher censored percentage results in the higher c-index of SURLS-SVM. The feature selection on SURLS-SVM contributes small improvement; furthermore, the replication informs the irrelevant predictors are often selected in SURLS-SVM model because the effect confounding. In application to the cervical cancer dataset, the significant features in Cox PHM are also the features that improve the c-index of SURLS-SVM after backward elimination was applied.

Acknowledgement. Authors thank to the reviewers for their advices. This research is supported by fundamental research scheme (PDUPT) in ITS number 871/PKS/ITS/2018 financed by DRPM DIKTI, Indonesian Ministry of Research, Technology and Higher Education (number 128/SP2H/PTNBH/DRPM/2018).

References

1. Kleinbaum, D.G., Klein, M.: Survival Analysis: A Self-Learning Text, 3rd edn. Springer, London (2012). https://doi.org/10.1007/978-1-4419-6646-9
2. Mahjub, H., Faradmal, J., Goli, S., Soltanian, A.R.: Performance evaluation of support vector regression models for survival analysis: a simulation study. IJACSA 7(6), 381–389 (2016)
3. Van Belle, V., Pelckmans, K., Suykens, J.A., Van Huffel, S.: Support vector machines for survival analysis. In: Proceedings of the Third International Conference on Computational Intelligence in Medicine and Healthcare (CIMED), Plymouth (2007)
4. Boser, B.E., Guyon, I.M., Vapnik, V.N.: A training algorithm for optimal margin classifiers. In: Proceedings of the Fifth Annual Workshop on Computational Learning Theory, pp. 144–152. ACM, Pittsburgh (1992)
5. Smola, A.J., Scholköpf, B.: A tutorial on support vector regression, statistics and computing. Stat. Comput. **14**(3), 192–222 (2004)
6. Van Belle, V., Pelckmans, K., Suykens, J.A., Van Huffel, S.: Additive survival least-squares support vector machines. Stat. Med. **29**(2), 296–308 (2010)
7. Van Belle, V., Pelckmans, K., Suykens, J.A., Van Huffel, S.: Support vector methods for survival analysis: a comparison between ranking and regression approaches. Artif. Intell. Med. **53**(2), 107–118 (2011)
8. Suykens, J.A., Vandewalle, J.: Least squares support vector machines classifiers. Neural Process. Lett. **9**(3), 293–300 (1999)

9. Goli, S., Mahjub, H., Faradmal, J.: Survival prediction and feature selection in patients with breast cancer using support vector regression. Comput. Math. Methods Med. **2016**, 1–12 (2016)
10. Khotimah, C., Purnami, S.W., Prastyo, D.D., Chosuvivatwong, V., Spriplung, H.: Additive survival least square support vector machines: a simulation study and its application to cervical cancer prediction. In: Proceedings of the 13th IMT-GT International Conference on Mathematics, Statistics and their Applications (ICMSA), AIP Conference Proceedings 1905 (050024), Kedah (2017)
11. Khotimah, C., Purnami, S.W., Prastyo, D.D.: Additive survival least square support vector machines and feature selection on health data in Indonesia. In: Proceedings of the International Conference on Information and Communications Technology (ICOIACT), IEEE Xplore (2018)
12. Haerdle, W.K., Prastyo, D.D., Hafner, C.M.: Support vector machines with evolutionary model selection for default prediction. In: Racine, J., Su, L., Ullah, A. (eds.) The Oxford Handbook of Applied Nonparametric and Semiparametric Econometrics and Statistics, pp. 346–373. Oxford University Press, New York (2014)
13. Chandrashekar, G., Sahin, F.: A survey on feature selection methods. Comput. Electr. Eng. **4** (1), 16–28 (2014)
14. Shieh, G.: Suppression situations in multiple linear regression. Educ. Psychol. Meas. **66**(3), 435–447 (2006)
15. Bender, R., Augustin, T., Blettner, M.: Generating survival times to simulate Cox proportional hazards models. Stat. Med. **24**(11), 1713–1723 (2005)
16. Haerdle, W.K., Prastyo, D.D.: Embedded predictor selection for default risk calculation: a Southeast Asian industry study. In: Chuen, D.L.K., Gregoriou, G.N. (eds.) Handbook of Asian Finance: Financial Market and Sovereign Wealth Fund, vol. 1, pp. 131–148. Academic Press, San Diego (2014)
17. Suhartono, Saputri, P.D., Amalia, F.F., Prastyo, D.D., Ulama, B.S.S.: Model selection in feedforward neural networks for forecasting inflow and outflow in Indonesia. In: Mohamed, A., Berry, M., Yap, B. (eds.) Soft Computing and Data Science 2017. Communications in Computer and Information Science, vol. 788, pp. 95–105. Springer, Singapore (2017). https://doi.org/10.1007/978-981-10-7242-0_8

VAR and GSTAR-Based Feature Selection in Support Vector Regression for Multivariate Spatio-Temporal Forecasting

Dedy Dwi Prastyo[1(✉)], Feby Sandi Nabila[1], Suhartono[1], Muhammad Hisyam Lee[2], Novri Suhermi[1], and Soo-Fen Fam[3]

[1] Department of Statistics, Institut Teknologi Sepuluh Nopember, Surabaya 60111, Indonesia
dedy-dp@statistika.its.ac.id
[2] Department of Mathematical Sciences, Universiti Teknologi Malaysia, Skudai, Malaysia
[3] Department of Technopreneurship, Universiti Teknikal Malaysia Melaka, Melaka, Malaysia

Abstract. Multivariate time series modeling is quite challenging particularly in term of diagnostic checking for assumptions required by the underlying model. For that reason, nonparametric approach is rapidly developed to overcome that problem. But, feature selection to choose relevant input becomes new issue in nonparametric approach. Moreover, if the multiple time series data are observed from different sites, then the location possibly play the role and make the modeling become more complicated. This work employs Support Vector Regression (SVR) to model the multivariate time series data observed from three different locations. The feature selection is done based on Vector Autoregressive (VAR) model that ignore the spatial dependencies as well as based on Generalized Spatio-Temporal Autoregressive (GSTAR) model that involves spatial information into the model. The proposed approach is applied for modeling and forecasting rainfall in three locations in Surabaya, Indonesia. The empirical results inform that the best method for forecasting rainfall in Surabaya is the VAR-based SVR approach.

Keywords: SVR · VAR · GSTAR · Feature selection · Rainfall

1 Introduction

Global warming has caused climate change which affected the rainfall. As a tropical country, Indonesia has various rainfall pattern and different amount of rainfall in each region. The rainfall becomes hard to predict because of this disturbance. The climate change that is triggered by the global warming causes the rainfall pattern becomes more uncertain. This phenomenon affects the agricultural productivity, for example, in East Java province, Indonesia [1], United State [2], and Africa [3]. The capital city of East Java, Surabaya, also suffers climate change as the effect of global warming.

The rainfall has a huge variance in spatial and time scale. Therefore, it is necessary to apply a univariate or multivariate modeling to predict rainfall. One of the multivariate

© Springer Nature Singapore Pte Ltd. 2019
B. W. Yap et al. (Eds.): SCDS 2018, CCIS 937, pp. 46–57, 2019.
https://doi.org/10.1007/978-981-13-3441-2_4

models commonly used is Vector Autoregressive Moving Average (VARMA), which is an expansion of ARMA model [4]. If the spatial effect from different locations is considered, then Generalized Space Time Autoregressive (GSTAR) model play into role.

In this research, we apply Vector Autoregressive (VAR) and GSTAR to model the rainfall. The VAR model does not involve location (spatial) information, while GSTAR model accommodates the heterogeneous locations by adding the weight to each location. The comparison and application of VAR and GSTAR models has already done Suhartono et al. [5] to determine the input in Feed-forward Neural Network (FFNN) as nonparametric approach. There are two types of time series prediction approach: parametric approach and nonparametric approach. Another nonparametric approach which is widely used is Support Vector Regression (SVR) as the modification of Support Vector Machine (SVM) [6–9] which handles the regression task. The main concept of SVR is to maximize the margin around the hyper plane and to obtain data points that become the support vectors.

This work does not handle outliers if they exist. This paper is organized as follows. Section 2 explains the theoretical part. Section 3 describes the methodology. Section 4 informs empirical results and discussion. At last, Sect. 5 shows the conclusion.

2 Literature Review

2.1 Vector Autoregressive (VAR) Model

The VAR model order one, abbreviated as VAR(1), is formulated in Eq. (1) [4]:

$$\dot{Y}_t = \Phi_0 + \Phi \dot{Y}_{t-1} + \alpha_t, \tag{1}$$

where $\dot{Y}_t = Y_t - \mu$, with $\mu = E(Y_t)$. The α_t is $m \times 1$ vector of residual at time t, $\dot{Y}_t$ is $m \times 1$ vector of variables at t, and $\dot{Y}_{t-1}$ is $m \times 1$ vector of variables at $(t-1)$. The parameter estimation is conducted using conditional least square (CLS). Given m series with T data points each, then VAR(p) model could be expressed by (2).

$$y_t = \delta + \sum_{i=1}^{p} \Phi_i y_{t-i} + a_t. \tag{2}$$

Equation (2) can also be expressed in the form of linear model as follows:

$$Y = XB + A \tag{3}$$

and

$$y = \left(X^T \otimes I_m\right)\beta + a, \tag{4}$$

with $\otimes$ is Kronecker product, $Y = (y_1, \ldots, y_T)_{(m \times T)}$, $B = \left(\delta, \Phi_1, \ldots, \Phi_p\right)_{(m \times (mp+1))}$, and $X = (X_0, \ldots, X_t, \ldots, X_{T-1})_{((mp+1) \times T)}$. The vector of data at time t is

$$X_t = \begin{pmatrix} 1 \\ y_t \\ \vdots \\ y_{t-p+1} \end{pmatrix}_{((mp+1)\times 1)}$$

and $A = (a_1, \ldots, a_T)_{(m \times T)}$, $y = (\text{vec}(Y))_{(mT \times 1)}$, $\beta = (\text{vec}(B))_{((m^2 p + m) \times 1)}$, and $a = (\text{vec}(A))_{(mT \times 1)}$. The *vec* denotes a column stacking operator such that:

$$\widehat{\beta} = \left(\left(X'X \right)^{-1} X' \otimes I_m \right) y. \tag{5}$$

The consistency property and asymptotic normality property of the CLS estimate $\widehat{\beta}$ is shown in the following equation.

$$\sqrt{T} \left(\widehat{\beta} - \beta \right) \xrightarrow{d} N \left(0, \Gamma_p^{-1} \otimes \sum \right), \tag{6}$$

where $X'X/T$ converges in probability towards Γ_p and $\xrightarrow{d}$ denotes the convergence in distribution. The estimate for Σ is given as follows:

$$\widehat{\Sigma} = (T - (mp+1))^{-1} \sum_{t=1}^{T} \widehat{a}_t \widehat{a}_t', \tag{7}$$

where $\widehat{a}_t$ is the residual vector.

2.2 Generalized Space Time Autoregressive (GSTAR) Model

Given a multivariate time series $\{Y(t) : t = 0, \pm 1, \pm 2, \ldots\}$ with T observations for each series, the GSTAR model for order one with 3 locations is given as [5, 10, 11]:

$$Y(t) = \Phi_{10} Y(t-1) + \Phi_{11} W^{(l)} Y(t-1) + a(t), \tag{8}$$

with $Y(t)$ is $(T \times 1)$ random vector at t, Φ_{10} is a matrix of coefficient, Φ_{11} is spatial coefficient matrix, and $W^{(l)}$ is an $(m \times m)$ weight matrix at spatial lag l. The weight must satisfy $w_{ii}^{(l)} = 0$ and $\sum_{i \neq j} w_{ij}^{(l)} = 1$. The $a(t)$ is vector of error which satisfies i.i.d and multivariate normally distributed assumption with 0 vector mean and variance-covariance matrix $\sigma^2 I_m$.

Uniform Weighting
Uniform weighting assumes that the locations are homogenous such that:

$$W_{ij} = \frac{1}{n_i}, \tag{9}$$

where n_i is the number of near location and W_{ij} is the weight location i and j.

Inverse Distance Weighting (IDW)
The IDW method is calculated based on the real distance between locations. Then, we calculate the inverse of the real distance and normalize it.

Normalized Cross-Correlation Weighting
Normalized cross-correlation weighting uses the cross-correlation between locations at the corresponding lags. In general, the cross-correlation between location i and location j at time lag k, i.e. the $corr\left[Y_i(t), Y_j(t-k)\right]$, is defined as follows:

$$\rho_{ij}(k) = \frac{\gamma_{ij}(k)}{\sigma_i \sigma_j}, k = 0, \pm 1, \pm 2, \ldots, \tag{10}$$

where $\gamma_{ij}(k)$ is cross-covariance in location i and location j. The sample cross-correlation can be computed using the following equation.

$$r_{ij}(k) = \frac{\sum_{t=k+1}^{T}\left(Y_i(t) - \overline{Y}_i\right)\left(Y_j(t-k) - \overline{Y}_j\right)}{\sqrt{\sum_{t=1}^{T}\left(Y_i(t) - \overline{Y}_i\right)^2 \sum_{t=1}^{T}\left(Y_j(t) - \overline{Y}_j\right)^2}}. \tag{11}$$

The weighting is calculated by normalizing the cross-correlation between locations. This process generally results in location weight for GSTAR (1_1) model, which is as follows:

$$w_{ij} = \frac{r_{ij}(1)}{\sum_{j \neq i}|r_{ij}(1)|} \text{ for } i \neq j. \tag{12}$$

2.3 Support Vector Regression (SVR)

The SVR is developed from SVM as a learning algorithm which uses hypothesis that there are linear functions in a high dimensional feature space [6–9]. SVM for regression uses $\varepsilon-$ insensitive loss function which is known as SVR. The regression function of SVR is perfect if and only if the deviation bound equals zero such that:

$$f(x) = w^T \varphi(x) + b, \tag{13}$$

where w is weight and b is bias. The notation $\varphi(x)$ denotes a point in feature space $\mathcal{F}$ which is a mapping result of x in an input space. The coefficients w and b is aimed to minimize following risk.

$$R(f(x)) = \frac{C}{n}\sum_{i=1}^{n} L_\varepsilon(y_i, f(x_i)) + \frac{1}{2}\|w\|^2 \tag{14}$$

Where

$$L_\varepsilon(y_i, f(x_i)) = \begin{cases} 0 & ; |y_i - f(x_i)| \le \varepsilon, \\ |y_i - f(x_i)| - \varepsilon & ; \text{otherwise.} \end{cases} \tag{15}$$

The L_ε is a ε–insensitive loss function, y_i is the vector of observation, C and ε are the hyper parameters. The function f is assumed to approximate all the points (x_i, y_i) with precision ε if all the points are inside the interval. While infeasible condition happens when there are several points outside the interval $f \pm \varepsilon$. The infeasible points can be added a slack variable ξ, ξ^* in order to tackle the infeasible constrain. Hence, the optimization in (14) can be transformed into the following.

$$\min \frac{1}{2} \|w\|^2 + C \frac{1}{n} \sum_{i=1}^{n} (\xi_i + \xi_i^*), \tag{16}$$

with constrains $(w^T \varphi(x_i) + b) - y_i \le \varepsilon + \xi_i^*; y_i - (w^T \varphi(x_i) - b) \le \varepsilon + \xi_i$ and $\xi, \xi^* \ge 0$, and $i = 1, 2, \ldots, n$. The optimization in that constrain can be solved using primal Lagrange:

$$L(w, b, \xi, \xi^*, \alpha_i, \alpha_i^*, \beta_i, \beta_i^*) =$$
$$\frac{1}{2} \|w\|^2 + C \left(\sum_{i=1}^{n} (\xi_i + \xi_i^*) \right) - \sum_{i=1}^{n} \beta_i [w^T \varphi(x_i) + b - y_i + \varepsilon + \xi_i^*] - \tag{17}$$
$$\sum_{i=1}^{n} \beta_i^* [y_i - w^T \varphi(x_i) - b + \varepsilon + \xi_i^*] - \sum_{i=1}^{n} (\alpha_i \xi_i + \alpha_i^* \xi_i^*)$$

The Eq. (17) is minimized in primal variables w, b, ξ, ξ^* and maximized in the form of non-negative Lagrangian multiplier $\alpha_i, \alpha_i^*, \beta_i, \beta_i^*$. Then, we obtain a dual Lagrangian with kernel function $K(x_i, x_j) = \varphi(x_i)^T \varphi(x_j)$. One of the most widely used kernel function is *Gaussian radial basis function* (RBF) formulated in (18) [6]:

$$K(x_i, x_j) = \exp\left(-\frac{\|x_i - x_j^2\|}{2\sigma^2} \right) \tag{18}$$

$$\partial(\beta_i, \beta_i^*) = \sum_{i=1}^{n} y_i(\beta_i - \beta_i^*) - \varepsilon \sum_{i=1}^{n} (\beta_i + \beta_i^*)$$
$$-\frac{1}{2} \sum_{i=1}^{n} \sum_{j=1}^{n} (\beta_i - \beta_i^*)(\beta_j - \beta_j^*) K(x_i, x_j). \tag{19}$$

Then, we obtain the regression function as follows.

$$f(x, \beta_i, \beta_i^*) = \sum_{i=1}^{l} (\beta_i - \beta_i^*) K(x_i, x_j) + b. \tag{20}$$

The SVM and SVR are extended for various fields. It is also developed for modeling and analyzing survival data, for example, done by Khotimah *et al.* [12, 13].

2.4 Model Selection

The model selection is conducted using out-of-sample criteria by comparing the multivariate *Root Mean Square Error* (RMSE). The RMSE of a model is obtained using the Eq. (11) for training dataset and (12) for testing dataset, respectively.

$$RMSE_{in} = \sqrt{MSE_{in}} = \sqrt{\frac{1}{n}\sum_{i=1}^{n}\left(Y_i - \widehat{Y}_i\right)^2}, \tag{21}$$

where n is the effective number of observation in training dataset.

$$RMSE_{out} = \sqrt{\frac{1}{n_{out}}\sum_{i=1}^{n_{out}}\left(Y_{n+l} - \widehat{Y}_n(l)\right)^2}, \tag{22}$$

with l is the forecast horizon.

3 Data and Method

The dataset that is used in this research is obtained from *Badan Meteorologi, Klimatologi, dan Geofisika* (BMKG) at Central of Jakarta. The rainfall is recorded from 3 stations: Perak I, Perak II, and Juanda for 34 years and 10 months. The dataset is divided into in-sample (training) and out-of-sample (testing) data. The in-sample spans from January 1981 to December 2013. The data from January 2014 to November 2015 is out-of-sample for evaluating the forecast performance.

The analysis is started by describing the rainfall pattern from 3 locations and model them using VAR and GSTAR. Once the right model with significant variables is obtained, it is continued with VAR-SVR and GSTAR-SVR modeling using the variables obtained from the VAR and GSTAR, respectively [5]. This kind of feature selection using statistical model was also studied by Suhartono *et al.* [14].

4 Empirical Results

4.1 Descriptive Statistics

The descriptive statistics of accumulated rainfall from three locations is visualized in Fig. 1. The means of rainfall at station Perak 1, Perak 2, and Juanda are respectively 45.6 mm, 43.1 mm, and 58.9 mm. These means are used as threshold to find period when the rainfall is lower or greater at each location. Figure 1 shows that from April to May there is a shift from rain season to dry season. There is a shift from dry season to rain season in November. The yellow boxplots show the rainfall average at that period is lower than overall mean, while the blue ones show the opposite. The yellow and blue boxplots are mostly in dry season and rain season, respectively.

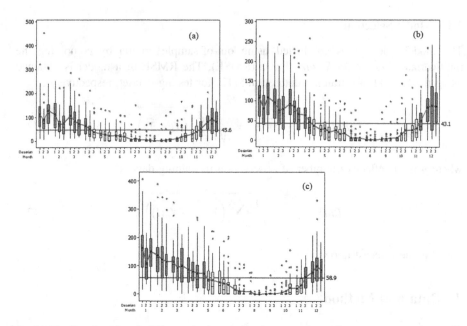

Fig. 1. The boxplots for rainfall per month and dasarian at station Perak 1 (a); Perak 2 (b); and Juanda (c) (Color figure online)

4.2 VAR Modeling

Order identification in VAR is conducted based on partial cross-correlation matrix from stationary data, after being differenced at lag 36. Lag 1 and 2 are significant such that we use non-seasonal order 2 in our model. We also use seasonal orders 1, 2, 3, 4, and 5 since we can see that lags 36, 72, 108, and 144 are still significant. Hence, we have 5 candidate models: VARIMA $(2,0,0)(1,1,0)^{36}$, VARIMA $(2,0,0)(2,1,0)^{36}$, VARIMA $(2,0,0)(3,1,0)^{36}$, VARIMA $(2,0,0)(4,1,0)^{36}$, and VARIMA $(2,0,0)(5,1,0)^{36}$.

VAR's residual must satisfy white noise and multivariate normality assumptions. The test results show none of the model satisfies the assumptions for $\alpha = 5\%$. The Root Mean Square Error (RMSE) of the out-of-sample prediction for five models is summarized in Table 1.

Table 1. Cross tabulation before and after merging stadium category.

Model	Location			Overall RMSE
	Perak 1	Perak 2	Juanda	
VARIMA $(2,0,0)(1,1,0)^{36}$	62.32484	47.51616	56.44261	55.76121
VARIMA $(2,0,0)(2,1,0)^{36}$	45.70456	41.19213	48.4053*	45.19871
VARIMA $(2,0,0)(3,1,0)^{36}$	40.13943	37.04678*	51.56591	44.76059
VARIMA $(2,0,0)(4,1,0)^{36}$	39.44743*	36.86216	49.98893	42.48063*
VARIMA $(2,0,0)(5,1,0)^{36}$	41.60190	37.73775	49.20983	43.11405

*Minimum RMSE

Table 1 shows that VARIMA $(2,0,0)(4,1,0)^{36}$ has the smallest overall RMSE. Hence, we choose it as the best model. The equation of VAR model for location Perak 1 is given as follows.

$$
\begin{aligned}
\widehat{y1}_t = \ & y1_{t-36} + 0.08576(y1_{t-1} - y1_{t-36}) - 0,1242(y1_{t-2} - y1_{t-38}) + \\
& 0.15702(y2_{t-2} - y2_{t-38}) + 0.0564(y3_{t-2} - y3_{t-38}) - 0.73164(y1_{t-36} - \\
& y1_{t-72}) - 0.60705(y1_{t-72} - y1_{t-108}) - 0.50632(y1_{t-108} - y1_{t-144}) + \\
& 0.14915(y2_{t-108} - y2_{t-144}) - 0.21933(y1_{t-144} - y1_{t-180})
\end{aligned}
$$

VAR model for location Perak 1 show that the rainfall in that location is also influenced by the rainfall in other location. The equation of VAR models for location Perak 2 and Juanda are given as follows, respectively.

$$
\begin{aligned}
\widehat{y2}_t = \ & y2_{t-36} + 0,07537(y1_{t-1} - y1_{t-36}) - 0.10323(y1_{t-2} - y1_{t-38}) + \\
& 0.09673(y2_{t-2} - y2_{t-38}) + 0.0639(y3_{t-2} - y3_{t-38}) + 0.16898(y1_{t-36} - \\
& y1_{t-72}) - 0.8977(y2_{t-36} - y2_{t-72}) + 0.07393(y1_{t-72} - y1_{t-108}) - \\
& 0.70884(y2_{t-72} - y2_{t-108}) - 0.38961(y2_{t-108} - y2_{t-144}) - \\
& 0.20648(y1_{t-144} - y1_{t-180})
\end{aligned}
$$

$$
\begin{aligned}
\widehat{y3}_t = \ & y3_{t-36} 0.0767(y1_{t-1} - y1_{t-36}) + 0.06785(y3_{t-1} - y3_{t-36}) - 0.09053(y1_{t-2} - y1_{t-38}) \\
& + 0.11712(y3_{t-2} - y3_{t-38}) - 0.74691(y3_{t-36} - y3_{t-72}) - \\
& 0.07787(y2_{t-72} - y2_{t-108}) - 0.58127(y3_{t-72} - y3_{t-108}) - \\
& 0.32507(y3_{t-108} - y3_{t-144}) - 0.16491(y3_{t-144} - y3_{t-180})
\end{aligned}
$$

The rainfall at station Perak 2 and Juanda are also influenced by the rainfall in other locations.

4.3   GSTAR Modeling

We choose GSTAR $([1,2,3,4,5,6,36,72]1)$-$I(1)(1)^{36}$ as our model. Residual assumption checking in GSTAR shows that this model does not satisfy assumptions for $\alpha = 5\%$. The prediction for out-of-sample is done with two scenarios: using all the variables and using only the significant variables. The results are shown in the Table 2.

Table 2. The RMSEs of out-of-sample from STAR $([1,2,36,72,108,144,180]1)$-$I(1)^{36}$

Location	Model with all variables			Model with only significant variables		
	Uniform	Inverse distance	Cross correlation	Uniform	Inverse distance	Cross correlation
Perak 1	271.2868	62.2626	61.7325	68.7310	61.7713	61.0599*
Perak 2	55.1563*	56.1579	56.1562	66.2657	56.1511	55.6316
Juanda	79.1952	75.5786*	76.776	109.9268	76.0599	76.1471
Total	166.2688	66.3322	66.2888*	84.0611	65.2016	64.8629*

*Minimum RMSE

The GSTAR model equations for locations Perak 1, Perak 2, and Juanda are given in the following, respectively.

$$
\begin{aligned}
\widehat{y1_t} = \ & y1_{t-36} + 0.0543608(y2_{t-1} - y2_{t-37}) + 0.042241(y3_{t-1} - y3_{t-37}) + \\
& 0.0444963(y2_{t-2} - y2_{t-38}) + 0.034576(y3_{t-2} - y3_{t-38}) + \\
& (-0.81419(y1_{t-36} - y1_{t-72})) + (-0.69679(y1_{t-72} - y1_{t-108})) + \\
& (-0.57013(y1_{t-108} - y1_{t-144}) + 0.039493(y2_{t-108} - y2_{t-144}) + \\
& 0.030688(y3_{t-108} - y3_{t-144}) + (-0.34571(y1_{t-144} - y1_{t-180})) + \\
& (-0.21989(y1_{t-180} - y1_{t-216})) + 0.038646(y2_{t-180} - y2_{t-216}) + \\
& 0.0300298(y3_{t-180} - y3_{t-216})
\end{aligned}
$$

and

$$
\begin{aligned}
\widehat{y2_t} = \ & y2_{t-36} + 0,035769(y1_{t-1} - y1_{t-37}) + 0.040401(y3_{t-1} - y3_{t-37}) + \\
& 0.029355(y2_{t-2} - y2_{t-38}) + 0.033157(y3_{t-2} - y3_{t-38}) + (-0.84879(y2_{t-36} - \\
& y2_{t-72})) + 0.022607(y1_{t-36} - y1_{t-72}) + 0.0255357(y3_{t-36} - y3_{t-72}) + \\
& (-0.72905(y2_{t-72} - y2_{t-108})) + (-0.55416(y2_{t-108} - y2_{t-144})) + \\
& (-0.36629(y2_{t-144} - y2_{t-180})) + (-0.20078(y2_{t-180} - y2_{t-216})).
\end{aligned}
$$

and

$$
\begin{aligned}
\widehat{y3_t} = \ & y3_{t-36} + 0.103666(y3_{t-1} - y3_{t-37}) + 0.089536(y3_{t-2} - y3_{t-38}) + \\
& (-0.78084(y3_{t-36} - y3_{t-72})) + (-0.6609(y3_{t-72} - y3_{t-108})) + \\
& (-0.44531(y3_{t-108} - y3_{t-144})) + (-0.31721(y3_{t-144} - y3_{t-180})) + \\
& (-0.18268(y3_{t-180} - y3_{t-216})).
\end{aligned}
$$

4.4   Forecasting Using VAR-SVR and GSTAR-SVR Model

The VAR-SVR and GSTAR-SVR modeling use grid search method to determine the hyper parameters, i.e. epsilon, sigma, and cost. Finding these hyper parameters values is in purpose of to obtain the minimum RMSE of out-of-sample data. VAR-SVR model uses the variables of VARIMA $(2,0,0)(4,1,0)^{36}$, which is the best VAR model, as the inputs. Then, GSTAR-SVR model uses the significant variables of GSTAR $([1,2,3,4,5,6,36,72]1)$-I(1)(1)^{36} with normalized cross-correlation weight. The prediction of the out-of-sample data (testing data) are given in Table 3. It shows that the RMSE of VAR-SVR model at Perak 2 is the smallest. It means that VAR-SVR model performs better at Perak 2 than other locations.

Table 3. The VAR-SVR model with smallest RMSE

Location	Epsilon	Cost	Sigma	RMSE Out sample
Perak 1	8.67×10^{-4}	2270	1.3×10^{-7}	38.57858
Perak 2	8.65×10^{-4}	2100.1	1.09×10^{-7}	34.03217
Juanda	8.69×10^{-4}	3001	1.08×10^{-7}	47.75733

The results in Table 4 also show that the RMSE of GSTAR-SVR model at Perak 2 is the smallest. Compared to GSTAR-SVR, the best model with the smallest overall RMSE is VAR-SVR. The VAR-SVR and GSTAR-SVR models are used to forecast the rainfall from November 2015 to November 2016. The forecast results in testing dataset as well as one year ahead forecasting are given in Figs. 2 and 3.

Table 4. The GSTAR-SVR model with smallest RMSE

Location	Epsilon	Cost	Sigma	RMSE out sample
Perak 1	9×10^{-5}	355	5×10^{-7}	41.68467
Perak 2	8×10^{-8}	450	3×10^{-7}	32.90443
Juanda	10^{-9}	280	7×10^{-7}	50.33458

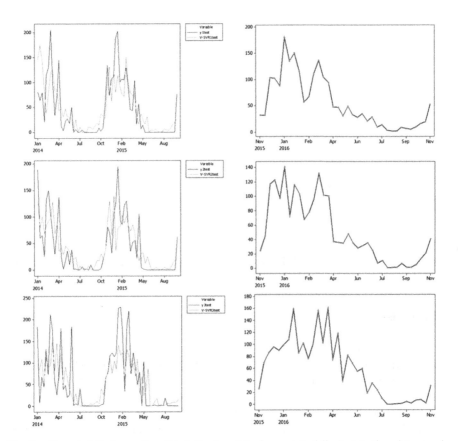

Fig. 2. The rainfall observation (black line) and its forecast (red line) at testing dataset using VAR-SVR model at station Perak 1 (top left); Perak 2 (middle left); Juanda (bottom left); and one-year forecasting (right) at each location. (Color figure online)

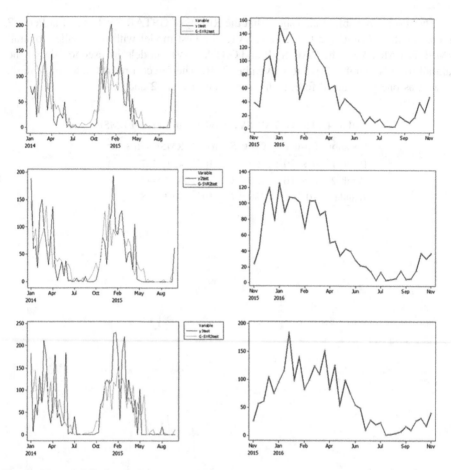

Fig. 3. The rainfall observation (black line) and its forecast (red line) at testing dataset using GSTAR-SVR model at station Perak 1 (top left); Perak 2 (middle left); Juanda (bottom left); and one-year forecasting (right) at each location. (Color figure online)

5 Conclusion

First, the best VARIMA model used to forecast rainfall in Surabaya is VARIMA $(2,0,0)(4,1,0)^{36}$. Second, the forecast of GSTAR ([1,2,3,4,5,6,36,72]1)-I(1)(1)^{36} using the only significant input (restricted form) and normalized cross-correlation weight resulted in the smallest RMSE than the other GSTAR forms. Third, the hybrid VAR-based SVR model with VARIMA $(2,0,0)(4,1,0)^{36}$ as feature selection produced smallest RMSE than other models. Thus, the spatial information does not improve the feature selection of SVR approach used in this analysis.

Acknowledgement. This research was supported by DRPM under the scheme of "Penelitian Dasar Unggulan Perguruan Tinggi (PDUPT)" with contract number 930/PKS/ITS/2018. The authors thank to the General Director of DIKTI for funding and to the referees for the useful suggestions.

References

1. Kuswanto, H., Salamah, M., Retnaningsih, S.M., Prastyo, D.D.: On the impact of climate change to agricultural productivity in East Java. J. Phys: Conf. Ser. **979**(012092), 1–8 (2018)
2. Adams, R.M., Fleming, R.A., Chang, C.C., McCarl, B.A., Rosenzweig, C.: A reassessment of the economic effects of global climate change on U.S. agriculture. Clim. Change **30**(2), 147–167 (1995)
3. Schlenker, W., Lobell, D.B.: Robust negative impacts of climate change on African agriculture. Environ. Res. Lett. **5**(014010), 1–8 (2010)
4. Tsay, R.S.: Multivariate Time Series Analysis. Wiley, Chicago (2014)
5. Suhartono, Prastyo, D.D., Kuswanto, H., Lee, M.H.: Comparison between VAR, GSTAR, FFNN-VAR, and FFNN-GSTAR models for forecasting oil production. Matematika **34**(1), 103–111 (2018)
6. Haerdle, W.K., Prastyo, D.D., Hafner, C.M.: Support vector machines with evolutionary model selection for default prediction. In: Racine, J., Su, L., Ullah, A. (eds.) The Oxford Handbook of Applied Nonparametric and Semiparametric Econometrics and Statistics, pp. 346–373. Oxford University Press, New York (2014)
7. Boser, B.E., Guyon, I.M., Vapnik, V.N.: A training algorithm for optimal margin classifiers. In: Proceedings of the Fifth Annual Workshop on Computational Learning Theory, pp. 144–152. ACM, Pittsburgh (1992)
8. Smola, A.J., Scholköpf, B.: A tutorial on support vector regression, statistics and computing. Stat. Comput. **14**(3), 192–222 (2004)
9. Suykens, J.A., Vandewalle, J.: Least squares support vector machines classifiers. Neural Process. Lett. **9**(3), 293–300 (1999)
10. Borovkova, S., Lopuhaä, H.P., Ruchjana, B.N.: Consistency and asymptotic normality of least squares estimators in Generalized STAR models. Stat. Neerl. **62**(4), 482–508 (2008)
11. Bonar, H., Ruchjana, B.N., Darmawan, G.: Development of generalized space time autoregressive integrated with ARCH error (GSTARI - ARCH) model based on consumer price index phenomenon at several cities in North Sumatra province. In: Proceedings of the 2nd International Conference on Applied Statistics (ICAS II). AIP Conference Proceedings 1827 (020009), Bandung (2017)
12. Khotimah, C., Purnami, S.W., Prastyo, D.D., Chosuvivatwong, V., Spriplung, H.: Additive survival least square support vector machines: a simulation study and its application to cervical cancer prediction. In: Proceedings of the 13th IMT-GT International Conference on Mathematics, Statistics and their Applications (ICMSA). AIP Conference Proceedings 1905 (050024), Kedah (2017)
13. Khotimah, C., Purnami, S.W., Prastyo, D.D.: Additive survival least square support vector machines and feature selection on health data in Indonesia. In: Proceedings of the International Conference on Information and Communications Technology (ICOIACT). IEEE Xplore (2018)
14. Suhartono, Saputri, P.D., Amalia, F.F., Prastyo, D.D., Ulama, B.S.S.: Model selection in feedforward neural networks for forecasting inflow and outflow in Indonesia. In: Mohamed, A., Berry, M., Yap, B. (eds.) SCDS 2017. CCIS, vol. 788, pp. 95–105. Springer, Singapore (2017). https://doi.org/10.1007/978-981-10-7242-0_8

Feature and Architecture Selection on Deep Feedforward Network for Roll Motion Time Series Prediction

Novri Suhermi[1(✉)], Suhartono[1], Santi Puteri Rahayu[1],
Fadilla Indrayuni Prastyasari[2], Baharuddin Ali[3],
and Muhammad Idrus Fachruddin[4]

[1] Department of Statistics, Institut Teknologi Sepuluh Nopember,
Kampus ITS Sukolilo, Surabaya 60111, Indonesia
novri@statistika.its.ac.id
[2] Department of Marine Engineering, Institut Teknologi Sepuluh Nopember,
Kampus ITS Sukolilo, Surabaya 60111, Indonesia
[3] Indonesian Hydrodynamic Laboratory, Badan Pengkajian Dan Penerapan
Teknologi, Surabaya 60111, Indonesia
[4] GDP Laboratory, Jakarta 11410, Indonesia

Abstract. The neural architecture and the input features are very substantial in order to build an artificial neural network (ANN) model that is able to perform a good prediction. The architecture is determined by several hyperparameters including the number of hidden layers, the number of nodes in each hidden layer, the series length, and the activation function. In this study, we present a method to perform feature selection and architecture selection of ANN model for time series prediction. Specifically, we explore a deep learning or deep neural network (DNN) model, called deep feedforward network, an ANN model with multiple hidden layers. We use two approaches for selecting the inputs, namely PACF based inputs and ARIMA based inputs. Three activation functions used are logistic sigmoid, tanh, and ReLU. The real dataset used is time series data called roll motion of a Floating Production Unit (FPU). Root mean squared error (RMSE) is used as the model selection criteria. The results show that the ARIMA based 3 hidden layers DNN model with ReLU function outperforms with remarkable prediction accuracy among other models.

Keywords: ARIMA · Deep feedforward network · PACF · Roll motion
Time series

1 Introduction

Artificial neural network (ANN) is one of nonlinear model that has been widely developed and applied in time series modeling and forecasting [1]. The major advantages of ANN models are their capability to capture any pattern, their flexibility form, and their free assumption property. ANN is considered as universal approximator such that it is able to approximate any continuous function by adding more nodes on hidden layer [2–4].

© Springer Nature Singapore Pte Ltd. 2019
B. W. Yap et al. (Eds.): SCDS 2018, CCIS 937, pp. 58–71, 2019.
https://doi.org/10.1007/978-981-13-3441-2_5

Many studies recently developed a more advanced architecture of neural network called deep learning or deep neural network (DNN). One of the basic type of DNN is a feedforward network with deeper layers, i.e. it has more than one hidden layer in its architecture. Furthermore, it has also been shown by several studies that DNN is very promising for forecasting task where it is able to significantly improve the forecast accuracy [5–10].

ANN model has been widely applied in many fields, including ship motion study. The stability of a roll motion in a ship is a critical aspect that must be kept in control to prevent the potential damage and danger of a ship such as capsizing [11]. Hence, the ship safety depends on the behavior of the roll motion. In order to understand the pattern of the roll motion, it is necessary to construct a model which is able to explain its pattern and predict the future motion. The modeling and prediction can be conducted using several approaches. One of them is time series model.

Many researches have frequently applied time series models to predict roll motion. Nicolau et al. [12] have worked on roll motion prediction in a conventional ship by applying time series model called artificial neural network (ANN). The prediction resulted in remarkable accuracy. Zhang and Ye [13] used another time series model called autoregressive integrated moving average (ARIMA) to predict roll motion. Khan et al. [14] also used both ARIMA and ANN models in order to compare the prediction performance from each model. The results showed that ANN model outperformed compared to ARIMA model in predicting the roll motion. Other researches have also shown that ANN model is powerful and very promising as its results in performing roll motion prediction [15, 16].

Another challenge in performing neural network for time series forecasting is the input or feature selection. The input used in neural network time series modeling is its significant lag variables. The significant lags can be obtained using partial autocorrelation function (PACF). We may choose the lags which have significant PACF. Beside PACF, another potential technique which is also frequently used is obtaining the inputs from ARIMA model [17]. First, we model the data using ARIMA. The predictor variables of ARIMA model is then used as the inputs of the neural network model. In this study, we will explore one of DNN model, namely deep feedforward network model, in order to predict the roll motion. We will perform feature selection and architecture selection of the DNN model to obtain the optimal architecture that is expected to be able to make better prediction. The architecture selection is done by tuning the hyperparameters, including number of hidden layers, the number of hidden nodes, and the activation function. The results of the selection and its prediction accuracy are then discussed.

2 Time Series Analysis: Concept and Methods

Time series analysis aims to analyze time series data in order to find the pattern and the characteristics of the data where the application is for forecasting or prediction task [18]. Forecasting or prediction is done by constructing a model based on the historical data and applying it to predict the future value. Contrast with regression model where it consists of response variable(s) Y and predictor variable(s) X, time series model uses the variable itself as the predictors. For instance, let Y_t a time series response variable at time t, then the predictor variables would be $Y_{t-1}, Y_{t-2}, Y_{t-3}, Y_{t-4}$. The variables $Y_{t-1}, Y_{t-2}, Y_{t-3}, Y_{t-4}$ are also called lag variables. There are many time series models that have been developed. In this section, we present two time series models which have been widely used for forecasting task, namely autoregressive integrated moving average (ARIMA) and artificial neural network (ANN). We also present several important and mandatory concepts in order to understand the idea of time series model. They are autocorrelation and partial autocorrelation.

2.1   Autocorrelation Function (ACF) and Partial Autocorrelation Function (PACF)

Let Y_t a time series process, the correlation coefficient between Y_t and Y_{t-k} is called autocorrelation at lag k, denoted by ρ_k, where ρ_k is a function of k only, under weakly stationarity assumption. Specifically, autocorrelation function (ACF) ρ_k is defined as follows [19]:

$$\rho_k = \frac{\text{Cov}(Y_t, Y_{t-k})}{\text{Var}(Y_t)}. \tag{1}$$

Hence, the sample autocorrelation is defined as follows:

$$\hat{\rho}_k = \frac{\sum_{t=k+1}^{T} (Y_t - \bar{Y})(Y_{t-k} - \bar{Y})}{\sum_{t=1}^{T} (Y_t - \bar{Y})^2}. \tag{2}$$

Then, partial autocorrelation function (PACF) is defined as the autocorrelation between Y_t and Y_{t-k} after removing their mutual linear dependency on the intervening variabels $Y_{t-1}, Y_{t-2}, \ldots, Y_{t-k+1}$. It can be expressed as $\text{Corr}(Y_t, Y_{t-k} \mid Y_{t-1}, Y_{t-2}, \ldots, Y_{t-k+1})$. PACF in stationary time series is used to determine the order of autoregressive (AR) model [20]. The calculation of sample partial autocorrelation is done recursively by initializing the value of partial autocorrelation at lag 1, $\hat{\phi}_{11} = \hat{\rho}_1$. Hence, the value of sample correlation at lag k can be obtained as follows [21, 22]:

$$\hat{\phi}_{k,k} = \frac{\hat{\rho}_k - \sum_{j=1}^{k-1} \hat{\phi}_{k-1,j} \hat{\rho}_{k-j}}{1 - \sum_{j=1}^{k-1} \hat{\phi}_{k-1,j} \hat{\rho}_j}. \tag{3}$$

PACF is used to determined the order p of an autoregressive process, denoted by AR (p), one of the special case of ARIMA(p, d, q) process, where $d = 0$ and $q = 0$. It is also used to determined the lag variables which are chosen as the inputs in ANN model [23].

2.2   The ARIMA Model

Autoregressive integrated moving average (ARIMA) is the combination of autoregressive (AR), moving average (MA), and the differencing processes. General form of ARIMA(p, d, q) model is given as follows [19]:

$$(1 - B)^d Y_t = \mu + \frac{\theta_q(B)}{\phi_p(B)} a_t, \tag{4}$$

where:

- $\phi_p(B) = 1 - \phi_1 B - \phi_2 B^2 - \cdots - \phi_p B^p$
- $\theta_q(B) = 1 - \theta_1 B - \theta_2 B^2 - \cdots - \theta_q B^q$
- $BY_t = Y_{t-1}$

Y_t denotes the actual value, B denotes the backshift operator, and a_t denotes the white noise process with zero mean and constant variance, $a_t \sim \mathrm{WN}(0, \sigma^2)$. $\phi_i(i = 1, 2, .., p)$, $\theta_j(j = 1, 2, \ldots, q)$, and μ are model parameters. d denotes the differencing order. The process of building ARIMA model is done by using Box-Jenkins procedure. Box-Jenkins procedure is required in order to identify p, d, and q; the order of ARIMA model, estimate the model parameters, check the model diagnostics, select the best model, and perform the forecast [24].

2.3 Artificial Neural Network

Artificial neural network (ANN) is a process that is similar to biological neural network process. Neural network in this context is seen as a mathematical object with several assumptions, among others include information processing occurs in many simple elements called neurons, the signal is passed between the neurons above the connection links, each connection link has a weight which is multiplied by the transmitted signal, and each neuron uses an activation function which is then passed to the output signal. The characteristics of a neural network consist of the neural architecture, the training algorithm, and the activation function [25]. ANN is a universal approximators which can approximate any function with high prediction accuracy. It is not required any prior assumption in order to build the model.

There are many types of neural network architecture, including feedforward neural network (FFNN), which is one of the architecture that is frequently used for time series forecasting task. FFNN architecture consist of three layers, namely input layer, hidden layer, and output layer. In time series modeling, the input used is the lag variable of the data and the output is the actual data. An example of an FFNN model architecture consisting of p inputs, a hidden layer consisting of m nodes connecting to the output, is shown in Fig. 1 [26].

The mathematical expression of the FFNN is defined as follows [27]:

$$f(\mathbf{x}_t, \mathbf{v}, \mathbf{w}) = g_2 \left\{ \sum_{j=1}^m v_j g_1 \left[\sum_{i=1}^n w_{ji} x_{it} \right] \right\}, \tag{5}$$

where $\mathbf{w}$ is the connection weight between the input layer and the hidden layer, $\mathbf{v}$ is the connection weight between the hidden layer and the output layer, $g_1(.)$ and $g_2(.)$ are the

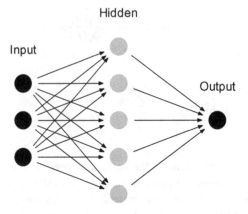

Fig. 1. The example of FFNN architecture.

activation functions. There are three activation functions that are commonly used, among others include logistic function, hyperbolic tangent (tanh) function, and rectified linear units (ReLU) function [28–30] The activations functions are given respectively as follows:

$$g(x) = \frac{1}{1 + e^{-x}},\tag{6}$$

$$g(x) = \frac{e^x - e^{-x}}{e^x + e^{-x}},\tag{7}$$

$$g(x) = \max(0, x).\tag{8}$$

2.4 Deep Feedforward Network

Deep feedforward network is a feedforward neural network model with deeper layer, i.e. it has more than one hidden layer in its architecture. It is one of the basic deep neural network (DNN) model which is also called deep learning model [31]. The DNN aims to approximate a function f^*. It finds the best function approximation by learning the value of the parameters θ from a mapping $y = f(x; \theta)$. One of the algorithm which is most widely used to learn the DNN model is stochastic gradient descent (SGD) [32]. The DNN architecture is presented in Fig. 2. In terms of time series model, the relationship between the output Y_t and the inputs $Y_{t-1}, Y_{t-2}, \ldots, Y_{t-p}$ in a DNN model with 3 hidden layers is presented as follows:

$$Y_t = \sum_{i=1}^{s} \alpha_i g\left(\sum_{j=1}^{r} \beta_{ij} g\left(\sum_{k=1}^{q} \gamma_{jk} g\left(\sum_{l=1}^{p} \theta_{kl} Y_{t-l}\right)\right)\right) + \varepsilon_t,\tag{9}$$

Input   Hidden   Hidden   Hidden

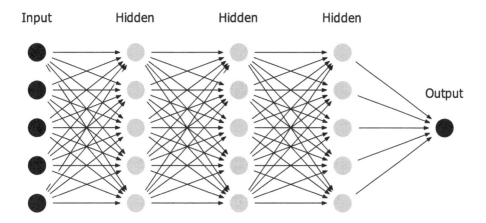

Output

Fig. 2. The Example of DNN architecture.

where ε_t is the error term, $\alpha_i(i = 1, 2, \ldots, s)$, $\beta_{ij}(i = 1, 2, \ldots, s; j = 1, 2, \ldots, r)$, $\gamma_{jk}(j = 1, 2, \ldots, r; k = 1, 2, \ldots, q)$, and $\theta_{kl}(k = 1, 2, \ldots, q; l = 1, 2, \ldots, p)$ are the model parameters called the connection weights, p is the number of input nodes, and q, r, s are the number of nodes in the first, second, and third hidden layers, respectively. Function $g(.)$ denotes the hidden layer activation function.

3 Dataset and Methodology

3.1 Dataset

In this study, we aim to model and predict the roll motion. Roll motion is one of ship motions, where ship motions consist of six types of motion, namely roll, yaw, pitch, sway, surge, and heave, which are also called as 6 degrees of freedom (6DoF). Roll is categorized as a rotational motion. The dataset used in this study is a roll motion time series data of a ship called floating production unit (FPU). It is generated from a simulation study conducted in Indonesian Hydrodynamic Laboratory. The machine recorded 15 data points in every one second. The total dataset contains 3150 data points. Time series plot of the data set is presented in Fig. 3.

3.2 Methodology

In order to obtain the model and predict the dataset, we split the data into there parts, namely training set, validation set, and test set. The training set which consists of 2700 data points is used to train the DNN model. The next 300 data points is set as validation set which is used for hyperparameter tuning. The remaining dataset is set as test set which is used to find the best model with the highest prediction accuracy (Fig. 4). In

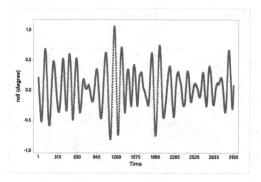

Fig. 3. Time series plot of roll motion.

order to calculate the prediction accuracy, we use root mean squared error (RMSE) as the criteria [33]. RMSE formula is given as follows:

$$\text{RMSE} = \sqrt{\frac{1}{L}\sum_{l=1}^{L}\left(Y_{n+l} - \hat{Y}_n(l)\right)^2}, \tag{10}$$

where L denotes the out-of-sample size, Y_{n+l} denotes the l-th actual value of out-of-sample data, and $\hat{Y}_n(l)$ denotes the l-th forecast.

The steps of feature selection and architecture selection is given as follows:

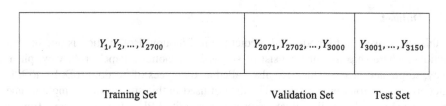

Fig. 4. The structure of dataset.

1. Feature selection based on PACF and ARIMA model, the significant lags of PACF and ARIMA model are used as the inputs in DNN model.
2. Hyperparameter tuning using grid search, where we use all combinations of the hyperparameters, including number of hidden layer: {1, 2, 3}, number of hidden nodes: [1,200], activation function: {logistic sigmoid, tanh, reLU}. The evaluation uses the RMSE of validation set.
3. Predict the test set using the optimal models which are obtained from the hyper-parameters tuning.
4. Select the best model based on RMSE criteria.

4 PACF Based Deep Neural Network Implementation

4.1 Preliminary Analysis

Our first approach is using PACF of the data for choosing the lag variables that will be set as the input on the neural network model. At first, we have to guarantee that the series satisfies stationarity assumption. We conduct several unit root tests, namely Augmented Dickey-Fuller (ADF) test [34], Phillips-Perron (PP) test [35], and Kwiatkowski-Phillips-Schmidt-Shin (KPSS) test [36, 37], which are presented in Table 1. By using significant level $\alpha = 0.05$, ADF test and PP test resulted in the p-values are below 0.01, which conclude that the series is significantly stationary. KPSS test also resulted in the same conclusion.

Table 1. Stationarity test using ADF test, PP test, and KPSS test.

Test	Test statistic	P-value	Result
ADF	−9.490	0.01	Stationary
PP	−35.477	0.01	Stationary
KPSS	0.030	0.10	Stationary

4.2 Feature Selection

Based on the PACF on Fig. 5, it shows the plot between the lag and the PACF value. We can see that the PACFs of lag 1 until lag 12 are significant, where the values are beyond the confidence limit. Hence, we will use the lag 1, lag 2, ..., lag 12 variables as the input of the model.

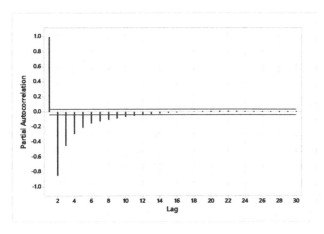

Fig. 5. PACF plot of roll motion series.

4.3   Optimal Neural Architecture: Hyperparameters Tuning

We perform grid search algorithm in order to find the optimal architecture by tuning the neural network hyperparameters, including number of hidden layers, number of hidden nodes, and activation functions [38]. Figure 6 shows the pattern of RMSE with respect to the number of hidden nodes from each architecture. From the chart, it is apparent that there is a significant decay as a result of increasing the number of hidden nodes. We can also see that the increase of number of hidden layers affects the stability of the RMSE decrease. For instance, it can be seen that the RMSEs of 1 hidden layer model with logistic function is not sufficiently stable. When we add more hidden layers, it significantly minimize the volatility of the RMSEs. Hence, we obtain the best architectures with minimal RMSE which is presented in Table 2.

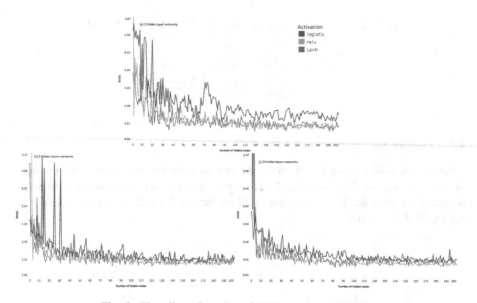

Fig. 6. The effect of number of hidden nodes to RMSE.

4.4   Test Set Prediction

Based on the results of finding the optimal architectures, we then apply theses architectures in order to predict the test set. We conduct 150-step ahead prediction which can be seen in Fig. 7 and we calculate the performance of the models based on the RMSE criteria. The RMSEs are presented in Table 3. The results show that 2 hidden layers model with ReLU function outperforms among other models. Unfortunately, the models with logistic function are unable to follow the actual data pattern such that the RMSEs are the lowest. Furthermore, the performance of the models with tanh function are also promising for the predictions are able to follow the actual data pattern although ReLU models are still the best.

Table 2. Optimal architectures of PACF based DNN.

Activation function	Number of hidden layers	Number of hidden nodes
Logistic	1	156
Logistic	2	172
Logistic	3	179
Tanh	1	194
Tanh	2	81
Tanh	3	80
ReLU	1	118
ReLU	2	119
ReLU	3	81

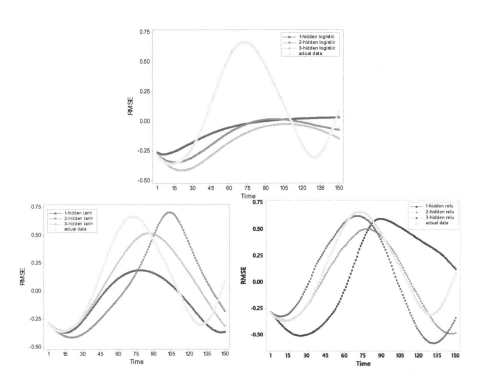

Fig. 7. Test set prediction of PACF based DNN models.

5   ARIMA Based Deep Neural Network

5.1   Procedure Implementation

We also use ARIMA model as another approach to choose the input for the model. The model is obtained by applying Box-Jenkins procedure. We also perform backward elimination procedure in order to select the best model where all model parameters are

Table 3. The RMSE of test set prediction of PACF based DNN models.

Architecture	RMSE
1-hidden layer logistic	0.354
2-hidden layers logistic	0.360
3-hidden layers logistic	0.407
1-hidden layer tanh	0.252
2-hidden layers tanh	0.406
3-hidden layers tanh	0.201
1-hidden layer ReLU	0.408
2-hidden layers ReLU	0.150
3-hidden layers ReLU	0.186

significant and it satisfies ARIMA model assumption which is white noise residual. Then, the final model we obtain is ARIMA ([1–4, 9, 19, 20], 0, [1, 9]) with zero mean. Thus, we set our DNN inputs based on the AR components of the model, namely $\{Y_{t-1}, Y_{t-2}, Y_{t-3}, Y_{t-4}, Y_{t-9}, Y_{t-19}, Y_{t-20}\}$.

We then conduct the same procedure as we have done in Sect. 4. The results are presented in Table 4 and Fig. 8.

Table 4. The RMSE of test set prediction of ARIMA based DNN models.

Architecture	RMSE
1-hidden layer logistic	0.218
2-hidden layers logistic	0.222
3-hidden layers logistic	0.512
1-hidden layer tanh	0.204
2-hidden layers tanh	0.274
3-hidden layers tanh	0.195
1-hidden layer ReLU	0.178
2-hidden layers ReLU	0.167
3-hidden layers ReLU	0.125

6   Discussion and Future Works

In Sects. 4 and 5, we see how the input features, the hidden layers, and the activation function affect the prediction performance of DNN model. In general, it can be seen that the DNN models are able to predict with good performance such that the prediction still follow the data pattern, except for the DNN model with logistic sigmoid function. In Fig. 7, it is shown that PACF based DNN models with logistic sigmoid function failed to follow the test set pattern. It also occured to the 3-hidden layers ARIMA based DNN model with logistic sigmoid function, as we can see in Fig. 8. Surprisingly, the models are significantly improved when we only used 1 or 2 hidden layers. The model

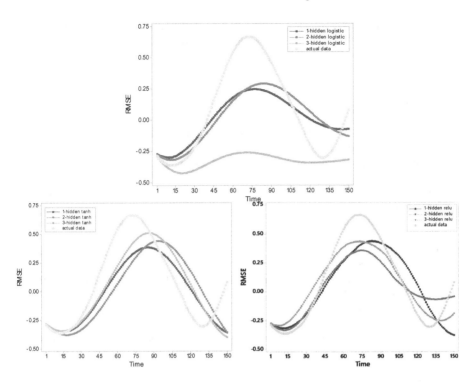

Fig. 8. Test set prediction of ARIMA based DNN.

suffers from overfitting when we used 3 hidden layers. In contrast, the other models with tanh function and ReLU function tend to outperform when we use more layers, as we can see in Tables 3 and 4. It is also shown that in average, ReLU function shows better performance, compared to other activation functions. Gensler et al. [39] also showed the same results where ReLU function outperformed than tanh function for forecasting using deep learning. Ryu et al. [40] also obtained the results that DNN with multiple hidden layers can be easily trained using ReLU function because of its simplicity; and performs better than simple neural network with one hidden layer.

Based on the input features, our study shows that the input from ARIMA model performs better than PACF based inputs. In fact, ARIMA based model has less features than the PACF based model. It is considered that adding more features in the neural input does not necessarily increase the prediction performance. Hence, it is required to choose correct inputs to obtain the best model. In time series data, using inputs based on ARIMA model is an effecctive approach to build the DNN architecture.

Based on the results of our study, it is considered that deep learning model is a promising model in order to handle time series forecasting or prediction task. In the future works, we suggest to apply feature and architecture selection for other advanced deep learning models such as long short term memory (LSTM) network. In order to prevent overfitting, it is also suggested to conduct regularization technique in the DNN architecture, such as dropout, L1, and L2.

Acknowledgements. This research was supported by ITS under the scheme of "Penelitian Pemula" No. 1354/PKS/ITS/2018. The authors thank to the Head of LPPTM ITS for funding and to the referees for the useful suggestions.

References

1. Zhang, G., Patuwo, B.E., Hu, M.Y.: Forecasting with artificial neural networks. Int. J. Forecast. **14**, 35–62 (1998)
2. Cybenko, G.: Approximation by superpositions of a sigmoidal function. Math. Control Sig. Syst. **2**, 303–314 (1989)
3. Funahashi, K.I.: On the approximate realization of continuous mappings by neural networks. Neural Netw. **2**, 183–192 (1989)
4. Hornik, K., Stinchcombe, M., White, H.: Multilayer feedforward networks are universal approximators. Neural Netw. **2**, 359–366 (1989)
5. Chen, Y., He, K., Tso, G.K.F.: Forecasting crude oil prices: a deep learning based model. Proced. Comput. Sci. **122**, 300–307 (2017)
6. Liu, L., Chen, R.C.: A novel passenger flow prediction model using deep learning methods. Transp. Res. Part C: Emerg. Technol. **84**, 74–91 (2017)
7. Qin, M., Li, Z., Du, Z.: Red tide time series forecasting by combining ARIMA and deep belief network. Knowl.-Based Syst. **125**, 39–52 (2017)
8. Qiu, X., Ren, Y., Suganthan, P.N., Amaratunga, G.A.J.: Empirical mode decomposition based ensemble deep learning for load demand time series forecasting. Appl. Soft Comput. **54**, 246–255 (2017)
9. Voyant, C., et al.: Machine learning methods for solar radiation forecasting: a review. Renew. Energy. **105**, 569–582 (2017)
10. Zhao, Y., Li, J., Yu, L.: A deep learning ensemble approach for crude oil price forecasting. Energy Econ. **66**, 9–16 (2017)
11. Hui, L.H., Fong, P.Y.: A numerical study of ship's rolling motion. In: Proceedings of the 6th IMT-GT Conference on Mathematics, Statistics and its Applications, pp. 843–851 (2010)
12. Nicolau, V., Palade, V., Aiordachioaie, D., Miholca, C.: Neural network prediction of the roll motion of a ship for intelligent course control. In: Apolloni, B., Howlett, Robert J., Jain, L. (eds.) KES 2007. LNCS (LNAI), vol. 4694, pp. 284–291. Springer, Heidelberg (2007). https://doi.org/10.1007/978-3-540-74829-8_35
13. Zhang, X.L., Ye, J.W.: An experimental study on the prediction of the ship motions using time-series analysis. In: The Nineteenth International Offshore and Polar Engineering Conference (2009)
14. Khan, A., Bil, C., Marion, K., Crozier, M.: Real time prediction of ship motions and attitudes using advanced prediction techniques. In: Congress of the International Council of the Aeronautical Sciences, pp. 1–10 (2004)
15. Wang, Y., Chai, S., Khan, F., Nguyen, H.D.: Unscented Kalman Filter trained neural networks based rudder roll stabilization system for ship in waves. Appl. Ocean Res. **68**, 26–38 (2017)
16. Yin, J.C., Zou, Z.J., Xu, F.: On-line prediction of ship roll motion during maneuvering using sequential learning RBF neural networks. Ocean Eng. **61**, 139–147 (2013)
17. Zhang, G.P.: Time series forecasting using a hybrid ARIMA and neural network model. Neurocomputing. **50**, 159–175 (2003)

18. Makridakis, S., Wheelwright, S.C., Hyndman, R.J.: Forecasting: Methods and Applications. Wiley, Hoboken (2008)
19. Wei, W.W.S.: Time Series Analysis: Univariate and Multivariate Methods. Pearson Addison Wesley, Boston (2006)
20. Tsay, R.S.: Analysis of Financial Time Series. Wiley, Hoboken (2002)
21. Durbin, J.: The fitting of time-series models. Revue de l'Institut Int. de Statistique/Rev. Int. Stat. Inst. **28**, 233 (1960)
22. Levinson, N.: The wiener (root mean square) error criterion in filter design and prediction. J. Math. Phys. **25**, 261–278 (1946)
23. Liang, F.: Bayesian neural networks for nonlinear time series forecasting. Stat. Comput. **15**, 13–29 (2005)
24. Box, G.E.P., Jenkins, G.M., Reinsel, G.C., Ljung, G.M.: Time Series Analysis: Forecasting and Control. Wiley, Hoboken (2015)
25. Fausett, L.: Fundamentals of Neural Networks: Architectures, Algorithms, and Applications. Prentice-Hall, Inc., Upper Saddle River (1994)
26. El-Telbany, M.E.: What quantile regression neural networks tell us about prediction of drug activities. In: 2014 10th International Computer Engineering Conference (ICENCO), pp. 76–80. IEEE (2014)
27. Taylor, J.W.: A quantile regression neural network approach to estimating the conditional density of multiperiod returns. J. Forecast. **19**, 299–311 (2000)
28. Han, J., Moraga, C.: The influence of the sigmoid function parameters on the speed of backpropagation learning. In: Mira, J., Sandoval, F. (eds.) IWANN 1995. LNCS, vol. 930, pp. 195–201. Springer, Heidelberg (1995). https://doi.org/10.1007/3-540-59497-3_175
29. Karlik, B., Olgac, A.V.: Performance analysis of various activation functions in generalized MLP architectures of neural networks. Int. J. Artif. Intell. Expert Syst. **1**, 111–122 (2011)
30. Nair, V., Hinton, G.E.: Rectified linear units improve restricted Boltzmann machines. In: Proceedings of the 27th International Conference on International Conference on Machine Learning. pp. 807–814. Omnipress, Haifa (2010)
31. Goodfellow, I., Bengio, Y., Courville, A.: Deep Learning. MIT Press, Cambridge (2016)
32. LeCun, Y.A., Bottou, L., Orr, G.B., Müller, K.-R.: Efficient BackProp. In: Montavon, G., Orr, G.B., Müller, K.-R. (eds.) Neural Networks: Tricks of the Trade. LNCS, vol. 7700, pp. 9–48. Springer, Heidelberg (2012). https://doi.org/10.1007/978-3-642-35289-8_3
33. De Gooijer, J.G., Hyndman, R.J.: 25 years of time series forecasting. Int. J. Forecast. **22**, 443–473 (2006)
34. Fuller, W.A.: Introduction to Statistical Time Series. Wiley, Hoboken (2009)
35. Phillips, P.C.B., Perron, P.: Testing for a Unit Root in Time Series Regression. Biometrika **75**, 335 (1988)
36. Hobijn, B., Franses, P.H., Ooms, M.: Generalizations of the KPSS-test for stationarity. Stat. Neerl. **58**, 483–502 (2004)
37. Kwiatkowski, D., Phillips, P.C.B., Schmidt, P., Shin, Y.: Testing the null hypothesis of stationarity against the alternative of a unit root. J. Econ. **54**, 159–178 (1992)
38. Hsu, C.W., Chang, C.C., Lin, C.J.: A practical guide to support vector classification. Presented at the (2003)
39. Gensler, A., Henze, J., Sick, B., Raabe, N.: Deep Learning for solar power forecasting — an approach using autoencoder and LSTM neural networks. In: 2016 IEEE International Conference on Systems, Man, and Cybernetics (SMC), pp. 002858–002865. IEEE (2016)
40. Ryu, S., Noh, J., Kim, H.: Deep neural network based demand side short term load forecasting. In: 2016 IEEE International Conference on Smart Grid Communications (SmartGridComm), pp. 308–313. IEEE (2016)

Acoustic Surveillance Intrusion Detection with Linear Predictive Coding and Random Forest

Marina Yusoff[1](✉) and Amirul Sadikin Md. Afendi[2]

[1] Advanced Analytic Engineering Center (AAEC),
Faculty of Computer and Mathematical Sciences, Universiti Teknologi MARA,
Shah Alam, Selangor, Malaysia
marinay@tmsk.uitm.edu.my
[2] Faculty of Computer and Mathematical Sciences,
Universiti Teknologi MARA, Shah Alam, Selangor, Malaysia

Abstract. Endangered wildlife is protected in remote land where people are restricted to enter. But intrusions of poachers and illegal loggers still occur due to lack of surveillance to cover a huge amount of land. The current usage of stealth ability of the camera is low due to limitations of camera angle of view. Maintenance such as changing batteries and memory cards were troublesome reported by Wildlife Conservation Society, Malaysia. Remote location with no cellular network access would be difficult to transmit video data. Rangers need a system to react to intrusion on time. This paper aims to address the development of an audio events recognition for intrusion detection based on the vehicle engine, wildlife environmental noise and chainsaw activities. Random Forest classification and feature extraction of Linear Predictive Coding were employed. Training and testing data sets used were obtained from Wildlife Conservation Society Malaysia. The findings demonstrate that the accuracy rates achieve up to 86% for indicating an intrusion via audio recognition. It is a good attempt as a primary study for the classification of a real data set of intruders. This intrusion detection will be beneficial for wildlife protection agencies in maintaining security as it is less power consuming than the current camera trapping surveillance technique.

Keywords: Audio classification · Feature extraction
Linear Predictive Coding · Random forest · Wildlife Conservation Society

1 Introduction

The protection of wildlife is becoming important as it grows smaller every year. This is can be evident from the poaching activities [1]. Wildlife Department officers hunt people who involving in poaching activities in Semporna, Sabah [1]. This is can be due to legal loggers sometimes break rules of entering the wildlife zones [2]. To overcome this issue, Sabah Forestry Department favors to set up a dedicated wildlife enforcement team as intruders became more daring in forests and reserve areas [3]. Even though, protection initiative has been made, but the numbers of wildlife species grew lower and

© Springer Nature Singapore Pte Ltd. 2019
B. W. Yap et al. (Eds.): SCDS 2018, CCIS 937, pp. 72–84, 2019.
https://doi.org/10.1007/978-981-13-3441-2_6

even near extinction for some species that reside in the sanctuary. Many approaches were used to protect wildlife and faced many challenges. A recent finding stressed on the urgent need for new or combined approaches that need to be taken up in the research challenges to enable better protection against poaching in wildlife zone [4]. One of the challenges is in the implementation of security in remote areas. It requires a special equipment such as camera trapping and it should be designed to endure the conditions of a rain forest. The use of the camera requires high maintenance due to the location as it has no power grid source, rely on its batteries for surveillance and high probability of being spotted by intruders [5]. The equipment and cameras can be stolen or destroyed by trespassers (WCS, 2017). The use of camera trapping surveillance by Wildlife Conservation Society (WCS), Malaysia acquired a high amount of memory for data storage and faced with fogs and blockages of the camera view. The stealth ability of the camera is low due to limitations of camera angle of view whereby the maintenance such as changing batteries and memory cards were troublesome. In addition, remote location with no cellular network access would be difficult to transmit video data.

There is a need to find a better solution to overcome this issue and consider the maintenance cost and security. Low investment in lack of protection Southeast Asia was a reason for the lack of protection of wildlife [6]. Thus, solution with less power consumption can be considered for less frequent maintenance and cost saving. There is effort in computing solution have been addressed to in detecting intruders mainly in acoustic surveillance. They detect the signals from the sound in the wildlife zone to classify them in two types; intrusion and non-intrusion. In this case, Fast Fourier Transform (FFT) spectrum of the voice signal extracts the information and calculate the similarity threshold to classify the intrusion.

Many researches focused on signal classification for several types of applications includes acoustic classification [7–15]. Machine learning methods are still used in acoustic signal solutions even though methods the recent method as such, as Convolution Neural Network and deep learning have been applied to the acoustic classifications [16, 17]. Quadratic discriminant analysis classifies audio signals of passing vehicles based on features based on short time energy, average zero cross rate, and pitch frequency of periodic segments of signals have demonstrated an acceptable accuracy with as compared to some methods in previous studies [18]. In addition, feature extraction of the audio signals is prime of importance task to determine features of audio. For instance, spectrum distribution and the second one on wavelet packet transform has shown different performance with the K-nearest neighbor algorithm, and support vector machine classifier [19]. This paper aims to identify a suitable technique to be efficient in identifying audio signals of an event of intrusion by the vehicle engine, environmental noise and chainsaw activities in wildlife reserves and evaluate an audio intrusion detection using data sets from WCS Malaysia.

2   Related Work

2.1   Signal Processing

The audio recording is a waveform whose frequency range is audible for humans. Stacks of the audio signs are used to define variance data formatting of stimulant audio signals [20]. To create an outline of the output signal, also analyses the stimulation signal and audio signal, classification systems are used which are helpful for catching the signal of any variation of a speech [21]. Prior to the classifications of audio signal, the features in the audio signal are extracted to minimize the amount of data [22]. Feature extraction is a numerical representation that later can be used to characterize a segment of audio signals. The valuable features can be used in the design of the classifier [23]. The audio signal features can be extracted as Mel Frequency Cepstral Coefficient (MFCC), pitch and sampling frequency [22].

MFCC represents the signals which are audio in nature are measured in a unit of Mel scale [24]. These features can be used for speech signal. MFCC is calculated by defining the STFT crescents of individual frame into sets of 40 consents using a set of the 40 weighting contours simulating the frequency sensing capability as humans. The Mel scale relates the frequency which is pre-received of a pure tone to its actual measured frequency.

Pitch determination is important for speech transforming algorithms [25]. Pitch is the quality of a sound in major correlations of the rate of vibration generating it, the amount of lowness or highness of the tone. The sound that comes from the vocal cords starts at the larynx and stops at the mouth. If unvoiced sounds are produced vocal cords do not shake and are open while the voiced sounds are being produced, the vocal cords vibrate and generate pulses known as glottal pulses [24].

2.2   Feature Extraction

One of the audio signal processing and speech processing is Linear Predictive Coding (LPC). It uses frequently in in extracting the spectral envelope of a digital signal of audio in a compact form factor. By applying information relevant to a linear predictive model. LPC provides very accurate speech parameter estimates for speech analysis [25]. LPC coefficient representation is normally used to extract features taking account of the spectral envelope of signals in the analog format [26]. Linear prediction is dependent on a mathematical computation whereas the upcoming values of a time discrete signal are specified as a linear function with consideration of previous samples. LPC is known as a subset of the filter theory in digital signal processing. LPC applies a mathematical operation such as autocorrelation method of, mhj autoregressive modeling allocating the filter coefficients. The feature extraction of LPC is quite sufficient for acoustic event detection tasks.

Selection of extracting features is important to get the optimized values from a set of features [27]. Selecting features from a large set of available features will allow a more scaled approach. These features will then use to determine the nature of the audio signal or classification purposes. It is used to select the optimum values to keep accuracy and performance level and minimizing computational cost altogether. It has resulted in drastic effects towards the accuracy and will require more computational cost if no optimum features were developed [28]. Reduction of features can improve the accuracy of prediction and may allow necessary, embedded, step of the prediction algorithm [29].

2.3 Random Forest Algorithm

Random forests are a type of ensemble method for predicting using the average over predictions of few independent base models [30]. The independent model is a tree as many trees make up a forest [31]. Random forests are built by combining the predictions of trees in which are trained separately [32]. The construct of random tree, it follows three choices [33].) as the following:

- Method for splitting the leaves.
- Type of predictor to use in each leaf.
- Method for injecting randomness into the trees.

The trees in random forest are randomized based regression trees. The combinations will form an aggregated regression estimate at the end [34]. Ensemble size or the number of trees to generate by the random forest algorithm is an important factor to consider as it shows to differentiate in different situations [35]. Past implementations of the random forest algorithm and their accuracy level of relevance to the ensemble size affect accuracy levels majorly. Bag of Features is the input data for predictions [36]. Sizes of the ensemble in this case show that there is a slightly better accuracy in setting the trees to a large number [37].

3 Development of an Audio Event Recognition for Intrusion Detection

3.1 System Architecture

The development of the audio events recognition for intrusion detection starts with the identification of system architecture. Figure 1 demonstrates the system architecture and explains the main components of the system generally in block diagram form. The system should be able to classify the audio as an intrusion or non-intrusive to allow accurate alarms of intrusions notify rangers. Figure 2 shows the system flow diagram consisting of a loop of real time recording of audio and classification.

3.2 Data Acquisition and Preparation

This section explains data processing and feature extraction processes. A set of recordings/signal dataset was provided by WCS Malaysia. The recording consists of 60 s of ambient audio of rainforest environment and vehicle engine revving towards the recording unit in the rainforest.

Since acquiring raw data are unstructured and unsuitable for machine learning the data requires a standard form to allow the system to be able to learn from this source.

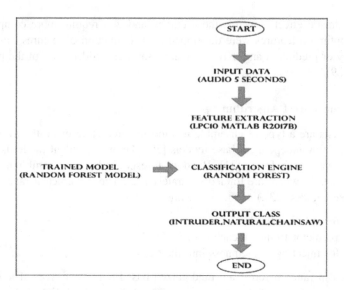

Fig. 1. System architecture

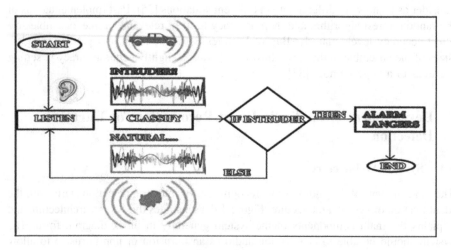

Fig. 2. System flow diagram

A standardized form has been formulated to allow a more lenient approach to solving the problem. The parameters are 5 s in duration, waveform audio files of the mono channel on the frequency of 44100 Hz. Two segments of 5 s from the raw audio file is combined using Sony Vegas an application for audio & video manipulation to resynthesize into training data. Independent audio files of vehicle engines and rainforest background environmental overlap in various combinations as described in scenarios below. The vehicle audio is lowered to produce various distances of vehicles between the devices. To produce a long-distance scenario the vehicle audio is reduced by 5 dB up to 20 dB. The composed audio is then verified again by human testing to validate further into logical terms of hearing ability and classification. In Figs. 3, 4, 5 and 6 visualize the 4 scenarios of resynthesizing of 2 layers of audio signals, namely the above audio is a natural environment and below is the vehicle engine audio segment.

Resynthesized audio files that are created as the training data are divided into three separate audio events. The recording acquired are altered using software to extract various five seconds of applicable audio indication of a vehicle or chainsaw activity and rainforest typical conditions. Data on vehicle audio activity consist of 4 × 4 vehicles moving since machine learning requires the data in the form of numbers the training audio data is not yet ready for modelling. The next step is to extract the feature of LPC from the audio files created before. The feature extraction of waveform audio files is done using MATLAB R2017b digital Signal processing toolbox using the LPC function.

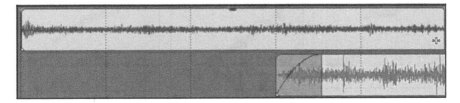

Fig. 3. Scenario 1, direct vehicle pass through

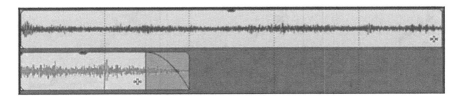

Fig. 4. Scenario 2, last 2 s vehicle pass through

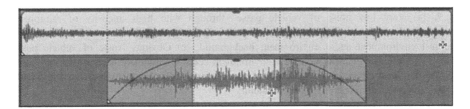

Fig. 5. Scenario 3, first 2 s vehicle pass through

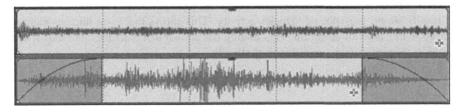

Fig. 6. Scenario 4, middle 3 s vehicle pass through

4   Results and Discussion

4.1   Audio Data Analysis Using Welch Power Spectral Density Estimate

To further examine the waveform audio files, it is converted from time domain to frequency domain. By using, Welch Power Spectral Density Estimate in MATLAB R2017b function, Figs. 7a–f, shows different scenarios and the representation of audio in which power spectral density estimation graph form.

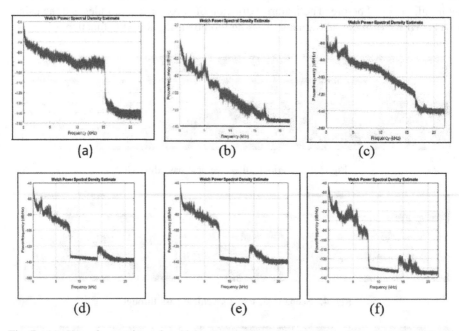

Fig. 7. (a) Very low noise of vehicle passes through with high intensity of rainforest environment background, (b) Low noise of vehicle passing through with medium intensity rainforest environment audio environment background, (c) Obvious Noise of vehicle pass through with the low intensity rainforest environment audio environment background, (d) Low intensity rainforest environment audio, (e) Medium intensity rainforest environment audio and (f) High intensity rainforest environment audio.

The composition is constructed from double environmental audio overlapped of a minus 20 dB of the engine activity. This audio file was validated by human testing, but the results are no presence of vehicles activity. This shows that even humans cannot hear up to this level of detection. This finding has shown that machines has shown the capability of performing surveillance accurately.

4.2   Results of a Random Forest Simulation

The simulation of the random forest used "sklearn" a python machine learning library and "Graphviz" a visualization library to create the decision trees. The simulation is done by producing 4 trees created by several subsets from the entire dataset. Gini index or entropy is normally used to create decision trees on each subset with random parameters. Testing is done for all 4 trees with the same input data to find most trees resulting the same output. Random Forest tree generation system is a series of random selection of the main training dataset into smaller subsets that consist of even classed data [27]. In this case it is broken up into 2 subsets and each subset is used to generate tree with Gini index and entropy method. It indicates that producing an ensemble of 4 trees can be used for predicting in random forest technique. Figure 8 displays the random forest dataset selection process and tree generation process.

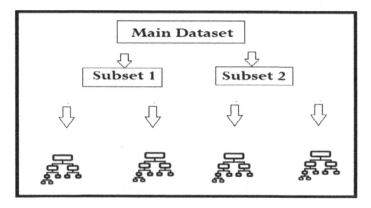

Fig. 8. Random Forest tree generation method

Test set A, B and C are features extracted from audio of the vehicle, the nature and chainsaw respectively. Variables L1, L2, L3, L4, L5, L6, L7, L8, L9 and L10 are the LPC extracted features from audio files. Table 1 shows the test inputs for the experiment. Figures 9 and 10 demonstrate the example of the generated and visualized tree.

Table 1. Test sets variables and target class

Set	L1	L2	L3	L4	L5	L6	L7	L8	L9	L10	Class
A	−3.414	5.191	−4.338	1.966	−0.412	−0.113	0.566	−0.890	0.646	−0.196	Vehicle
B	−3.138	4.848	−4.781	3.799	−2.810	1.630	−0.247	−0.486	0.382	−0.102	Nature
C	−3.619	6.700	−6.888	5.800	−4.580	3.367	−1.640	0.108	0.364	−0.154	Chainsaw

Each test set A, B and C will be tested in all 4 trees generated. The majority class will be the most similar results among tree results. Table 2 shows the results for each tree and test set respectively. It can be concluded that the results prove that as trees could produce false results the whole ensemble will allow better interpretation of the overall prediction. This shows that a cumulative result of a majority will help avoid false positives.

Table 2. Result of random forest simulation

Input Set	Decision tree results (Output class)				Majority class	Confidence (%)	Target class
	1	2	3	4			
A	Nature	Vehicle	Vehicle	Vehicle	Vehicle	75	Vehicle
B	Nature	Nature	Nature	Nature	Nature	100	Nature
C	Chainsaw	Chainsaw	Chainsaw	Vehicle	Chainsaw	75	Chainsaw

Results of MATLAB 2017b Tree bagger classifier in the Classification Learner App and A series of test has been done to find results on the WEKA platform is shown in Table 3. On both platforms, it shows an average of 86% positive prediction based on the 10 variables of LPC features. The results obtained is promising enough as the training data is limited.

Table 3. Results using MATLAB 2017b tree bagger function.

Size of ensemble	Tree bagger classifier		WEKA platform	
	Time to construct (seconds)	Accuracy (%)	Time to construct (seconds)	Accuracy (%)
300	22.04	84.6	0.35	86.4
200	13.366	86.0	0.17	85.7
100	6.7436	86.0	0.07	86.4
50	3.7142	87.5	0.04	85.7
25	2.1963	84.6	0.01	87.1
10	1.2386	84.6	0.01	87.1

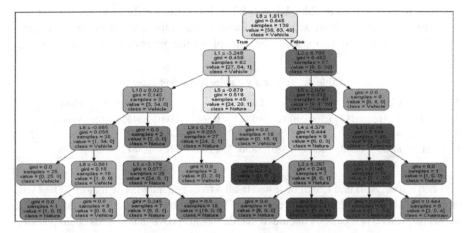

Fig. 9. Tree 1 generated and visualized

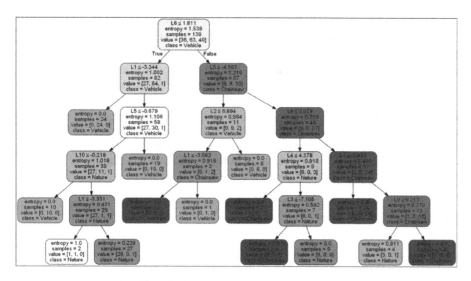

Fig. 10. Tree 2 generated and visualized

By using Classification Learner App in MATLAB 2017b allow to run many classifiers. It is found that Linear Discriminant method is more accurate in predicting LPC extraction of audio files that consist of events such as vehicle, chainsaws and natural acoustic events. Basic decision tree results may differ based on their maximum splits that could be controlled to produce diversity of results. The performance of each type of tree is assessed on the entire data set. Fine Tree is defined by increasing the maximum splits allowed in the generation process. Medium tree is in between a fine tree and a coarse tree with just enough maximum splits allow. A Coarse tree allows low numbers of total splits. Table 4 shows the total results of all basic decision trees generated with their respective parameters.

Table 4. Basic decision trees of gini diversity index result on LPC dataset.

Fine tree		Medium tree		Coarse tree	
Max split	Accuracy	Max split	Accuracy (%)	Max split	Accuracy (%)
100	81.0	20	81.7	4	76.3%
150	81.0	40	81.0	8	83.5%
200	81.0	60	81.0	10	84.2%

5   Conclusions

Random Forest technique with Linear Predictive coding feature extraction has been found to be efficient. The combinations of linear predictive coding feature extraction and random forest classification is the best combination with past studies. The current study only achieved 86%. It is believed to be connected to the data variance and amount collected for training the model. Thus, it could be concluded in the implementation of random forest require a decent data set for training to allow better results. LPC extracting and classification of audio signals are very light in requirements of computing power. In future, the evaluation of other techniques as such of deep learning and different type of signal datasets can be applied for a better solution.

Acknowledgement. The authors express a deep appreciation to the Ministry of Education, Malaysia for the grant of 600-RMI/FRGS 5/3 (0002/2016), Institute of Research and Innovation, Universiti Teknologi MARA and the Information System Department, Faculty of Computer and Mathematical Sciences, Universiti Teknologi MARA, Shah Alam, Malaysia for providing essential support and knowledge for the work.

References

1. Wildlife.gov.my: Latar Belakang PERHILITAN. http://www.wildlife.gov.my/index.php/2016-04-11-03-50-17/2016-04-11-03-57-37/latar-belakang. Accessed 30 Apr 2018
2. Pei, L.G.: Southeast Asia marks progress in combating illegal timber trade. http://www.flegt.org/news/content/viewItem/southeast-asia-marks-progress-in-combating-illegal-timber-trade/04-01-2017/75. Accessed 30 Apr 2018
3. Inus, K.: Special armed wildlife enforcement team to be set up to counter poachers, 05 November 2017. https://www.nst.com.my/news/nation/2017/10/294584/special-armed-wildlife-enforcement-team-be-set-counter-poachers. Accessed 30 June 2018
4. Kamminga, J., Ayele, E., Meratnia, N., Havinga, P.: Poaching detection technologies—a survey. Sensors **18**(5), 1474 (2018)
5. Ariffin, M.: Enforcement against wildlife crimes in west Malaysia: the challenges. J. Sustain. Sci. Manag. **10**(1), 19–26 (2015)
6. Davis, D., Lisiewski, B.: U.S. Patent Application No. 15/296, 136 (2018)
7. Davis, E.: New Study Shows Over a Third of Protected Areas Surveyed are Severely at Risk of Losing Tigers, 04 April (2018). https://www.worldwildlife.org/press-releases/new-study-shows-over-a-third-of-protected-areas-surveyed-are-severely-at-risk-of-losing-tigers. Accessed 30 June 2018
8. Mac Aodha, O., et al.: Bat detective—deep learning tools for bat acoustic signal detection. PLoS computational Biol. **14**(3), e1005995 (2018)
9. Maijala, P., Shuyang, Z., Heittola, T., Virtanen, T.: Environmental noise monitoring using source classification in sensors. Appl. Acoust. **129**, 258–267 (2018)
10. Zhu, B., Xu, K., Wang, D., Zhang, L., Li, B., Peng, Y.: Environmental Sound Classification Based on Multi-temporal Resolution CNN Network Combining with Multi-level Features. arXiv preprint arXiv:1805.09752 (2018)
11. Valada, A., Spinello, L., Burgard, W.: Deep feature learning for acoustics-based terrain classification. In: Bicchi, A., Burgard, W. (eds.) Robotics Research. SPAR, vol. 3, pp. 21–37. Springer, Cham (2018). https://doi.org/10.1007/978-3-319-60916-4_2
12. Heittola, T., Çakır, E., Virtanen, T.: The machine learning approach for analysis of sound scenes and events. In: Virtanen, T., Plumbley, M., Ellis, D. (eds.) Computational Analysis of Sound Scenes and Events, pp. 13–40. Springer, Cham (2018). https://doi.org/10.1007/978-3-319-63450-0_2
13. Hamzah, R., Jamil, N., Seman, N., Ardi, N, Doraisamy, S.C.: Impact of acoustical voice activity detection on spontaneous filled pause classification. In: Open Systems (ICOS), pp. 1–6. IEEE (2014)

14. Seman, N., Roslan, R., Jamil, N., Ardi, N.: Bimodality streams integration for audio-visual speech recognition systems. In: Abraham, A., Han, S.Y., Al-Sharhan, S.A., Liu, H. (eds.) Hybrid Intelligent Systems. AISC, vol. 420, pp. 127–139. Springer, Cham (2016). https://doi.org/10.1007/978-3-319-27221-4_11

15. Seman, N., Jusoff, K.: Acoustic pronunciation variations modeling for standard Malay speech recognition. Comput. Inf. Sci. 1(4), 112 (2008)

16. Dlir, A., Beheshti, A.A., Masoom, M.H.: Classification of vehicles based on audio signals using quadratic discriminant analysis and high energy feature vectors. arXiv preprint arXiv: 1804.01212 (2018)

17. Aljaafreh, A., Dong, L.: An evaluation of feature extraction methods for vehicle classification based on acoustic signals. In: 2010 International Conference on Networking, Sensing and Control (ICNSC), pp. 570–575. IEEE (2010)

18. Baelde, M., Biernacki, C., Greff, R.: A mixture model-based real-time audio sources classification method. In: IEEE International Conference on Acoustics, Speech and Signal Processing, pp. 2427–2431. IEEE (2017)

19. Dilber, D.: Feature Selection and Extraction of Audio, pp. 3148–3155 (2016). https://doi.org/10.15680/IJIRSET.2016.0503064. Accessed 30 Apr 2018

20. Xia, X., Togneri, R., Sokel, F., Huang, D.: Random forest classification based acoustic event detection. In: 2017 IEEE International Conference on Multimedia and Expo (ICME), pp. 163–168. IEEE (2017)

21. Lu, L., Jiang, H., Zhang, H.: A robust audio classification and segmentation method. In: Proceedings of the Ninth ACM International Conference on Multimedia, pp. 203–211. ACM (2001)

22. Anselam, A.S., Pillai, S.S.: Performance evaluation of code excited linear prediction speech coders at various bit rates. In: 2014 International Conference on Computation of Power, Energy, Information and Communication (ICCPEIC), April 2014, pp. 93–98. IEEE (2014)

23. Chamoli, A., Semwal, A., Saikia, N.: Detection of emotion in analysis of speech using linear predictive coding techniques (LPC). In: 2017 International Conference on Inventive Systems and Control (ICISC), pp. 1–4. IEEE (2017)

24. Grama, L., Buhuş, E.R., Rusu, C.: Acoustic classification using linear predictive coding for wildlife detection systems. In: 2017 International Symposium on Signals, Circuits and Systems (ISSCS), pp. 1–4. IEEE (2017)

25. Homburg, H., Mierswa, I., Möller, B., Morik, K., Wurst, M.: A benchmark dataset for audio classification and clustering. In: ISMIR, September 2005, vol. 2005, pp. 528–531 (2005)

26. Jaiswal, J.K., Samikannu, R.: Application of random forest algorithm on feature subset selection and classification and regression. In: 2017 World Congress on Computing and Communication Technologies (WCCCT), pp. 65–68. IEEE (2017)

27. Kumar, S.S., Shaikh, T.: Empirical evaluation of the performance of feature selection approaches on random forest. In: 2017 International Conference on Computer and Applications (ICCA), pp. 227–231. IEEE (2017)

28. Tang, Y., Liu, Q., Wang, W., Cox, T.J.: A non-intrusive method for estimating binaural speech intelligibility from noise-corrupted signals captured by a pair of microphones. Speech Commun. 96, 116–128 (2018)

29. Balili, C.C., Sobrepena, M.C.C., Naval, P.C.: Classification of heart sounds using discrete and continuous wavelet transform and random forests. In: 2015 3rd IAPR Asian Conference on Pattern Recognition (ACPR), pp. 655–659. IEEE (2015)

30. Denil, M., Matheson, D., De Freitas, N.: Narrowing the gap: random forests in theory and in practice. In: International Conference on Machine Learning, January 2014, pp. 665–673 (2014)

31. Behnamian, A., Millard, K., Banks, S.N., White, L., Richardson, M., Pasher, J.: A systematic approach for variable selection with random forests: achieving stable variable importance values. IEEE Geosci. Remote Sens. Lett. **14**(11), 1988–1992 (2017)
32. Biau, G.L., Curie, M., Bo, P.V.I., Cedex, P., Yu, B.: Analysis of a random forests model. J. Mach. Learn. Res. **13**, 1063–1095 (2012)
33. Phan, H., et al.: Random regression forests for acoustic event detection and classification. IEEE/ACM Trans. Audio Speech Lang. Process. **23**(1), 20–31 (2015)
34. Xu, Y.: Research and implementation of improved random forest algorithm based on Spark. In: 2017 IEEE 2nd International Conference on Big Data Analysis (ICBDA), pp. 499–503. IEEE (2017)
35. Zhang, Z., Li, Y., Zhu, X., Lin, Y.: A method for modulation recognition based on entropy features and random forest. In: IEEE International Conference on Software Quality, Reliability and Security Companion (QRS-C), pp. 243–246. IEEE (2017)
36. Abuella, M., Chowdhury, B.: Random forest ensemble of support vector regression models for solar power forecasting. In: Power & Energy Society Innovative Smart Grid Technologies Conference (ISGT), pp. 1–5. IEEE (2017)
37. Manzoor, M.A., Morgan, Y.: Vehicle make and model recognition using random forest classification for intelligent transportation systems. In: 2018 IEEE 8th Annual Computing and Communication Workshop and Conference (CCWC), pp. 148–154. IEEE (2018)

Timing-of-Delivery Prediction Model to Visualize Delivery Trends for Pos Laju Malaysia by Machine Learning Techniques

Jo Wei Quah[✉], Chin Hai Ang[✉], Regupathi Divakar[✉],
Rosnah Idrus[✉], Nasuha Lee Abdullah[✉], and XinYing Chew[✉]

School of Computer Sciences, Universiti Sains Malaysia, 11800 Penang,
Malaysia
{jowei, chinhai, divakar.regupathi}@student.usm.my,
{irosnah, nasuha, xinying}@usm.my

Abstract. The increasing trend in online shopping urges the need of continuous enhancing and improving user experience in many aspects and on-time delivery of goods is one of the key area. This paper explores the adoption of machine learning in predicting late delivery of goods on Malaysia national courier service named Poslaju. The prediction model also enables the visualization of the delivery trends for Poslaju Malaysia. Meanwhile, data extraction, transformation, experimental setup and performance comparison of various machine learning methods will be discussed in this paper.

Keywords: Supervised machine learning · Naïve Bayes · Decision tree
K-nearest neighbors · Poslaju

1 Introduction

Online shopping plays an important role in business world nowadays. Survey [1] reveals that more than 50% of American prefers online shopping and 95% of them do online shopping at-least once yearly. This is become prevalent in Malaysia as well where 83% of Malaysian have shopped online [2]. Development and deployment of Ecommerce Marketplaces such as 11street, Shopee, Lazada (to name a few) [3] provide a platform for buyers and sellers to carry out online shopping in a simple and efficient manner. This further accelerates the adoption of online shopping and is expected to be a trend moving forward. Numerous works on online shopping have been conducted over the years, such as the ones made in [4–8], to name a few. Online shopping involves several parties. Figure 1 shows a typical online shopping flow with an online marketplace.

One important component in the above flow is the shipping process. Survey done in [2] showed that 90% of online shopper are willing to wait for a maximum period of 1 week for their purchases while 46% of them expects delivery within 3 days. This highlights the importance of on-time delivery service to meet customer satisfaction.

Poslaju [9] is Malaysia's national courier service that provides express mail and parcel delivery. The service level is next working day (D + 1) delivery for selected

© Springer Nature Singapore Pte Ltd. 2019
B. W. Yap et al. (Eds.): SCDS 2018, CCIS 937, pp. 85–95, 2019.
https://doi.org/10.1007/978-981-13-3441-2_7

Fig. 1. Online shopping process flow

areas and within 2–3 working days for the standard delivery. This paper explores the use of machine learning techniques to predict late courier delivery with the aim to determine the relevant factors contributing to late delivery. By doing so, further improvements on overall delivery service in Malaysia can be achieved. To our best knowledge, this paper is the first attempt to apply machine learning methods in courier delivery service domain.

The other sections of this paper are organized as follows. Section 2 explains extract, transform and load (ETL) process of the proposed solution. Section 3 discusses feature selection and list of machine learning methods to explore. Experiments and prediction results will be shown in Sect. 4. Sections 5 and 6 will conclude the paper and future work respectively.

2 Extract, Transform and Load

Similar to other data mining tasks, extract, transform and load (ETL) [10] is used. Figure 2 shows the ETL process used in this paper.

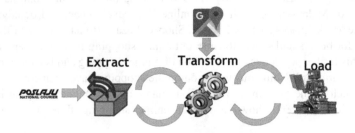

Fig. 2. Extract, transform, load progress

Each process will be illustrated in the following sub-sections.

2.1   Extract Process

In this stage, delivery data is crawled from the data source [9]. Each delivery is assigned with a unique tracking identifier. Figure 3 shows the format of Poslaju tracking identifier. The first two characters can be a combination of any letters (A–Z); the subsequent 9-digits are incremental numbers and the code at the end dictates domestic or international delivery. This can support humongous amount of delivery tracking (*volume*).

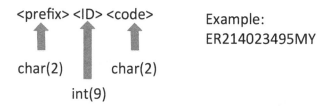

Fig. 3. Poslaju delivery tracking identifier format

Figure 4 shows an example of delivery tracking status. It comprises of date/time, process (status of goods delivery) and event (location of goods). This is an unstructured or semi-structured data where the number of entries varies per tracking identifier (variety). Moreover, the textual description isn't standardized and requires certain extend of text mining to extract some useful information from it. At the same time, several thousands (if not tens of thousand) of goods are dispatched out (velocity). Therefore, this can be viewed as a big data analytic problem [11].

*Date / Time	Process	Event
19 Dec 2017, 04:52:52 PM	Item delivered to rohani	Caw. Serahan Pengkalan Chepa
19 Dec 2017, 10:43:00 AM	Item out for delivery	Caw. Serahan Pengkalan Chepa
19 Dec 2017, 10:10:00 AM	Arrive at delivery facility at	Caw. Serahan Pengkalan Chepa
19 Dec 2017, 08:29:07 AM	Arrive at delivery facility at	Pos Laju Kota Bharu
18 Dec 2017, 11:33:29 PM	Consignment dispatch out from Transit Office	Pos Laju Butterworth
18 Dec	Item processed	Pos Laju

Fig. 4. Example of Poslaju delivery tracking

Scripts developed in Python were used to crawl the above information. Figure 5 shows the data extraction process. Python HTTP Request [12] is used to perform HTTP POST transaction to retrieve the tracking information. The raw HTML content is processed further by Python BeautifulSoup package [13] to store the intended output in comma separated value (CSV) format. The information stored will feed the next transform process.

Fig. 5. Poslaju data extraction process

2.2   Transform Process

Unstructured or semi-structured data are processed further to produce data in tabular form so that they can be consumed by a later machine learning task. In addition, more data fields are derived such as the distance between sender and receiver town by extrapolating using Google distance API [14]. Postal code information is extracted from Google API too and is used to determine the service level agreement (next day delivery or standard delivery) as assured by Poslaju. To consider public holidays, a list of public holidays was generated and captured into the transformation process to determine if a delivery is around holiday season. Number of transit offices are determined and represented as hop_count. A label is assigned to each record to indicate late delivery (yes/no) based on the following business logic in Table 1.

Table 1. Business logic to determine late delivery

```
days_taken = days(end_date – start_date)

IF sender_postcode AND receiver_postcode is within next day delivery zone
   IF days_taken > 1 + is_weekend
     late_delivery = yes
   ELSE
     late_delivery = no
ELSE
   IF days_taken > 3 + is_weekend
     late_delivery = yes
   ELSE
   late_delivery = no
```

The output of transformation process is a CSV (comma separate value) file which consists of data fields as shown in Table 2.

Table 2. Data field/feature sets

No	Data attribute	Type
1	delivery_id	Categorical (unique identifier)
2	start_dest	Categorical
3	start_date	Categorical (date)
4	end_dest	Categorical
5	end_date	Categorical (date)
6	days_taken	Numeric
7	hop_count	Numeric
8	is_weekend	Boolean
9	pub_hol	Boolean
10	st_town	Categorical
11	st_state	Categorical
12	st_country	Categorical
13	ed_town	Categorical
14	ed_state	Categorical
15	ed_country	Categorical
16	dist_meter	Numeric
17	is_next_day_delivery	Boolean
18	late_delivery	Boolean

2.3 Load Process

In a typical data warehousing process, load process refers to loading records into a database of sorts. In the context of this paper, loading process is taking the transformed datasets and load into machine learning methods.

Figure 6 shows a typical machine learning process. During data preparation stage, the dataset is split into train and test dataset by percentage ratio. In addition, data clean up and missing value handling is carried out at this stage. For model training, train dataset with a list of identified features will feed a chosen machine learning method via Python's "scikit-learn" [15] library. Once a model is produced, test dataset will be used to evaluate the model performance (accuracy, precision, recall, to name a few). Model tuning is carried out to find the best performing model.

Fig. 6. Typical machine learning process

The entire process has feed-forward and feedback flow as indicated in Fig. 2. Feedback flow is needed when user need to fine-tune the data extraction and/or transformation process.

3   Feature Selection and Machine Learning Methods

The objective is to determine late delivery (yes = late, no = on-time delivery) of a given tracking number, therefore this is a binary classification, supervised learning problem. Label is named "late_delivery", a Boolean field indicating 1 (late) or 0 (on-time).

Feature selection is done by examining the data field based on the semantic. Elimination strategy is used in this paper. The "delivery_id" isn't a good feature as it is a unique identifier. Correlated features such as "start_date", "end_date" and "days_-taken" will be discarded as they are used to determine the label "late_delivery". This analysis focuses on domestic delivery, therefore "st_country" and "ed_country" can be eliminated too (single value). "start_dest" and "end_dest" are similar to the derived fields "st_town", "st_state", "ed_town" and "ed_state" and will be discarded. Derived fields will be used which has cleaner and consistent value.

To the best knowledge of the authors, there is no prior art in applying machine learning methods for courier delivery service prediction. Since there is no baseline for comparison, this paper will leverage on the principle of Occam's Razor [16] that recommends going for simpler methods which may yield better result. Therefore, simple supervised learning methods are selected for use in this paper. From our feature selection, Naïve Bayes was selected from parametric algorithm list to evaluate from the perspective of feature independence. Decision Tree and KNN were selected from the non-parametric list to investigate feature relevance. With no assumption on data, Decision Tree and KNN may yield better performance. Each of the supervised machine learning method will be discussed in the following sub-section.

3.1   Naïve Bayes (NB)

Naïve Bayes is a probabilistic based classifier, exists since 1950 [17]. The "naïve" aspect of this machine learning method is that it simply assumes that each feature are independent from each other. Some recent research on Naïve Bayes include [18–22], to name a few.

As a result, probability function for a list of features (assumed to be independent) can be calculated easily. Figure 7 shows the posterior probability for target c for a given set of features $x_1, \ldots, x_n$.

There are 3 categories of Naïve Bayes event model: Gaussian, Multinomial and Bernoulli [17]. Gaussian model assumes that a feature follows Gaussian normal distribution. Multinomial model takes in the count or frequency of occurrences for a given feature, whereas Bernoulli model is based on binomial distribution.

With the assumption of independency among all features, Naïve Bayes classifier is simple, efficient and runs fast. It requires less training data for modeling to achieve good prediction outcome. By using different distribution model, Naïve Bayes can

Likelihood

Class Prior Probability

$$P(c \mid x) = \frac{P(x \mid c)P(c)}{P(x)}$$

Posterior Probability

Predictor Prior Probability

$$P(c \mid X) = P(x_1 \mid c) \times P(x_2 \mid c) \times \cdots \times P(x_n \mid c) \times P(c)$$

Fig. 7. Posterior probability

handle categorical and numerical value well. This will be a good machine learning method to attempt with for this paper.

3.2 Decision Tree (DT)

Decision Trees are a non-parametric supervised learning method mostly used in classification problems and applicable for both categorical and continuous input and output. In decision tree, it performs recursive actions to arrive the result. It is called as decision tree because it maps out all possible decision path in the form of a tree. In recent years, [23–27] have done some research work by applying Decision Tree Algorithm (Fig. 8).

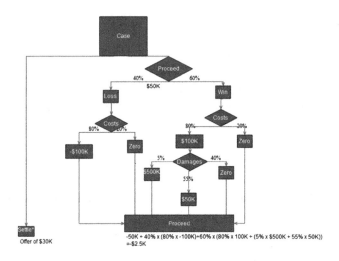

Fig. 8. Decision tree example [28]

Decision tree is simple to understand and to interpret, making it applicable to our daily life and activities. Therefore, it is a good method to start with in this paper too.

3.3   K-Nearest Neighbors (KNN)

K-Nearest Neighbor (KNN) is a type of supervised machine learning technique that is used for classification and regression [29]. It is a non-parametric, lazy learning algorithm [30]. This means that it does not make any generalization, inference or interpretation of the raw data distribution. Therefore, it should be considered for classification analysis where there is minimal prior knowledge to the distribution of data. Some recent study on KNN algorithm included [31–35], to name a few.

KNN is a collection of data where data points are separated into multiple classes to predict the classification of a new sample point. It is based on how "similar" or close a feature resembles its neighbors (Fig. 9).

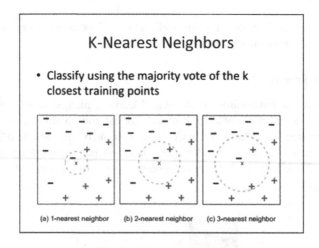

Fig. 9. KNN example [36]

KNN is simple to implement and is flexible on determining the number of neighbors to use on the data set and is also versatile, capable of classification or regression.

4   Results

A subset of 400K records were extracted from Poslaju tracking website. Table 3 shows the class distribution based on the class label. With 35% of late delivery, this is an unbalanced class therefore precision and recall will be used as performance measurement instead of accuracy.

Table 4 shows the results of applying different machine learning algorithm. Features used include hop_count, st_town, ed_town, st_state, ed_state, dist_meter, is_next_day_delivery and is_weekend. 70% of the data set is allocated as training set while the remaining 30% of the data set is allocated as test set.

Table 3. Class distribution by late_delivery

late_delivery	Count
0	253771
1	141825
Total	**395596**

Table 4. Comparison results for Naive Bayes, decision tree and KNN (k = 1)

	Naïve Bayes	Decision tree	KNN (k = 1)
Performance metrics			
Precision	0.6738	0.7385	0.7193
Recall	0.6778	0.7409	0.7142
Run time			
Train time	0.16 s	1.73 s	143.45 s
Test time	0.07 s	0.07 s	22.44 s

Results show that Decision Tree yields the best performance although with slightly longer train time. Different K parameter is tried for KNN and the result is shown in Table 5. Precision and recall improves with higher number of K, approaching similar performance as decision tree.

Table 5. Comparison among different K settings (KNN)

	k = 1	k = 3	k = 5	k = 11
Performance metrics				
Precision	0.7193	0.7287	0.7309	0.7338
Recall	0.7142	0.7270	0.7304	0.7334
Run time				
Train time	143.45 s	166.68 s	167.32 s	151.56 s
Test time	22.44 s	26.38 s	30.35 s	27.43 s

5   Conclusion

The machine learning model has been built to predict late delivery in Poslaju, a national courier service in Malaysia. This is the first research paper that works on leveraging on machine learning to predict late deliver for delivery service in Malaysia. A lot of data clean-up has been carried out during data preparation stage such as text mining to look for certain keywords was necessary to extract and transform into meaningful and useful dataset. Result shows that decision tree and KNN (with higher K value) method has better precision and recall measure compared to Naïve Bayes method.

6 Future Work

This paper represents an initial step towards improving delivery service within Malaysia. Instead of working on our own, collaborating with Poslaju to obtain features such as maximum items per delivery, parcel size, employee rotation and delivery patterns is important. This will help re-evaluate the feature selection phase and use higher complexity machine learning algorithms such as neural network(s) to obtain higher precision and recall measure. From there, potential improvements such as optimized travel routes, package size(s) and courier optimization planning such as employee training can be built.

Acknowledgement. The authors would like to thank Universiti Sains Malaysia for supporting the publication of this paper through USM Research University Grant scheme 1001/PKOMP/ 814254.

References

1. E-commerce Trends: 147 Stats Revealing How Modern Customers Shop in 2017. https://www.bigcommerce.com/blog/ecommerce-trends/. Accessed 1 Aug 2018
2. Malaysia online shopping trends in 2017. http://news.ecinsider.my/2016/12/5-malaysia-online-shopping-trends-2017.html. Accessed 1 Aug 2018
3. Compares Malaysia E-commerce Marketplaces. https://www.webshaper.com.my/compare-ecommerce-marketplaces/. Accessed 1 Aug 2018
4. Pappas, I.O., Kourouthanassis, P.E., Giannakos, M.N., Lekakos, G.: The interplay of online shopping motivations and experiential factors on personalized e-commerce: a complexity theory approach. Telematics Inform. **34**(5), 730–742 (2017)
5. Cao, Y., Ajjan, H., Hong, P.: Post-purchase shipping and customer service experiences in online shopping and their impact on customer satisfaction: an empirical study with comparison. Asia Pac. J. Mark. Logist. **30**, 400–412 (2018)
6. Kuoppamäki, S.M., Taipale, S., Wilska, T.A.: The use of mobile technology for online shopping and entertainment among older adults in Finland. Telematics Inform. **34**(4), 110–117 (2017)
7. Kawaf, F., Tagg, S.: The construction of online shopping experience: a repertory grid approach. Comput. Hum. Behav. **72**(C), 222–232 (2017)
8. Wang, M., Qu, H.: Review of the research on the impact of online shopping return policy on consumer behavior. J. Bus. Adm. Res. **6**(2), 15 (2017)
9. Poslaju. http://www.poslaju.com.my/. Accessed 1 Aug 2018
10. Extract, Transform and Load (ETL), Wikipedia. https://en.wikipedia.org/wiki/Extract,_transform,_load. Accessed 1 Aug 2018
11. Yin, S., Kaynak, O.: Big data for modern industry: challenges and trends [point of view]. Proc. IEEE **103**(2), 143–146 (2015)
12. Requests: HTTP for Humans. http://docs.python-requests.org/en/master/. Accessed 1 Aug 2018
13. Beautiful Soup. https://www.crummy.com/software/BeautifulSoup/. Accessed 1 Aug 2018
14. Google distance matrix API (web services). https://developers.google.com/maps/documentation/distance-matrix/intro. Accessed 1 Aug 2018
15. Scikit-learn. http://scikit-learn.org/. Accessed 1 Aug 2018
16. Occam's Razor, Wikipedia. https://en.wikipedia.org/wiki/Occam%27s_razor. Accessed 1 Aug 2018

17. Naïve Bayes Classifier, Wikipedia. https://en.wikipedia.org/wiki/Naive_Bayes_classifier. Accessed 1 Aug 2018
18. Shinde, T.A., Prasad, J.R.: IoT based animal health monitoring with Naive Bayes classification. IJETT **1**(2) (2017)
19. Chen, X., Zeng, G., Zhang, Q., Chen, L., Wang, Z.: Classification of medical consultation text using mobile agent system based on Naïve Bayes classifier. In: Long, K., Leung, V.C. M., Zhang, H., Feng, Z., Li, Y., Zhang, Z. (eds.) 5GWN 2017. LNICST, vol. 211, pp. 371–384. Springer, Cham (2018). https://doi.org/10.1007/978-3-319-72823-0_35
20. Wu, J., Zhang, G., Ren, Y., Zhang, X., Yang, Q.: Weighted local Naive Bayes link prediction. J. Inf. Process. Syst. **13**(4), 914–927 (2017)
21. Krishnan, H., Elayidom, M.S., Santhanakrishnan, T.: Emotion detection of tweets using Naïve Bayes classifier. Emotion, Int. J. Eng. Technol. Sci. Res. **4**(11) (2017)
22. Mane, D.S., Gite, B.B.: Brain tumor segmentation using fuzzy c-means and k-means clustering and its area calculation and disease prediction using Naive-Bayes algorithm. Brain, Int. J. Eng. Technol. Sci. Res. **6**(11) (2017)
23. Sim, D.Y.Y., Teh, C.S., Ismail, A.I.: Improved boosted decision tree algorithms by adaptive apriori and post-pruning for predicting obstructive sleep apnea. Adv. Sci. Lett. **24**(3), 1680–1684 (2018)
24. Tayefi, M., et al.: hs-CRP is strongly associated with coronary heart disease (CHD): a data mining approach using decision tree algorithm. Comput. Methods Programs Biomed. **141** (C), 105–109 (2017)
25. Li, Y., Jiang, Z.L., Yao, L., Wang, X., Yiu, S.M., Huang, Z.: Outsourced privacy-preserving C4.5 decision tree algorithm over horizontally and vertically partitioned dataset among multiple parties. Clust. Comput., 1–13 (2017)
26. Yang, C.H., Wu, K.C., Chuang, L.Y., Chang, H.W.: Decision tree algorithm-generated single-nucleotide polymorphism barcodes of rbcL genes for 38 Brassicaceae species tagging. Evol. Bioinform. Online **14**, 1176934318760856 (2018)
27. Zhao, H., Li, X.: A cost sensitive decision tree algorithm based on weighted class distribution with batch deleting attribute mechanism. Inf. Sci. **378**(C), 303–316 (2017)
28. Decision tree, Wikipedia. https://en.wikipedia.org/wiki/Decision_tree. Accessed 1 Aug 2018
29. k-nearest neighbors algorithm, Wikipedia. https://en.wikipedia.org/wiki/K-nearest_neighbors_algorithm. Accessed 1 Aug 2018
30. A Detailed Introduction to K-Nearest Neighbor (KNN) Algorithm. https://saravanan thirumuruganathan.wordpress.com/2010/05/17/a-detailed-introduction-to-k-nearest-neighbor-knn-algorithm/. Accessed 1 Aug 2018
31. Mohammed, M.A., et al.: Solving vehicle routing problem by using improved K-nearest neighbor algorithm for best solution. J. Comput. Sci. **21**, 232–240 (2017)
32. Ha, D., Ahmed, U., Pyun, H., Lee, C.J., Baek, K.H., Han, C.: Multi-mode operation of principal component analysis with k-nearest neighbor algorithm to monitor compressors for liquefied natural gas mixed refrigerant processes. Comput. Chem. Eng. **106**, 96–105 (2017)
33. Chen, Y., Hao, Y.: A feature weighted support vector machine and K-nearest neighbor algorithm for stock market indices prediction. Expert Syst. Appl. **80**(C), 340–355 (2017)
34. García-Pedrajas, N., del Castillo, J.A.R., Cerruela-García, G.: A proposal for local *k* values for *k*-nearest neighbor rule. IEEE Trans. Neural Netw. Learn. Syst. **28**(2), 470–475 (2017)
35. Bui, D.T., Nguyen, Q.P., Hoang, N.D., Klempe, H.: A novel fuzzy K-nearest neighbor inference model with differential evolution for spatial prediction of rainfall-induced shallow landslides in a tropical hilly area using GIS. Landslides **14**(1), 1–17 (2017)
36. Rudin, C.: MIT, Spring (2012). https://ocw.mit.edu/courses/sloan-school-of-management/15-097-prediction-machine-learning-and-statistics-spring-2012/lecture-notes/MIT15_097S12_lec06.pdf. Accessed 1 Aug 2018

Image Processing

Cervical Nuclei Segmentation in Whole Slide Histopathology Images Using Convolution Neural Network

Qiuju Yang[1], Kaijie Wu[1(✉)], Hao Cheng[1], Chaochen Gu[1], Yuan Liu[2], Shawn Patrick Casey[1], and Xinping Guan[1]

[1] Department of Automation, Key Laboratory of System Control and Information Processing, Ministry of Education of China, Shanghai Jiao Tong University, Shanghai 200240, China
{napolun279,kaijiewu,jiaodachenghao,jacygu, shawncasey,xpguan}@sjtu.edu.cn
[2] Pathology Department, International Peace Maternity and Child Health Hospital of China Welfare Institute, Shanghai 200030, China
sean_han@163.com

Abstract. Pathologists generally diagnose whether or not cervical cancer cells have the potential to spread to other organs and assess the malignancy of cancer through whole slide histopathology images using virtual microscopy. In this process, the morphology of nuclei is one of the significant diagnostic indices, including the size, the orientation and arrangement of the nuclei. Therefore, accurate segmentation of nuclei is a crucial step in clinical diagnosis. However, several challenges exist, namely a single whole slide image (WSI) often occupies a large amount of memory, making it difficult to manipulate. More than that, due to the extremely high density and variant shapes, sizes and overlapping nuclei, as well as low contrast, weakly defined boundaries, different staining methods and image acquisition techniques, it is difficult to achieve accurate segmentation. A method is proposed, comprised of two main parts to achieve lesion localization and automatic segmentation of nuclei. Initially, a U-Net model was used to localize and segment lesions. Then, a multi-task cascade network was proposed to combine nuclei foreground and edge information to obtain instance segmentation results. Evaluation of the proposed method for lesion localization and nuclei segmentation using a dataset comprised of cervical tissue sections collected by experienced pathologists along with comparative experiments, demonstrates the outstanding performance of this method.

Keywords: Nuclei segmentation · Whole slide histopathology image
Deep learning · Convolutional neural networks · Cervical cancer

1 Introduction

Worldwide, cervical cancer is both the fourth-most common cause of cancer and cause of death from cancer in women, and about 70% of cervical cancers occur in low and middle-income countries [1]. Its development is a long-term process, from precancerous

© Springer Nature Singapore Pte Ltd. 2019
B. W. Yap et al. (Eds.): SCDS 2018, CCIS 937, pp. 99–109, 2019.
https://doi.org/10.1007/978-981-13-3441-2_8

changes to cervical cancer, which typically takes 10 to 20 years [1]. In recent years, with the widespread use of cervical cancer screening programs which allows for early detection and intervention, as well as helping to standardize treatment, mortality has been dramatically reduced [2]. With the development of digital pathology, clinicians routinely diagnose disease through histopathological images obtained using whole slide scanners and displayed using virtual microscopy. In this approach, the morphology of nuclei is one of the significant diagnostic indices for assessing the degree of malignancy of cervical cancer. It is of great significance to make accurate nuclei segmentation in order to provide essential reference information for pathologists. Currently, many hospitals, particularly primary medical institutions lack experienced experts, which influences diagnostic efficiency and accuracy. Therefore achieving automatic segmentation of nuclei is necessary to reduce the workload on pathologists and help improve efficiency, as well as to assist in the determination of treatment plans and recovery prognosis.

Whole slide images (WSI) with high resolution usually occupies large amounts of memory. Therefore, it is difficult to achieve high efficiency and throughput if WSI are directly processed. Due to overlapping, variant shape and sizes, extremely high density of nuclei, as well as factors such as low contrast, weakly defined boundaries, and the use of different staining methods and image acquisition techniques, accurate segmentation of nuclei remains a significant challenge.

In recent years, with the application of deep learning methods for image segmentation, a significant amount of research has been devoted to the development of algorithms and frameworks to improve accuracy, especially in areas of non-biomedical images. Broadly speaking, image segmentation includes two categories; semantic and instance segmentation methods. The semantic method achieves pixel-level classification, which transforms traditional CNN [3] models into end-to-end models [4] such as existing frameworks including FCN [5], SegNet [6], CRFs [7], DeepLab [8], U-Net [9], and DCAN [10]. Based upon semantic segmentation, the instance segmentation method identifies different instances, and includes MNC [11], FCIS [12], Mask RCNN [13], R-FCN [14], and similar implementations. Although these methods achieved considerable results, their application in the field of biomedical images with complex background is relatively poor, with the exception of U-Net [9]. U-Net [9] is a caffe-based convolutional neural network which is often used for biomedical image segmentation and obtains more than acceptable results in many practical applications.

In the case of whole slide images of cervical tissue sections, recommendation of a pathologists' clinical diagnostic process was followed, localizing lesions and segmenting nuclei for diagnosing diseases. The method relies upon two steps with the first being localization and segmentation of lesions in WSI using the U-Net [9] model (Fig. 1, Part1). The second step, nuclei segmentation, builds a multi-task cascade network to segment the nuclei from lesions areas, hereinafter referred to as MTC-Net (Fig. 1, Part2). Similar to DCAN [10], MTC-Net leverages end-to-end training which reduces the number of parameters in the fully connected layer and improves computational efficiency. MTC-Net combines nuclei foreground and edge information for accurate instance segmentation results. However it differs from DCAN [10] in that an intermediate learning process, a noise reduction network of nuclei foreground and a distance transformation learning network, are added. A nuclei segmentation dataset of stained cervical sections was used for comparative study, and the results show that segmentation accuracy has been improved by using this method, especially in the case of severely overlapping nuclei.

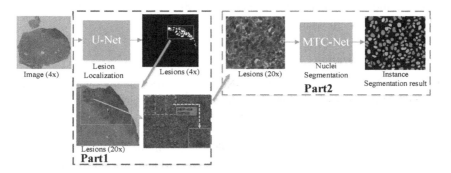

Fig. 1. The overview of the proposed method. Part1 is lesion localization using U-Net [9], the input is a cervical cell image at 4x magnification. The output is a probability map of the input. The lesion region with its coordinates, are chosen and mapped to the same image at 20x magnification. In Part2, a randomly cropped nuclei image from the lesion localized in Part1 is used as the input image of MTC-Net, finally obtaining the instance segmentation result.

2   Experiments

In this section, we describe in detail the preparation of our dataset, detailed explanation of the network structure and loss function of every stage.

2.1   Dataset and Pre-processing

All of the cervical tissue section images in our WSI dataset were collected from the pathology department of International Peace Maternity & Child Health Hospital of China welfare institute (IPMCH) in Shanghai. The dataset contains 138 WSI of variant size, with each sample imaged at 4x and 20x magnification and all ground truth annotations labeled by two experienced pathologists.

Images at 4x magnification were chosen for the initial portion of the algorithm using U-Net [9]; ninety for training/validation and 48 images for testing. Pathologists labeled lesions present in all images in white with the rest of image, viewed as the background region, masked in black. All training/validation images were resized to *512 * 512* in order to reduce computational and memory overhead.

Taking into account the time-consuming nature of labeling nuclei, while implementing the second step MTC-Net, fifty randomly cropped images from the lesions of the WSI dataset were prepared as our nuclei segmentation dataset, with a size of *500 * 500* pixels at 20x magnification. Then pathologists marked nuclei in every image with different colors in order to distinguish between different instances. Ground truth instance and boundary labels of nuclei were generated from pathologists' labels in preparation for model training. We chose 35 images for the training/validation and 15 images for the testing portion. Given the limited number of images, the training/validation dataset was enlarged using a sliding window with a size of *320 * 320* pixels, cropping in increments of 50 pixels. After obtaining small tiles using the sliding window, each tile was processed with data augmentation strategies including vertical/horizontal flip and rotation (0°, 90°, 180°, 270°). Finally, there were 3124 training images in total.

2.2   Lesion Localization

A fully convolutional neural network, U-Net [9], was used as the semantic segmentation model to separate the lesions from the whole slide images (Fig. 2). The input is an *RGB* image at 4x magnification, and the output of this network is a probability map of grayscale pixel values varying from 0 to 1, with a threshold set to 0.6 in order to obtain final segmentation result which is binary. When comparing with the binary ground truth label with pixel values are 0 (background) and 1 (lesions), the semantic segmentation loss function L_l is defined as:

$$L_l(\theta_l) = L_{bce}(output, label) \tag{1}$$

L_{bce} is the binary cross entropy loss function, θ_l denotes the parameters of the semantic segmentation network U-Net [9].

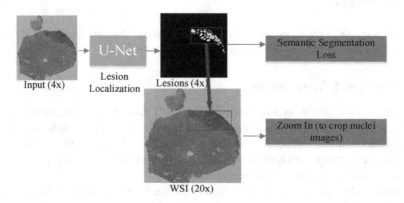

Fig. 2.   Procedure of lesion localization. Input is an *RGB* image and the output is a probability map with grayscale pixel values varying from 0 to 1.

2.3   Nuclei Segmentation

Loss Function

The training details of this network (Fig. 3) is divided into four stages, where UNET1 and UNET2 are both U-Net [11] models. The whole loss function L_{seg} is defined as:

$$L_{seg} = \begin{cases} L_1 & stage1 \\ L_1 + L_2 & stage2 \\ L_1 + L_2 + L_3 & stage3 \\ L_1 + L_2 + L_3 + L_4 & stage4 \end{cases} \quad (2)$$

L_1 is the binary cross entropy loss of UNET1, L_2 is the mean squared error loss of stack Denoising Convolutional Auto-Encoder (sDCAE) [15], L_3 is the mean squared error loss of UNET2, L_4 is the binary cross entropy loss of Encoder-Decoder (ED) [16].

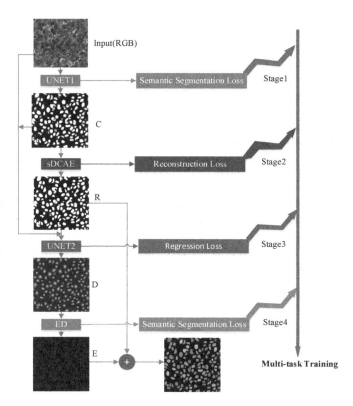

Fig. 3. The procedure of Cervical nuclei segmentation using a multi-task cascaded network (MTC-Net).

Training and Implementation Details
During training stages, the network in each stage focuses on the learning of a sub-task and relies upon the previous output. Therefore, the whole training process is a multi-task cascaded network (MTC-Net). The first stage implements UNET1 for foreground extraction network to isolate the nuclei from the complex background, as much as possible. The input is an *RGB* image, and the semantic output *C* is the preliminary segmentation image, with semantic segmentation loss L_1 defined as:

$$L_1(\theta_1) = L_{bce}(C, input(RGB)) \tag{3}$$

L_{bce} is the binary cross entropy loss function, θ_1 denotes the parameters of UNET1.

The second stage implements sDCAE [15] as the noise reduction network to reconstruct nuclei foreground and segments edges from the semantic output C. As an end-to-end training, fully convolutional network, sDCAE [15] is not sensitive to the size of input images and more efficient with less parameters when compared to fully connected layers. The input is semantic output C and the output R is the reconstruction image after noise reduction, semantic reconstruction loss is defined as:

$$L_2(\theta_2) = L_{mse}(R, C) \tag{4}$$

L_{mse} is the mean squared error loss function, θ_2 denotes the parameters of sDCAE [15].

The third stage is using UNET2 as the distance transformation learning network of the nuclei. Inputs are the RGB image, C and R, with the output D is a distance transformation image. At the same time, distance transformation is used to convert the ground truth instance labels into distance transformation labels (DT). Then making a regression on DT and D, so regression loss L_3 is defined as:

$$L_3(\theta_3) = L_{mse}(D, DT) \tag{5}$$

L_{mse} is the mean squared error loss function, θ_3 denotes the parameters of UNET2.

The last stage uses ED [16] as the edge learning network of the nuclei. The construction of ED [16] uses conventional convolution, deconvolution and pooling layers. The input is D and output is the prediction segmentation mask E of nuclei. According to ground truth boundary label B, the semantic segmentation loss L_4 is defined as:

$$L_4(\theta_4) = L_{bce}(E, B) \tag{6}$$

L_{bce} is the binary cross entropy loss function, θ_4 denotes the parameters of ED [16].

When generating the final instance result of the input image, the predicted probability maps of R and E were fused, and the final segmentation mask seg is defined as:

$$seg(i,j) = \begin{cases} 1 & E(i,j) \geq \lambda \text{ and } R(i,j) \geq \omega \\ 0 & otherwise \end{cases} \tag{7}$$

where $seg(i, j)$ is one of the pixel of seg, $E(i, j)$ and $R(i, j)$ are the pixels at coordinate (i, j) of the nuclei segmentation prediction mask E and the predicted probability maps R respectively, λ and ω are thresholds, set to 0.5 empirically. Then each connected domain in seg is filled with different values to show the instance segmentation result of nuclei.

The whole framework is implemented under the open-source deep learning network Torch. Every stages' weights were initially set as 0, the learning rate was set as $1e^{-4}$ initially and multiplied by 0.1 every 50 epochs.

3 Evaluation and Discussion

To illustrate the superiority and provide effective evaluation metrics for our model, the winning model of the Gland Segmentation Challenge Contest in MICCAI 2015– DCAN [10] was chosen as a baseline to perform a comparative experiment.

3.1 Evaluation Metric

In the initial step (Lesion Localization), U-Net [9] used the common metric IoU to evaluate the effect of localization. IoU is defined as:

$$IoU(G_w, S_w) = (|G_w \cap S_w|)/(|G_w| \cup |S_w|) \tag{8}$$

where $|G_w|$ and $|S_w|$ are the total number of pixels belonging to the ground truth lesions and the semantic segmentation result of lesions respectively.

In second step (Nuclei Segmentation), the evaluation criteria include traditional dice coefficient D_1 and ensemble dice D_2. D_1 measures the overall overlapping between the ground truth and the predicted segmentation results. D_2 captures mismatch in the way the segmentation regions are split, while the overall region may be very similar. The two dice coefficients will be computed for each image tile in the test dataset. The *Score* for the image tile will be the average of the two dice coefficients. The score for the entire test dataset will be the average of the scores for the image tiles. D_1 and D_2 are defined as:

$$\begin{cases} D_1(G_n, S_n) = (|G_n \cap S_n|)/(|G_n| \cup |S_n|) \\ D_2 = 1 - \frac{|G_n - S_n|}{|G_n| \cup |S_n|} \\ Score = \frac{D_1 + D_2}{2} \end{cases} \tag{9}$$

Where $|G_n|$ and $|S_n|$ are the total number of pixels belonging to the nuclei ground truth annotations and the nuclei instance segmentation results respectively, *Score* is the final comprehensive metric of the method.

3.2 Results and Discussion

Some semantic segmentation results of testing data in lesion localization, and the visualization of the comparative instance segmentation results in nuclei segmentation, were analyzed.

The architecture of U-Net [9] combines low-level features to ensure the resolution and precision of the output and high-level features used to earn different and complex features for accurate segmentation at the same time. Another advantage is that U-Net [9] utilizes the auto-encoder framework to strengthen the boundary recognition capabilities by adding or removing noise automatically.

U-Net [9] in Part1 can accurately localize and segment the lesions from WSI (Fig. 4). The semantic segmentation results of the network with the threshold set to 0.6 are almost the same as the ground truth, and the results achieved the *IoU* above 97%, which laid the foundation for the subsequent work of nuclei instance segmentation to obtain good results.

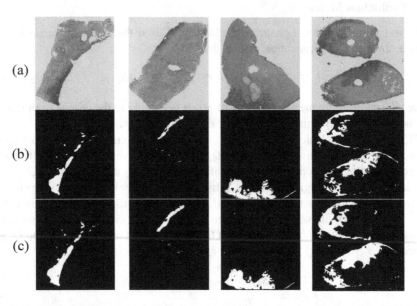

Fig. 4. Semantic segmentation results of testing data in lesion localization. (a): WSI at 4x magnification. (b): ground truth masks of WSI. (c): segmented images.

Nuclei instance segmentation results compared with DCAN [10] (Fig. 5), with MTC-Net exhibiting higher sensitivity for nuclei with severe overlap or blurred boundaries. The application of UNET2 enhanced the segmentation edges and improved the model sensitivity of nuclei edges, and then improved the accuracy of this model.

Quantitative comparative results between DCAN [10] and MTC-Net on the nuclei segmentation dataset were obtained (Table 1), with thresholds λ and ω both set to 0.5. In order to account for possible errors from edge segmentation in nuclei foreground, both segmentation results of DCAN [10] and MTC-Net were operated by morphological expansion. MTC-Net achieves better performance, with the final score about 3% higher than DCAN [10]. The comparative results demonstrate MTC-Net is more effective than DCAN [10] in the field of nuclei segmentation.

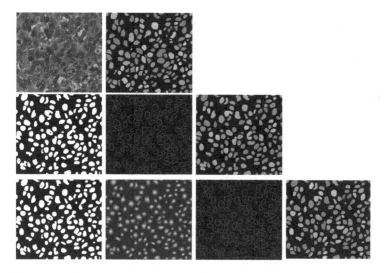

Fig. 5. The comparative nuclei segmentation results using DCAN [10] and MTC-Net. The first row are original image and the ground truth segmentation of this image (left to right). The second row are segmentation results of nuclei foreground, nuclei edges and instance segmentation results (left to right) using model DCAN [10]. The third row are nuclei foreground noise reduction segmentation results, the distance transformation results, nuclei edges segmentation results and the instance segmentation results (left to right) using MTC-Net.

Table 1. The quantitative comparative results between DCAN [10] and MTC-Net on our nuclei segmentation dataset.

Method	Performance		
	D1	D2	Score
DCAN [10]	0.7828	0.7021	0.7424
MTC-Net	**0.8246**	**0.7338**	**0.7792**

4 Conclusions

A two-part method for lesion localization and automatic nuclei segmentation of WSI images of stained cervical tissue sections was introduced. A U-Net [9] model to localize and segment lesions was implemented. A multi-task cascaded network, named MTC-Net, was proposed to segment nuclei from lesions, which is potentially a crucial step for clinical diagnosis of cervical cancer. Similar to DCAN [10], MTC-Net combines nuclei foreground and edge information to obtain instance segmentation results, but the difference is that MTC-Net adds intermediate learning process in the form of a noise reduction network of nuclei foreground and a distance transformation learning network of nuclei. Comparative results were obtained based on our nuclei segmentation dataset, which demonstrated better performance of MTC-Net. After practical application, it was found to some extent that this work provides essential reference information for pathologists in assessing the degree of malignancy of cervical cancer, which can reduce the workload on pathologists and help improve efficiency. Future work will continue to optimize MTC-Net and focus on training with a larger dataset to achieve higher segmentation accuracy.

Acknowledgements. This work is supported by National Key Scientific Instruments and Equipment Development Program of China (2013YQ03065101) and partially supported by National Natural Science Foundation (NNSF) of China under Grant 61503243 and National Science Foundation (NSF) of China under the Grant 61521063.

References

1. Mcguire, S.: World cancer report 2014. Geneva, Switzerland: world health organization, international agency for research on cancer, WHO Press, 2015. Adv. Nutr. **7**(2), 418 (2016)
2. Canavan, T.P., Doshi, N.R.: Cervical cancer. Am. Fam. Physician **61**(5), 1369 (2000)
3. LeCun, Y.: http://yann.lecun.com/exdb/lenet/. Accessed 16 Oct 2013
4. Saltzer, J.H.: End-to-end arguments in system design. ACM Trans. Comput. Syst. (TOCS) **2** (4), 277–288 (1984)
5. Shelhamer, E., Long, J., Darrell, T.: Fully convolutional networks for semantic segmentation. IEEE Trans. Pattern Anal. Mach. Intell. **39**(4), 640–651 (2014)
6. Badrinarayanan, V., Kendall, A., Cipolla, R.: SegNet: a deep convolutional encoder-decoder architecture for image segmentation. IEEE Trans. Pattern Anal. Mach. Intell. **12**(39), 2481–2495 (2017)
7. Zheng, S., Jayasumana, S., Romera-Paredes, B., Vineet, V., Su, Z., Du, D., et al.: Conditional random fields as recurrent neural networks. In: IEEE International Conference on Computer Vision (ICCV), pp. 1529–1537 (2015)
8. Chen, L.C., Papandreou, G., Kokkinos, I., et al.: DeepLab: semantic image segmentation with deep convolutional nets, atrous convolution, and fully connected CRFs. IEEE Trans. Pattern Anal. Mach. Intell. **40**(4), 834–848 (2018)
9. Ronneberger, O., Fischer, P., Brox, T.: U-Net: convolutional networks for biomedical image segmentation. In: Navab, N., Hornegger, J., Wells, W.M., Frangi, A.F. (eds.) MICCAI 2015. LNCS, vol. 9351, pp. 234–241. Springer, Cham (2015). https://doi.org/10.1007/978-3-319-24574-4_28
10. Chen, H., Qi, X., Yu, L., Heng, P.A.: DCAN: deep contour-aware networks for accurate gland segmentation. In: IEEE Conference on Computer Vision and Pattern Recognition (CVPR), pp. 2487–2496 (2016)
11. Dai, J., He, K., Sun, J.: Instance-aware semantic segmentation via multi-task network cascades. In: IEEE Conference on Computer Vision and Pattern Recognition (CVPR), pp. 3150–3158 (2015)
12. Li, Y., Qi, H., Dai, J., Ji, X., Wei, Y.: Fully convolutional instance-aware semantic segmentation. In: IEEE Conference on Computer Vision and Pattern Recognition (CVPR), pp. 4438–4446 (2017)
13. He, K., Gkioxari, G., Dollár, P., et al.: Mask R-CNN. In: IEEE International Conference on Computer Vision (ICCV), pp. 2980–2988 (2017)
14. Dai, J., Li, Y., He, K., et al.: R-FCN: Object detection via region-based fully convolutional networks. Advances in Neural Information Processing Systems 29 (NIPS) (2016)

15. Vincent, P., Larochelle, H., Lajoie, I., Bengio, Y., Manzagol, P.A.: Stacked denoising autoencoders: learning useful representations in a deep network with a local denoising criterion. J. Mach. Learn. Res. **11**(12), 3371–3408 (2010)
16. Cho, K., Van Merrienboer, B., Gulcehre, C., Bahdanau, D., Bougares, F., Schwenk, H.: Learning phrase representations using RNN encoder-decoder for statistical machine translation. Computer Science (2014)

Performance of SVM and ANFIS for Classification of Malaria Parasite and Its Life-Cycle-Stages in Blood Smear

Sri Hartati[1(✉)], Agus Harjoko[1], Rika Rosnelly[2], Ika Chandradewi[1], and Faizah[1]

[1] Universitas Gadjah Mada, Sekip Utara, Yogyakarta 55281, Indonesia
shartati@ugm.ac.id
[2] Department of Informatics, University of Potensi Utama, Medan, Indonesia

Abstract. A method to classify Plasmodium malaria disease along with its life stage is presented. The geometry and texture features are used as Plasmodium features for classification. The geometry features are area and perimeters. The texture features are computed from GLCM matrices. The support vector machine (SVM) classifier is employed for classifying the Plasmodium and its life stage into 12 classes. Experiments were conducted using 600 images of blood samples. The SVM with RBF kernel yields an accuracy of 99.1%, while the ANFIS gives an accuracy of 88.5%.

Keywords: Malaria · Geometry · Texture · GLCM · RBF

1 Introduction

Malaria is a highly hazardous disease to humans because it can cause death. Malaria is caused by parasites which are transmitted by the female Anopheles mosquito. These mosquitoes bite infected Plasmodium from a person previously infected with the parasite. Plasmodium is divided into four types: Plasmodium ovale, Plasmodium malaria, Plasmodium falciparum, and Plasmodium vivax. Plasmodium vivax is often found in patients with malaria disease. Plasmodium falciparum is the cause of deaths of nearly 90% of the patient with malaria disease in the world.

Microscopic examination is required to determine the parasite Plasmodium visually by identifying directly at the patient's blood dosage. The microscopic examination result is highly dependent on the expertise of the laboratory worker (health analyst) that identifies the parasite Plasmodium. The microscopic examination technique is the gold standard for the diagnosis of malaria. Among some techniques which can be used for malaria diagnosis the peripheral blood smear (PBS), quantitative buffy coat (QBC), rapid diagnosis test (RDT), Polymerase Chain Reaction (PCR), and Third Harmonic Generation (THG) [1, 2]. The PBS technique is the most widely used malaria diagnosis even though has limitations of human resistance due to the time required.

To diagnose malaria parasite, a manual calculation process that uses a microscopic examination of Giemsa-stained thick and thin blood smears is carried out. This process

© Springer Nature Singapore Pte Ltd. 2019
B. W. Yap et al. (Eds.): SCDS 2018, CCIS 937, pp. 110–121, 2019.
https://doi.org/10.1007/978-981-13-3441-2_9

requires a long time and is a tedious process. It is very susceptible to the capabilities and skills of technicians. Its potential for mistakes made by humans is significant [3].

As an illustration, a trained technician requires about 15 min to count 100 cells. Worldwide, technicians have to deal with millions of patients every year [4]. To overcome a long and tedious process, several studies have been conducted to develop automated microscopic blood cell analysis. Some early studies showed limited performance, which leads to classifying the types of parasites present in blood cells but has not been able to show the entire stage of malaria life [5]. Similar studies were conducted with various methods to increase the accuracy of identification of infectious parasites, mainly only identifying 2–4 Plasmodium parasites that can infect humans [6]. Without specifying the life stages of malarial parasites, whereas each parasite has three different life stages, namely trophozoite, schizoite, and gametocytes [3]. Therefore, the study of the classification of the life stages of malarial parasites poses a challenge to the study [7], and successfully detects three stages of the Plasmodium parasite while in the human host, trophozoite, schizont, and Plasmodium falciparum gametocytes, even though it has not been able to detect other species. Plasmodium that can form human infection has four species: falciparum, vivax, ovale, and malaria. Each species is divided into four distinct phases, which are generally distinguishable: rings, trophozoites, schizonts, and gametocytes, so that there are sixteen different classes. This paper discusses methods for classifying 12 classes that include three types of Plasmodium and each with four life stages.

2 Data Collections

A total of 600 malaria image data of Giemsa - stained thin blood smears is obtained from Bina Medical Support Services (BPPM) in Jakarta. The malaria image data size is 2560×1920 pixels. The manual plasmodium classification is carried out by laboratory workers of the parasitology Health Laboratory of the North Sumatra Province, Indonesia, which provide the ground truth for the proposed method. Each image is given a label associated with the name of the parasite, i.e., Plasmodium malaria, Plasmodium falciparum, Plasmodium vivax) along with its life-cycle-stage (ring, trophozoite, schizont, or gametocyte). None of the 600 image data consist of Plasmodium ovale. Therefore the 600 image data consist of 12 classes. Figure 1 shows different Plasmodium, and their life-stages.

3 Method

The classification process of the malaria parasite is shown in Fig. 2. A blood smear is performed on the blood sample. The region of interest (ROI) is then determined to locate the area, which contains parasite. Next, three basic image processing steps are carried out, that is, preprocessing, segmentation, and feature extraction. Following that, the image classification and detection of infected red blood cells (RBC), that is called parasitemia, are carried out. In this work, the malaria images consist of three types of

Plasmodium and each has four different life stages, i.e., ring, schizont, trophozoite, and gametocyte stages.

3.1 Preprocessing

The aim of the preprocessing step is to obtain images with lower noise and higher contrast than the original images for further processing. Blood smear images might be affected by the illumination and color distribution of blood images due to the camera setting and staining variability. Most of the microscopes yield blood cells with quite similar colors. Therefore, image enhancement and noise reduction operations are required. Low intensities of light might decrease the contrast of blood image [8]. Therefore the contrast image has to be improved using a contrast enhancement method.

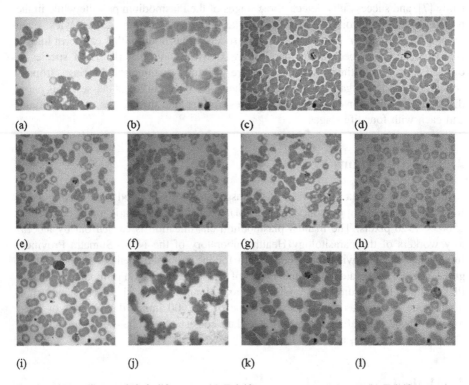

(a)   (b)   (c)   (d)

(e)   (f)   (g)   (h)

(i)   (j)   (k)   (l)

Fig. 1. Plasmodium and their life stage. (a) Falcifarum, gametocyte stage (b) Falcifarum, ring stage (c) Falcifarum, schizont stage (d) Falcifarum, trophozoite stage (e) Malariae, gametocyte stage (f) Malariae, ring stage (g) Malariae, schizont stage (h) Malariae, trophozoite stage (i) Vivax, gametocyte stage (j) Vivax, ring stage (k) Vivax, schizont stage (l) Vivax, trophozoite stage.

After image enhancement is performed, the region of interest (ROI) is carried out by manually cropping the infected RBC, because the image contains infected not only

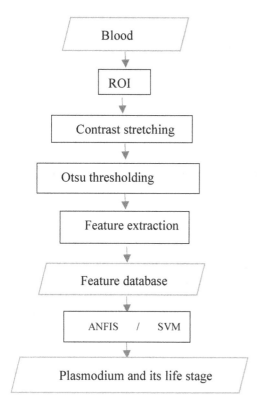

Blood

ROI

Contrast stretching

Otsu thresholding

Feature extraction

Feature database

ANFIS / SVM

Plasmodium and its life stage

Fig. 2. Detection of the malaria parasite and its life stage.

red blood cells but also normal red blood cells, white blood cells, platelets, and artifacts. Experts validate the process of determining ROI. Experience indicates that the appropriate size for ROI is 256×256 pixels. These preprocessing produces an image with good contrast.

3.2 Segmentation

Segmentation attempts to subdivide an image into sub-images or segments such that each segment fulfills certain characteristics. In this case, as the malaria parasite affects the red blood cells, the segmentation is carried out to separate red blood cells from the rest, and the result is the red blood cells in the microscopic images of the blood sample. Initially, the RGB image of ROI is converted into the gray image since the red blood cells can be distinguished from the rest of its gray level value. In this research, Otsu's thresholding method is used for its ability to determine threshold automatically. An example is depicted in Fig. 3.

After thresholding, the morphological closing and opening are performed to extract the hole inside the infected cell and eliminate the unwanted artifacts [9]. These segmented cells are further processed and then the infected red blood cells are identified.

3.3 Features Extraction

Many studies concerning the analysis of red blood cells recently use texture features [5, 9], and color features [10, 11], to differentiate normal cells and infected cells. In this research texture and geometry, features are used. Geometry features are selected for analyzing blood since hematologist uses these features. The selected geometric features are area and perimeter. The area is defined as the number of pixels of the object that indicates the size of the object and is calculated using

$$Area = \sum_x \sum_y f(x, y). \tag{1}$$

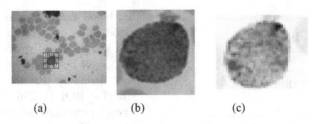

(a)   (b)   (c)

Fig. 3. (a) Initial image, (b) Region of Interest (ROI) (c) grayscale of ROI.

The perimeter is expressed as the continuous line forming the boundary of a closed geometric object. It can be calculated as

$$Perimeter = \sum_x \sum_y {}_{x,y \in Boundary\ region} f(x,y), \tag{2}$$

The texture features are computed from the Gray-Level Co-occurrence Matrix (GLCM) of the ROI image. The GLCM is used to calculate the co-occurrence of a pair of pixels with gray-level value and in a particular direction. A GLCM element Pθ, d(i, j) is the joint probability of the gray level pairs i and j in a given direction θ separated by a distance of d units. In this research, the GLCM features are extracted using one distance (d = {1}), and three directions (θ = {45°, 90°, 135°}). These texture based features can be calculated as follows:

1. *Contrast* is the measure of intensity contrast between a pixel and the neighboring pixel over the complete image.

$$\sum_{i,j}^{N-1} p_{i,j}(i-j)^2 \tag{3}$$

2. *Entropy*
   Entropy is the measure of the complexity of the image, and it represents the amount of information contained in data distribution. The higher the entropy value, the higher the complexity of the image.

$$\sum_{i,j}^{N-1} p_{i,j}(-\ln p_{i,j})^2 \tag{4}$$

3. *Energy*
   Energy is a measure of the pixel intensities in grayscale value. Energy is computed by summing all squared elements in the GLCM matrix,

$$\sum_{i,j}^{n-1} p_{i,j}{}^2 \tag{5}$$

4. Homogeneity is the measure of the homogeneity of a particular region. This value is high when all pixels have the same values or uniform.

$$\sum_{i,j=0}^{N-1} \frac{p_{i,j}}{1+(i-1)^2} \tag{6}$$

5. Correlation indicates how a pixel is correlated with the neighboring pixels in a particular area

$$\sum_{i,j=0}^{N-1} p_{i,j} \left[\frac{(i-\mu_i)(i-\mu_j)}{\sqrt{\sigma_i^2 \sigma_j^2}} \right] \tag{7}$$

3.4 Classification Using ANFIS

A specific approach in neuro-fuzzy development is the adaptive neuro-fuzzy inference system (ANFIS), which has shown significant results in modeling nonlinear functions. The ANFIS learn features in the data set and adjusts the system parameters according to a given error criterion. In this research, the ANFIS is a fuzzy Sugeno model. To present the ANFIS architecture, fuzzy if-then rules based on a first-order Sugeno model are considered. The output of each rule can be a linear combination of input variables and a constant term or can be only a constant term. The final output is the weighted average of each rule's output. Basic architecture with two inputs x and y and one output z is shown in Fig. 4.

Suppose that the rule base contains two fuzzy if-then rules of

Rule 1: If x is A_1 and y is B_1, then $f_1 = p_1 x + q_1 y + r_1$,
Rule 2: If x is A_2 and y is B_2, then $f_2 = p_2 x + q_2 y + r_2$.

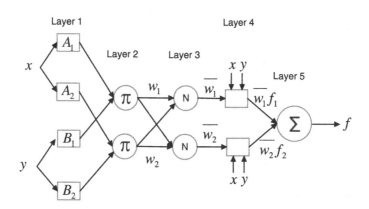

Fig. 4. The architecture of ANFIS.

Layer 1: Every node i in this layer is an adaptive node with a node function

$$O_i = \mu_{A_i} \tag{8}$$

where x is the input to node i, and A_i is the linguistic label (small, large, etc.) associated with this node function. In other words, Eq. (8) is the membership function of specifies the degree to which the given x satisfies the quantifier A_i. Usually, it equals to 1 and minimum equal to 0, such as choose $\mu_{Ai}(x)$ to be bell-shaped with maximum

$$\mu_{A_i}(x) = \frac{1}{1 + \left[\left(\frac{x-x_i}{a_i}\right)^2\right]} \tag{9}$$

$$\mu_{A_i}(x) = e^{\left\{-\left(\frac{x-x_i}{a_i}\right)^2\right\}} \tag{10}$$

where a_i is the parameter set. As the values of these parameters change, the bell-shaped functions vary accordingly, thus exhibiting various forms of membership functions on linguistic label A_i. In fact, any continuous and piecewise differential functions, such as trapezoidal or triangular shaped membership functions, can also be used for node functions in this layer. Parameters in this layer are referred to as premise parameters.

Layer 2: Every node in this layer is a fixed node labeled Π which multiplies the incoming signals and sends the product out. For instance,

$$w_i = \mu_{A_i}(x) + \mu_{B_i}(y), \ i \leq 2 \tag{11}$$

Each node output represents the firing strength of a rule.

Layer 3: Every node in this layer is a circle node labeled N. The ith node calculates the ratio of i to the sum of all rules firing strengths. For convenience, outputs of this layer will be called as normalized firing strengths

$$\bar{w}_i = \frac{w_i}{w_1 + w_2} \tag{12}$$

Layer 4: Every node i in this layer is a square node with a node function

$$O_i = \bar{w}_i f_1 = \bar{w}_i (p_1 x + q_1 y + r_1) \tag{13}$$

where w_i is the output of layer 3, and $\{p_1, q_1, r_1\}$ parameter set. Parameters in this layer will be referred to consequent parameters.

Layer 5: The single node in this layer is a circle node labeled as $\sum$ that computes the overall output as the summation of all incoming signals, i.e.

$$O_i = \sum_i \bar{w}_i f_1 = \frac{\sum_i w_i f_i}{\sum_i w_i} \tag{14}$$

Learning Algorithm

In the ANFIS structure, it is noticed that given the values of premise parameters, the final output can be expressed as a linear combination of the consequent parameters. The output f can be written as

$$f = \frac{w_1}{w_1 + w_2} f_1 + \frac{w_2}{w_1 + w_2} f_2 \tag{15}$$

$$w_1 f_1 + w_2 f_2 = (\overline{w_1}x)p_1 + (\overline{w_1}x)q_1 + (\overline{w_1}x)r_1 + (\overline{w_2}x)p_2 + (\overline{w_2}x)q_2 + (\overline{w_2}x)r_2 w_1 w_2$$

where f is linear in the consequent parameters (p_1, q_1, r_1, p_2, q_2, r_2). In the feedforward learning process, consequent parameters are identified by the least squares estimate. In the backward learning process, the error signals, which are the derivatives of the squared error with respect to each node output, propagate backward from the output layer to the input layer. In this backward pass, the premise parameters are updated by the gradient descent algorithm.

3.5   Classification Using SVM

Support Vector Machines (SVMs) are state-of-the-art classification methods based on machine learning theory [12]. Compared with other methods such as artificial neural networks, decision trees, and Bayesian networks, SVMs have significant advantages because of their high accuracy, elegant mathematical tractability, and direct geometric interpretation. Besides, they do not need a large number of training samples to avoid overfitting. The support vector machine (SVM) is selected to classify the Plasmodium type along with its life stage. There are 12 possible classes since there are three types of Plasmodium and four life stages. Two different kernels are implemented, and their performances are compared.

Before the SVM is used for classification, it is trained using training data. In the process of training, the SVM uses feature matrix, as the training input, which is obtained in the features extraction process. The training data classification process is to seek support vector and bias of input data. The following is the training algorithm for each binary SVM:

Input: Z is a matrix of Plasmodium features obtained from feature extraction process. Output: Strain vector as a target. Y_{train} vector is a column vector for classification of the first class, where all images of blood preparations of the first class will be symbolized by number 1, all images of blood smears from other classes with number -1. In this study, a Gaussian kernel function with variance (σ) = one is used. The next step is to calculate Hessian matrix, i.e., multiplication of a Gaussian kernel with Y_{train}. Y_{train} is a vector that contains values of 1 and -1. Hessian matrix is later used as input variables in quadratic programming. The training steps are described as follows:

1. Determine input ($Z = X_{train}$) and Target (Y_{train}) as a pair of training from two classes.
2. Calculating Gaussian kernel

$$K(Z, Z_i) = \exp\left(\frac{-|Z - Z_i|^2}{2\sigma^2}\right) \tag{16}$$

3. Calculate Hessian matrix

$$H = K(Z, Z_i) * Y * YT \tag{17}$$

Assign c and *epsilon*. The term c is a constant in Lagrangian multipliers and epsilon (cost parameter) is the upper limit value of α, which serves to control classification error. This study used value of $c = 100000$ and *epsilon* $= 1 \times 10^{-7}$.
4. Assign vector e as a unit vector which has the same dimension with the dimension of Y.
5. Calculating quadratic programming solutions

$$L(\alpha) = \frac{1}{2}\alpha^+ H\alpha + e^T\alpha \tag{18}$$

In testing process, data that have never been used for training are used. Results of this process are an index value of the largest decision function, stating the class of the testing data. If a class in the classification test match the test data classes, classification is stated to be correct. The final result of classification is an image of blood that matches with an index value of decision function using SVM one against all.

Having an input data feature vector T for test data (w, x, b), and k number of classes, the input data then is used for the testing process. The input is generated in the process of feature extraction, The process of testing is as follows:

1. Calculate Kernel Gaussian

$$K(T, x_i) = \exp\left(\frac{-|T - x_i|^2}{2\sigma^2}\right) \tag{19}$$

2. Calculate

$$f_i = K(T, x_i)w_i + b_i \tag{20}$$

3. Repeat steps 1, 2 for $i = 1$ to k.
4. Determining the maximum value of f_i
5. A class i is a class from T which has the largest value of f_i

The performance of both the proposed method is measured regarding accuracy, sensitivity, and specificity. The true positive (TP) shows the image of blood smears correctly identified. False positive (FP) is the image of Plasmodium classified incorrectly. The true negative (TN) indicates the number of images that is not a member of a class and is correctly identified as not a member of class (NV). False negative (FN) showed the number image of blood smears that should not be members of class but identified as a member of class.

$$Accuracy = (TP + TN)/(TP + TN + FP + FN),$$
$$Sensitivity = TP/(TP + FN),$$
$$Specificity = TN/(FP + TN)$$

4 Experimental Results

Experiments were conducted to evaluate the performance of the proposed classification method. A total of 600 image data from Bina Medical Support Services (BPPM), Jakarta, Indonesia were used. The resolution of the image is 2560×1920 pixels. Parasite labeling was carried out by a professional from a parasitology health laboratory in North Sumatra, Indonesia. There are three types of parasites, i.e., Plasmodium malariae, Plasmodium falciparum, and Plasmodium vivax. Each plasmodium is distinguished into four life stages, i.e., ring, trophozoite, schizont, or gametocyte.

The ANFIS neural network is used for classifying the Plasmodium type along with its life stages which makes a total combination of 12 classes. The testing process utilizes k-fold cross-validation model were adopted with $k = 1, 2, 3, 4, 5$. Table 1 shows the experimental results for the algorithm.

Table 1. Experimental results for ANFIS algorithm.

	K = 1	K = 2	K = 3	K = 4	K = 5
Accuracy (%)	89.29	84.82	90.62	91.07	86.74
Precision (%)	89.30	83.28	90.62	92.10	86.65
Sensitivity (%)	89.31	98.00	90.62	89.60	85.86
Specificity (%)	89.32	86.30	90.62	91.00	88.33

As seen in Table 1, the ANFIS gives an average accuracy of 88,503%. While as seen in Table 2, the SVM with linear kernel gives an average accuracy of 57% which is not satisfactory. The highest accuracy, which is 62%, was obtained when $k = 3$. As shown in Table 3, SVM with RBF kernel yields a much better results with an average accuracy of 99.1%.

Table 2. Experimental results for SVM classifier with linear kernel.

	K = 1	K = 2	K = 3	K = 4	K = 5
Accuracy (%)	53.0	52.0	62.0	60.0	56.0
Precision (%)	33.0	34.4	45.3	37.8	44.0
Sensitivity (%)	38.9	37.4	45.4	44.1	43.4
Specificity (%)	95.4	95.6	95.5	96.3	95.7

Table 3. Experimental results for SVM classifier with RBF kernel.

	K = 1	K = 2	K = 3	K = 4	K = 5
Accuracy (%)	100	98.0	100	100	98.0
Precision (%)	100	96.2	100	100	97.9
Sensitivity (%)	100	99.1	100	100	97.0
Specificity (%)	100	99.8	100	100	99.8

5   Conclusion

A method to classify plasmodium of malaria disease along with its life stage is presented. The geometry and texture features are used for classification. The texture features are computed from GLCM matrices. The SVM classifier is employed for classifying the Plasmodium and its life stage into 12 classes. The SVM with linear kernel gives the accuracy of 57%; the ANFIS gives an accuracy of 88.5% whereas SVM with RBF kernel yields an accuracy of 99.1%.

Acknowledgment. The authors would like to thank the Directorate General of Higher Education, the Ministry of Research and Higher Education of the Republic of Indonesia for sponsoring this research. The authors would also like to thank the parasitology Health Laboratory of the North Sumatra Province and Bina Medical Support Services (BPPM), Jakarta, for supporting this research.

References

1. World Health Organization: Basic Malaria Microscopy, Part I Learners Guide, 2nd edn. World Health Organization, Geneve (2010). https://doi.org/10.1016/0169-4758(92)90107-D
2. Jain, P., Chakma, B., Patra, S., Goswami, P.: Potential biomarkers and their applications for rapid and reliable detection of malaria. BioMed Res. Int., 201–221 (2014). https://doi.org/10.1155/2014/852645
3. McKenzie, F.E.: Dependence of malaria detection and species diagnosis by microscopy on parasite density. Am. J. Trop. Med. Hyg. **69**(4), 372–376 (2003)
4. Tek, F.B., Dempster, A.G., Kale, I.: Malaria parasite detection in peripheral blood images. In: 17th International Conference British Machine Vision Conference Proceedings, pp. 347–356. British Machine Vision Association, Edinburgh (2006). https://doi.org/10.1109/ACCESS.2017.2705642
5. Ross, N.E., Pittchard, C.J., Rubbin, D.M., Duse, A.G.: Automated image processing method for the diagnosis and classification of malaria on thin blood smears. Med. Biol. Eng. Comput. **44**(5), 427–436 (2006). https://doi.org/10.1109/ICSIPA.2013.6708035
6. Komagal, E., Kumar, K.S., Vigneswaran, A.: Recognition and classification of malaria plasmodium diagnosis. Int. J. Eng. Res. Technol. **2**(1), 1–4 (2013)
7. Nugroho, H.A., Akbar, S.A., Muhandarwari, E.E.H.: Feature extraction and classification for detection malaria parasites in thin blood smear. In: 2nd International Conference on Information Technology, Computer, and Electrical Engineering Proceedings, pp. 198–201. IEEE, Semarang (2015). https://doi.org/10.1109/ICITACEE.2015.7437798

8. Khatri, E.K.M., Ratnaparkhe, V.R., Agrawal, S.S., Bhalchandra, A.S.: Image processing approach for malaria parasite identification. Int. J. Comput. Appl. 5–7 (2014)
9. Kumar, A., Choudhary, A., Tembhare, P.U., Pote, C.R.: Enhanced identification of malarial infected objects using Otsu algorithm from thin smear digital images. Int. J. Latest Res. Sci. Technol. 1(159), 2278–5299 (2012)
10. Ahirwar, N., Pattnaik, S., Acharya, B.: Advanced image analysis based system for automatic detection and classification of malaria parasite in blood images. Int. J. Inf. Technol. Knowl. Manag. 5(1), 59–64 (2012)
11. Chen, T., Zhang, Y., Wang, C., Ou, Z., Wang, F., Mahmood, T.S.: Complex local phase based subjective surfaces (CLAPSS) and its application to DIC red blood cell image segmentation. J. Neurocomputing 99, 98–110 (2013). https://doi.org/10.1016/j.neucom.2012.06.015
12. Bhavsar, T.H., Panchal, M.H.: A review on support vector machine for data classification. Int. J. Adv. Res. Comput. Eng. Technol. 1(10), 185–189 (2012)

Digital Image Quality Evaluation for Spatial Domain Text Steganography

Jasni Mohamad Zain[1(✉)] and Nur Imana Balqis Ramli[2]

[1] Advanced Analytics Engineering Centre, Fakulti Sains Komputer dan Matematik, UiTM Selangor (Kampus Shah Alam), 40450 Shah Alam, Selangor, Malaysia
jasni@tmsk.uitm.edu.my
[2] Fakulti Sains Komputer dan Matematik, UiTM Selangor (Kampus Shah Alam), 40450 Shah Alam, Selangor, Malaysia
girloy912@gmail.com

Abstract. Steganography is one of the techniques that can be used to hide information in any file types such as audio, image, text and video format. The image steganography is about concealing the hidden data into digital images that alter the pixel of the image. This paper will examine how steganography affect the quality of digital images. Two types of images were selected and different capacities of text documents from 4 kB to 45 kB were used as secret messages. The secret message is embedded in the least significant bits of the images and the distortion is measured using peak signal to noise ratio (PSNR). The results show that for small capacity, it is possible to embed in the second most significant bit (LSB 6) while maintaining a good quality image of more than 30 dB, while for a bigger capacity up to 45 kB, embedding in the fourth least significant bit is possible.

Keywords: Steganography · Spatial · Least significant bit

1 Introduction

The meaning of steganography in Greek is "Covered or Concealed Writing". The process of hiding information in steganography involves cover medium redundant bit identification. It does not only hide the information of the messages but as well as the presence of the messages. The most crucial elements in steganography include the secret message's size that can hide, prevention method for the attacker and the number of changes in media before the messages are being seen [1].

The element of steganography can be seen in Fig. 1. The capacity is the amount of secret data that 5 can be embedded without deterioration of image quality [2]. When using the capacity element for detection, the data hidden must be so small that it cannot be seen by human eyes. Another element is imperceptibility. The detection of the image alteration should be done without anyone being able to see it and there are no techniques that being able to sense it. Aside from that, robustness is also part of the elements of steganography. All of the hidden information is saved from being removed. One of the example is watermarking.

© Springer Nature Singapore Pte Ltd. 2019
B. W. Yap et al. (Eds.): SCDS 2018, CCIS 937, pp. 122–133, 2019.
https://doi.org/10.1007/978-981-13-3441-2_10

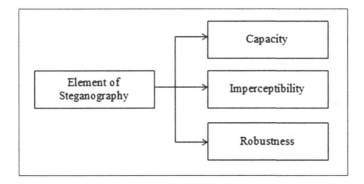

Fig. 1. Element of steganography.

Steganography can be divided into text, audio or sound, image, and protocol steganography. Since the digital images have a high redundancy, it becomes a well-known cover media. Text steganography hides secret messages via printed natural language meanwhile video steganography uses video frames to hide the messages and audio steganography aims to hide the messages that exceed the human hearing into the cover audio file [3].

One of the problems that occur in the steganography is the size of the bits of the secret data. Increasing the bit in LSB algorithm can distort the stego images [4]. Besides, when changing the quantity of the secret image inserted, it might be visible to anyone. Thus, it can lead to a suspicious content of the images, for example. Aside from that, the level of data security needs to be high to avoid the untrusted person read or see the content of the secret message that is hidden as the quality of the image is concerned. Increasing only two or more bit bits will affect the image resolution thus decreasing the image quality [5].

Besides, Sharma and Kumar states that by reducing the embedding data, the detectable artefacts will also reduce [6]. So the selection of the cover object and length of the embedded secret message is very important in protecting the embedding algorithm. In steganography algorithm, data rate and imperceptibility are contrasted to each other. When the capacity of data rate is higher, the robustness will be lower and vice versa. To ensure the quality of the stego image, it needs a worth PSNR value. Another problem is when having too much modification on the cover image affecting the modification of the secret message as the method is really sensitive.

2   Literature Review

This section will review work regarding image steganography. Basic components of digital image steganography is discussed. The next subsection will look at the evaluations criteria for digital image steganography, followed by digital image definition.

2.1   Image Steganography

An image steganography is a steganography that uses a cover object on the images due to the commonness of the images on the internet [6]. It can hide text or images in the cover images. Thus, it is unknown to people if the images contain secret data or not.

Different file formats have different algorithm, for example, least significant bit insertion, Masking and filtering, Redundant Pattern Encoding, Encrypt and Scatter, Algorithms and transformations [7].

There are several basic components of digital image steganography which can be seen in Fig. 2 [8].

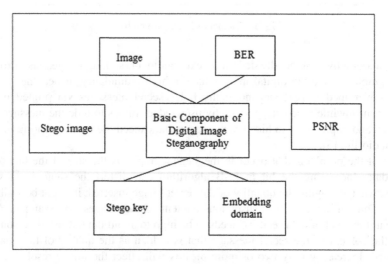

Fig. 2. Basic component of digital image steganography [8].

One of them is the image; it signifies graphic view of an object, scene, person or abstraction. Another one is the cover image; an image that stores secret message securely and used to in embedding process. Next is the Stego image which is the image with the secret data after the embedding process. It has smallest differences from the cover image and requires by the receiver to reveal the message. The Stego key is a key that is used when the receiver wants to retrieve the secret message which can be any random number or password.

Other than that, the embedding domain which exploiting the characteristic of the cover image for the embedding process is one of the basic components. It can be in spatial or transform domain which directly embeds the secret message into the cover image, and the cover image is converted into the frequency domain and the embedding process is being done with the converted cover image respectively.

Another basic component is the Peak Signal to Noise Ratio (PSNR); determine the perceptual transparency of the stego image with respect to the cover image by measuring the quality of the image. Last but not least the Bit Error Rate (BER). Error measurement that calculated while recovered the message. It occurs when the communication for the suitable channel between the sender and receiver is lacked.

2.2 Evaluation Criteria for Image Steganography

There are several factors that are observed in order to make a good steganographic algorithm as shown in Fig. 3 [9]. Not all of these factors can be observed in an algorithm as it shall have weakness if not one [9].

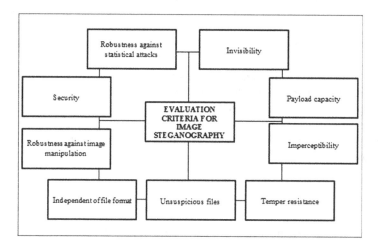

Fig. 3. Evaluation criteria for image steganography [9]

Imperceptibility should be high as the image shall not have any visual on it. The image shall not be visible to the human eyes however if the image can be seen easily by human eyes, it may be because the algorithm is not good. Bit per pixels, payload capacity need to have the ability to hide a good amount of data in the cover image. Another factor is security. The image needs to survive from attacks, noise, cropping, scaling or filtering. The image also needs to withstand the statistical attacks as many are trying to uncover the image in order to find out the hidden messages. The image manipulation needs to be handled with careful so the hidden message in the image do not destroy or lose. Furthermore, a good algorithm can hide the message in different format of file as it can be confusing when someone tries to uncover it. The files that are used do not need to be suspicious as it can gain attention. "Tamper resistance means the survival of the embedded data in the stego-image when attempt is done to modify it. Finally, computational complexity refers to the computational cost of embedding and extraction" has to be low.

2.3 Image Definition

The object of a logical arrangement of colour(s) is called an image meanwhile "a two dimensional function i(x, y), where x and y are plane coordinators pointing to a unique value, corresponding to light's intensity at that point, and stored as raw data inside persistent storage which gets its meaning from the header that precede and relates it to a specific file format" is called the digital image [10].

The numbers that assembly in different areas that create a different amount of light is called an image. Thus, creating grids and individual points that are being represented by the numeric form called pixels. In the image, the pixel is shown "horizontally row by row" [11].

The amount of bits in color scheme that are used for each of the pixels is referred to the bit depth. According to the same author, it is said that the smallest value is 8 bits which define the color of each pixel in an image. Hence, for 8 bits image, there will be 256 colors. For example, monochrome and grayscale images show 256 various shades of grey. In addition, the true color which is digital color image uses RGB color and is saved as a 24-bit file [12].

Different image file formats have its specific use in the digital image field and for each of them have different algorithms [13]. The reasons of using digital image are it is a popular medium that is being used nowadays, takes advantages of the limitation of human eyes towards the color, as the computer graphic power grows, this field is continually grow parallel to it, and there are a lot of program that are available to apply the steganography.

3 Methodology

This section will discuss the methods used to carry out the experiments to evaluate the image degradation by embedding text files as secret message into an image. The selection of images will be described, then the sizes of text files were chosen. Embedding steps using least significant bit manipulation will be explained. The flow of the system is then being laid out and the metric measurement of quality is selected.

3.1 Cover Images Selection

There are three categories of images that are tested in this dissertation. The categories that are being used are the random images and textured images. The images dimension that has been tested is 512×512 and for the PNG format images. Table 1 shows the images that will be used in this study.

3.2 Secret Message

For the size of text, there are several sizes that are tested, for example starting with 4 kB, 12 kB, 22 kB, until 45 kB. Table 2 shows the text messages that is used in this project.

3.3 Least Significant Bit (LSB) Method

The methods that are chosen for this project are the Least Significant Bit (LSB) in the spatial domain steganography. The advantages and disadvantages of the spatial domain

Table 1. Images used.

Images	Random		Texture
Rand1.png		Texture1.png	
Rand2.png		Texture2.png	
Rand3.png		Texture3.png	
Rand4.png		Texture4.png	
Rand5.png		Texture5.png	

Table 2. Text document as secret message.

Secret message type	Size
Text document	4 kB
Text document	12 kB
Text document	22 kB
Text document	32 kB
Text document	45 kB

LSB method. Advantages of the spatial LSB method are it is hard to degrade the original images and the images can store more information that can be stored in an image meanwhile disadvantages of the spatial LSB method are low robustness and an attack can be done by anyone [14–16].

The spatial steganography that will be mentioned in this section is the LSB-Based steganography. The main idea is to replace the LSB of the cover image with the message bits secretly without damaging the properties of the image. It is stated that this method is the hardest due to its difficulty of distinguishing between the cover image and stego image. Some of the advantages of the spatial LSB domain are, "degradation of the original image is not easy" and an image can store more data in it. In spite of that, the drawbacks of this method are low robustness and it can be destroyed by a simple attack [17–19].

According to [13], 3 bits of each red, blue, and green color can be kept in the pixel on the image of 24-bit color causing secret message has 1,440,000 bits on 800 × 600 pixel image. The following example shows an image that contains 3 pixels of 24 bits color image.

Pixel 1 : 11011101 11001001 01011101

Pixel 2 : 10011111 01110011 00100010

Pixel 3 : 00111100 01010111 11110110

The secret message that will be inserted into the above image is 10100100 and the result should be:

Pixel 1 : 11011101 11001000 01011101

Pixel 2 : 10011110 01110010 00100011

Pixel 3 : 00111100 01010110 11110110

From the result above, out of 24-bit pixel, only 5 bit that need to be changed and by using 24-bit image in which having a larger space, the secret message is successfully hidden. Meanwhile, if the 8-bit image is used, the selective image needs to be handled carefully and it has to be in grayscale possibly, in order for the eyes cannot differentiate the differences.

3.4 Experimental Design

Figure 4 shows the flowchart of the system. It is to assist to understand the system better.

To start the process, an image and text size to be embedded are determined. After that, the text are being embedded in the image which resulting the stego image is produced using basic LSB algorithm. Then, the PSNR value is being calculated. If the value of PSNR is equal or less than 30 dB, the system will exit but if not the bit sizes need to be adjusted lower or higher.

Next, the new bit size will be embedded into the original image to calculate the PSNR value which called stego images. Continually, it will be compared with the original image. This process will be repeated until it reaches around 30 dB.

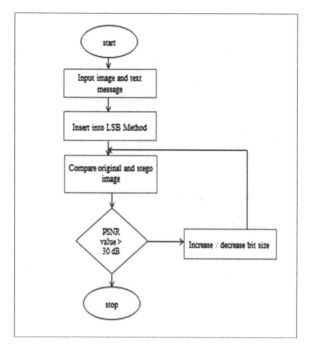

Fig. 4. Flow of the system

3.5 Pixel Differences Based Measure

Peak Signal-to-Noise Ratio (PSNR) and Mean Square Error (MSE), are the measurements that are being used. PSNR and MSE are the pixel differences based measurement. The MSE and PSNR are relatively related to one another. MSE calculates the average of the original and stego images by using the formula below.

$$\text{MSE} = \frac{1}{RS} \sum_{i-0}^{S-1} \sum_{j-0}^{R-1} e(i,j)^2 \tag{1}$$

Where $e(i,j)$ indicates the error of the original and affected image. Meanwhile, SNR calculates the differences between the image pixels of two images. The following is the formula of PSNR.

$$\text{PSNR} = 10 \log \frac{a^2}{MSE} \tag{2}$$

Where a, is 255 of the 8-bit image. In conclusion of PSNR, is the sum of SNR that when all the pixel and maximum possible value is equal. For images and video, PSNR ratio between 30 dB–50 dB is acceptable [4].

4 Results

As mentioned in Sect. 3, the tested image is 512×512 of the PNG image and the sizes of the secret text message are 4 kB, 12 kB, 22 kB, 32 kB and 45 kB. The images used are from random colored images and textured images.

From the Table 3 above the size of the secret text document used is 4 kB. For 4 kB embedding text size, the highest PSNR value is 69.94 dB which is Rand2.png image at bit 0 meanwhile Texture4.png holds the lowest PSNR value which is 25.34 dB at bit 6. All random colored images maintain the quality at >30 dB except Rand5.png, meanwhile only Texture2.png passed the quality test with 33.77 dB at bit 6.

Table 3. PSNR value for 4 kB embedding text

Images	LSB value (PSNR in dB)						
	0	1	2	3	4	5	6
Rand1.png	69.89	61.48	54.37	47.8	41.51	34.21	30.16
Rand2.png	69.94	61.52	54.51	47.97	42.05	39.36	30.04
Rand3.png	69.86	61.55	54.48	47.84	42.11	40.33	32.02
Rand4.png	69.88	60.43	53.49	47.06	40.79	38.69	30.11
Rand5.png	68.73	60.19	53.37	46.77	40.4	38.54	29.24
Texture1.png	68.88	60.39	53.39	47.1	40.67	37.58	28.6
Texture2.png	68.83	60.47	53.5	46.48	41.2	39.26	33.77
Texture3.png	68.61	60.04	52.98	46.5	40.15	39.18	29.97
Texture4.png	68.52	60.01	52.52	47.39	40.01	32.62	25.38
Texture5.png	68.76	60.27	53.25	46.84	40.48	39.57	29.89

From the Table 4, the highest PSNR value is 65.31 dB. Again, the image that holds that value is Rand2.png at bit 0. Despite that, the lowest PSNR value is 31.45 dB of Texture4.png image at LSB bit 5. The PSNR value is decreasing as the bit increased but all of the images are good quality.

Table 4. PSNR value for 12 kB embedding text

Images	LSB value (PSNR in dB)					
	0	1	2	3	4	5
Rand1.png	65.28	56.76	49.66	43.2	37.02	34.21
Rand2.png	65.31	56.82	49.86	43.28	37.33	34.86
Rand3.png	65.19	56.82	50.01	43.43	37.33	35.8
Rand4.png	64.13	55.63	48.67	42.17	35.92	33.76
Rand5.png	64.03	55.5	48.56	41.95	35.74	33.88
Texture1.png	64.05	55.6	48.66	42.31	35.89	32.86
Texture2.png	64.14	55.67	48.78	41.66	36.47	34.72
Texture3.png	63.85	55.23	48.21	41.75	35.45	34.48
Texture4.png	63.82	55.23	47.79	42.55	35.38	31.45
Texture5.png	63.97	55.48	48.48	42.03	35.59	35.11

Table 5 shows the results of the images for 22 kB embedding text. The highest value of PSNR at bit 0 is 62.8 of Rand1.png image. The bit that holds the lowest value is bit 4, a bit lower than previous at 12 kB embedding text.

Table 5. PSNR value for 22 kB embedding text

Images	LSB value (PSNR in dB)				
	0	1	2	3	4
Rand1.png	62.8	54.02	46.76	40.44	34.17
Rand2.png	62.44	54.03	47.03	40.47	34.5
Rand3.png	62.41	54.01	47.21	40.56	34.56
Rand4.png	61.32	52.87	45.92	39.45	33.22
Rand5.png	61.21	52.63	45.66	39.19	32.89
Texture1.png	61.28	52.81	45.86	39.51	33.11
Texture2.png	61.32	52.86	46	38.88	33.74
Texture3.png	61.07	52.51	45.46	38.99	32.67
Texture4.png	61.04	52.39	44.9	39.94	32.5
Texture5.png	61.2	52.72	45.72	39.25	32.85

Table 6 shows the results of the images for 32 kB embedding text. The highest PSNR value is also Rand1.png which holds 60.96 dB and the lowest PSNR value holds the PSNR value of 30.12 of Texture3.png image.

Table 6. PSNR value for 32 kB embedding text

Images	LSB value (PSNR in dB)				
	0	1	2	3	4
Rand1.png	60.96	52.21	44.97	38.66	32.49
Rand2.png	60.73	52.31	45.29	38.77	32.68
Rand3.png	60.74	52.3	45.43	38.89	32.8
Rand4.png	59.64	51.2	44.22	37.77	31.55
Rand5.png	59.42	50.87	43.93	37.53	31.23
Texture1.png	59.63	51.16	44.22	37.86	31.44
Texture2.png	59.67	51.2	44.36	37.22	32.12
Texture3.png	59.32	50.74	43.7	37.23	30.12
Texture4.png	59.32	50.67	43.16	38.33	30.8
Texture5.png	59.5	51.03	44	37.53	31.11

Table 7 shows the results of the images for 45 kB embedding text. For this embedding text, there are a lot of PSNR values that is below than 30 dB. The bit that holds those values is the bit 4. The texture images hold the most value below than 30 dB. The highest value is 59.41 of Rand1.png and the lowest value is 29.27 dB of Texture3.png image.

Table 7. PSNR value for 45 kB embedding text

Images	LSB value (PSNR in dB)				
	0	1	2	3	4
Rand1.png	59.41	50.77	43.59	37.11	30.92
Rand2.png	59.23	50.75	43.76	37.25	31.14
Rand3.png	59.26	50.78	43.88	37.36	31.22
Rand4.png	58.06	49.6	42.62	36.15	29.89
Rand5.png	57.95	49.25	42.44	36.06	29.58
Texture1.png	58.03	49.56	42.6	36.24	29.84
Texture2.png	58.1	49.6	42.76	35.6	30.5
Texture3.png	57.75	49.13	42.07	53.58	29.27
Texture4.png	57.79	49.16	41.68	36.63	29.33
Texture5.png	57.95	49.45	42.43	35.95	29.54

5   Conclusion

From the experiments, it is shown that for images of size 512×512, we could embed 45 kB of text document in the four least significant bits. If the capacity is small, seven least significant bits can be manipulated.

This paper also showed that the more colored and the finer the texture of an image will increase the capacity for embedding and at the same time will maintain the quality of the image.

References

1. Al-Mazaydeh, W.I.A.: Image steganography using LSB and LSB+ Huffman code. Int. J. Comput. Appl. (0975–8887) **99**(5), 17–22 (2014)
2. Liew, S.C., Liew, S.-W., Zain, J.M.: Tamper localization and lossless recovery watermarking scheme with ROI segmentation and multilevel authentication. J. Digit. Imaging **26**(2), 316–325 (2013)
3. Awad, A., Mursi, M.F.M., Alsammak, A.K.: Data hiding inside JPEG images with high resistance to steganalysis using a novel technique: DCT-M3. Ain Shams Eng. J. (2017, in press)
4. Gupta, H., Kumar, P.R., Changlani, S.: Enhanced data hiding capacity using LSB-based image steganography method. Int. J. Emerg. Technol. Adv. Eng. **3**(6), 212–214 (2013)
5. Vyas, K., Pal, B.L.: A proposed method in image steganography to improve image quality with LSB technique. Int. J. Adv. Res. Comput. Commun. Eng. **3**(1), 5246–5251 (2014)
6. Sharma, P., Kumar, P.: Review of various image steganography and steganalysis techniques. Int. J. Adv. Res. Comput. Sci. Softw. Eng. **6**(7), 152–159 (2016)
7. Chitradevi, B., Thinaharan, N., Vasanthi, M.: Data hiding using least significant bit steganography in digital images. In: Statistical Approaches on Multidisciplinary Research, vol. I, pp. 144–150 (2017). (Chapter 17)
8. Rai, P., Gurung, S., Ghose, M.K.: Analysis of image steganography techniques: a survey. Int. J. Comput. Appl. (0975–8887) **114**(1), 11–17 (2015)

9. Jain, R., Boaddh, J.: Advances in digital image steganography. In: International Conference on Innovation and Challenges in Cyber Security, pp. 163–171 (2016)
10. Rafat, K.F., Hussain, M.J.: Secure steganography for digital images meandering in the dark. (IJACSA) Int. J. Adv. Comput. Sci. Appl. 7(6), 45–59 (2016)
11. Al-Farraji, O.I.I.: New technique of steganography based on locations of LSB. Int. J. Inf. Res. Rev. 04(1), 3549–3553 (2017)
12. Badshah, G., Liew, S.-C., Zain, J.M., Ali, M.: Watermark compression in medical image watermarking Using Lempel-Ziv-Welch (LZW) lossless compression technique. J. Digit. Imaging 29(2), 216–225 (2016)
13. Michael, A.U., Chukwudi, A.E., Chukwuemeka, N.O.: A cost effective image steganography application for document security. Manag. Sci. Inf. Technol. 2(2), 6–13 (2017)
14. Kaur, A., Kaur, R., Kumar, N.: A review on image steganography techniques. Int. J. Comput. Appl. (0975–8887) 123(4), 20–24 (2015)
15. Qin, H., Ma, X., Herawan, T., Zain, J.M.: DFIS: a novel data filling approach for an incomplete soft set. Int. J. Appl. Math. Comput. Sci. 22(4), 817–828 (2012)
16. Ainur, A.K., Sayang, M.D., Jannoo, Z., Yap, B.W.: Sample size and non-normality effects on goodness of fit measures in structural equation models. Pertanika J. Sci. Technol. 25(2), 575–586 (2017)
17. Aliman, S., Yahya, S., Aljunid, S.A.: Presage criteria for blog credibility assessment using Rasch analysis. J. Media Inf. Warfare 4, 59–77 (2011)
18. Zamani, N.A.M., Abidin, S.Z.Z., Omar, N., Aliman, S.: Visualizing people's emotions in Facebook. Int. J. Pure Appl. Math. 118(Special Issue 9), 183–193 (2018)
19. Yusoff, M., Ariffin, J., Mohamed, A.: Discrete particle swarm optimization with a search decomposition and random selection for the shortest path problem. J. Comput. Inf. Syst. Ind. Manag. Appl. 4, 578–588 (2012)

Exploratory Analysis of MNIST Handwritten Digit for Machine Learning Modelling

Mohd Razif Shamsuddin, Shuzlina Abdul-Rahman$^{(\boxtimes)}$,
and Azlinah Mohamed$^{(\boxtimes)}$

Faculty of Computer and Mathematical Sciences, Universiti Teknologi MARA,
40450 Shah Alam, Selangor, Malaysia
razif@tmsk.uitm.edy.my,
{shuzlina,azlinah}@tmsk.uitm.edu.my

Abstract. This paper is an investigation about the MNIST dataset, which is a subset of the NIST data pool. The MNIST dataset contains handwritten digit images that is derived from a larger collection of NIST data which contains handwritten digits. All the images are formatted in 28×28 pixels value with grayscale format. MNIST is a handwritten digit images that has often been cited in many leading research and thus has become a benchmark for image recognition and machine learning studies. There have been many attempts by researchers in trying to identify the appropriate models and pre-processing methods to classify the MNIST dataset. However, very little attention has been given to compare binary and normalized pre-processed datasets and its effects on the performance of a model. Pre-processing results are then presented as input datasets for machine learning modelling. The trained models are validated with 4200 random test samples over four different models. Results have shown that the normalized image performed the best with Convolution Neural Network model at 99.4% accuracy.

Keywords: Convolution Neural Network · Handwritten digit images
Image recognition · Machine learning · MNIST

1 Introduction

The complexity of data in the future is increasing rapidly, consistent with the advances of new technologies and algorithms. Due to the advancements of research in computer vision, machine learning, data mining and data analytics, the importance of having a reliable benchmark and standardized datasets cannot be ignored. Benchmark and standardized datasets help to provide good platforms to test the accuracy of different algorithms [1–4]. Comparing the accuracies of different algorithms can be conducted without having to necessarily recreate previously tested models.

As the behaviors and features of different datasets vary significantly, the capabilities of different machine learning models have always been evaluated differently. This evaluation always happens in isolated research experiments where created models were always biased to a specific dataset. Thus, the perseverance of a differing suite of benchmarks is exceptionally important in enabling a more effective way to deal with

© Springer Nature Singapore Pte Ltd. 2019
B. W. Yap et al. (Eds.): SCDS 2018, CCIS 937, pp. 134–145, 2019.
https://doi.org/10.1007/978-981-13-3441-2_11

surveying and assessing the execution of a calculation or newly created model. There are several standardized datasets in the machine learning community, which is widely used and have become highly competitive such as the National Institute of Standards and Technology (NIST) and the Modified National Institute of Standards and Technology (MNIST) datasets [1, 2]. Other than the two datasets, the Standard Template Library (STL)-10 dataset, Street View House Numbers (SVHN) dataset, Canadian Institute for Advanced Research (CIFAR-10) and (CIFAR-100) datasets, are among the famous and widely used datasets to evaluate the performance of a newly created model [5]. Additionally, a good pre-processing method is also important to produce good classification results [12, 13].

The above past studies have shown the importance of pre-processing methods. However, very little attention was given to compare binary and normalized pre-processed images datasets and its effects on the performance of the models. Therefore, this study aims to explore the different pre-processing methods on image datasets with several different models. The remainder of this paper is organized as follows: The next section presents the background study on handwritten images, NIST and MNIST datasets. The third section describes the image pre-processing methods for both normalized and binary datasets. The fourth section discusses the results of the experiments, and finally in Sect. 5 is the conclusion of the study.

2   Handwritten Images

It is a known fact that handwritten dataset has been widely utilized as a part of machine learning model assessments. Numerous model classifiers utilize primarily the digit classes. However, other researchers handle the alphabet classes to demonstrate vigor and scalability. Each research model tackles the formulation of the classification tasks in a slightly different manner, varying fundamental aspects and algorithm processes. The research model is also varied according to their number of classes. Some vary the training and testing splits while others conduct different pre-processing methods of the images.

2.1   NIST Dataset

The NIST Special Database 19 was released in 1995 by the National Institute of Standards and Technology [1, 2]. The institute made use of an encoding and image compression method based on the CCITT Group 4 algorithm. Subsequently, the compressed images are packed into a patented file format. The initial release of the compressed image database includes codes to extract and process the given dataset. However, it remains complex and difficult to compile and run these given tools on modern systems. Due to these problematic issues, an initiative was made as a direct response catered to the problems. A second edition of the NIST dataset was successfully published in September 2016 [2] and contained the same image data encoding using the PNG file format.

The objective of creating the NIST dataset was to provide multiple optical character recognition tasks. Therefore, NIST data has been categorized under five separate organizations referred to as data hierarchies [5]. The hierarchies are as follows:

- By Page: Full page binary scans of many handwriting sample forms are found in this hierarchy. Other hierarchies were collected through a standardized set of forms where the writers were asked to complete a set of handwritten tasks.
- By Author: Individually segmented handwritten characters images organized by writers can be found in this hierarchy. This hierarchy allows for tasks such as identification of writers but is not suitable for classification cases.
- By Field: Digits and characters sorted by the field on the collection are prepared while preserving the unique feature of the handwriting. This hierarchy is very useful for segmenting the digit classes due to the nature of the images which is in its own isolated fields.
- By Class: This hierarchy represents the most useful group of data sampling from a classification perspective. This is because in this hierarchy, the dataset contains the segmented digits and characters arranged by its specific classes. There are 62 classes comprising of handwritten digits from 0 to 9, lowercase letters from a to z and uppercase letters from A to Z. This dataset is also split into a suggested training and testing sets.
- By Merge: This last data hierarchy contains a merged data. This alternative on the dataset combines certain classes, constructing a 47-class classification task. The merged classes, as suggested by the NIST, are for the letters C, I, J, K, L, M, O, P, S, U, V, W, X, Y and Z. This merging of classifications addresses a fascinating problem in the classification of handwritten digits, which tackles the similarity between certain uppercase and lowercase letters such as lowercase letter u and uppercase letter U. Empirically, this kind of classification problems are often understandable when examining the confusion matrix resulting from the evaluation of any learning models.

The NIST dataset is considered challenging to be accessed and utilized. The limitations of storage and high cost during the creation of the NIST dataset have driven it to be stored in an amazingly efficient and compact manner. This however, has made it very hard to be manipulated, analyzed and processed. To cope with this issue, a source code is provided to ease the usage of the dataset. However, it remains challenging for more recent computing systems. Inevitably, as mentioned earlier, NIST has released a second edition of the dataset in 2016 [1, 5, 9]. It is reported that the second edition of the NIST dataset is easily accessible. However, the organization of the image datasets contained in this newly released NIST is different from the MNIST dataset. The MNIST dataset offers a huge training set of sixty thousand samples which contains ten-digit classifications. Moreover, the dataset also offers ten thousand testing samples for further evaluation of any classification models. Further discussions and analysis on MNIST dataset will be elaborated in the next section.

2.2   MNIST Dataset

The images contained in MNIST is a downsized sampled image from 128^2 pixel to 28^2 pixel. The image format of the 282 pixel MNIST dataset is an 8-bit grayscale resolution. Next, the pre-processed grey level image is centered by computing the center mass pixel. Finally, it is positioned to the center of the 282 pixel sized images resulting in the consistent formats of the MNIST dataset. The dataset is ready to be manipulated and pre-processed further for analysis and experiment. Although the original NIST dataset contains a larger sampling of 814,255 images, MNIST takes only a small portion of the total sampling as it merely covers ten classification of handwritten digits from number zero to nine. The readiness of MNIST data makes it very popular to be used as a benchmark to analyze the competency of classification models. Thousands of researchers have used, manipulated and tested the dataset which proves its reliability and suitability for testing newly created models. The easy access and widespread usage make it easier for researchers to compare the results and share their findings. Table 1 lists a few recent studies on machine learning using MNIST dataset.

Table 1. Similar works that used MNIST dataset as benchmark

Author (Year)	Description of research
Shruti *et al.* (2018)	Used a network that employed neurons operating at sparse biological spike rates below 300 Hz, which achieved a classification accuracy of 98.17% on the MNIST dataset [3]
Jaehyun *et al.* (2018)	Using Deep Neural Networks with weighted spikes, the author showed that the proposed model with weighted spikes achieved significant reduction in classification latency and number of spikes. This led to faster and more energy-efficient than the conventional spiking neural network [4]
Gregory *et al.* (2018)	A research that conducted an extension to MNIST dataset. They created a new dataset that covered more classification problems. The newly created datasets was named EMNIST [5]
Mei-Chin *et al.* (2018)	The author performed a systematic device-circuit-architecture co-design for digit recognition with the MNIST handwritten digits dataset to evaluate the feasibility of the model. The device-to-system simulations introduced by the author indicated that the proposed skyrmion-based devices in deep SNNs could possibly achieve huge improvements in energy consumption [6]
Shah *et al.* (2018)	Created a handwritten characters recognition via Deep Metric Learning. The author created a new handwritten dataset that followed the MNIST format known as the Urdu-Characters with sets of classes suitable for deep metric learning [7]
Paul *et al.* (2018)	The author used Sparse Deep Neural Network Processor for IoT Applications which measured high classification accuracy (98.36% for the MNIST test set) [8]
Jiayu *et al.* (2018)	The author used Sparse Representation Learning with variation Auto-Encoder for MNIST data Anomaly Detection [9]
Amirreza *et al.* (2018)	Used an Active Perception with Dynamic Vision Sensors to classify N-MNIST dataset, which achieved a 2.4% error rate [10]

3   Image Pre-processing

In this paper, the original MNIST dataset is created and divided into two different pre-processed datasets. The first dataset is in grayscale with normalized values while the second dataset is in grayscale with binary values. Both pre-processing methods were chosen because they allow the dataset to be converted to a low numeric value while preserving their aspect ratio. To run the experiments, MNIST dataset with two different pre-processing formats were constructed. The idea of preparing two sets of pre-processed data samples is to observe the performance of the machine learning models learning accuracy with different pre-processed images. This will help researchers to understand how machine learning behave with different image pre-process formats. The input format values of the neural network will depend on how the pre-processing of the dataset is executed. The created models will be fed with the pre-processed datasets.

3.1   Normalized Dataset

Each of the pre-processed data categories is segmented into ten groups of classifications. The data category is a set of ten numbers consisting of numbers varying from zero to nine with a dimension size of 28×28 pixels in grayscale format. Grayscale images allow more detailed information to be preserved in an image. However, the representative values of the images contain an array of values from 0 to 255. The activation of the network is expected to be slightly unstable as there will be more variation elements in the network input ranges. Thus, to prevent a high activation of the learning models, the grayscale values are normalized using a min max function with values between zero to one as shown in Eq. (1).

$$y = (x - min)/(max - min) \tag{1}$$

Figure 1 shows nine random samplings of the pre-processed MNIST dataset. This visualization shows that the min max normalization preserves the small details that belong to each individual sample. The representation of the normalized grayscale images is smoother as it preserves the features and details of the handwritten digits. Smoother images mean more details and less jagged edges. These smoother images will help the training models to learn the input patterns with a smaller input activation which is in the range of values from 0 to 1.

3.2   Binary Dataset

Figure 2 shows nine random samplings of the binary MNIST dataset. This visualization shows that converting the data sampling to binary format preserves the shape of the digits. However, the small details that belong to some individual samples can be seen missing. This is due to the threshold that was set at a certain value to classify two regions that belong to either 0 or 1. In this experiment, the threshold is set at 180 to preserve the shape of the digits while avoiding the data having too much noise.

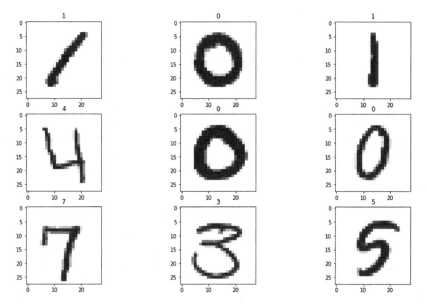

Fig. 1. Nine random MNIST samplings of 28 × 28 pixel dimension in grayscale format.

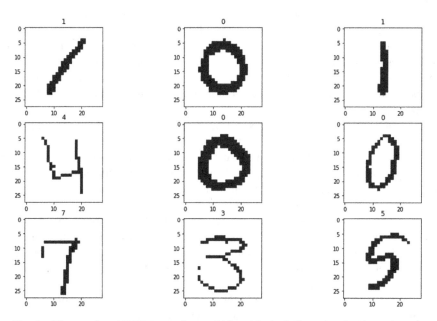

Fig. 2. Nine random MNIST samplings of 28 × 28 pixel dimension in binary format.

3.3   Machine Learning Models

The pre-processed MNIST datasets are tested with four machine learning models on both binary and normalized images. The accuracy of these models is then compared with several measures. Below are a few short explanations of the models used in this experiment.

Logistic regression is very similar to linear regression. It utilizes probability equation to represent its output classification. In short, logistic regression is a probabilistic linear classifier. By projecting an input onto a set of hyperplanes, classification is possible by identifying the input that corresponds to the most similar vector. Some research has successfully performed a logistic regression model with satisfactory accuracy [11].

Random Forest is a supervised classification algorithm that grows many classification trees [14]. Random forest is also known as random decision trees. It is a group of decision trees used for regression, classification and other task. Random forest works by creating many decision trees during training, which will produce either the classification of the generated classes of regression of an individual tree. Random forest also helps correct the possibility of overfitting problem in decision trees. By observation, a higher number of trees generated can lead to better classification. This generation somehow shows the relation of tree size with the accurate number of classification that a random forest can produce.

Extra Trees classifier, also known as an "Extremely randomized trees" classifier, is a variant of Random Forest. However, unlike Random Forest, at each step, the entire sample is used and decision boundaries are picked at random rather than the best one. Extra Trees method produces piece-wise multilinear approximations. The idea of using a piece-wise multilinear approximation is a good idea as it is considered productive. This is because in the case of multiple classification problems it is often linked to better accuracy [15].

Convolution Neural Network (CNN) is a Deep Neural Network made up of a few convolutional layers. These layers contain a pool of feature maps with a predefined size. Normally, the size of the feature maps is cut in half in the subsequent convolutional layer. Thus, as the network goes deeper, a down-sampled feature map of the original input is created during the training session. Finally, at the end of the convolution network is a fully connected network that works like a normal feed forward network. These networks apply the same concept of a SVM/Softmax loss function. Figure 3 shows the architecture of the created CNN. As depicted in the figure, the created CNN contains three convolutional layers, and two layers of a fully connected layer at the end. The last layer contains only ten outputs that use a softmax function in order to classify ten numbers.

From the input datasets as shown in Figs. 1 and 2, each dataset is supplied with the aforementioned four machine learning models. This is to test how the pre-processing of each test dataset affects the accuracy of the training and validation of the models above.

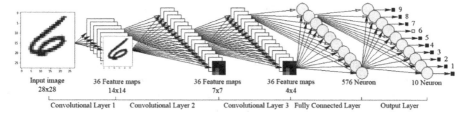

Fig. 3. Architecture of the created Convolutional Neural Network

4 Experiments and Results

In this section, we discuss the experimental results and findings from this study. All four machine learning models that were discussed earlier were both tested with the normalized and binary datasets.

4.1 Experimental Setup

We have set up four machine learning models to be trained with the pre-processed MNIST dataset. Each learning model was analyzed for its training and validation accuracy for both normalized and binary datasets. Further discussions on the analysis of the accuracy is explained in the next subsection.

4.2 Machine Learning Model Accuracy

The outcome of the experiment shows fascinating results. In both datasets, all four models would have no or minimal difficulties of training the classification of the handwritten digits. Almost all models manage to get a training and validation accuracy of greater than 90%. However, this does not mean that the errors produced by some of the models are actually good. For 4200 validation samplings, a mere 10% inaccuracies may cost up to 400 or more misclassifications.

The experiment results show that the machine learning models had misclassified some of the training and validation data. This misclassification may be due to some of the training data instances having similar features but classified with a totally different label. The misclassification issue is elaborated further in the next section. Table 2 shows CNN having the least overfitting over other training results as it has the least differences between the training and validation accuracies for both normalized and binary dataset. This is probably due to the design and architecture of the CNN itself that produces a less overfitting models as reported by [16]. Although Extra Trees shows a better training accuracy of 100%, a big difference of its validation and training results mean that there is a possible overfitting in the created model. However, Random Forest, having the highest accuracy for binary dataset of 1.9%, is slightly higher than the CNN model.

Table 2. MNIST model accuracy comparison

Model	MNIST normalized		MNIST binary	
	Training	Validation	Training	Validation
Logistic regression	94%	92%	93.3%	89.5%
Random forest	99.9%	94%	99.9%	91%
Extra trees	100%	94%	100%	92%
Convolution Neural Network	99.5%	99.4%	90.6%	90.1%

4.3   CNN Accuracy and Loss

Figure 4 depicts the training and validation of graph patterns. A close observation of the results show that the normalized dataset generates a better learning curve. The learning of patterns is quite fast as the graph shows a steep curve at the beginning of the training. In Fig. 4(a), as the log step increases, the training and validation accuracies of the model become stable at an outstanding accuracy of 99.43%. The binary dataset shows a good validation and loss at an earlier epoch. Nevertheless, as the training continued, the CNN training model began to decline in its accuracy.

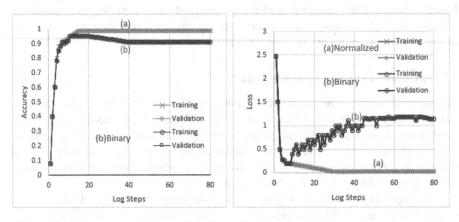

Fig. 4. Training accuracy & loss of (a) Normalized dataset (b) Binary dataset fed to CNN

The training declination can be seen as shown in Fig. 4(b). This declination may be caused by the noise and data loss in the binary images that make it difficult for the CNN to learn. Some features of the training and testing images were lost during the process of changing them to binary values. Further analysis of the misclassification of the CNN models of normalized datasets shows that only 24 out of 4200 validation sets are false predictors. More information in the misclassification of the handwritten digits are shown in the Table 3.

Table 3. CNN confusion matrix

Predicted Digit	0	1	2	3	4	5	6	7	8	9
True Digit										
0	412		1				1			
1		470								
2			420					1		
3				432						
4					410			2		3
5				1		391	1		1	2
6	1						431			
7				1				420		4
8		1				1		1	400	
9					1				1	390
Total	413	471	421	434	411	392	433	424	402	399

Further investigation on the results was performed by analyzing the confusion matrix output. From the table, we can see that the CNN model is having a difficulty in classifying digit nine, having the highest misclassification rate. It is clearly stated that some numbers that should be classified as nine may be misinterpreted by the CNN models as a seven, five and four. Other examples of misclassifications are where seven is interpreted as two, four and eight. Figure 5 shows all of the false predictor images.

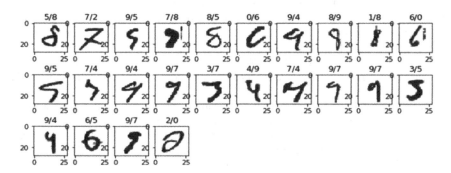

Fig. 5. False predictors

5 Conclusions

This study has demonstrated the importance of pre-processing methods prior to machine learning modelling. Two different pre-processed images namely the binary and normalized images were fed into four machine learning models. The experiments revealed that both the selection of machine learning models, with regards to the appropriate pre-processing methods, would yield better results. Our experiments show that CNN has better results with 99.6% accuracy for normalized dataset and Extra

Trees gives an accuracy of 92.4% for binary dataset. Moreover, it could also be concluded that normalized datasets from all models out-performed binary datasets. These results suggest that normalized dataset preserves meaningful data in image recognition.

Acknowledgement. The authors are grateful to the Research Management Centre (RMC) UiTM Shah Alam for the support under the national Fundamental Research Grant Scheme 600-RMI/FRGS 5/3 (0002/2016).

References

1. Grother, P., Hanaoka, K.: NIST special database 19 hand printed forms and characters 2nd Edition, National Institute of Standards and Technology (2016) Available: http://www.nist.gov/srd/upload/nistsd19.pdf. Accessed 20 July 2018
2. Grother, P.: NIST special database 19 hand printed forms and characters database. National Institute of Standards and Technology, Technical report (1995). http://s3.amazonaws.com/nist-srd/SD19/1stEditionUserGuide.pdf,last. Accessed 20 July 2018
3. Kulkarni, S.R., Rajendran, B.: Spiking neural networks for handwritten digit recognition, supervised learning and network optimization (2018)
4. Kim, J., Kim, H., Huh, S., Lee, J., Choi, K.: Deep neural networks with weighted spikes. Neurocomputing (2018)
5. Cohen, G., Afshar, S., Tapson, J., van Schaik, A.: EMNIST: an extension of MNIST to handwritten letters. Comput. Vis. Pattern Recognit. (2017)
6. Chen, M.C., Sengupta, A., Roy, K.: Magnetic skyrmion as a spintronic deep learning spiking neuron processor. IEEE Trans. Mag. **54**, 1–7 (2018). IEEE Early Access Articles
7. Shah, N., Alessandro, C., Nisar, A., Ignazio, G.: Hand written characters recognition via deep metric learning. In: 2018 13th IAPR International Workshop on Document Analysis Systems (DAS), IEEE Conferences, pp. 417–422. IEEE (2018)
8. Paul, N.W., Sae, K.L., David, B., Gu-Yeon, W.: DNN engine: a 28-nm timing-error tolerant sparse deep neural network processor for IoT applications. IEEE J. Solid-State Circuits **53**, 1–10 (2018)
9. Jiayu, S., Xinzhou, W., Naixue, X., Jie, S.: Learning sparse representation with variational auto-encoder for anomaly detection. IEEE Access, 1 (2018)
10. Amirreza, Y., Garrick, O., Teresa, S.G., Bernabé, L.B.: Active perception with dynamic vision sensors. minimum saccades with optimum recognition. IEEE Trans. Biomed. Circuits Syst. **14**, 1–13 (2018). IEEE Early Access Articles
11. Yap, B.W., Nurain, I., Hamzah, A.H., Shuzlina, A.R., Simon, F.: Feature selection methods: case of filter and wrapper approaches for maximising classification accuracy. Pertanika J. Sci. Technol. **26**(1), 329–340 (2018)
12. Mutalib, S., Abdullah, M.H., Abdul-Rahman, S., Aziz, Z.A: A brief study on paddy applications with image processing and proposed architecture. In: 2016 IEEE Conference on Systems, Process and Control (ICSPC), pp. 124–129. IEEE (2016)
13. Azlin, A., Rubiyah, Y., Yasue M.: Identifying the dominant species of tropical wood species using histogram intersection method. In: Industrial Electronics Society, IECON 2015-41st Annual Conference of the IEEE, pp. 003075–003080. IEEE (2015)

14. Bernard, S., Adam, S., Heutte, L.: Using random forests for handwritten digit recognition. In: Proceedings of the 9th IAPR/IEEE International Conference on Document Analysis and Recognition ICDAR 2007, pp. 1043–1047. IEEE (2007)
15. Geurts, P., Ernst, D., Wehenkel, L.: Extremely randomized trees. Mach. Learn. **63**, 3–42 (2006). Engineering, computing & technology: Computer science
16. LeNet-5, convolutional neural networks, http://yann.lecun.com/exdb/lenet/. Accessed 20 July 2018

Financial and Fuzzy Mathematics

Improved Conditional Value-at-Risk (CVaR) Based Method for Diversified Bond Portfolio Optimization

Nor Idayu Mat Rifin[1], Nuru'l-'Izzah Othman[2(✉)],
Shahirulliza Shamsul Ambia[1], and Rashidah Ismail[1]

[1] Faculty of Computer and Mathematical Sciences, Shah Alam, Malaysia
`noridayumatrifin@gmail.com`,
`{sliza, shidah}@tmsk.uitm.edu.my`
[2] Advanced Analytics Engineering Center (AAEC), Faculty of Computer and
Mathematical Sciences, Universiti Teknologi MARA, 40450 Shah Alam,
Selangor, Malaysia
`nurul@tmsk.uitm.edu.my`

Abstract. In this study, an improved CVaR-based Portfolio Optimization Method is presented. The method was used to test the performance of a diversified bond portfolio in providing low expected loss and optimal CVaR. A hypothetical diversified bond portfolio, which is a combination of Islamic bond or *Sukuk* and conventional bond, was constructed using bonds issued by four banking institutions. The performance of the improved method is determined by comparing the generated returns of the method against the existing CVaR-based Portfolio Optimization Method. The simulation of the optimization process of both methods was carried out by using the Geometric Brownian Motion-based Monte Carlo Simulation method. The results of the improved CVaR portfolio optimization method show that by restricting the upper and lower bounds with certain floor and ceiling bond weights using volatility weighting schemes, the expected loss can be reduced and an optimal CVaR can be achieved. Thus, this study shows that the improved CVaR-based Portfolio Optimization Method is able to provide a better optimization of a diversified bond portfolio in terms of reducing the expected loss, and hence maximizes the returns.

Keywords: Value-at-Risk (VaR) · Conditional Value-at-Risk (CVaR)
CVaR optimization · Bond · *Sukuk*

1 Introduction

Capital markets are markets where securities such as equities and bonds are issued and traded in raising medium to long-terms funds [1]. Securities are important components in a financial system, which are issued by public or private companies and entities including governments. Islamic capital markets carry the same definition as the conventional capital markets, except that all transaction activities are *Shariah* compliant.

© Springer Nature Singapore Pte Ltd. 2019
B. W. Yap et al. (Eds.): SCDS 2018, CCIS 937, pp. 149–160, 2019.
https://doi.org/10.1007/978-981-13-3441-2_12

Bond is a type of debt investment, which is basically a transaction of loan that involves a lender (investor) and a borrower (issuer). There are two types of bonds which are conventional bond and Islamic bond or *Sukuk*. In the capital markets the *Sukuk* has been established as an alternative financial instrument to the conventional bond. The *Sukuk* differs from the conventional bond in the sense that *Sukuk* must comply with the *Shariah* principles, while the conventional bond involves debt upon sale which is prohibited in Islam.

From the bond issuance perspective, the issuer will either issue a conventional bond or *Sukuk* to the investor in order to finance their project(s). Based on the agreement that has been agreed upon by both parties, the issuer will make regular interest payments to the investor at a specified rate on the amount that have been borrowed before or until a specified date. As with any investment, both conventional bonds and *Sukuk* carry risks such as market and credit risks. A known technique to manage risk is diversification. Diversification is a risk management technique that is designed to reduce the risk level by combining a variety of investment instruments which are unlikely to move in the same direction within a portfolio [2]. To move in different directions here means that the financial instruments involved in a diversified portfolio are negatively correlated and have different price behaviours between them. Hence, investing in a diversified portfolio affords the possibility of reducing the risks as compared to investing in an undiversified portfolio.

Value-at-Risk (VaR) is an established method for measuring financial risk. However, VaR has undesirable mathematical characteristics such as lack of sub-additivity and convexity [3]. The lack of sub-additivity means that the measurement of a portfolio VaR might be greater than the sum of its assets [4]. While, convexity is the characteristics of a set of points in which, for any two points in the set, the points on the curve joining the two points are also in the set [5]. [6, 7] have shown that VaR can exhibit multiple local extrema, and hence does not behave well as a function of portfolio positions in determining an optimal mix of positions. Due to its disadvantages, VaR is considered a non-coherent risk measure.

As an alternative, [3] proved that CVaR has better properties than VaR since it fulfils all the properties (axioms) of a coherent risk measure and it is convex [8]. By using the CVaR approach, investors can estimate and examine the probability of the average losses when investing in certain transactions [9]. Although it has yet to be a standard in the finance industry, CVaR appears to play a major role in the insurance industry. CVaR can be optimized using linear programming (LP) and non-smooth optimization algorithm [4], due to its advantages over VaR.

The intention of this study was to improve the CVaR-based portfolio optimization method presented in [4]. In this paper, the improved CVaR portfolio optimization method is introduced in Sect. 2. The method finds the optimal allocation (weight) of various assets or financial instruments in a portfolio when the expected loss is minimized, thus maximizing the expected returns. The results of the implementation of the existing CVaR-based method in [4] and the improved CVaR-based method of this study are presented and discussed in Sect. 3 and concluded in Sect. 4.

2 Conditional Value-at-Risk (CVaR) - Based Portfolio Optimization Method for Diversified Bond Portfolio

Diversification has been established as an effective approach in reducing investment risk [2]. Portfolio optimization is considered a useful solution in investment diversification decision making where the investors will be able to allocate their funds in many assets (portfolios) with minimum loss at a certain risk level. Hence, the CVaR-based Portfolio Optimization Method has been developed in [4] to find the optimum portfolio allocation with the lowest loss at a certain risk level.

2.1 CVaR-Based Portfolio Optimization Method

In this study, the portfolio optimization problem using the CVaR-based Portfolio Optimization Method in [4] is solved by applying the approach presented in [2], which uses linear programming. The optimization problem is described as follows:

$$\min \; - w^T \bar{y}$$

subject to

$$w \in W, \varphi \in \Re$$

$$\varphi + \frac{1}{J(1-\beta)} \sum_{j=1}^{J} s_j \leq \delta \tag{1}$$

$$s_j \geq 0, \qquad j = 1, \ldots, J$$

$$w^T r_j + \varphi + s_j \geq 0, \qquad j = 1, \ldots, J$$

where w represents the weight, $\bar{y}$ is the expected outcome of r, r_j is the vector representing returns, φ is the value-at-risk (VaR), δ is the conditional value-at-risk (CVaR) limit, β is the level of confidence, J is the number of simulations and s is the auxiliary variable. The computation for the optimization of (1) to find the portfolio allocation when loss is minimized (or return is maximized) within a certain CVaR (risk) limit is implemented using the MATLAB fmincon function. The fmincon function is a general constraint optimization routine that finds the minimum of a constrained multivariable function and has the form

$$[w, fval] = \text{fmincon} \, (objfun, \, w_0, \, A, \, b, \, Aeq, \, beq, \, LB, \, UB, \, [\,], \, options),$$

where the return value $fval$ is the expected return under the corresponding constraints.

To use the fmincon function, several parameters of the linear programming formulation of (1) need to be set up which are described as follows:

i. Objective Function

The aim of the formulation is to minimize the loss $-w^T \bar{y}$ in order to maximize the expected returns.

ii. Decision variables

The decision variables of this formulation are $w_1, w_2, \ldots, w_N$ which represent the weights for N assets of the optimal portfolio.

iii. Constraints

(a) Inequality Constraints

The linear inequality of this formulation takes the form of $Aw \leq b$, where w is the weight vector. Matrix A represents the constraint coefficient which consists of the asset weights $(w_1, w_2, \ldots, w_N)$, VaR (φ) and the auxiliary variables $(s_1, s_2, \ldots, s_j)$ as expressed in (1). Matrix b describes the constraints level. Following (1), matrix A and b can be expressed as follows:

$$A = \begin{pmatrix} \overset{w_1}{0} & \overset{w_2}{0} & \overset{\cdots}{\cdots} & \overset{w_N}{0} & \overset{\varphi}{1} & \overset{s_1}{\frac{1}{J*(1-\beta)}} & \overset{s_2}{\frac{1}{J*(1-\beta)}} & \overset{\cdots}{\cdots} & \overset{s_j}{\frac{1}{J*(1-\beta)}} \\ -r_{11} & -r_{12} & \cdots & -r_{1N} & -1 & -1 & 0 & \cdots & 0 \\ -r_{21} & -r_{22} & \cdots & -r_{2N} & -1 & 0 & -1 & \cdots & 0 \\ \vdots & \vdots & \ddots & \vdots & \vdots & \vdots & \vdots & \ddots & \vdots \\ -r_{j1} & -r_{j2} & \cdots & -r_{jN} & -1 & 0 & 0 & \cdots & -1 \end{pmatrix}$$

$$b = \begin{pmatrix} -\delta \\ 0 \\ 0 \\ \vdots \\ 0 \end{pmatrix}.$$

The first row in matrix A and b represents the condition $\varphi + \frac{1}{J(1-\beta)} \sum_{j=1}^{J} s_j \leq \delta$ in (1), while the remaining rows represent the condition $w^T r_j + \varphi + s_j \geq 0$. Since the objective of the formulation is to minimize the loss, then the returns must be multiplied by -1. N and J in matrix A represents the number of bonds in a portfolio and the number of simulations respectively.

(b) Equality Constraints

The equality constraints in this formulation are of the form $Aeq * w = beq$. The equality matrices Aeq and beq are used to define

$$\sum_{i=1}^{N} w_i = 1,$$

which means that the sum of all the asset weights is equal to 1 or 100%. The equality matrices can be represented in the following matrix form:

$$Aeq = (1 \quad 1 \quad \cdots \quad 1 \quad 0 \quad 0 \quad 0 \quad \cdots \quad 0).$$

$$beq = (1).$$

iv. Lower and Upper Bounds

The lower and upper bounds in this formulation follow the formulation in [2] and are not restricted to the condition that any asset in a portfolio can have a maximum of 100% of the portfolio weight and must be greater than 0. Matrices UB (upper bound) and LB (lower bound) can be in the form of:

$$
\begin{array}{ccccccccc}
& w_1 & w_2 & \cdots & w_N & \varphi & s_1 & s_2 & \cdots & s_j \\
UB = & (UB_1 & UB_2 & \cdots & UB_N & \inf & \inf & \inf & \cdots & \inf). \\
LB = & (LB_1 & LB_2 & \cdots & LB_N & 0 & 0 & 0 & \cdots & 0).
\end{array}
$$

The constraint is defined as $s_j \geq 0$, where $j = 1, \ldots, J$ and $s_1, s_2, \ldots, s_j = 0$ in LB.

v. Initial Parameter

The initial parameter for the fmincon needs to be set up first before it is used by the optimizer. The initial parameter is the vector w_0, consists of the values $w_1, w_2, \ldots, w_N$ that are initialized by $\frac{1}{N}$, the initial values of $s_1, s_2, \ldots, s_j$, which are all zeros and the initial value for φ, which is the quantile of the equally weighted portfolio returns, namely VaR_0. Given these initial value w_0 can be described as

$$w_0 = \left(\frac{1}{N} \quad \frac{1}{N} \quad \cdots \quad \frac{1}{N} \quad VaR_0 \quad 0 \quad 0 \quad \cdots \quad 0 \right).$$

Various CVaR limits (δ) were used to see the changes in the returns. The optimization computations the weight vector w of the optimal portfolio where $w_1, w_2, \ldots, w_N$ are the corresponding weights of N assets. Meanwhile, w_{N+1} is the corresponding VaR and *fval* is the expected return.

2.2 Improved CVaR-Based Portfolio Optimization Method

Asset allocation of a portfolio is one of the important key strategies in minimizing risk and maximizing gains. Since the asset allocation in a portfolio is very important [10], thus, an improvement of the existing CVaR-based Portfolio Optimization Method is proposed in this paper. The improved CVaR-based Portfolio Optimization Method focused on determining the upper and lower limits of the bond weight in a diversified portfolio. In estimating the upper and lower limits of each bond weight, the volatility weighting schemes have been used in this study due to the close relationship between volatility and risk. Bond portfolio weight can be obtained by applying the formula in [11] as follows:

$$w_i = k_i \sigma_i^{-1} \tag{2}$$

where

w_i = weight of bond i,

σ_i = volatility of returns of bond i,

k_i = variable that controls the amount of leverage of the volatility weighting such that

$$k_i = \frac{1}{\sum\limits_{i=1}^{n} \sigma_i^{-1}} \tag{3}$$

in a diversified portfolio for $i = 1, 2, \ldots, n$. The weight of each bond in the diversified portfolio in (2) is used as an indication in setting the upper and lower limits by setting the respective floor and ceiling values as follows:

$$\lfloor w_i \rfloor \leq w_i \leq \lceil w_i \rceil. \tag{4}$$

The floor and ceiling values of w_i are rounded to the nearest tenth due the values of w_i being in percentage form, which have been evaluated using Microsoft Excel. Thus, the improved CVaR-based Portfolio Optimization Method can be presented as follows:

$$\min - w^T \bar{y}$$

subject to

$$w \in W, \varphi \in \Re \tag{5}$$

$$\varphi + \frac{1}{J(1 - \beta)} \sum_{j=1}^{J} s_j \leq \delta$$

$$s_j \geq 0, \qquad j = 1, \ldots, J$$

$$w^T r_j + \varphi + s_j \geq 0, \qquad j = 1, \ldots, J$$

$$\lfloor w_i \rfloor \leq w_i \leq \lceil w_i \rceil$$

2.3 Simulation of Existing and Improved CVaR-Based Portfolio Optimization Methods

The simulation of the optimization process of both the existing CVaR-based and the improved CVaR-based Portfolio Optimization Methods in generating the returns were carried out using the Monte Carlo Simulation method. The Geometric Brownian Motion (GBM), or the stochastic pricing model of bonds, was used in the simulation to generate future price of bond. GBM, which is also known as Exponential Brownian Motion, is a continuous-time stochastic process that follows the Wiener Process, and is defined as the logarithm of the random varying quantity.

The diversified or multiple asset bond portfolios of this study comprises of bonds issued by four banking institutions namely the Export-Import Bank of Malaysia Berhad (EXIM), Commerce International Merchant Bankers (CIMB) Malaysia, European Investment bank (EIB) and Emirates National Bank of Dubai (Emirates NBD). EXIM and EIB issued the *Sukuk* while CIMB and Emirates NBD issued the conventional bonds. Each bond price evolves according to the Brownian motions that are described in (6):

$$S(\Delta t)_1 = S(0)_1 \exp\left[\left(\mu_1 - \frac{\sigma_1^2}{2}\right)\Delta t + \left(\sigma_1\sqrt{\Delta t}\right)\varepsilon_1\right]$$
$$S(\Delta t)_2 = S(0)_2 \exp\left[\left(\mu_2 - \frac{\sigma_2^2}{2}\right)\Delta t + \left(\sigma_2\sqrt{\Delta t}\right)\varepsilon_2\right]$$
$$\vdots$$
$$S(\Delta t)_i = S(0)_i \exp\left[\left(\mu_i - \frac{\sigma_i^2}{2}\right)\Delta t + \left(\sigma_i\sqrt{\Delta t}\right)\varepsilon_i\right] \tag{6}$$
$$\vdots$$
$$S(\Delta t)_N = S(0)_N \exp\left[\left(\mu_N - \frac{\sigma_N^2}{2}\right)\Delta t + \left(\sigma_N\sqrt{\Delta t}\right)\varepsilon_N\right]$$

for $i = 1, 2, \ldots, N$, where

$S(\Delta t)_i$ = Simulated bond price for bond i.
$S(0)_i$ = Initial bond price for bond i.
μ_i = Drift rate of returns over a holding period for bond i.
σ_i = Volatility of returns over a holding period for bond i.
Δt = Time step for a week.

The random numbers $\varepsilon_1, \varepsilon_2, \ldots, \varepsilon_N$ are correlated, whereby their correlation patterns depend on the correlation patterns of bonds returns [12]. By using Cholesky factorization of variance-covariance matrix, the correlated asset paths are generated from the given correlation matrix. The Cholesky factorization can be described as follows:

$$C = U^T U. \tag{7}$$

Correlated random numbers are generated with the help of the upper triangular matrix (with positive diagonal elements) U as follows:

$$R_{r,c} = W_{r,c} * U_{c,c}. \tag{8}$$

Before (8) can be applied, the uncorrelated random numbers W need to be generated first, followed by the construction of bond prices paths using (6) for all bonds. The Cholesky factorization procedure is available in many statistical and computational software packages such as ScaLAPACK [13] and MATLAB. In this study, Cholesky factorization was evaluated by repeating the procedure 3000, 5000, 10000, 20000 times to obtain a distribution of the next period's portfolio price. The simulation for the correlated bond prices based on the existing CVaR-based and the improved CVaR-based Profolio Optimization Methods were generated in MATLAB using a source code modified from [2] (Refer Appendix A).

The results of the simulated bond prices were presented in the form of T-by-N-by-J dimensional matrix where each row represent a holding period $(t_1, t_2, \ldots, t_T)$, each column represents a different bond $(a_1, a_2, \ldots, a_N)$ and each slice in the third dimension represents the number of simulations $(S_1, S_2, \ldots, S_N)$. The returns from the simulated prices were calculated using the log-normal formula which is expressed as follows:

$$R_i = \ln \left| \frac{P_i}{P_{i-1}} \right|, \tag{9}$$

where

R_i = Bond returns at week i.
P_i = Bond price at week i.
P_{i-1} = Bond price at week $i - 1$.

3 Results

The performance of the existing and the improved CVaR-based Portfolio Optimization Methods in optimizing the diversified bond portfolio of this study were compared in order to determine which of the two methods provides a better optimization. The existing and the improved CVaR-based Portfolio Optimization Methods are summarized in Table 1.

Table 1. CVaR portfolio optimization method and the improved CVaR portfolio optimization method

	Existing CVaR portfolio optimization by Rockafellar and Uryasev [4]	Improved CVaR portfolio optimization
Method	$\min \ -w^T \bar{y}$ subject to $w \in W, \varphi \in \Re$ $\varphi + \frac{1}{J(1-\beta)} \sum_{j=1}^{J} s_j \leq \delta$ $s_j \geq 0, \qquad j = 1, \ldots, J$ $w^T r_j + \varphi + s_j \geq 0, \qquad j = 1, \ldots, J$	$\min \ -w^T \bar{y}$ subject to $w \in W, \varphi \in \Re$ $\varphi + \frac{1}{J(1-\beta)} \sum_{j=1}^{J} s_j \leq \delta$ $s_j \geq 0, \qquad j = 1, \ldots, J$ $w^T r_j + \varphi + s_j \geq 0, \qquad j = 1, \ldots, J$ $\lfloor w_i \rfloor \leq w_i \leq \lceil w_i \rceil$

Table 2 shows that the results of the optimal CVaR and the expected loss generated using the improved method, which has restricted condition for the upper and lower bounds, are lower than that of the existing method in [4], which has no restricted conditions. The correct choice of maximum and minimum bond weight when performing the optimization process can help reduce the portfolio's VaR and CVaR along with the expected loss.

As demonstrated by the results in Table 3, the inclusion of the upper and lower bounds for each bond in the diversified portfolio shows that each bond plays a significant role in reducing the expected loss resulting in a more balanced portfolio as compared to the optimization using the existing method. However, the Sukuk appears to provide more benefits to investors and issuers in producing a balanced diversified portfolio due to the reduced CVaR. The results obtained from the existing CVaR-based Portfolio Optimization Method show unbalanced bond weight allocations of the diversified portfolio leading to a bias towards the positive drift rate.

Table 2. Results generated by existing CVaR portfolio optimization method and the improved CVaR portfolio optimization method

		Existing CVaR portfolio optimization method	Improved CVaR portfolio optimization method
Results	Risk limit	−2.50	
	Confidence level	99.9	
	Expected loss	−0.0264	−0.0194
	VaR portfolio	−0.0125	−0.0125
	CVaR portfolio	−0.0148	−0.013

Table 3. Assets weights generated by existing CVaR portfolio optimization method and the improved CVaR portfolio optimization method in the diversified portfolio

		Generated assets weights	
		Existing CVaR portfolio optimization method	Improved CVaR portfolio optimization method
Results	EXIM Sukuk (%)	0.013	19.49
	EIB Sukuk (%)	0.1777	29.96
	CIMB (%)	99.789	39.97
	Emirates NBD (%)	0.0193	10.58

4   Conclusion

In conclusion, this study has successfully improved the existing CVaR-based method for optimizing a diversified portfolio presented in [4] by using the approach presented in [2]. The need to improve the existing method is due to the possibility of the method resulting in an unbalanced bond weight allocation for a diversified portfolio. The improved method proposed in this study appears to overcome this problem. The method is found to be more helpful in allocating the optimal weight of bonds in a diversified portfolio in order to minimize the loss for a certain risk level. The improved CVaR-based Optimization Method minimizes the loss by introducing new constraint level on the upper and lower limit of the bond weight. The constraint is based on the volatility weighting scheme for the optimization formulation since there is a strong relationship between volatility and risk. Given the results, it can be concluded that the improved CVaR-based Optimization Method is able to provide positive results in terms of lower expected loss and optimal CVaR.

Acknowledgement. This work was supported by the LESTARI grant [600-IRMI/DANA 5/3/LESTARI (0127/2016)], Universiti Teknologi MARA, Malaysia

APPENDIX A

Source Code
A.1: Simulated Price and Return to Run A.2

```
function[S,r] = Simulated(S0,drift,vol,corr,steps,nsims)

    nAssets = length(S0);
    dt=1/52;%time steps for one week%
     %to stimulate correlated asset path (bond prices) based on MCS%
    R = chol(corr);%cholesky factorization%
    S = nan(steps+1,nsims,nAssets);
    for irand = 1:nsims
        x = randn(steps,size(corr,2));
        ep = x*R;
        S(:,irand,:) = [ones(1,nAssets); ...
     cumprod(exp(repmat(drift*dt,steps,1)+ep*diag(vol)*sqrt(dt)))]*
        diag(S0);
    end

    nAssets=size(S,3);
    nsims=size(S,2);
    %to generate return from simulated prices%
    r=nan(nsims,nAssets);
    for iSim = 1: nAssets
        k = squeeze (S(:,:, iSim ));
        rSim = log(k(end,:)./k(1 ,:));
        r(:,iSim) = rSim;
    end

end
```

A.2: CVaR Portfolio Optimization

```
function Optimization_CVaR (r,beta,CVaRLimit,UB,LB)
    % Sizes
    [nsims,nAssets]=size(r);
    % Inequality constraints
    A1=[zeros(1,nAssets) 1 1/(1-beta)*1/nsims*
  ones(1,nsims)];
    A2=-r;
    A3=-ones(nsims,1);
    A4=-eye(nsims,nsims);
    A=[A2 A3 A4];
    A=[A1;A];
    b=[-CVaRLimit zeros(1,nsims)];
    b=b';
    % Equality constraints --> sum of weights has to be
  100%
    Aeq = [ones(1,nAssets) zeros(1,nsims+1)];
    beq = [1];
    % Upper and lower bounds
    if UB==1
        UB=[repmat(UB,1,nAssets) +Inf*ones(1,nsims+1)];
    else
        UB=[UB +Inf*ones(1,nsims+1)];
    End

    if LB==0
        LB = [repmat(LB,1,nAssets) zeros(1,nsims+1)];
    else
        LB = [LB zeros(1,nsims+1)];
    end
    % Initial weights and initial VaR
    w0=[(1/nAssets)*ones(1,nAssets)];
    VaR0=quantile(r*w0',beta);
    w0=[w0 VaR0 zeros(1,nsims)];
    % Objective function
    objfun = @(w) -mean(r(:,1:nAssets))*w(1: nAssets)';
    options = optimoptions(@fmincon,'Algorithm',
  'interior-point');
    options = optimoptions(options,'MaxFunEvals',
  100000);
    % Optimization %
    [w,fval,exitflag,output]=fmincon(objfun,w0,A,b,Aeq,
  beq,LB,UB,[],options);
    history = [];

    wopt=w(1:nAssets)'; % Optimal weight%
    Asset_Weight_Optimal=wopt*100
    ExpectedReturn=-fval % Expected Return %
    ropt=r*wopt; % Optimal Return %
    VaR_OptPort=-w(nAssets+1)/100 %Optimal VaR%
    p=sort(ropt,'descend');
    CVaR_OptPort= mean(ropt(ropt<VaR_OptPort));
     % Optimal CVaR%
    display (CVaR_OptPort);
end
```

References

1. Lexicon.ft.com.: Capital Markets Definition from Financial Times Lexicon. http://lexicon.ft.com/Term?term=capital-markets
2. Kull, M.: Portfolio optimization for constrained shortfall risk: implementation and it architecture considerations. Master thesis, Swiss Federal Institute of Technology, Zurich, July 2014
3. Artzner, P., Delbaen, F., Eber, J.M., Heath, D.: Coherent measures of risk. Math. Financ. 9 (3), 203–228 (1999)
4. Rockafellar, R.T., Uryasev, S.: Optimization of conditional value-at-risk. J. Risk 2(3), 21–42 (2000)
5. Follmer, H., Schied, A.: Convex and risk coherent measures (2008). http://citeseerx.ist.psu.edu/viewdoc/summary?doi=10.1.1.335.3202
6. McKay, R., Keefer, T.E.: VaR is a dangerous technique. euromoney's corporate finance (1996). https://ralphmckay.wordpress.com/1996/08/03/
7. Mausser, H., Rosen, D.: Beyond VaR: from measuring risk to managing risk. ALGO. Res. Quarter. 1(2), 5–20 (1999)
8. Kisiala, J.: Conditional value-at-risk: theory and applications. Dissertation, University of Edinburgh, Scotland (2015). https://arxiv.org/abs/1511.00140
9. Forghieri, S.: Portfolio optimization using CVaR. Bachelor's Degree Thesis, LUISS Guido Carli (2014). http://tesi.luiss.it/id/eprint/12528
10. Ibbotson, R.G.: The importance of asset allocation. Financ. Anal. J. 66(2), 18–20 (2010)
11. Asness, C.S., Frazzini, A., Pedersen, L.H.: Leverage aversion and risk parity. Financ. Anal. J. 68(1), 47–59 (2012)
12. Cakir, S., Raei, F.: Sukuk vs. Eurobonds: Is There a Difference in Value-at-Risk? IMF Working Paper, vol. 7, no. 237, pp. 1–20 (2007)
13. Chois, J., Dongarrasl, J.J., Pozoj, R., Walkers, D.W.: ScaLAPACK: a Scalable Linear Algebra Library for Distributed Memory Concurrent Computers. In: 4th Symposium on the Frontiers of Massively Parallel Computation. IEEE Computer Society Press (1992). https://doi.org/10.1109/FMPC.1992.234898

Ranking by Fuzzy Weak Autocatalytic Set

Siti Salwana Mamat[1], Tahir Ahmad[1,2(✉)], Siti Rahmah Awang[3],
and Muhammad Zilullah Mukaram[1]

[1] Department of Mathematical Sciences, Faculty of Science,
Universiti Teknologi Malaysia, 81310 Johor Bahru, Malaysia
[2] Centre of Sustainable Nanomaterials,
Ibnu Sina Institute for Scientific and Industrial Research,
Universiti Teknologi Malaysia, 81310 Johor Bahru, Malaysia
`tahir@ibnusina.utm.my`
[3] Department of Human Resource Development, Faculty of Management,
Universiti Teknologi Malaysia, 81310 Johor Bahru, Malaysia

Abstract. A relation between objects can be presented in a form of a graph. An autocatalytic set (ACS) is a directed graph where every node has incoming link. A fuzzy weak autocatalytic set (FWACS) is introduced to handle uncertainty in a ranking. The FWACS is found to be comparable to eigenvector method (EM) and potential method (PM) for ranking purposes.

Keywords: Ranking · Fuzzy graph · Fuzzy weak autocatalytic set

1 Introduction

The study of decision problems has a long history. Mathematical modeling has been used by economist and mathematicians in decision making problems, in particular multiple criteria decision making (MCDM) (Rao 2006; Lu and Ruan 2007). In early 1950s, Koopmans (1951) worked on MCDM and Saaty (1990) introduced analytic hierarchy process (AHP) which brought advances to MCDM techniques.

In general, there are many situations in which the aggregate performance of a group of alternatives must be evaluated based on a set of criteria. The determination of weights is an important aspect of AHP. The ranks of alternatives are obtained by their associated weights (Saaty 1978; 1979). In AHP, the eigenvector method (EM) is used to calculate the alternative weights. The following section is a review on EM.

2 Eigenvector Method

The AHP is based on comparing n alternatives in pair with respect to their relative weights. Let $C_1, \ldots, C_n$ be n objects and their weights by $W = (w_1, \ldots, w_m)^T$. The pairwise comparisons can be presented in a form of a square matrix $A(a_{ij})$.

B. W. Yap et al. (Eds.): SCDS 2018, CCIS 937, pp. 161–172, 2019.
https://doi.org/10.1007/978-981-13-3441-2_13

$$A = (a_{ij})_{n \times n} = \begin{array}{c} \\ C_1 \\ C_2 \\ \vdots \\ C_n \end{array} \begin{array}{cccc} C_1 & C_2 & \cdots & C_n \\ \begin{bmatrix} a_{11} & a_{12} & \cdots & a_{1n} \\ a_{21} & a_{22} & \cdots & a_{2n} \\ \vdots & \vdots & \ddots & \vdots \\ a_{n1} & a_{n2} & \cdots & a_{nn} \end{bmatrix} \end{array},$$

where $a_{ij} = 1/a_{ji}$ and $a_{ii} = 1$ for $i,j = 1, 2, \ldots, n$.

Saaty (1977) proposed the EM to find the weight vector from pairwise comparison. He developed the following steps.

Step 1: From the pairwise comparison matrix A, the weight vector W can be determined by solving the following equation.

$$AW = \lambda_{max} W$$

where λ_{max} is the largest eigenvalue of A.

Step 2: Calculate the consistency ratio (CR). This is the actual measure of consistency. It is defined as follows.

$$CR = \frac{(\lambda_{max} - n)/(n-1)}{RI}$$

where RI is the consistency index. Table 1 shows the RI values for the pairwise comparison matrices. The pairwise comparison matrix is consistent if $CR \le 0.1$, otherwise it need to be revised.

Table 1. Random Index for matrices of various size (Saaty 1979)

n	1	2	3	4	5	6	7	8	9	10	11
RI	0.0	0.0	0.58	0.90	1.12	1.24	1.32	1.41	1.45	1.49	1.51

Step 3: The overall weight of each alternative is calculated using the following formula.

$$w_{A_i} = \sum_{j=1}^{m} w_{ij} w_j, \quad i = 1, \ldots, n$$

where $w_j (j = 1, \ldots, m)$ are the weights of criteria, $w_{ij} (j = 1, \ldots, n)$ are the weights of alternatives with respect to criterion j, and $w_{A_i} (j = 1, \ldots, n)$ are the overall weights of alternatives.

Further, a ranking function using preference graph, namely Potential Method (PM) was introduced by Lavoslav Čaklović in 2002. The following section is a brief review on PM.

3   Potential Method

The Potential Method is a tool in a decision making process which utilizes graph, namely preference graph. A preference graph is a structure generated by comparing on a set of alternatives (Čaklović 2002). Čaklović (2002; 2004) used preference graph to model pairwise comparisons of alternatives. Suppose V be a set of alternatives in which some preferences are being considered. If an alternative u is preferred over alternative v (denoted as $u \succ v$), it can be presented as a directed edge from vertex v to vertex u. The edge is denoted as (u, v) (Fig. 1).

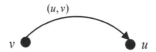

(u,v)

v u

Fig. 1. An alternative u is preferred than alternative v

The preference is described with an intensity from a certain scale (e.g. equal, weak, moderate, strong, or absolute preference) which is expressed by a nonnegative real number, $\mathbb{R}$. The directed edge from v to u has a weight, i.e., it has a preference flow denoted by $F_{(u,v)}$. The formal definition of a preference graph is stated as below.

Definition 1 Čaklović and Kurdija (2017).
A preference graph is a triple $G = (V, E, F)$ where V is a set of $n \in \mathbb{N}$ vertices (representing alternatives), $E \subseteq V \times V$ is a set of directed edges, and $F : E \to \mathbb{R}$ is a preference flow which maps each edge (u, v) to the corresponding intensity $F_{(u,v)}$. The following are the steps to determine weights and ranks by PM.

Step 1: Build a preference graph $G = (V, E, F)$ for a given problem.
Step 2: Construct incidence, A and flow difference, F matrices.
      An $m \times n$ incidence matrix is given by

$$A_{\alpha,v} = \begin{cases} -1, & \text{if the edge } \alpha \text{ leaves } v \\ 1, & \text{if the edge } \alpha \text{ enters } v \\ 0, & \text{otherwise} \end{cases} \tag{1}$$

Step 3: Build the Laplacian matrix, L
      The Laplacian matrix is $L = A^T A$ with entries define as

$$L_{i,j} = \begin{cases} -1, & \text{if the edge } (i,j) \text{ or } (j,i), \\ \deg(i), & \text{if } i = j, \\ 0, & \text{else.} \end{cases} \tag{2}$$

such that $\deg(i)$ is the degree of vertex i.

Step 4: Generate the flow difference, ∇.

Let the flow difference be $\nabla := A^T F$. The component of ∇ is determined as below.

$$\begin{aligned}
\nabla_v &= \sum_{\alpha=1}^{m} A_{v.\alpha}^T F_\alpha \\
&= \sum_{\alpha \text{ enters } v} F_\alpha - \sum_{\alpha \text{ leaves } v} F_\alpha
\end{aligned} \tag{3}$$

whereby ∇_v is the difference between the total flow which enters v and the total flow which leaves v.

Step 5: Determine potential, X

Potential, X is a solution of the Laplacian system

$$LX = \nabla \tag{4}$$

such that $\sum X_v = 0$ on its connected components.

Step 6: Check the consistency degree, $\beta < 12^0$

The measure of inconsistency is defined as

$$\text{Inc}(F) = \frac{\|F - AX\|_2}{\|AX\|_2} \tag{5}$$

where $\| . \|_2$ denotes 2-norm and $\beta = \arctan(\text{Inc}(F))$ is the angle of inconsistency. The ranking is considered acceptable whenever $\beta < 12^0$.

Step 7: Determine the weight, w. The following equation is used to obtain the weight.

$$w = \frac{a^X}{\|a^x\|_1} \tag{6}$$

where $\| . \|_1$ represents l_1-norm and parameter a is chosen to be 2 suggested by Čaklović (2002).

Step 8: Rank the objects by their associated weights.

The PM is meant for crisp edges (Čaklović 2004). It is not equipped for fuzzy edges. The following section introduces a special kind of graph, namely weak autocatalytic set (WACS) as a tool for ranking purposes.

4   Weak Autocatalytic Set

Jain and Krishna introduced the concept of autocatalytic set (ACS) set in form of a graph in 1998. An ACS is described by a directed graph with vertices represent species and the directed edges represent catalytic interactions among them (Jain and Krishna 1998; 1999). An edge from vertex j to vertex i indicates that species j catalyses i. The formal definition of an ACS is given as follows.

Definition 2 (Jain and Krishna 1998).

An ACS is a subgraph, each of whose nodes has at least one incoming link from vertices belonging to the same subgraph (Fig. 2).

Fig. 2. Some examples of ACS

A weak form of an ACS i.e. WACS was proposed by Mamat et al. (2018). A WACS allows some freedom in connectivity of its vertices in a system. The WACS is defined as follows.

Definition 3 (Mamat *et al.* 2018).

A WACS is a non-loop subgraph which contains a vertex with no incoming link (Fig. 3).

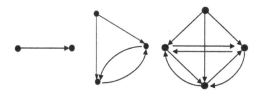

Fig. 3. Several WACS

Some uncertainties may happen in a WACS. The fuzzification of WACS has led to a new structure namely Fuzzy Weak Autocatalytic Set (FWACS). The definition of a FWACS is formalized in Definition 4 as follows.

Definition 4 (Mamat *et al.* 2018)

A FWACS is a WACS such that each edge e_i has a membership value $\mu(e_i) \in [0, 1]$ for $e_i \in E$ (Fig. 4).

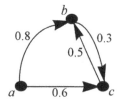

Fig. 4. A FWACS

A FWACS is used for ranking. The following section describes the propose method.

5 Ranking by FWACS

This section presents an algorithm for ranking by FWACS. The input are the membership values of edges obtained in pairwise comparison of objects. The orientation of edges can be represented by an incidence matrix, A. The membership values of edges denoted by F are represented by a $m \times 1$ matrix. The procedure of ranking with FWACS is given as follows.

1. Build a FWACS, $G = (V, E_\mu)$ for a given problem and determine the membership value for edges. The V is a set of vertices and E_μ is the corresponding fuzzy edges.
2. Construct incidence matrix, A and fuzzy flow matrix, F_μ. A $m \times n$ incidence matrix is given by Eq. 1.
3. Define Laplacian matrix, L using Eq. 2.
4. Generate flow difference, D_μ using Eq. 3.
5. By using Eq. 4, the potential, X is calculated.
6. Check the consistency ($\beta < 12^0$) by solving Eq. 5.
7. Determine the weight, w using Eq. 6.
8. Rank the objects with respect to their associated weights.

The ranking procedure is illustrated in the following flowchart in Fig. 5 which is followed by its algorithm in Fig. 6.

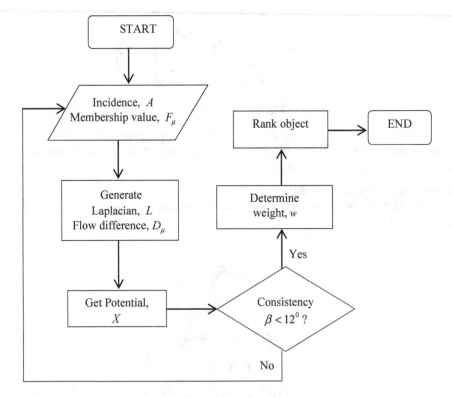

Fig. 5. Ranking flowchart

Algorithm 1 Ranking with FWACS

Begin

Input: $A = (a_{ij})_{m \times n}$ Incidence matrix

         $F = (f_1, f_2, f_3, \ldots, f_m)$ Flow matrix

Output: $w = (w_1, w_2, w_3, \ldots, w_n)$ Criteria weights

  1: **Procedure 1:** [Define laplacian, L]

  2: $L = (l_{ij})_{n \times n}$

  3: **return** L

  4: **Procedure 2:** [Generate flow difference, D]

  5: $D = (D_1, D_2, D_3, \ldots, D_n)$

  6: **return** D

  7: **Procedure 3:** [Get potential, X]

  8: $X = (x_1, x_2, x_3, \ldots, x_n)$

  9: **return** X

10: **Procedure 4:** [Consistency degree, β]

11: β

12: **return** β

13: **Procedure 5:** [Determine weight, w]

14: $w = (w_1, w_2, w_3, \ldots, w_n)$

15: **return** w

End

Fig. 6. Ranking algorithm

An implementation of ranking using FWACS on a problem described in Morano *et al.* (2016) is presented in the following section.

6 Implementation on Culture Heritage Valorization

The Rocca Estate is located in the municipality of Finale Emilia which was erected in 1213 as a defense tower to the city. The building is characterized over the centuries by different interventions, which ended the recovery activities in 2009. However, in 2012 an earthquake struck which caused serious damage to the fortress. An urgent action was needed to restore the building.

The main task is to identify the "total quality" of the building with the support of evaluator (see Fig. 7). The "total quality" takes into account the compatibility of the alternative respect to multiple instances described through the criteria at level 2. The criteria are derived from expertise in different aspects namely technical, economic, legal, social and others. The alternatives are given in level 3.

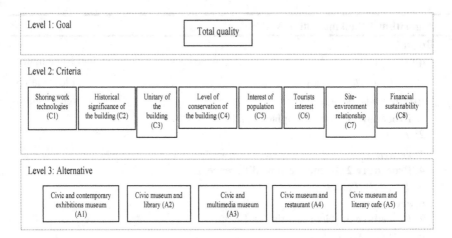

Fig. 7. The hierarchy of decision levels

The evaluation matrix for the goal is given in Table 2 and Fig. 8 illustrates the FWACS for the identified goal.

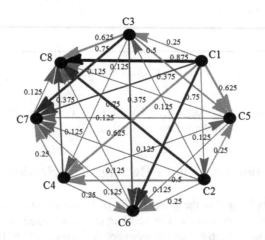

Fig. 8. The FWACS for culture heritage valorization goal

There are 8 criteria need to be considered in order to achieve the goal. Hence, a pairwise comparison within each criterion is made. There exist 28 comparisons in this level. The comparison is represented by an incidence matrix. An arrow pointing from C1 to C2 in Fig. 8 signifies that C2 is more preferred than C1. The incidence matrix and its corresponding membership values are given as follow.

$$A = \begin{bmatrix}
-1 & 1 & 0 & 0 & 0 & 0 & 0 & 0 \\
-1 & 0 & 1 & 0 & 0 & 0 & 0 & 0 \\
-1 & 0 & 0 & 1 & 0 & 0 & 0 & 0 \\
-1 & 0 & 0 & 0 & 1 & 0 & 0 & 0 \\
-1 & 0 & 0 & 0 & 0 & 1 & 0 & 0 \\
-1 & 0 & 0 & 0 & 0 & 0 & 1 & 0 \\
-1 & 0 & 0 & 0 & 0 & 0 & 0 & 1 \\
0 & -1 & 1 & 0 & 0 & 0 & 0 & 0 \\
0 & -1 & 0 & 1 & 0 & 0 & 0 & 0 \\
0 & -1 & 0 & 0 & 1 & 0 & 0 & 0 \\
0 & -1 & 0 & 0 & 0 & 1 & 0 & 0 \\
0 & -1 & 0 & 0 & 0 & 0 & 1 & 0 \\
0 & -1 & 0 & 0 & 0 & 0 & 0 & 1 \\
0 & 0 & -1 & 1 & 0 & 0 & 0 & 0 \\
0 & 0 & -1 & 0 & 1 & 0 & 0 & 0 \\
0 & 0 & -1 & 0 & 0 & 1 & 0 & 0 \\
0 & 0 & -1 & 0 & 0 & 0 & 1 & 0 \\
0 & 0 & -1 & 0 & 0 & 0 & 0 & 1 \\
0 & 0 & 0 & -1 & 1 & 0 & 0 & 0 \\
0 & 0 & 0 & -1 & 0 & 1 & 0 & 0 \\
0 & 0 & 0 & -1 & 0 & 0 & 1 & 0 \\
0 & 0 & 0 & -1 & 0 & 0 & 0 & 1 \\
0 & 0 & 0 & 0 & -1 & 1 & 0 & 0 \\
0 & 0 & 0 & 0 & -1 & 0 & 1 & 0 \\
0 & 0 & 0 & 0 & -1 & 0 & 0 & 1 \\
0 & 0 & 0 & 0 & 0 & -1 & 1 & 0 \\
0 & 0 & 0 & 0 & 0 & -1 & 0 & 1 \\
0 & 0 & 0 & 0 & 0 & 0 & -1 & 1
\end{bmatrix} \quad \text{and} \quad F = \begin{bmatrix}
0.125 \\ 0.25 \\ 0.625 \\ 0.625 \\ 0.75 \\ 0.375 \\ 0.875 \\ 0.125 \\ 0.5 \\ 0.25 \\ 0.25 \\ 0.125 \\ 0.75 \\ 0.125 \\ 0.5 \\ 0.375 \\ 0.75 \\ 0.625 \\ 0.125 \\ 0.25 \\ 0.25 \\ 0.375 \\ 0.125 \\ 0.125 \\ 0.125 \\ 0.125 \\ 0.125 \\ 0.125
\end{bmatrix}$$

The potential, X of $[-0.453 \quad -0.234 \quad -0.25 \quad -0.031 \quad 0.141 \quad 0.188 \quad 0.203 \quad 0.375]^T$ is determined by solving Eq. 4. In this paper, we made a comparison result using EM taken from Morano et al. (2016) with the result using PM and FWACS. The EM weights are listed alongside our calculated PM and FWACS weights in Table 2.

Table 2. Pairwise comparisons for goal

Criteria	C1	C2	C3	C4	C5	C6	C7	C8	Priority vector		
									EM	PM	FWACS
C1	1	1/2	1/3	1/6	1/6	1/7	1/4	1/8	0.024	0.005	0.090
C2	2	1	1/2	1/5	1/3	1/3	1/2	1/7	0.044	0.015	0.105
C3	3	2	1	1/2	1/5	1/4	1/7	1/6	0.046	0.014	0.103
C4	6	5	2	1	1/2	1/3	1/3	1/4	0.095	0.066	0.126
C5	6	3	5	2	1	1/2	1/2	1/2	0.135	0.122	0.136
C6	7	3	4	3	2	1	1/2	1/2	0.169	0.158	0.140
C7	4	2	7	3	2	2	1	1/2	0.203	0.172	0.142
C8	8	7	6	4	2	2	2	1	0.285	0.447	0.159

Table 2 presented the weights for each criterion for goal. The weights obtained using EM, PM and FWACS signified that the criterion C8 has the highest weight whereas the lowest weight is assigned to criterion C1.

Then, the comparison for alternatives with respect to each criterion is made. The pairwise comparisons of criteria are presented in Table 3.

Table 3. Pairwise comparisons of each criterion (Morano *et al.* 2016)

C1 Shoring work technologies						C2 Historical significance of building				
	A1	A2	A3	A4	A5		A1	A2	A3	A4	A5
A1	1	1/3	1/8	1/6	1/9	A1	1	1/2	1/6	1/2	1/4
A2	3	1	1/5	1/3	1/7	A2	2	1	1/4	3	2
A3	8	5	1	5	1/2	A3	6	4	1	5	3
A4	6	3	1/5	1	1/6	A4	2	1/3	1/5	1	2
A5	9	7	2	6	1	A5	4	1/2	1/3	1/2	1

C3 Unitary of building						C4 Level of conservation of the building				
	A1	A2	A3	A4	A5		A1	A2	A3	A4	A5
A1	1	1	3	5	6	A1	1	2	7	8	9
A2	1	1	3	5	6	A2	1/2	1	6	7	8
A3	1/3	1/3	1	2	4	A3	1/7	1/6	1	2	3
A4	1/5	1/5	1/2	1	2	A4	1/8	1/7	1/2	1	4
A5	1/6	1/6	1/4	1/2	1	A5	1/9	1/8	1/3	1/4	1

C5 Interest of population						C6 Touristic interest				
	A1	A2	A3	A4	A5		A1	A2	A3	A4	A5
A1	1	1/3	1/2	1/4	1/7	A1	1	3	1/5	1/4	1/8
A2	3	1	2	2	1/3	A2	1/3	1	1/7	1/7	1/9
A3	2	1/2	1	1/2	1/6	A3	5	7	1	1/3	1/3
A4	4	1/2	2	1	1/3	A4	4	7	3	1	1/3
A5	7	3	6	3	1	A5	8	9	3	3	1

C7 site-environment relationship						C8 Financial stability				
	A1	A2	A3	A4	A5		A1	A2	A3	A4	A5
A1	1	3	1/6	1/4	1/5	A1	1	3	1/3	1/5	1/6
A2	1/3	1	1/7	1/5	1/7	A2	1/3	1	1/6	1/8	1/9
A3	6	7	1	2	1/3	A3	3	6	1	1/2	1/4
A4	4	5	1/2	1	1/3	A4	5	8	2	1	1/5
A5	5	7	3	3	1	A5	6	9	4	5	1

The comparison between EM from Morano et al. (2016), PM and FWACS weights of alternatives with respect to each criterion are given in Table 4.

Table 4. Comparison between EM, PM and FWACS weights

Priorities		C1	C2	C3	C4	C5	C6	C7	C8
EM	A1	0.03	0.06	0.36	0.48	0.05	0.06	0.07	0.06
	A2	0.06	0.20	0.36	0.34	0.20	0.03	0.04	0.03
	A3	0.32	0.49	0.15	0.08	0.09	0.17	0.27	0.14
	A4	0.12	0.12	0.08	0.07	0.16	0.26	0.17	0.22
	A5	0.47	0.13	0.05	0.03	0.49	0.47	0.45	0.54
PM	A1	0.002	0.025	0.431	0.654	0.017	0.009	0.019	0.014
	A2	0.010	0.117	0.431	0.327	0.119	0.002	0.006	0.002
	A3	0.290	0.710	0.094	0.010	0.039	0.115	0.307	0.073
	A4	0.032	0.059	0.031	0.007	0.104	0.175	0.134	0.145
	A5	0.666	0.089	0.013	0.002	0.721	0.689	0.534	0.766
FWACS	A1	0.132	0.167	0.238	0.281	0.160	0.157	0.165	0.166
	A2	0.162	0.202	0.238	0.258	0.204	0.132	0.143	0.132
	A3	0.246	0.252	0.197	0.167	0.178	0.215	0.233	0.204
	A4	0.187	0.185	0.172	0.159	0.201	0.226	0.210	0.223
	A5	0.273	0.195	0.155	0.136	0.256	0.269	0.249	0.274

The priorities listed in Table 4 for PM and FWACS are aggregated with the weights identified in Table 2 using Eq. 6. Table 5 lists the overall priority vectors.

Table 5. Priority vector for goal

Alternatives	Overall Priority vector					
	FWACS	RANK	PM	RANK	EM (Morano et al. 2016)	RANK
A1	0.18283	4	0.02919	4	0.115	4
A2	0.17940	5	0.01081	5	0.108	5
A3	0.20186	3	0.13020	3	0.181	3
A4	0.20731	2	0.16876	2	0.182	2
A5	0.22859	1	0.66104	1	0.414	1

The results are summarized in Table 5, whereby A5 is the dominant. The result is in order $A5 \succ A4 \succ A3 \succ A1 \succ A2$. Furthermore, the outcome is in agreement with Morano et al. (2016).

The weights differences between A4 and A3 is 0.001 using EM. However, the weights are different by 0.03856 and 0.00545 by PM and FWACS, respectively. The differences between A1 and A2 is 0.007, 0.01838 and 0.00343 by EM, PM and FWACS respectively.

7 Conclusion

The aim of this paper is to introduce a method for ranking of uncertainty environments. A problem posted in Morano et al. (2016) is considered. The result obtained from FWACS is found to be comparable to EM and PM. Furthermore, FWACS can accommodate the uncertainty environment.

Acknowledgement. This work is supported by FRGS vote 4F756 from Ministry of High Education (MOHE) and MyBrainSc scholarship.

References

Čaklović, L.: Decision making via potential method. preprint (2002)

Čaklović, L.: Interaction of criteria in grading process. In: Knowledge Society-Challenges to Management Globalization Regionalism and EU Enlargement, pp. 273–288. Koper, Slovenia (2004)

Čaklović, L., Kurdija, A.S.: A universal voting system based on the potential method. Eur. J. Oper. Res. **259**(2), 677–688 (2017)

Jain, S., Krishna, S.: Autocatalytic sets and the growth of complexity in an evolutionary model. Phys. Rev. Lett. **81**(25), 5684 (1998)

Jain, S., Krishna, S.: Emergence and growth of complex networks in adaptive systems. Comput. Phys. Commun. **121–122**, 116–121 (1999)

Koopmans, T.C.: Activity analysis of production as an efficient combination of activities. In: Activity Analysis of Production and Allocation, vol. 13. Wiley, New York (1951)

Lu, J., Ruan, D.: Multi-objective Group Decision Making: Methods, Software and Applications with Fuzzy Set Techniques, 6th edn. Imperial College Press, London (2007)

Morano, P., Locurcio, M., Tajani, F.: Cultural heritage valorization: an application of ahp for the choice of the highest and best use. Proc.-Soc. Behav. Sci. **223**, 952–959 (2016)

Rao, R.V.: A decision-making framework model for evaluating flexible manufacturing systems using digraph and matrix methods. Int. J. Adv. Manuf. Technol. **30**(11–12), 1101–1110 (2006)

Saaty, T.L.: A scaling method for priorities in hierarchical structures. J. Math. Psychol. **15**(3), 234–281 (1977)

Saaty, T.L.: Exploring the interface between hierarchies, multiple objectives and fuzzy sets. Fuzzy Sets Syst. **1**(1), 57–68 (1978)

Saaty, T.L.: Applications of analytical hierarchies. Math. Comput. Simul. **21**(1), 1–20 (1979)

Saaty, T.L.: How to make a decision: the analytic hierarchy process. Eur. J. Oper. Res. **48**(1), 9–26 (1990)

Mamat, S.S., Ahmad, T., Awang, S.R.: Transitive tournament as weak autocatalytic set. Indian J. Pure Appl. Math. (2018) (Submitted and under review)

Fortified Offspring Fuzzy Neural Networks Algorithm

Kefaya Qaddoum$^{(\boxtimes)}$

Higher Colleges of Technology, Abu Dhabi, Al Ain, UAE
Kqaddoum@hct.ac.ae

Abstract. Our research here suggests a fortified Offspring fuzzy neural networks (FOFNN) classifier developed with the aid of Fuzzy C-Means (FCM). The objective of this study concerns the selection of preprocessing techniques for the dimensionality reduction of input space. Principal component analysis (PCA) algorithm presents a pre-processing phase to the network to shape the low-dimensional input variables. Subsequently, the effectual step to handle uncertain information by type-2 fuzzy sets using Fuzzy C-Means (FCM) clustering. The proposition (condition) phase of the rules is formed by two FCM clustering algorithms, which are appealed by spending distinct values of the fuzzification coefficient successively resulting in valued type-2 membership functions. The simultaneous parametric optimization of the network by the evolutionary algorithm is finalized. The suggested classifier is applied to some machine learning datasets, and the results are compared with those provided by other classifiers reported in the literature.

Keywords: Fuzzy C-Means · Fuzzy neural networks · Artificial bee colony
Principal Component Analysis · Type-2 fuzzy set

1 Introduction

Neural classifiers has proven to have tangible benefits for learning abilities, and robustness. These classifiers, multilayer perceptrons (MLPs) including flexible nature of hidden layers have been widely used. It is shown that the MLPs can be trained to approximate complex functions to any required accuracy [1]. Since then, radial basis function neural networks (RBFNNs) came as a sound alternative to the MLPs. RBFNNs reveal more advantages including optimal global approximation and classification capabilities, and rapid convergence of the learning procedures [2, 3].

Fuzzy neural networks (FNNs) have shown an impact in many areas of research yielded from fuzzy logic and neural networks. It utilizes the best of the two methodologies [4, 5]. The fuzzy set theory has been introduced [6, 7] to deal with uncertain or indefinite characteristics. Since its launch, the research of fuzzy logic has been a pivotal topic of various studies and proven many meaningful results both in theory and application [8, 9]. The essential advantage of neural networks is in their adaptive network nature and learning abilities. To create the maximum synergy effect with both fields, the FNN combines fuzzy rules represented as "if-then" clause with neural networks that are learned to employ the standards back-propagation [10, 11].

© Springer Nature Singapore Pte Ltd. 2019
B. W. Yap et al. (Eds.): SCDS 2018, CCIS 937, pp. 173–185, 2019.
https://doi.org/10.1007/978-981-13-3441-2_14

Type-2 fuzzy sets have been widely used in a different application, which requires more than using only type-1 fuzzy sets [12–15]. Still, type-2 fuzzy sets increase computational complexity comparing to type-1. Additionally, type-2 TSK fuzzy logic system (FLS) only uses back propagation-based learning to update successive parameters (coefficients). Nonetheless, the advantages of type-2 fuzzy sets, which are known to deal more effectively with the uncertainty correlated with the given problems balance these downsides [14–23]. In addition, type-2 fuzzy sets are combined with FNNs to promote the accuracy of FNNs. Some new methodologies such as self-evolving or self-learning have been anticipated to boost the powers of FNNs [24–30]. The fuzzy clustering algorithm is used to decrease dimensionality. Fuzzy clustering forms fuzzy ground considering the feature of the specified dataset; thus fuzzy clustering prevents the production of unnecessary fuzzy rules (domain) that do not affect the accuracy of a model. Furthermore, the FCM clustering yields different shapes of membership functions depending upon the values of the fuzzification coefficient. These membership functions could be regarded in the form of a single type-2 fuzzy set, especially an interval-valued fuzzy set. Like this, the FCM algorithm generates a footprint of uncertainty (FOU) of the type-2 fuzzy set [17, 18]. Parametric factors: two different fuzzification coefficients (m1 and m2) of FCM, and two learning rates (ηc and ηs) as well as two attributes terms (αc and αc) for BP.

Here we suggest the following: preprocessing, proposition, and inference phase. The preprocessing phase is to decrease the dimensionality of input variables as well as to promote the execution of the suggested network. Data preprocessing is vital at this phase. The representative algorithm is Principal Component Analysis (PCA). PCA is based on the covariance of the entire set of patterns. Therefore, PCA is preferred since it minimizes the loss of information. The proposition phase of the suggested rule-based classifier is realized with the aid of parameter-variable FCM clustering methods to form type membership functions [17, 18]. In the successive (condition) phase, the coefficients of a linear function are updated employing the BP algorithm. In the inference phase, Karnik and Mendel's algorithm serves as a type reduction mechanism to decrease fuzzily type-set into a fuzzy set of type-1 [31–34].

The other influencing phase is applying the ABC to identify parameters of the network and provides a consistent approach to promote the global and local exploration capabilities [18, 35–39]. We utilize ABC to optimize the preprocessing, the number of transformed (feature) data, the learning rate, attributes coefficient, and fuzzification coefficient used by the FCM. The optimal amount of the feature data should be selected mainly for minimizing the preprocessing time. Since the fuzzy neural network is learned by gradient descent method [18, 40–43], the values of the learning rate and attributes are incredibly fitting to the value of the resulting neural network.

The paper is structured as follows. In the next section we start with PCA, then the general architecture of the fortified Offspring fuzzy neural networks (FOFNN) classifier and discuss learning procedure is engaging the FCM shown in Sect. 3. In Sect. 4, we consider the essentials of the ABC and show its usage to the variety of parameters. Experimental results are presented in Sect. 5. Conclusion shows in Sect. 6.

2 Preprocessing Phase

Principal Component Analysis (PCA) used in the preprocessing phase is regarded as a data preprocessing module to transform initially highly dimensional input data into feature data of under dimensionality. PCA maximizes the ratio of the determinant of the class scatter matrix, and the within-class scatter matrix of projected samples of given data [19]. As the patterns often contain redundant information, we represent them to a feature space of under dimensionality with the intent of removing the existing redundancy. In this paper, we use the independent transformation that involves maximizing the ratio of overall variance to within-class variance. First, we calculate a global covariance matrix and within-class, two different fuzzification coefficients (m1 and m2) of FCM, and two learning rates (ηc and ηs), as well as two, attributes terms (αc and αc) for BP. The suggested network.

Principal Component Analysis (PCA) used in the preprocessing phase is regarded as a data preprocessing module to transform initially highly dimensional input data into feature data of under dimensionality. PCA maximizes the ratio of the determinant of the class scatter matrix, and the within-class scatter matrix of projected samples of given data. As the patterns often contain redundant information, we represent them to a feature space of under dimensionality with the intent of removing the existing redundancy. In this paper, we use the independent transformation that involves maximizing the ratio of overall variance to within-class variance. First, we calculate a global covariance matrix and within-class, two different fuzzification coefficients (m1 and m2) of FCM, and two learning rates (ηc and ηs), as well as two, attributes terms (αc and αc) for BP. The suggested network consists of three functional modules such as preprocessing, proposition, and inference phase.

Table 1. Classification rate of two classifiers

Classifier	C1 rate	C2 rate
2	98.00 (3)	99.00 (3)
3	100.0 (0)	100.0 (0)
4	99.33 (3)	99.0 (0)
5	99.0 (0)	100.0 (0)

The proposition phase of the suggested rule-based classifier is realized with the aid of parameter-variable FCM clustering methods to form type membership functions [36, 37]. In the conditioning phase, the coefficients of a linear function are updated employing the BP algorithm. Since the fuzzy neural network is learned by gradient descent method, the values of the learning rate and impetus are highly relevant to the quality of the resulting neural network. As the shape of the membership functions depends on the benefits of the fuzzification coefficient, a proper choice of this coefficient is important. We Calculate the covariance matrix, and within-class scatter matrix for the given data, where cs, N and Nc denote the number of classes, total data, and data of each class, respectively. m stands for the average value of entire class while mj indicates the average value of each class.

The fuzzification coefficient m1, while u2 is the Where cs, N and Nc denote the number of classes, total, data, and data of each class, respectively.

This feature vector XP is regarded as a new input to the fortified Offspring fuzzy neural network. Calculate the mean M and covariance C of input data, where wk denotes the feature vector (eigenvector). To obtain W, we have to select the feature vector corresponding to a phase eigenvalue and store it in the transformation matrix W.

The model output y^p is a fuzzy set. The output is defuzzified (decoded) by using the average of yp and yp.

Calculate the feature data XP using transformation matrix and input data this feature vector XP is regarded as a new input to the fortified Offspring fuzzy neural network.

3   The Architecture of Fortified Offspring FNN

The suggested Fortified Offspring fuzzy neural networks (FOFNN) classifier is used for each functional module.

$$\mu_{ij} = \frac{1}{\sum\limits_{k=1}^{N} \left(\frac{\|x_i - c_j\|}{\|x_i - c_k\|} \right)^{\frac{2}{m-1}}}. \tag{1}$$

- D presents data points.
- N presents clusters.
- m is a fuzzy matrix that shows the critical membership cluster.
- x_i is the ith item.
- c_j is the focus of the jth cluster.
- μ_{ij} is the membership degree of x_i in the jth cluster.
- Set the cluster membership, μ_{ij}.
- Compute the core cluster:

    Update μ_{ij}

$$J_m = \sum_{i=1}^{D} \sum_{j=1}^{N} \mu_{ij}^m \|x_i - c_j\|^2, \tag{2}$$

μ_{ij} = compute, J_m.

- Reiterate to reach a threshold.

    The result is calculated as

$$\text{Final Output} = \frac{\sum\limits_{i=1}^{N} w_i z_i}{\sum\limits_{i=1}^{N} w_i} \tag{3}$$

Principal Component Analysis (PCA) used in the preprocessing phase is considered as a pre-processing data component to transform initially highly dimensional input data into feature data of under dimensionality.

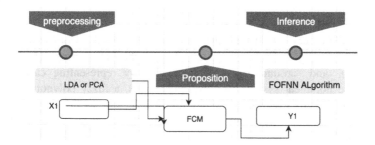

Fig. 1. The architecture of the fortified Offspring fuzzy neural networks classifier.

The architecture of the suggested classifier (Fig. 1) is represented through a collection of fuzzy rules coming in the following form.

$$\text{Rp: If x is } u^{\sim}i \text{ then } Y p = Cp + Cp\, x1 + Cp\, x2 + \cdots + Cp\, xn \tag{4}$$

where $ui(x)$ and $u^-i(x)$ are the bounds of the membership ratings of pattern x belonging to cluster vi, cp stands for the center (mean) of Cp and sp denote the spread of Cp. In the suggested classifier, the membership intervals are obtained from the membership ratings produced by the two FCM methods being realized for different values of the fuzzification coefficients.

The FCM algorithm [37] is a representative fuzzy clustering algorithm. It is used to split the data found in the input space into c fuzzy collections. The objective function Q guiding a formation of fuzzy clusters is expressed as a sum of the distances of data from the corresponding prototypes. In clustering, we assign patterns $xk \in X$ into c clusters, which are represented by their prototypes $vi \in Rn$, $1 \leq i \leq c$. The assignment to individual clusters is stated concerning phases. The minimization of Q is realized iteratively by adjusting both the prototypes and the entries of the membership matrix, that is we count the minimization task, min Q(U, v1, v2,..., vc). There are different crucial parameters of the FCM that affect the formed scores. These parameters include the number of clusters, the value of the fuzzification coefficient and a form of the distance function. As mentioned previously, FCM clustering is carried out for two values of m, say to m1 and m2. If the nonlinear labels have chosen to be f1(x), we obtained the over, and under bounds f1(x) and f1(x) series approach discussed previous, both of them are in the form of polynomials we use following fuzzy rules to interpret the modeling process:

$$\text{Rule 1 :   IF f1}(x)\text{is around f1}(x),$$
$$\text{THEN f1}(x) = \text{f1}(x),$$
$$\text{Rule 2 :   IF f1}(x)\text{ is around f1}(x),$$
$$\text{THEN f1}(x) = \text{f1}(x).$$

The membership functions are exploited to combine the fuzzy rules. To calculate the ratings of membership, we employ the following relations:

$$\text{f1}(x) = \mu M1(x)f$$

Where $\mu M1(x)$ and $\mu M2(x)$ are the ratings of membership corresponding to the fuzzy terms M1 and M2, respectively. In this case, the fuzzy terms M1 and M2 are "around f1(x)" and "around f1(x)", respectively. By representing each nonlinear labeling of the nonlinear system by polynomial terms, a fuzzy polynomial model is eventually established. It is worth mentioning that as long as the polynomial terms decreased to 1, the fuzzy polynomial model will turn out to be a T-S fuzzy model, which demonstrates that the fuzzy polynomial model has better chance to characterize the nonlinearity in the system than the T-S fuzzy model does. The overall form of the fuzzy model will be introduced in the following sections.

Denote the under and over ratings of membership overseen by their under and over membership functions, respectively.

$$\text{Rule j: IF x1}(t) \text{ THEN u}(t) = \text{Gjx}(t),$$

After combining all the fuzzy rules, we have constancy settings we have:

$$u(t) = m1G1x(t) + m2G2x(t).$$

Successively, to get membership functions into the stability conditions, No need for infinite stability conditions, we split the running domain Φ into L connected sub-domains, $\Phi l, l = 1, 2,..., L$ such that, the under and over bound of the IT2 membership function in the l-th subdomains, respectively, satisfying 0.

The membership functions are chosen as:

$$w2(x1) = 1 - w1(x1) - w3(x1), m1(x1) = \max(\min(1, (4.8 - x1)/10), 0), m1(x1)$$

Function max is to elite the leading element and min mean to elite the lightest one. The IT2 membership functions for the fuzzy model and fuzzy controller shown in Fig. 2: the bold and normal black curves are for w1(x1) and w1(x1); the bold and normal green curves are for w2(x1) and w2(x1); the bold and normal red curves are for w3(x1) and w3(x1); the bold and normal cyan curves are for m1(x1) and m1(x1); the bold and normal magenta curves are for m2(x1) and m2(x1).

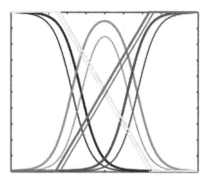

Fig. 2. Gradual membership function (Color figure online)

During the simulations, we set mp = 0.85 kg and Mc = 19 kg. 8 the number of the polynomial functions is 6 and the feedback gains have been achieved can be found in Table 1 and δij are 0.1366, 0.0408, 0.3403, 0.1501, 0.0698, 0.0874, 0.1119, 0.0738, respectively. The number of sub-domains is 10, and the order of the polynomial functions is 2 (Table 2).

Table 2. Polynomial function gains.

$h_{3,2,l}$	$k = 1$	$k = 2$	$k = 3$	$k = 4$
x_1^4	5.0251×10^{-8}	1.3316×10^{-4}	-2.4135×10^{-3}	-5.5157×10^{-4}
x_1^3	1.6670×10^{-6}	1.9714×10^{-3}	1.7446×10^{-2}	1.8813×10^{-2}
x_1^2	1.7135×10^{-5}	1.0296×10^{-2}	8.4027×10^{-4}	-2.4186×10^{-1}
	9.3061×10^{-5}	2.4812×10^{-2}	3.0593×10^{-2}	1.3900×10

4 The Optimization Process for Fortified Offspring Fuzzy Neural Network Classifier

The FCM utilize the data set in the input domain. Where function Q directing the creation of fuzzy clusters is articulated as a sum of the distances of data from the matching prototypes. There are several essential parameters of the FCM that affect the produced results. These parameters include the number of clusters, the value of the fuzzification coefficient and a form of the distance function. The fuzzification coefficient reveals a remarkable effect on the outline of the developed clusters. The frequently used value of m is equal to 2. As mentioned previously, FCM clustering is carried out for two values of m, say to m1 and m2.

The following step is using the artificial bee colony [11]. The idea of ABC algorithms tracks different bees as a phase of a big community and may contribute to the search cosmos. Commonly, three sets of bees are considered in the colony. They are commissioned bees, observers, and prospectors. As for ABC outline, it is assumed to have only one artificial commissioned bee for each feed supply. The position of a feed supply links to a feasible solution in the problem's solution space, and the fluid amount of a feed supply denotes the quality of the correlated answer. Every round in ABC entails three different steps: sending the commissioned bee onto their feed supplies and calculating their fluid amounts; after sharing the fluid information of feed supplies, the selection of feed supplies regions by the observers and assess the fluid quantity of the feed supplies; determining the prospector bees and then sending them arbitrarily onto potential new feed supplies. In general, the technique for the ABC algorithm for constant problems can be described as follows:

The initialization phase: The initial solutions are n-dimensional real vectors generated randomly. The active bee phase: Each commissioned bee is associated with a solution, and they apply a random modification (local search) on the solution (assigned feed supply) to find a new solution (new feed supply). As soon as the feed supply is found, it will be valued against former ones. If the fitness of the current approach is better than the former, the bee will forget the old feed supply and memorize the new one. Otherwise, she will keep applying modifications until the abandonment criterion is reached.

The onlooker bee phase: When all commissioned bees have completed their local search, they share the fluid information of their feed supply with the observers, each of whom will then select a feed supply in a probabilistic manner. The probability by which an onlooker bee will choose a feed supply is calculated by:

$$pi = \frac{fi}{\sum_{i-1}^{SN} fi} + 1 \qquad (5)$$

Where pi is the probability by which an onlooker chooses a feed supply I, SN is the total number of feed supplies, and fi is the fitness value of the feed supply i. The onlooker bees tend to choose the feed supplies with better fitness value (higher amount of fluid). The prospector bee phase: If the quality of a solution can't be promoted after a scheduled number of experiments, the feed supply is abandoned, and the corresponding commissioned bee becomes a prospector. This prospector will then produce a randomly generated feed supply. These steps are repeated until another termination status is fulfilled.

The main idea behind the ABC is about a population-based search in which bees representing possible solutions carry out a collective search by exchanging their findings while taking into account their previous knowledge and assessing it. ABC contains two challenging search tactics. First, the bees disregard their current knowledge and adjust their behavior according to the successful practice of bees occurring in their neighborhood. Second, the cognition aspect of the search underlines the importance of the bee's experience: the bees focus on its execution and makes adjustments accordingly. ABC is conceptually simple, easy to implement, and computationally efficient. The design framework of fortified Offspring fuzzy neural network classifier comprises the following steps. The input-output data are split into training and testing phase by 5-fcv. The training data is used to construct the suggested classifier. Next, testing takes place to evaluate the quality of the classifier. Successively determine the optimal parameters of the suggested classifier using ABC algorithm. As previously indicated, the parameters of the model, as well as its optimization environments such as the fuzzification coefficient of the FCM as well as the learning rate and the attributes label of the Back Propagation (BP) algorithm, are determined by using the ABC algorithm. Here a selection of the type of pre-processing data algorithm is completed, where a range is setting the real number between 0 and 1. For example, if the integer value is close to zero (a threshold 0.9 is set), PCA pre-processing phase. Otherwise, PCA is exploited to realize pre-processing of the input data.

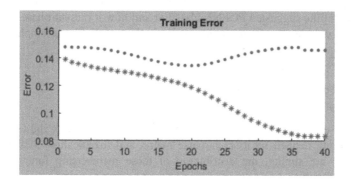

Fig. 3. Fuzzification coefficient rate during training phase

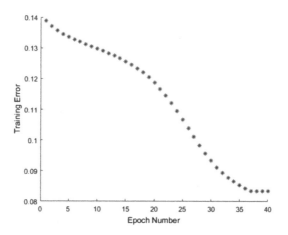

Fig. 4. Error rate during training phase

The number of feature vectors has an interval starting from two. The consequential fuzzification coefficient of the FCM clustering stands between 2.3 and 4.7. We composed classifier, then totaled the classification rate, so afterward that rate is used as the feed value of the objective function of ABC. When the threshold criterion has been achieved, the optimization procedure becomes absolute (Figs. 3 and 4).

5 Experimental Results

Experiments reported here involve two UCL datasets Iris, Balance, Heart, and Seeds data, where the execution of the suggested FOFNN classifier was evaluated and compared to the execution of other classifiers stated in the literature. To evaluate the classifiers, we use the classification rate of the classifier. Five, and the number of iterations of BP equals 300. The initial values of parameters of ABC employed. The best convergence appeared within many trials. Beginning with two-dimensional artificial examples waiting for the variables to converge using PCA. Here we show the classification of the suggested FOFNN classifier and how it present phase space of the collections of data involve 2 and 3 classes. Each class of the first example consists of 79 patterns:

If x is u~1 then y1r1 = 0.0061 + 0.0035x1 + 0.0056x2
If x is u~3 then y1 = −0.3487 + 0.8549x1 − 1.0231x2
If x is u~4 then y1 = 0.1229 − 1.1433x1 − 0.5397x2

for any other example, 80 patterns were revealed. In every group, the Gaussian distribution entirely defined by its covariance matrix and fuzzification coefficients (m1, m2, and m3) are similar, the distribution of those membership functions appears respectively (Fig. 5).

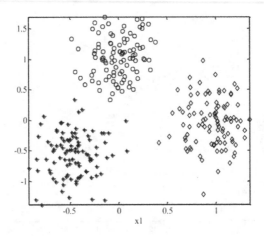

Fig. 5. Fuzzification coefficient distribution

Within the Iris data, the finest execution of the suggested classifier is 97.97% for the testing data. Both training and testing of FOFNN classifiers are improved. The experimental results of the Fortified Offspring FNN are improved. This emphasizes that using type-2 fuzzy set is used to classify iris data in comparison of the type-1 fuzzy set. Moreover, adding pre-processing techniques results in the decline of the dimensionality of input space. The overall results of testing data for Iris, Balance, Heart, and Seeds data is better than the execution of FNN and defined the 5-fcv test. Variables count establishing a phase in case of FNN is equal to the number of parameters enhanced by ABC equals 9 resulting from FOFNN.

6 Conclusion

This paper presented the fortified Offspring fuzzy neural networks (FOFNN) classifier established with the support of the pre-processing algorithm, FCM clustering, and the fuzzy inference using type-2 fuzzy sets. Before making the proposition phase of the suggested classifier, the pre-processing phase helped to decrease the dimensionality of the input domain aside from fostering the execution of the suggested network. For the proposition phase of the rules of the classifier, FCM clustering algorithm used with values of the fuzzification coefficient are measured to build the fuzzy set. The learning rate and the attributes are optimized using ABC algorithm. Numerous shapes of the membership function are devised based on the optimal fuzzification coefficients produced by the ABC, and We revealed a better execution of the suggested classifier assessed with previous existing classifiers. The suggested approach could be utilized in biometrics and recognition that involves uncertainty and bias. As future work, we want to shorten the learning function within a given rule.

References

1. Lippman, R.P.: An introduction to computing with neural nets. IEEE ASSP Mag. **4**, 4–22 (1981)
2. Mali, K., Mitra, S.: Symbolic classification, clustering and fuzzy radial basis function network. Fuzzy Sets Syst. **152**, 553–564 (2005)
3. Huang, W., Oh, S.-K., Pedrycz, W.: Design of Offspring radial basis function neural networks (HRBFNNs) realized with the aid of hybridization of fuzzy clustering method (FCM) and polynomial neural networks (PNNs). Neural Netw. **60**, 66–181 (2014)
4. Buckley, J.J., Hayashi, Y.: Fuzzy neural networks: a survey. Fuzzy Sets Syst. **66**, 1–13 (1994)
5. Gupta, M.M., Rao, D.H.: On the principles of fuzzy neural networks. Fuzzy Sets Syst. **61**(1), 1–18 (1994)
6. Zadeh, L.A.: Fuzzy sets. Inf. Control **8**, 338–353 (1965)
7. Zadeh, L.A.: Outline of a new approach to the analysis of complex systems and decision processes. IEEE Trans. Syst. Man Cybern. **3**, 28–44 (1973)
8. Zimmermann, H.-J.: Fuzzy Set Theory and Its Applications. Kluwer, Norwell (1996)
9. Lee, B.-K., Jeong, E.-H., Lee, S.-S.: Context-awareness healthcare for disease reasoning based on fuzzy logic. J. Electr. Eng. Technol. **11**(1), 247–256 (2016)
10. Nguyen, D.D., Ngo, L.T., Pham, L.T., Pedrycz, W.: Towards Offspring clustering approach to data classification: multiple kernels based interval-valued Fuzzy C-Means algorithm. Fuzzy Sets Syst. **279**(1), 17–39 (2015)
11. Karaboga, D., Akay, B.: Artificial bee colony (ABC), harmony search and bees algorithms on numerical optimization. In: 2009 Innovative Production Machines and Systems Virtual Conference (2009)

12. Wu, G.D., Zhu, Z.W.: An enhanced discriminability recurrent fuzzy neural network for temporal classification problems. Fuzzy Sets Syst. **237**(1), 47–62 (2014)
13. Karnik, N.N., Mendel, J.M.: Operations on type-2 fuzzy sets. Fuzzy Sets Syst. **122**(2), 327–348 (2001)
14. Runkler, T., Coupland, S., John, R.: Type-2 fuzzy decision making. Int. J. Approx. Reason. **80**, 217–224 (2017)
15. Dash, R., Dash, P.K., Bisoi, R.: A differential harmony search based Offspring interval type2 fuzzy EGARCH model for stock market volatility prediction. Int. J. Approx. Reason. **59**, 81–104 (2015)
16. Karnik, N.N., Mendel, J.M.: Centroid of a type-2 fuzzy set. Inf. Sci. **132**, 195–220 (2001)
17. Livi, L., Tahayori, H., Rizzi, A., Sadeghian, A., Pedrycz, W.: Classification of type-2 fuzzy sets represented as sequences of vertical slices. IEEE Trans. Fuzzy Syst. **24**(5), 1022–1034 (2016)
18. Ekong, U., et al.: Classification of epilepsy seizure phase using type-2 fuzzy support vector machines. Neurocomputing **199**, 66–76 (2016)
19. Salazar, O., Soriano, J.: Convex combination and its application to fuzzy sets and interval-valued fuzzy sets II. Appl. Math. Sci. **9**(22), 1069–1076 (2015)
20. Hwang, C., Rhee, F.: Uncertain fuzzy clustering: the type-2 fuzzy approach to C-Means. IEEE Trans. Fuzzy Syst. **15**(1), 107–120 (2007)
21. Rhee, F.: Uncertain fuzzy clustering: insights and recommendations. IEEE Comput. Intell. Mag. **2**(1), 44–56 (2007)
22. McLachlan, G.J.: Discriminant Analysis and Statistical Pattern Recognition. Wiley-Interscience, Hoboken (2004)
23. Jolliffe, I.T.: Principal Component Analysis. Springer, New York (2002). https://doi.org/10.1007/b98835
24. Daqi, G., Jun, D., Changming, Z.: Integrated Fisher linear discriminants: an empirical study. Pattern Recogn. **47**(2), 789–805 (2014)
25. Li, L., Qiao, Z., Liu, Y., Chen, Y.: A convergent smoothing algorithm for training max-min fuzzy neural networks. Neurocomputing **260**, 404–410 (2017)
26. Lin, C.-M., Le, T.-L., Huynh, T.-T.: Self-evolving function-link type-2 fuzzy neural network for nonlinear system identification and control. Neurocomputing **275**, 2239–2250 (2018)
27. Wu, D., Mendel, J.M.: Enhanced Karnik–Mendel algorithm for type-2 fuzzy sets and systems. In: Fuzzy Information Processing Society, pp. 184–189 (2007)
28. Mendel, J.M.: Introduction to Rule-Based Fuzzy Logic System. Prentice-Hall, Upper Saddle River (2001)
29. Kennedy, J., Eberhart, R.: Phase swarm optimization. In: Proceedings of the IEEE International Conference on Neural Networks IV, pp. 1942–1948 (1995)
30. Liu, F., Mendel, J.M.: Aggregation using the fuzzy weighted average, as calculated by the KM algorithms. IEEE Trans. Fuzzy Syst. **16**, 1–12 (2008)
31. Oh, S.-K., Kim, W.-D., Pedrycz, W., Park, B.-J.: Polynomial-based radial basis function neural networks (P-RBF NNs) realized with the aid of phase swarm optimization. Fuzzy Sets Syst. **163**(1), 54–77 (2011)
32. Weka. http://www.cs.waikato.ac.nz/ml/weka/
33. Vapnik, V.: The Nature of Statistical Learning Theory. Springer, New York (1995). https://doi.org/10.1007/978-1-4757-2440-0
34. Tipping, M.E.: The relevance vector machine. Adv. Neural. Inf. Process. Syst. **12**, 652–658 (2000)
35. Yang, Z.R.: A novel radial basis function neural network for discriminant analysis. IEEE Trans. Neural Netw. **17**(3), 604–612 (2006)

36. Tahir, M.A., Bouridane, A., Kurugollu, F.: Simultaneous feature selection and feature weighting using Offspring Tabu Search/K-nearest neighbor classifier. Pattern Recogn. Lett. **28**(4), 438–446 (2007)
37. Mei, J.P., Chen, L.: Fuzzy clustering with weighted medoids for relational data. Pattern Recogn. **43**(5), 1964–1974 (2010)
38. Oh, S.K., Kim, W.-D., Pedrycz, W.: Design of radial basis function neural network classifier realized with the aid of data preprocessing techniques: design and analysis. Int. J. Gen. Syst. **45**(4), 434–454 (2016)
39. Ulu, C., Guzelkaya, M., Eksin, I.: A closed-form type reduction method for piece wise linear type-2 fuzzy sets. Int. J. Approx. Reason. **54**, 1421–1433 (2013)
40. Chen, Y., Wang, D., Tong, S.: Forecasting studies by designing Mamdani type-2 fuzzy logic systems: with the combination of BP algorithms and KM algorithms. Neurocomputing **174** (Phase B), 1133–1146 (2016)
41. Qiao, J.-F., Hou, Y., Zhang, L., Han, H.-G.: Adaptive fuzzy neural network control of wastewater treatment process with a multiobjective operation. Neurocomputing **275**, 383–393 (2018)
42. Han, H.-G., Lin, Z.-L., Qiao, J.-F.: Modeling of nonlinear systems using the self-organizing fuzzy neural network with adaptive gradient algorithm. Neurocomputing **266**, 566–578 (2017)
43. Lu, X., Zhao, Y., Liu, M.: Self-learning type-2 fuzzy neural network controllers for trajectory control of a Delta parallel robot. Neurocomputing **283**, 107–119 (2018)

Forecasting Value at Risk of Foreign Exchange Rate by Integrating Geometric Brownian Motion

Siti Noorfaera Karim and Maheran Mohd Jaffar[(⊠)]

Faculty of Computer and Mathematical Sciences, Universiti Teknologi MARA, Shah Alam, Selangor Darul Ehsan, Malaysia
maheran@tmsk.uitm.edu.my

Abstract. Foreign exchange is one of the most important financial assets for all countries around the world including Malaysia. After recovering from the Asian financial crisis, Malaysia tried to build a strong currency in order to maintain the economic performance. The study focuses on Malaysia foreign exchange rate and foreign exchange risk between ten currencies, which are CNY, SGD, JPY, EUR, USD, THB, KRW, IDR, TWD and AUD. Unpredictability of the foreign exchange rate makes the traders hard to forecast the future rate and the future risk. The study implements the parametric approach in the Value at Risk (VaR) method and the geometric Brownian motion (GBM) model. The objectives of the study are to integrate the VaR model with the GBM model in order to compute or forecast the VaR. By using parametric approach, the study successfully computes the VaR of foreign exchange rate for different confidence levels. The GBM model is suitable to forecast the foreign exchange rate accurately using less than one year input data and using the log volatility formula. Lastly, the study verifies the feasibility of the integrated model for a one month holding period using the data shifting technique. In conclusion, the prediction of future foreign exchange rate and foreign exchange risk is important in order to know the performance of a country and to make better decision on investment.

Keywords: Forecasting · Foreign exchange rate · Parametric approach
Value at risk · Geometric Brownian motion

1 Introduction

The near-breakdown of the European Exchange Rate Mechanism in 1992–1993, the Latin American Tequila Crisis following Mexico's peso devaluation in 1994–1995 and the Asian financial crisis in 1997–1998 were several episodes of currency turmoil in 1990s [1]. In view of Asian's currency turmoil, Thailand, Korea, Indonesia and also Malaysia were among the countries that were affected. A strong currency is able to form a shield against any possible problem with the economy of a country.

Malaysia Ringgit denoted as MYR is the national currency of Malaysia federation. The three letter system of codes in ISO 4217 is introduced by the international organization for standardization to define the currency [2]. Besides that, currency trades in

© Springer Nature Singapore Pte Ltd. 2019
B. W. Yap et al. (Eds.): SCDS 2018, CCIS 937, pp. 186–198, 2019.
https://doi.org/10.1007/978-981-13-3441-2_15

pairs, therefore, Malaysia deals a lot with China, Singapore, Japan, European Union, United States, Thailand, Korea, Indonesia, Taiwan and Australia [3]. Foreign exchange rate is the monetary value of one currency in terms of another currency. Foreign exchange rate has become more volatile during the past decades. It also gives big influence on the whole economy and the country itself. Foreign exchange transaction nowadays involves greater foreign exchange risk.

According to [4], the foreign exchange risk refers to the risk that the value of trading return may change due to the fluctuation of exchange rate. It can occur because of the international obligations span time between the day of transactions and payment. Value at risk (VaR) is the most popular method in the risk management department. VaR can simply be defined as a measure of potential loss of some risk value associated with the general market movements over a defined period of time with a given confidence interval.

One of the earliest past researches in VaR of exchange rates was by [5] that examined the model of conditional autoregressive VaR (CAViaR) that was proposed by [6]. A study [7] states the risk value for currency market can be predicted by using the variance covariance model. It concludes that the proposed model is approved of its accuracy in valuation the risk of the forex market. Nevertheless, VaR is essential and most of the models calculate the VaR for the current time. Hence, to be able to forecast the VaR accurately can lead to better decisions.

In this study, the focus is on the VaR method using parametric approach. The objectives of this study are to integrate the VaR model with the GBM model in order to compute the VaR for currencies for different confidence levels, to forecast the foreign exchange rate, for example, between CNY, SGD, JPY, EUR, USD, THB, KRW, IDR, TWD and AUD with MYR using GBM model and to identify the feasibility of the integrated VaR model with the GBM model.

2   Mathematical Models

Parametric and non-parametric models are the most common model in VaR method. The study applies the parametric model based on statistical parameter of the risk factor distribution. This model considers the rate of returns of foreign exchange rate as the risk factor that follows a normal distribution curve as in Eq. (1) below [8–10]:

$$v = AS(\mu \delta t - \sigma \delta t^{\frac{1}{2}} \cdot \alpha(1 - c)). \tag{1}$$

Based on the above VaR model, the terms A and S are the number of portfolios and the foreign exchange rate respectively. It is followed by the terms

$$\mu \delta t - \sigma \delta t^{\frac{1}{2}} \alpha(1 - c).$$

The quantity $\mu \delta t$ refers to the average annual return μ of the foreign exchange rate with the timestep δt is equal to 1/252. The quantity σ in the term $\sigma \delta t^{\frac{1}{2}}$ is the standard deviation with timestep $\delta t^{\frac{1}{2}}$. The last term $\alpha(1 - c)$ is the value of quartiles of the standard normal variable in a given confidence level c as in Table 1.

Table 1. The value of lower quartile of normal distribution

C	$\alpha(1 - c)$
99.9%	−3.090
99%	−2.326
97.5%	−1.960
95%	−1.645
90%	−1.282

Source: [11]

The study computes the VaR on foreign exchange rate using the above parameters.

From the historical data, the relative daily return of the ith day, R_i is computed using equation below [9, 11]:

$$R_i = \frac{S_{i+1} - S_i}{S_i} \tag{2}$$

where S_i is the foreign exchange rate on the ith day. Then, the values of the average daily return $\mu\delta t$ are calculated using equation as below [10, 11, 15]:

$$\mu\delta t = \overline{R} = \frac{1}{M}\sum_{i=1}^{M} R_i \tag{3}$$

where M is the number of foreign exchange rate return. Then, the standard deviation of daily return $\sigma\delta t^{\frac{1}{2}}$ is calculated based on

$$\sigma\delta t^{\frac{1}{2}} = \sqrt{\frac{1}{(M-1)}\sum_{i=1}^{M}((\log S_i - \log S_{i-1})^2}. \tag{4}$$

The quantity σ is the log volatility.

Equations (3) and (4) are used to calculate the VaR in Eq. (1). By using Eq. (1), the VaR is calculated for one day holding period $v(1)$ for five different confidences. In order to compute the future VaR in foreign exchange trading, the study focused on using the historical data and the foreign exchange rate Malaysia Ringgit was chosen as the domestic currency. The study [13] focused on secondary data that was obtained from the session at 12.00 pm and used the middle rate of data. The data had information on the foreign exchange rate among various countries.

VaR can also be calculated using the root function $v(h)$ as below [14]:

$$v(h) = v(1) \cdot \sqrt{h} \tag{5}$$

where h is equal to the number of the holding period.

This study proposes to forecast VaR by using the forecast foreign exchange rate. In order to find the forecast value of the foreign exchange rate, the equation of the log normal random walk is used [8, 9, 11, 12] as follows:

$$S(t) = S(0) \, e^{[\mu - \frac{1}{2}\sigma^2]t + \sigma(x(t) - x(0))} \tag{6}$$

where $S(0)$ is actual foreign exchange rate at $t = 0$, μ is equal to drift, σ is equal to volatility, t is equal to timestep and $x(t)$ is equal to the random number at time t.

Here, the study integrates VaR model with GBM model. It substitutes Eq. (6) into (1) with $A = 1$. An integrated VaR is

$$v(t) = A \big(S(0) \, e^{[\mu - \frac{1}{2}\sigma^2]t + \sigma(x(t) - x(0))} \big) \cdot \big(\mu \delta t - \sigma \delta t^{\frac{1}{2}} \cdot \alpha(1 - c) \big) \tag{7}$$

where the forecast foreign exchange rate is used in order to forecast the VaR accurately.

In order to verify this model, the study compared both values of VaR calculated using the forecast and the actual foreign exchange rate by using the mean absolute percentage error (MAPE) as a model of accuracy in Eq. (8) [11]:

$$E = \sum_{t=1}^{n} \frac{\left| \left(\frac{e_t}{y_t} \right) * 100 \right|}{n} \tag{8}$$

where n is the effective data points and $\left| \left(\frac{e_t}{y_t} \right) * 100 \right|$ is the absolute percentage error with, $e_t = y_t - \hat{y}_t$, y_t is the actual value and $\hat{y}_t$ is the forecast value. In order to judge the accuracy of the model, a scale based on the MAPE measure was used as in Table 2.

Table 2. A scale of judgement of forecast accuracy.

MAPE	Judgement of forecast accuracy
Less than 10%	Highly accurate
11% to 20%	Good forecast
21% to 50%	Reasonable forecast
51% or more	Inaccurate forecast

Source: [11]

Therefore the study compares the VaR of the historical data and the VaR of forecast foreign exchange rates.

3 Methodology

The integrated model of VaR and GBM that produces Eq. (8) can be verified by using the foreign exchange rate data.

3.1 Data Collection

There are many currencies in the world, but in this study only eleven currencies were selected. The countries that had been chosen were Malaysia (MYR), China (CNY), Singapore (SGD), Japan (JPY), European Union (EUR), United State (USD), Thailand (THB), Korea (KRW), Indonesia (IDR), Taiwan (TWD) and Australia (AUD). These are the countries that deal regularly with Malaysia in international trading, investment and others [15, 16].

In order to calculate the VaR and forecast the foreign exchange rate, the rates that had been chosen are Malaysia Ringgit as the domestic currency. The study focused on secondary data because it was more reliable than other sources. The data were obtained from [13] that had provided three sessions of data which were taken at 9.00 am, 12.00 pm and 5.00 pm. There are slight differences of foreign exchange rates between the three sessions. It also provided three different types of rate, which were buying rate, middle rate and selling rate. The study focused on the session at 12.00 pm and used the middle rate of data. According to the interview with the senior executive of foreign exchange at Bank Negara Malaysia, the session at 12.00 pm is the most active trading time in Malaysian market.

In this study, the data were obtained from 2nd May 2013 until 27th August 2014. All the historical data within the covered period was used to calculate the VaR. For the forecast foreign exchange rate, data from 2nd May 2013 until 30th May 2014 was considered as input data that was used to generate initial forecasts. Data from 2nd June 2014 until 27th August 2014 was used as comparison with forecasting values. From the historical data, the study analyzed its characteristic and performance for each currency.

3.2 Computation of Value at Risk Using Parametric Approach

In order to analyze the risk in foreign exchange rate, the VaR using the parametric approach was selected. The VaR measures were expressed in terms of currency, which is Ringgit Malaysia (RM). The probability of maximum loss is usually about 10% and it depends on the degree of choosing confidence level. The degrees of the confidence level of this stage are 99.9%, 99%, 97.5%, 95% and 90%.

Firstly, the study used one day VaR as the holding period and thirteen months historical data to calculate the VaR. The VaR today can be calculated using the previous historical data. Then, the study calculated the average of VaR from the 90% until 99.9% confidence level. The currency is ranked in decreasing order to identify the most risky country in foreign exchange trading pairs. Secondly, the study analyzed and compared the VaR for different holding periods. The chosen holding periods are 1-day,

5-days, 20-days, 40-days and 60-days with the fixed confidence level of 99%. The study calculated the VaR by shifting the 13 months historical data usage using Eq. (1). It shifted the historical data usage by 5, 20, 40 and 60 days in order to calculate VaR today for the next 5, 20, 40 and 60 days respectively, and the results were compared with the VaR calculation using the root function (5).

3.3 Identify the Feasibility of Integrated Value at Risk Model with the Geometric Brownian Motion Model

At this stage, the aim was to measure the feasibility of integrating VaR model with GBM model. The VaR model for foreign exchange rate was calculated using (1). The VaR calculation method by shifting the historical data was selected. The VaR was calculated using a confidence level of 99% and different holding periods that are 1-day, 5-days, 20-days, 40-days and 60-days. Therefore, the study compared the VaR that uses totally historical data (HD) and the VaR from mixed data with the GBM forecast rate. The model of accuracy, MAPE in (8) was selected and the result was analyzed based on Table 2.

4 Results and Discussion

4.1 Analysis of Data

It was found that the most volatile currency was AUD and the less volatile was KRW. This could be shown from the value of R^2 and movement of the currencies itself. The upward movement of the currencies means that the currency is depreciating while the downward movement means that the currency becomes a little stronger currency. The movement of the foreign exchange rates affects the daily profit and loss. IDR had shown a different pattern of daily returns from the other currencies. The daily returns produced were equal for certain dates. The normal distribution of daily returns produced did not provide a right fit to the foreign exchange data, but at the same time it still maintained the bell shape curve. All currencies produced the short and wide curve since the value of standard deviation is large within the covered period.

4.2 Value at Risk Using the Parametric Approach

Parametric approach is the simplest and convenient method to compute the VaR. The study applied the value of lower quartiles of the normal distribution of returns to calculate VaR of the foreign exchange rates. The study compute the 1-day VaR using Eq. (1) for five confidence levels, which are 90%, 95%, 97.5%, 99% and 99.9%. All the steps were repeated in order to calculate the VaR for SGD, JPY, EUR, USD, THB, KRW, IDR, TWD and AUD and rank them. The result is shown in Table 3.

Table 3. VaR of 1-day holding period

Currency	VaR of 1-day holding period (RM)						
	Confidence levels						
	90%	95%	97.5%	99%	99.9%	Average	Rank
CNY	0.0032	0.0040	0.0048	0.0057	0.0075	0.0050	6
SGD	0.0107	0.0136	0.0162	0.0191	0.0253	0.0170	10
JPY	0.0298	0.0382	0.0455	0.0540	0.0717	0.0478	1
EUR	0.0295	0.0375	0.0444	0.0524	0.0691	0.0466	4
USD	0.0201	0.0257	0.0305	0.0360	0.0476	0.0320	5
THB	0.0460	0.0596	0.0714	0.0852	0.1138	0.0752	9
KRW	0.0017	0.0022	0.0026	0.0030	0.0040	0.0027	7
IDR	0.0002	0.0002	0.0003	0.0004	0.0005	0.0003	3
TWD	0.0573	0.0731	0.0868	0.1027	0.1360	0.0912	8
AUD	0.0225	0.0290	0.0346	0.0412	0.0548	0.0364	2

Table 3 shows the results of VaR for all currencies. Here, there exists a linear relationship between VaR and confidence levels. The largest confidence level within the period will produce the largest VaR. Moreover, the VaR for all currencies show a rapid growth of the movement between 99% and 99.9% confidence levels. Overall, the changes in VaR with respect to the change in the confidence levels are the same for all the foreign exchange rate at any time t. The study also ranks the currencies from larger to smaller risk in order to know the risky currency. The most risky currency within the covered period is JPY. Then, followed by the AUD, IDR, EUR, USD, CNY, KRW, TWD, THB and SGD. Based on the average of VaR the study ranked the currencies from larger to smaller risk in order to know the risky currency. Table 4 shows the currency rank.

Table 4. Currency rank

Rank	Currency	Initial portfolio (RM), y	Average VaR (RM), x	$\frac{x}{y} \times 100\%$ Percentage VaR
1	JPY	3.1655	0.0478	1.51
2	AUD	2.9954	0.0364	1.22
3	IDR	0.0277	0.0003	1.08
4	EUR	4.3737	0.0466	1.07
5	USD	3.2150	0.0320	0.99
6	CNY	0.5150	0.0050	0.98
7	KRW	0.3150	0.0027	0.86
8	TWD	10.7217	0.0912	0.85
9	THB	9.8078	0.0752	0.77
10	SGD	2.5624	0.0170	0.66

Even though, the JPY is a more risky currency, Japan was still on the top three of Malaysian trading partners due to the demand and supply of certain products at that time.

Then, the study computes the VaR for different holding periods. From the model of parametric approach in (1), the study calculated the 1 day of VaR, $v(1)$. It shifted the historical data usage by 5, 20, 40 and 60 days in order to calculate VaR for the next 5, 20, 40 and 60 days respectively. The VaR using shifted historical data, HD and VaR using root function (RF) are calculated using Eqs. (1) and (5) respectively.

From the results of the MAPE, the large value of error and the study concludes that the RF model in (5) for different holding periods is inaccurate forecast for foreign exchange rate for both confidence levels. Besides that, the study finds that VaR of HD and RF is not close to each other for both confidence levels. It found that the graph of VaR using the HD method is smooth for the 95% and 99% confidence level for all currencies. In conclusion, the VaR calculate using HD is more reliable in order to obtain the actual VaR in the real situation. In the real situation, the VaR depends on the fluctuation of the foreign exchange rate. The VaR that is computed from Eq. (5) is only for 1-day holding period because the square root rule is very unreliable over a longer horizon for the foreign exchange rates. The VaR from the parametric approach with the shifted data decreases as holding period increases. The VaR using the root function by [20] increases with the increasing holding period. Therefore, RF model does not portray the real situation of risk on a definite holding period.

4.3   Future Foreign Exchange Rate Using the Geometric Brownian Motion Model

GBM model is a model of time series data that deals with the randomness. Based on the assumption of GBM model, the randomness of the data must be normally distributed in order to get accurate forecast value. The study assumes that the length of input data gives the different value of accuracy. The study found that the value of MAPE for ten currencies with 13 observations is less than 5%. The MAPE of GBM model is highly accurate for all observations. The time span for forecast value was less than one year and highly accurate for the initial three months. Although the result produced was highly accurate for all observations, the study must obtain the best of duration of daily data used in getting the most accurate forecast. The result of best duration of daily data for each currency is shown in Table 4. The MAPE accuracy model produces almost the same results of the best durations.

Based on Table 5, the duration of observation may be different among the ten currencies. The best duration of observations to forecast CNY is to use 6 months observations, SGD and TWD use 5 months observations, JPY and KRW use 1 month observation, EUR, USD and AUD use 2 months observations, IDR was 3 months observations and lastly the longest observations is 12 months for THB. Table 6 shows the forecast foreign rate for the currencies using the best durations for CNY, SGD, JPY, EUR and USD.

Table 5. The best duration of observations

Currency	Duration (Months)	Average MAPE	Log volatility
CNY	6	0.7776	0.0219
SGD	5	0.6053	0.0143
JPY	1	1.1797	0.0268
EUR	2	0.9951	0.0257
USD	2	0.8928	0.0211
THB	12	1.6522	0.0238
KRW	1	0.8493	0.0175
IDR	3	1.5325	0.0298
TWD	5	0.7406	0.0175
AUD	2	1.1250	0.0250

Table 6. The forecast value of foreign exchange rate using the best durations of CNY, SGD, JPY, EUR and USD

Date	CNY		SGD		JPY		EUR		USD	
	Actual	Forecast	Actual	Forecast	Actual	Forecast	Actual	Forecast	Actual	Forecast
2/6	0.5159	0.5221	2.5668	2.5553	3.1597	3.1742	4.3933	4.3993	3.2235	3.1872
3/6	0.5168	0.5200	2.5703	2.5609	3.1522	3.2010	4.3912	4.3383	3.2280	3.1771
4/6	0.5169	0.5226	2.5701	2.5667	3.1468	3.1930	4.4014	4.3828	3.2335	3.2169
5/6	0.5169	0.5210	2.5714	2.5654	3.1525	3.1481	4.3962	4.3874	3.2330	3.1858
6/6	0.5155	0.5179	2.5712	2.5851	3.1485	3.1465	4.4013	4.3823	3.2220	3.2100
9/6	0.5125	0.5232	2.5563	2.5570	3.1183	3.1313	4.3628	4.3855	3.1975	3.1932
10/6	0.5137	0.5213	2.5602	2.5733	3.1288	3.1932	4.3518	4.3612	3.2020	3.1967
11/6	0.5144	0.5157	2.5626	2.5825	3.1325	3.1786	4.3355	4.2925	3.2035	3.2060
.	.	.	.	.	.	.	.	.	.	.
.	.	.	.	.	.	.	.	.	.	.
19/8	0.5138	0.5160	2.5346	2.5525	3.0728	3.1388	4.2115	4.1851	3.1528	3.1581
20/8	0.5155	0.5110	2.5383	2.5466	3.0707	3.0697	4.2160	4.2391	3.1685	3.1200
21/8	0.5159	0.5158	2.5346	2.5523	3.0536	3.0729	4.2021	4.2459	3.1725	3.1520
22/8	0.5136	0.5081	2.5336	2.5716	3.0487	3.0969	4.2029	4.2179	3.1635	3.1322
25/8	0.5150	0.5120	2.5324	2.5370	3.0397	3.1056	4.1833	4.2544	3.1680	3.1519
26/8	0.5140	0.5175	2.5295	2.5694	3.0448	3.1124	4.1758	4.2570	3.1625	3.1478
27/8	0.5128	0.5102	2.5248	2.5482	3.0323	3.0848	4.1493	4.2548	3.1525	3.1572

4.4 Feasibility of Integrated Value at Risk Model with Geometric Brownian Motion Model

This study integrates VaR model with the GBM model in order to forecast the VaR. It means that the study calculates the VaR from the distribution of returns that includes the GBM forecast foreign exchange rate. All the steps to compute the VaR is similar for VaR using HD, but now, the data usage includes the forecast GBM foreign exchange rate.

In this section, the study uses confidence level of 99% with the holding period of 1-day, 5-days, 20-days, 40-days and 60-days. The historical data used from 2nd May 2013 to 27th August 2014 while the use of forecast GBM foreign exchange rates were from 2nd June 2014 until 27th August 2014. The steps of integrating the VaR with GBM model are shown in Fig. 1.

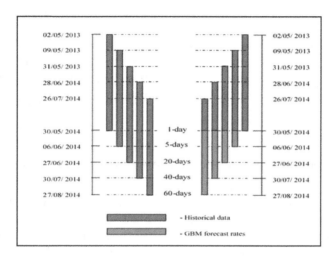

Fig. 1. Historical data for GBM forecast

There are two non-working days in a week. Hence, 5-days, 20-days, 40-days, and 60-days of the holding periods mean a duration on 1 week, 1 month, 2 months, and 3 months respectively. Based on the Fig. 1, the overall historical data used to calculate VaR was from 2nd May 2013 until 27th August 2014. The historical data used to calculate 1-day VaR was from 2nd May 2013 until 30th May 2014. For 5-days VaR, the historical data used was from 9th May 2013 until 6th June 2014. Then, for 20-days VaR was from 31st May 2013 until 27th June 2014. Followed by the 40-days VaR was from 28th June 2013 until 30th July 2014. Lastly, 60-days VaR was from 26th July 2013 until 27th August 2014.

The study compares the VaR using actual historical data and the VaR that integrates the forecast GBM foreign exchange rate in Eq. (7). The MAPE is used to determine the accuracy of the forecast VaR model. Tables 7, 8 and 9 show the results of VaR using actual and forecast exchange rates of 10 currencies with the error values.

Based on Tables 7, 8 and 9, the MAPE of VaR with GBM increases proportionally with the holding periods. The VaR with HD decreases while the VaR with GBM increases within the holding period. The 1-day VaR is the same for both the actual and the forecast exchange rate because both use the same value of the initial exchange rate. The 5-days and 20-days VaR produce highly accurate forecast, which are 3% and 9% respectively. For 40-day VaR and 60-days VaR, the study concludes that VaR with GBM are reasonable forecast. The movement of VaR with GBM is close for the 1-day,

5-days and 20-days holding period than after that the forecast VaR diverges from the VaR that uses HD.

Table 7. VaR using actual and forecast exchange rates of CNY, SGD, JPY and EUR

	CNY			SGD			JPY			EUR		
	Actual	F'cast	E%	Actual	F'cast	E%	Actual	F'cast	E%	Actual	F'cast	E%
1-day	0.0057	0.0057	0	0.0191	0.0191	0	0.0540	0.0540	0	0.0524	0.0524	0
5-days	0.0054	0.0056	3	0.0176	0.0180	2	0.0515	0.0532	3	0.0511	0.0522	2
20-days	0.0053	0.0057	9	0.0171	0.0189	10	0.0502	0.0549	9	0.0496	0.0583	18
40-days	0.0050	0.0066	34	0.0163	0.0210	29	0.0436	0.0522	20	0.0454	0.0580	28
60-days	0.0049	0.0073	49	0.0156	0.0228	46	0.0410	0.0556	36	0.0410	0.0616	50

F'cast – Forecast E – MAPE

Table 8. VaR using actual and forecast exchange rates of USD, THB, KRW and IDR

	USD			THB			KRW			IDR		
	Actual	F'cast	E%	Actual	F'cast	E%	Actual	F'cast	E%	Actual	F'cast	E%
1-day	0.0360	0.0360	0	0.0852	0.0852	0	0.0030	0.0030	0	0.0004	0.0004	0
5-days	0.0344	0.0356	3	0.0793	0.0827	4	0.0029	0.0031	6	0.0003	0.0004	5
20-days	0.0334	0.0358	7	0.0777	0.0959	23	0.0029	0.0031	9	0.0003	0.0004	17
40-days	0.0314	0.0377	20	0.0730	0.1031	41	0.0028	0.0035	26	0.0003	0.0004	21
60-days	0.0304	0.0399	31	0.0713	0.1223	71	0.0026	0.0036	36	0.0003	0.0005	40

F'cast – Forecast E – MAPE

Table 9. VaR using actual and forecast exchange rates of TWD and AUD

	TWD			AUD		
	Actual	F'cast	E%	Actual	F'cast	E%
1-day	0.1027	0.1027	0	0.0412	0.0412	0
5-day	0.0962	0.1004	4	0.0405	0.0422	4
20-days	0.0955	0.1064	11	0.0398	0.0425	7
40-days	0.0907	0.1109	22	0.0372	0.0435	17
60-days	0.0886	0.1187	34	0.0346	0.0455	31

F'cast – Forecast E – MAPE

5 Conclusion and Recommendation

The use of input data can affect the forecast values and in forecasting the foreign exchange rate, the duration of input data is determined for each of the considered currencies. There are currencies that are sharing the best duration of input data. The best duration of input data chosen is based on the lowest MAPE.

The study is able to forecast VaR for one month holding period for most of the country currencies. The VaR using forecast exchange rate is closer to the VaR using HD due to the better forecasting GBM model in currency. Each currency had produced different accuracy of MAPE since the VaR was depending on their foreign exchange rate.

The prediction of the future foreign exchange rate is important in order to know the future performance of the country and to be able to manage the foreign exchange risk in trading. As a developing country, Malaysia must be able to manage the foreign exchange risk.

It is recommended to use other VaR models and other forecasting model [15] in calculating the foreign exchange. In order to hedge the foreign exchange risk, the study recommends doing a swap currency and this needs more quantitative research in swap derivatives.

Acknowledgement. This study is partially funded by the Fundamental Research Grant Scheme (FRGS), Ministry of Higher Education Malaysia that is managed by the Research Management Centre (RMC), IRMI, Universiti Teknologi MARA, 600-IRMI/FRGS 5/3 (83/2016).

References

1. Pesenti, P.A., Tille, C.: The economics of currency crises and contagion: an introduction. Econ. Policy Rev. **6**(3), 3–16 (2000)
2. Gotthelf, P.: Currency Trading: How to Access and Trade the World's Biggest Market. Wiley, Mississauga (2003)
3. Department of Statistics Malaysia Homepage. http://www.statistics.gov.my/main/main.php. Accessed 28 Aug 2014
4. Jorion, P.: Value at Risk: The New Benchmark for Managing Financial Risk, 2nd edn. McGraw-Hill International Edition, New York City (2002)
5. Duda, M., Schmidt, H.: Evaluation of various approaches to Value at Risk: empirical check. Master thesis, Lund University, Sweden (2009)
6. Engle, R.F., Manganelli, S.: CAViaR: Conditional autoregressive Value at Risk by regression quartiles. J. Bus. Econ. Stat. **22**(4), 367–381 (2004)
7. Aniūnas, P., Nedzveckas, J., Krušinskas, R.: Variance-covariance risk value model for currency market. Eng. Econ.: Econ. Eng. Decis. **1**(61), 18–27 (2009)
8. Wilmott, P.: Introduces Quantitative Finance, 2nd edn. Wiley, Chichester (2007)
9. Abdul Hafiz, Z., Maheran, M.J.: Forecasting value at risk of unit trust portfolio by adapting geometric Brownian motion. Jurnal Kalam. Jurnal Karya Asli Lorekan Ahli Matematik **9**(2), 24–36 (2016)
10. Aslinda, A.: Estimating Value at Risk of stock exchange and unit trust by using variance covariance method. Master thesis of M.Sc. (Applied Mathematics). Universiti Teknologi MARA, Malaysia (2018)
11. Siti Nazifah, Z.A., Maheran, M.J.: Forecasting share prices of small size companies in Bursa Malaysia using geometric Brownian motion. Appl. Math. Inf. Sci. **8**(1), 107–112 (2014)
12. Nur Aimi Badriah, N., Siti Nazifah, Z.A., Maheran, M.J.: Forecasting share prices accurately for one month using geometric Brownian Motion. Pertanika J. Sci. Technol. **26**(4) (2018)
13. Bank Negara Malaysia Homepage. http://www.bnm.gov.my/. Accessed 1 July 2014

14. Dowd, K.: Measuring Market Risk. Wiley, Chichester (2005)
15. Department of Statistics Malaysia. http://www.statistics.gov.my/main/main.php. Accessed 1 July 2014
16. Mohd Alias, L.: Introductory Business Forecasting: A Practical Approach, 3rd edn. University Publication Centre (PENA), UiTM Shah Alam, Selangor (2011)

Optimization Algorithms

Fog of Search Resolver for Minimum Remaining Values Strategic Colouring of Graph

Saajid Abuluaih[1(⊠)], Azlinah Mohamed[1,2(⊠)],
Muthukkaruppan Annamalai[1,2(⊠)], and Hiroyuki Iida[3(⊠)]

[1] Faculty of Computer and Mathematical Sciences,
Universiti Teknologi MARA, Shah Alam, Selangor, Malaysia
saajid.59@gmail.com, {azlinah,mk}@tmsk.uitm.edu.my
[2] Faculty of Computer and Mathematical Sciences, Advanced Analytic
Engineering Center (AAEC), Universiti Teknologi MARA,
Shah Alam, Selangor, Malaysia
[3] School of Information Science, Japan Advanced Institute of Science
and Technology (JAIST), Ishikawa 923-1292, Japan
iida@jaist.ac.jp

Abstract. Minimum Remaining Values (MRV) is a popular strategy used along with Backtracking algorithm to solve Constraint Satisfaction Problems such as the Graph Colouring Problem. A common issue with MRV is getting stuck on search plateaus when two or more variables have the same minimum remaining values. MRV breaks the tie by arbitrarily selecting one of them, which might turn out to be not the best choice to expand the search. The paper relates the cause of search plateaus in MRV to 'Fog of Search' (FoS), and consequently proposes improvements to MRV to resolve the situation. The improved MRV+ generates a secondary heuristics value called the Contribution Number, and employs it to resolve a FoS. The usefulness of the FoS resolver is illustrated on Sudoku puzzles, a good instance of Graph Colouring Problem. An extensive experiment involving ten thousand Sudoku puzzles classified under two difficulty categories (based on the Number of clues and the Distribution of the clues) and five difficulty levels (ranging from Extremely Easy to Evil puzzles) were conducted. The results show that the FoS resolver that implements MRV+ is able to limit the FoS situations to a minimal, and consequently drastically reduce the number of recursive calls and backtracking moves that are normally ensued in MRV.

Keywords: Fog of Search · Search plateau · Constraint satisfaction problem
Graph colouring problem · Minimum remaining values · Contribution number
Sudoku puzzles

© Springer Nature Singapore Pte Ltd. 2019
B. W. Yap et al. (Eds.): SCDS 2018, CCIS 937, pp. 201–215, 2019.
https://doi.org/10.1007/978-981-13-3441-2_16

1 Introduction

Backtracking (BT) algorithms are widely adopted for solving Constraint Satisfaction Problems (CSPs), which includes the Graph Colouring Problem [1]. BT algorithm builds partial solutions (variable assignments) recursively in a process called 'labelling', and abandons an assignment as soon as it fails to be part of a valid solution in process called 'backtracking'. In order to improve the performance of the brute-force algorithms, heuristic strategies are applied to dynamically reorder the variables for labelling [2]. The idea is to reduce the number of backtracking to a minimum, and the Minimum Remaining Value (MRV) strategy is an efficient and popular strategy to that [4].

MRV deliberately selects a variable with the smallest domain size (least number of values) to expand a heuristic search. It uses Forward-Checking (FC) strategy to check in advance whether a labelling is doomed to fail.

A problem arises when MRV nominates more than one variable (with same minimum remaining values) for labelling because its heuristics is incapable of distinguishing the most promising variable for labelling. This uncertainty often arises in MRV due to what we call 'Fog of Search' (FoS) that is attributed to inadequacy of information to make a definite decision. Consequently, the paper presents a FoS resolver that helps to resolve FoS situations in MRV by employing an additional heuristics called the Contribution Number.

The rest of the paper is organised as follows. Section 2 describes the related works. The case study: Sudoku is presented in Sect. 3. The notion 'Fog of Search' is explained in Sect. 4. The improved MRV strategy called MRV+ that the FoS resolver implements is detailed in Sect. 5. The experiment and its results are discussed in Sect. 6, and finally Sect. 7 concludes the paper.

2 Related Works

The section briefly describe the key concepts that are related to our study, namely CSP, Graph Colouring and the MRV strategy, on which the proposed improvement is based.

2.1 Constraint Satisfaction Problem

Constraints Satisfaction Problem (CSP) is a well-studied example of NP-complete family of problems and exceedingly used by experts to model and solve complex classes of computational problems in artificial intelligence [3]. Finding a complete solution for this type of problems involves a search process to find a finite set of valid answers (or values) among the given candidates for a finite set of questions (or variables), without violating a finite set of restrictions (or constraints).

A CSP is defined mathematically by a triple (V, D, C) where V, D and C denote sets of variables, domains and candidates, respectively. $V = \{v_i\}_{i=1}^{n}$ is a finite set of n variables. Each variable v_i is associated with a set of potential candidates with which the variable can be labelled with, i.e., the domain of v_i or $d(v_i)$. Consequently, $D = \{d(v_i)\}_{i=1}^{n}$ is a set of domains for each of the n variables. $C = \{c_i\}_{i=1}^{m}$ is a set of m constraints where each constraint $c_i = \langle s_i, r_i \rangle$ is a pair of relation r_i over a subset of variables $s_i = \{v_j\}_{j=1}^{k}$. The set of variables tightly associated through predefined constraints s_i, is normally referred to as 'peers'.

A CSP can be illustrated graphically as a Constraint Satisfaction Network such as one shown in Fig. 1, where $V = \{E, F, G, H\}$ whose respective domains are $d(E) = \{1, 2\}$, $d(F) = \{1, 3\}$, $d(G) = \{2, 4\}$ and $d(H) = \{2, 3, 4\}$. In this example, $\langle s', r' \rangle$ is an instance of a constraint c' involving variables $s' = \{F, H\}$ and relation $r' = \{F \geq H\}$. In this example, the constrained variables F and H are peers.

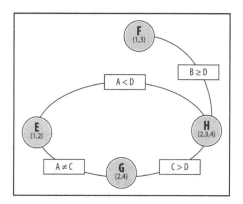

Fig. 1. An example constraint satisfaction network.

Graph Colouring Problem is a special subclass of CSP where the peers must not be labelled using same value; thus, only one type of logical relation, i.e., 'not equal to' ($\neq$) is applied to constrain the peers.

2.2 Solving Graph Colouring Problem

Solvers devoted to solving Graph Colouring Problems and CSPs in general can be classified under two main categories [4]: Deductive and Brute-force search algorithms.

Deductive search algorithm performs iterative improvements on variables' domains by implementing a set of deductive rules. The process of eliminating irrelevant values from a variable's domain emulates human deductive behaviour. At times, this approach fails to find a solution.

On the other hand, the brute-force BT search algorithm always finds solutions when there is one. In the worst case scenario it attempts all possible assignments on all unassigned variables until a solution is found or the possibilities ran out.

While the fundamental differences between these two approaches are significant, there are persistent efforts to merge their advantageous [5], which is also the aim of this paper.

A typical BT algorithm is incapable of ordering the variables right, which leads to trashing and affects the efficiency of the algorithm. As a consequence, the solving takes advantage of appropriate heuristics to prioritise the variables with the aim of pruning down the search space and to limit the occurrence of thrashing [6]. In place of a static variable order, a responsive selection mechanism that progressively reorders the variables as the problem solving process evolves, is often applied.

2.3 Minimum Remaining Values

The Minimum Remaining Values (MRV) strategy, which heuristically selects variable with fewest candidates to expand, is an existing popular strategy for Graph Colouring Problem [4]. MRV prioritises unassigned variables dynamically based on the number of available values that they hold, i.e., the candidates in the variables domains. According to its simple heuristics, the less the number of candidates in a variable's domain, the higher priority it receives as potential variable for search.

The counter-argument is if a variable with a large domain size is selected, the probability of assigning an incorrect candidate to it, is high. It could result in wasteful exploration of search space before the preceding bad assignment is realised. Poor variable selection also causes repeated failures.

On the contrary, MRV is a 'fail-first' heuristic strategy that helps to confirm if an assignment is doomed to fail at the early stages of the search. MRV applies Forward-Checking (FC) to preserve the valid candidates for the unassigned variables as the solving process progresses. While backtracking still occurs with MRV, it is considerably reduced by FC. As a result, the MRV strategy has been shown to accelerate the problem solving process by factor of more than a thousand (1000) times compared to static or random variable selection [4].

3 Sudoku as Case Study

Sudoku is a common Graph Colouring Problem example. It is a logic-based, combinatorial number-placement puzzle that has become popular pencil and paper game [14]. It is also regarded as a good example of difficult problems in computer science and computational search.

Basically, Sudoku is a group of cells that composes a board or also known as 'main grid' (see Fig. 2(a)). The main grid consists of a × b boxes or also known as sub-grids. Each sub-grid has a cells on width (row) and b cells on length (column). Subsequently, the main grid has a × b rows and a × b columns with a total of (a × b) × (a × b) cells (see Fig. 2(b)). The summation of the numbers placed in any row, column, or sub-grid is equal to the constant value of $\left(\sum_{i=1}^{a \times b} i \right)$, which in classical 9 × 9 board is equal to 45 [14]. In this paper, we consider the classical Sudoku board that has 9 (3 × 3) sub-grids, 9 rows, 9 columns, and 81 cells. The puzzle creator provides a partially completed grid where some of these empty cells are pre-assigned with values known as 'clues' whereas the rest of the cells are left blank (see Fig. 2(c)). The objective is to place a single value out of a set of numbers {1, 2, 3...9} into the remaining blank cells such that each row, column and sub-grid contains all of the numbers 1 through 9 that total to 45 (see Fig. 2(d)).

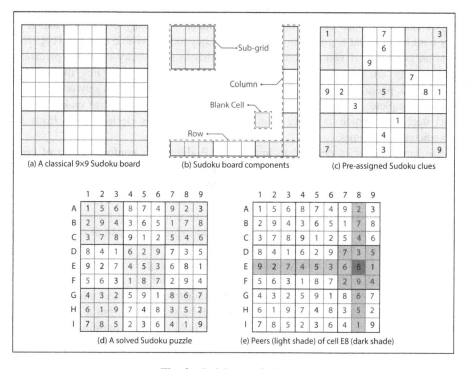

Fig. 2. Sudoku puzzle layout.

A 9×9 empty Sudoku board could generate $6{,}670 \times 10^{21}$ valid completed configurations. It has been shown that for creating a puzzles that has only one solution, at least 17 clues are required [15]. However, there is still no guarantee that a puzzle with 17 or more clues will have a unique solution [7, 8].

The constraints structure of classical Sudoku is such that each cell in the board is tightly associated with twenty (20) other cells or 'peers' (see Fig. 2(e)). Each cell has its own domain of potential values or candidates that can occupy the cell according to the candidates the peers are going to hold. The size of domain of a blank cell is 9, whose candidates are 1, 2, .., 9. Therefore, the domain of cell k, D_k can be defined mathematically as shown in Eq. 1, where DR_k, DC_k, and DS_k are sets of candidates of the assigned peers located on row, column, and sub-grid of cell k, respectively.

$$D_k = \{1, 2, .., 9\} \backslash \{DR_k \cup DC_k \cup DS_k\} \qquad (1)$$

4 Fog of Search (FoS)

In military operations, gathering intelligence during on-going combats could be a serious challenge since the operational environment is partially observable and it is very hard to tell what is going on the other side beyond the visible distance [10]. The Prussian general Carl von Clausewitz realized that in all military conflicts, precision and certainty are unattainable goals and he introduced the term 'Fog of War' to describe this phenomenon [11]. During such situations, commanders rely on however small, incomplete and imperfect information that has been gathered to make 'intelligent' decisions, which is better than making spontaneous decision that leads to unpredictable outcomes.

Similarly, strategies devoted to improve CSP algorithms confront a sort of confusion when the best available choices have same heuristics value; a phenomenon known as 'search plateau' [12]. In the MRV strategy for instance, the search reaches a plateau if there are two or more variables holding the same minimum number of values or candidates, i.e., when the strategy is unable to discern the most variable among the them. We coined the term 'Fog of Search' (FoS) to express this state of confusion that hampers a strategy from progressing deterministically.

Consider the constraint satisfaction network shown in Fig. 1. Solving it using MRV will confront FoS at the very first assignment! Except for variable H that has three candidates in its domain, the rest of the variables have two candidates each. In this case, the strategy will exclude H from 'next variable to be solved' list, but a FoS situation arises because there are three other variables that hold the same minimum remaining value of 2. MRV is not designed to deal with the kind of ambiguity associated with FoS. In the example, MRV simply breaks the tie by selecting one of the variables E, F or G, in an arbitrary manner. When a strategy resorts to random actions to advance, it only tells the strategy is incompetent to deal with the problem, FoS in this case.

We know that the order in which the algorithm selects the 'next variable to be solved' significantly impacts its search performance. The question to ask is: can MRV make use the available information to break the tie among the best available choices in a FoS situation? The paper answers this question and proposes an improvement to MRV to help avoid the arbitrary selection of variable that occurs.

5 Minimum Remaining Values Plus (MRV+)

Typically, the MRV strategy iterates through all unassigned variables in a CSP, and compares each of their domain sizes before selecting a variable with the minimum remaining values or candidates as the 'next variable to be solved'. If there is only one variable with the optimal heuristic value, the variable is selected and labelled, and the search continues. However, if there is a FoS, MRV deals with the situation in two ways: (a) select a variable based on pre-assigned static order, i.e., the first variable found with the desired optimal heuristic value will become the new frontier even if there are other variables holding the same heuristic value; (b) select a variable randomly among a group of variables that hold same optimal heuristic value.

Applied to solving Sudoku puzzles, the first approach is described by Algorithm 1 where the first cell that is found to have the minimum remaining value will be selected (see lines 6–9), while Algorithm 2 describes the second approach where one of the variables with minimum remaining value is selected randomly (see lines 23–25).

What is common with both approaches is the arbitrary selection of variables that does not effectively help to advance the search.

Algorithm 1 MRV Static Cell Selection	Algorithm 2 MRV Random Cell Selection
1: **Procedure** SelectNextState()	1: **Procedure** SelectNextState()
2: LessMRV ← int.MaximumValue	2: LessMRV ← int.MaximumValue
3:	3: PotentialCellsList ← null
4: **For each** Cell **in** SudokuBoard **do**	4:
5: **If** Cell.Value = NotAssignedCell **AND**	5: **For each** Cell **in** SudokuBoard **do**
Cell.Candidates.Count < LessMRV **Then**	6: **If** Cell.Value = NotAssignedCell **AND**
6: potentialCell ← Cell	Cell.Candidates.Count < LessMRV **Then**
7: LessMRV ← Cell.Candidates.Count	7: PotentialCellsList ← NewList()
8: **ENDIF**	8: PotentialCellsList.Add(Cell)
9: **End For each**	9: LessMRV ← Cell.Candidates.Count
10:	10: **Else If** Cell.Value = NotAssignedCell **AND**
11: **If** potentialCell = null **Then**	Cell.Candidates.Count = LessMRV **Then**
12: //The current partial solution is inconsistent. Backtracking has to be committed.	11: PotentialCellsList.Add(Cell)
13: **Return** null	12: **ENDIF**
14: **Else**	13: **ENDIF**
15: **Return** potentialCell	14: **End For each**
16: **ENDIF**	15: **If** PotentialCellsList.count < 1 **Then**
17:	16: //The current partial solution is inconsistent.Backtracking has to be committed.
18:	17: **Return** null
19:	18: **ENDIF**
20:	19: **If** PotentialCellsList.count = 1 **Then**
21:	20: //No FoS has been encountered, return the first cell in the list.
22:	21: **Return** potentialCellsList[0]
23:	22: **ENDIF**
24:	23: **if** PotentialCellsList.count > 1 **Then**
25:	24: //The strategy faces FoS. Return random cell .
26:	25: **Return** potentialCellsList[random(0, potentialCellsList.count)]
	26: **ENDIF**

The paper proposes to involve a secondary heuristics strategy that is invoked upon detection of FoS in MRV. New heuristic values are generated to re-evaluate each of the indeterminate MRV choice variables. The secondary heuristics proposed is called Contribution Number (CtN), and it takes advantage of existing information to resolve FoS. Technically, the MRV+ strategy comprises MRV and CtN.

The CtN heuristics work by identifying the variables that have potentially valid candidates in common with their peers. The more candidates in common a variable has with respect to its peers, the greater is its contribution number. The argument is that by labelling a variable with the highest contribution number, will result in the deduction of most number of candidates from its peers' domains; thus, solving the problem quickly by hastening fail-first. Therefore, when MRV encounters a FoS, the 'next variable to be solved' is the one with minimum remaining value and maximum contribution number. The mathematical definition of the contribution number of variable k, CtN_k is given by Eq. 2 where U_k denotes the set of unassigned peers associated with variable k, and D_k is the domain of variable k. The function iterates through the domains of each unassigned peers of variable k and counts the number of candidates they have in common.

$$CtN_k = \sum_{i=1}^{|U_k|} \sum_{j=1}^{|D_i|} \left(d_j \in D_k \right) \tag{2}$$

$$U_k = P_k \backslash \{AR_k \cup AC_k \cup AS_k\} \tag{3}$$

In the context of Sudoku, the set of unassigned peers associated with variable of cell k is described by Eq. 3, where P_k is the set of peers associated with cell k (in the case of classical Sudoku P_k consists of 20 peers), and AR_k, AC_k, and AS_k are sets of assigned cells located on row, column, and sub-grid of cell k, respectively.

Algorithm 3 describes the application of MRV+ to Sudoku. When MRV detects FoS, the 'FogResolver' function that implements CtN is invoked (see line 25). The function receives a list of cells with same minimum remaining values (PotentialCellsList) as argument, and evaluates each cell's contribution number (see lines 31–41). Finally, the cell with the maximum contribution number is selected as a new frontier for MRV+ to explore.

Algorithm 3 MRV+

```
1:   Procedure  SelectNextState()                                    27:  Procedure  FogResolver(PotentialCellsList)
2:      LessMRV ← int.MaximumValue                                   28:     SelectedCell ← null
3:      PotentialCellsList ← null                                    29:     CtNOfSelectedCell ← 0
4:                                                                   30:
5:      For each Cell in SudokuBoard do                              31:     For each Cell in PotentialCellsList do
6:         If Cell.Value = NotAssignedCell AND                       32:        Cell.CtN ← 0
            Cell.Candidates.Count < LessMRV Then                     33:        For each Peer in Cell.Peers do
7:            PotentialCellsList ← NewList()                         34:           If Peer.Value = NotAssignedCell Then
8:            PotentialCellsList.Add(Cell)                           35:              For each PeerCandidate in Peer.Candidates do
9:            LessMRV ← Cell.Candidates.Count                        36:                 If PeerCandidate is In Cell.Candidate Then
10:        Else If Cell.Value = NotAssignedCell AND                  37:                    Cell.CtN ← Cell.CtN +1
            Cell.Candidates.Count = LessMRV Then                     38:              ENDIF
11:           PotentialCellsList.Add(Cell)    .                      39:           End For each
12:        ENDIF                                                     40:        ENDIF
13:     ENDIF                                                        41:     End For each
14:     End For each                                                 42:
15:     If PotentialCellsList.count < 1 Then                         43:     If Cell.CtN > CtNOfSelectedCell Then
16:        //The current partial solution is inconsistent.Backtracking has to be committed.   44:        SelectedCell ← Cell
17:        Return  null                                              45:        CtNOfSelectedCell ← Cell.CtN
18:     ENDIF                                                        46:     ENDIF
19:     If PotentialCellsList.count = 1 Then                         47:  End For each
20:        //No FoS has been encountered, return the first cell in the list.   48:
21:        Return  potentialCellsList[0]                             49:  Return  SelectedCell
22:     ENDIF                                                        50:
23:     if PotentialCellsList.count > 1 Then                         51:
24:        //The strategy faces FoS. Return the most promising one.  52:
25:        Return  FogResolver(potentialCellsList)                   53:
26:     ENDIF                                                        54:
```

Figure 3(a) illustrates the dense distribution of large domain sizes for an instance of a difficult Sudoku puzzle. The darker a shaded cell, the larger is its domain size, i.e., it holds more candidates compared to a lightly shaded cell. In this illustrated example, MRV identifies three cells with same minimum remaining values of two candidates in each, namely D1{6,9}, E6{4,8}, and I2{8,9}. These cells are the most lightly shaded cells on the board. Among them, MRV+ selects D1 as the most promising choice to start the search because it has the maximum contribution number among them; $CtN_{D1} = 20$, $CtN_{E6} = 15$ and $CtN_{I2} = 14$. In this case, the candidates in the domain of D1 {6,9} also appear in twelve of its peers' domains: D2{6,8,9}, D3{6,8,9}, D5{4,5,6,9}, D7{3,5,6,8}, D8{3,5,6,8}, C1{1,6,9}, F1, {1,2,6,9}, G1{2,4,5, 6,9}, H1{2,4,5,6,9}, I1{2,5,9}, E2{6,7,8}, and F3{1,2,6,8,9}.

Thus, labelling D1 before E6 or I2 will result in a greater reduction of the domain sizes in the problem. As the solving progresses, the domain sizes in the problem keeps shrinking until a solution is found, i.e., when the domain sizes of all unassigned cells is a singleton. Figure 3 graphically illustrates the dwindling unassigned cells and the concomitant shrinking of their domain sizes as the puzzle evolves from difficult to medium (Fig. 3(b)) to easy (Fig. 3(c)) problem in the solving process.

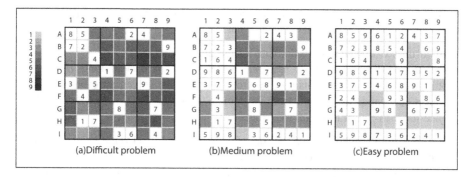

Fig. 3. The density and distribution of domain sizes of unassigned cells in a 9 × 9 Sudoku problem being solved. The darkest cell has nine candidates while the lightest cell has one candidate.

It is noteworthy to mention that the MRV+ strategy could still face FoS when the contribution numbers of the selected variables are same, in which case the tie at the second level has to be broken in an arbitrary manner. Such a situation happens when there is 'forbidden rectangle' or 'forbidden triangle' on a Sudoku board where the corner cells in the rectangle or triangle have same candidates [8], in which case their labels can be swapped. However, such incidents are rare. Moreover, these puzzles do not have unique solutions, and so are not regarded as valid puzzles.

6 Experiments, Results and Discussion

As part of our empirical experiment to evaluate the performance of MRV+ in relation to MRV, we encoded a solver that implements the BT algorithm extended with the MRV and MRV+ heuristic strategies. The MRV code was adapted from Peter Norvig's Python program [14]. MRV+ incorporates the CtN code within MRV.

The purpose of the experiment is: (a) To determine the number of times the MRV and MRV+ strategies confront FoS. For this, we implemented a monitoring function that records information related to the FoS occurrence; and, (b) To compare the performance of MRV and MRV+ in terms of the number of recursion and backtracking operations executed to solve a puzzle.

6.1 Performance Measures

Recursion and Backtracking are common performance measures of BT algorithms.

In our study, Recursion denotes the steps involved in the labelling of a cell whose domain size is two or more (Note: Assignment of 'naked single' is not counted):

- Select a cell with minimum remaining values (randomly selected in the case of MRV and strategically selected in the case of MRV+), then assign to it a candidate chosen from its domain; and,
- Perform FC and update the domains of its peers.

Backtracking denotes the steps carried out to undo an inconsistent labelling that occurs when certain constraint(s) is/are violated:

- Undo the FC updates to the domains of the peers; and,
- Free the candidate previously assigned to the cell. Upon backtracking, if there are other candidates in the domain of the freed cell then the solver performs Recursion with a new candidate chosen from its domain, otherwise it performs Backtracking once more to return to a previous state.

It is important to mention that the concept of neutralisation [13] has been adopted in this study, where a puzzle is considered solved once the main-grid is neutralised, i.e., when that the remaining unassigned cells are all are all 'naked single' cells. The assignment of 'naked single' candidates is trivial.

6.2   Simulation Data

The experiment uses simulation as a way to gain empirical insight towards problem solving. The advantage of the simulation approach is that it can be quick and easy to analyse the performance of the heuristics strategies. Large number of random simulations will find results close to the real behaviour of the heuristics. For this, we generated ten thousand (10000) Sudoku puzzles under two difficulty categories: Number of Clues [15] and Distribution of Clues [9].

- Number of Clues. Five thousand (5000) puzzles are randomly generated based on the number of clues. These puzzles are further divided into five difficulty levels, each with one thousand (1000) puzzles. They are Extremely Easy (50–61 clues), Easy (36–49 clues), Medium (32–35 clues), Difficult (28–31 clues) and Evil (22-27 clues) puzzles.
- Distribution of Clues. Five thousand (5000) puzzles are randomly generated based on the distribution of clues on the main grid. These puzzles are also divided into five difficulty levels, each with one thousand (1000) puzzles. They are Extremely Easy (each row, column, and sub-grid contains 5 clues), Easy (each row, column, and sub-grid contains 4 clues), Medium (each row, column, and sub-grid contains 3 clues), Difficult (each row, column, and sub-grid contains 2 clues), and Evil (each row, column, and sub-grid contains 1 clue).

The Evil puzzles in the Number of Clues category, which have at least 22 clues, are comparably easier to solve than the Difficult puzzles in the Distribution of Clues category, which have exactly 18 clues. The Evil level puzzles in the Distribution of Clues category, which have exactly 9 clues, are much harder to solve, not only because of the scanty clues but also because they are sparsely distributed. It should be noted that puzzles with 16 clues or less cannot have a unique solution [8], which includes the Evil puzzles in the Distribution of Clues category. In such cases where there can be more than one solution, the solver has been programmed to stop after finding the first solution.

6.3   Performance of MRV and MRV+

Tables 1 and 2 list the average number of FoS encountered by MRV and MRV+ for the Sudoku puzzles generated based on the Number of Clues and the Location of Clues categories, respectively. The 5,000 puzzles under each category are organised according to their difficulty levels where each level comprises 1,000 puzzles.

Table 1. Average FoS in solving 5,000 Sudoku puzzles generated based on the Number of Clues for the MRV and MRV+ strategies.

Strategy	Difficulty level (1,000 puzzles in each level)				
	Ext. easy Clues: 50–61	Easy Clues: 49–36	Medium Clues: 35–32	Difficult Clues: 31–28	Evil Clues: 27–22
MRV	17.9	33.4	44.2	53.7	68
MRV+	0	0	0	1	3

Table 2. Average FoS in solving 5,000 Sudoku puzzles generated based on the Location of Clues for the MRV and MRV+ strategies.

Strategy	Difficulty level (1,000 puzzles in each level)				
	Ext. Easy Clues (5)	Easy Clues (4)	Medium Clues (3)	Difficult Clues (2)	Evil Clues (1)
MRV	18.8	34.5	45	53.9	68.2
MRV+	0	0	0	2	5

The performances of MRV and MRV+ are measured in terms of the number of Recursion (R) and the number of Backtracking (B) as described in Sect. 6.1. The average number of recursion and backtracking executed for solving the puzzles according to their difficulty levels are shown in Tables 3 and 4. Table 3 lists the results for the Sudoku puzzles generated based on Number of Clues, while Table 4 lists the results for puzzles generated based on the Location of Clues. The latter are harder to

Table 3. Number of Recursion and Backtracking in solving 5,000 Sudoku puzzles generated based on the Number of Clues for the MRV and MRV+ strategies.

Strategies	Difficulty level (1,000 puzzles in each level)									
	Ext. easy Clues: 50–61		Easy Clues: 49–36		Medium Clues: 35–32		Difficult Clues: 31–28		Evil Clues: 27–22	
	R	B	R	B	R	B	R	B	R	B
MRV	19	0	35.7	0.8	53.5	9	80	31.5	195	139
MRV+	9.3	0	27.5	0.5	47.3	5.7	63.7	16.8	103.8	50.3

solve because of fewer clues and their distributedness. Therefore, the number of Recursion and Backtracking (in Table 4) are necessarily higher compared to their counterparts in Table 3.

Table 4. Number of Recursion and Backtracking in solving 5,000 Sudoku puzzles generated based on the Location of Clues for the MRV and MRV+ strategies.

Strategies	Difficulty level (1,000 puzzles in each level)									
	Ext. easy Clues (5)		Easy Clues (4)		Medium Clues (3)		Difficult Clues (2)		Evil Clues (1)	
	R	B	R	B	R	B	R	B	R	B
MRV	20	0	36	1	61	16	160.5	107	284	223
MRV+	10.6	0	28	0.5	54	11	95	44	121	61.5

In Extremely Easy and Easy puzzles, MRV targets unassigned 'naked single' cells first where FoS does not arise; selecting any of the cells with a single minimum remaining value will not give cause to backtracking. The FC strategy eliminates the assigned value from the domains of the peers. As a result, most of the remaining unassigned cells will eventually become 'naked single' cells too. Recall that a puzzle is considered solved (neutralised) when all the unassigned cells are 'naked single' cells, so the search is deliberately halted before all the cells in the main-grid are filled.

Even in few cases where FoS occurs in Easy puzzles, we observe that there are at most two minimum remaining values, and MRV almost always picks the right value to label during Recursion, so there is little or no backtracks. This explains the nearly equal numbers of Recursion and FoS in the Extremely Easy and Easy puzzles, under both Difficulty categories.

In more complex Medium, Difficult and Evil puzzles where the domain sizes of the variables with minimum remaining values are much larger (i.e., up to a maximum of nine in many instances of Evil puzzles), there are relatively lesser FoS situations. However, the chances of committing to wrong labelling using values from a large domain, is high. The more mistakes the solver makes, the more backtracks and retries it must perform. For this reason, the numbers of Recursion and Backtracking in the complex puzzles have increased dramatically.

The experiment demonstrates that MRV+ out-performs MRV to drastically reduce the FoS situations. In fact, MRV+ encountered no FoS for the Extremely Easy, Easy and Medium puzzles in both Difficulty categories. Even for the more complex Difficult and Evil puzzles, the FoS in MRV+ is negligible. For example, in the Number of Clues category, MRV+ on the average encountered only 1 and 3 FoS situations for the Difficult and Evil puzzles. These counts are extremely small compared to 53.9 and 68 average FoS situations that MRV encountered for the corresponding difficulty levels (see Table 1). The result is consistent in the Location of Clues category (see Table 2).

The much fewer FoS in MRV+ compared to MRV indicates that the second level CtN heuristics is able to differentiate the unassigned cells according to their influences on their peers and decisively select a more promising cell in Recursion. Subsequently, the numbers of Recursion and Backtracking are consistently lower for MRV+ compared to MRV (see Tables 3 and 4). The efficiency of MRV+ is more distinct in Difficult and Evil puzzles where the number of Recursion and Backtracking of MRV+ are less by more than half of that of MRV.

The results tabulated in Tables 3 and 4 are graphically illustrated in Figs. 4 and 5 graphically, respectively. The graphs illuminate that MRV+ has consistently low numbers of Recursion and Backtracking compared to MRV. The difference between their numbers of Recursion (see Figs. 4(a) and 5(a)) and their numbers of Backtracking (see Figs. 4(b) and 5(b)) are significant in the Difficult and Evil puzzles.

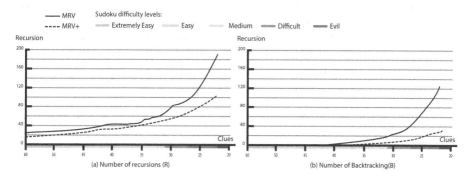

Fig. 4. Performance comparison between MRV and MRV+ for solving Sudoku puzzles generated based on the Number of Clues.

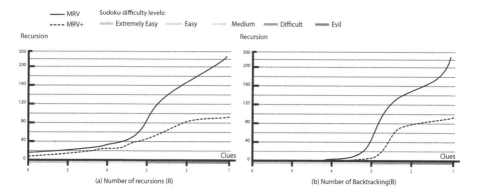

Fig. 5. Performance comparison between MRV and MRV+ for solving Sudoku puzzles generated based on the Location of Clues.

7 Conclusion

The Fog of Search (FoS) situation defines a state of confusion that a search strategy encounters when more than one variable shares the same optimal heuristic value. In the case of MRV, the optimal heuristics is the minimum remaining values, where the

common practice to select a variable arbitrarily. Moreover, the reason behind using heuristics in the first place is to rank the alternatives such that each gets rated based on how promising it is worth exploring given the limited resource (time, memory, and computing power) and being caught in a FoS means that the heuristic function has failed to achieve its purpose of design. Therefore, addressing FoS helps to overcome the failure of the existing heuristics.

The paper presents a secondary heuristics called Contribution Number (CtN) that enables MRV to make a resolute decision to resolve FoS. The function FogResolver implements the modified MRV+ strategy, which re-evaluates the choice variables that have same minimum remaining values (fewest number of candidates), then selects one that has greatest influence on its peers; the one with the maximum contribution number.

The results of an extensive experiment involving 10,000 puzzles under two difficulty categories and multiple difficulty levels show that MRV+ consistently outperforms MRV. The results indicate that the MRV+ strategy that fortifies MRV with CtN heuristics is resourceful in resolving FoS, and consequentially returns the solution with significantly lower number of Recursion and Backtracking than MRV.

In future work we plan to extend the application of CtN to value selection, i.e., to label the most promising variable with the most promising candidate as well, which we believe will further improve the efficiency of MRV+. We also plan to provide the proof of correctness of the generalised MRV+ for solving Graph Colouring Problems.

References

1. Poole, D.L., Mackworth, A.K.: Artificial Intelligence: Foundations of Computational Agents Artificial. Cambridge University Press (2010)
2. Edelkamp, S., Schrodl, S.: Heuristic Search: Theory and Applications. Morgan Kaufmann Publishers Inc. (2011)
3. Habbas, Z., Herrmann, F., Singer, D., Krajecki, M.: A methodological approach to implement CSP on FPGA. In: IEEE International Workshop on Rapid System Prototyping Shortening Path from Specification to Prototype (1999). https://doi.org/10.1109/iwrsp.1999.779033
4. Russell, S., Norvig, P.: Artificial Intelligence A: Modern Approach, 3rd edn. Pearson (2010)
5. Sudo, Y., Kurihara, M., Yanagida, T.: Keeping the stability of solutions to dynamic fuzzy CSPs. In: IEEE International Conference on Systems, Man and Cybernetics, pp. 1002–1007 (2008)
6. Haralick, R.M., Shapiro, L.G.: The consistent labeling problem: Part I. IEEE Trans. Pattern Anal. Mach. Intell. 173–184 (1979). https://doi.org/10.1109/tpami.1979.4766903
7. Jilg, J., Carter, J.: Sudoku evolution. In: 2009 International IEEE Consumer Electronics Society's Games Innovations Conference, pp. 173–185 (2009). https://doi.org/10.1109/icegic.2009.5293614
8. Mcguire, G., Tugemann, B., Civario, G.: There is no 16-clue sudoku: solving the sudoku minimum number of clues problem via hitting set enumeration. Exp. Math. 23, 190–217 (2014)
9. Jiang, B., Xue, Y., Li, Y., Yan, G.: Sudoku puzzles generating: from easy to evil. Chin. J. Math. Pract. Theory 39, 1–7 (2009)
10. Kiesling, E.C.: On war without the fog. Mil. Rev. 85–87 (2001)

11. Shapiro, M.J.: The fog of war. Secur. Dialogue **36**, 233–246 (2005). https://doi.org/10.1177/0967010605054651
12. Asai, M., Fukunaga, A.: Exploration among and within plateaus in greedy best-first search. In: International Conference on Automated Planning Schedule, pp. 11–19 (2017)
13. Abuluaih, S., Mohamed, A.H., Annamalai, M., Iida, H.: Reordering variables using contribution number strategy to neutralize sudoku sets. In: International Conference on Agents Artificial Intelligence, pp. 325–333 (2015). https://doi.org/10.5220/0005188803250333
14. Norvig, P.: Solving Every Sudoku Puzzle (2010). http://www.norvig.com/sudoku.html
15. Lee, W.: Programming Sudoku, 1st edn. Apress (2006)

Incremental Software Development Model for Solving Exam Scheduling Problems

Maryam Khanian Najafabadi[✉] and Azlinah Mohamed

Advanced Analytics Engineering Centre, Faculty of Computer and Mathematical
Sciences, Universiti Teknologi MARA, Shah Alam, Malaysia
{maryam,azlinah}@tmsk.uitm.edu.my

Abstract. Examination scheduling is a challenging and time consuming
activity among academic administrators of colleges and universities. This is
because it involves scheduling a set of exams within a limited number of
timeslots, assigning invigilators for each exam and satisfying a set of defined
constraints. Scheduling is done to avoid cases in which students sit for more
than one exam at the same time or invigilators invigilate more than one exam in
different examination venue at the same time or the exams set exceeded the
venue capacity. To overcome these challenges, we developed an incremental
software model based on greedy algorithm to structure, plan and control the
process of an automated schedule construction. Incremental development model
using greedy algorithm (IMGA) is used to prioritize the hard and soft constraints
and optimize exam scheduling problems. IMGA assigns exams to resources
(e.g.: time periods and venues) based on a number of rules. When rules defined
are not applicable to the current partial solution, a backtracking is executed in
order to find a solution which satisfies all constraints. These processes are done
through adaptation of greedy algorithm. Our algorithm iteratively makes one
choice after another in order to minimize the conflicts that may have arisen. The
advantage of IMGA is that it provides clear-cut solutions to smaller instances of
a problem and hence, makes the problem easier to be understood.

Keywords: Timetabling · Exam scheduling · Incremental development
Artificial intelligence

1 Introduction

Examination scheduling is one of the most important administrative activities in colleges and universities. It is a time-consuming task which occurs quarterly or annually in
faculties. Often, the manual ways of managing exams with paperwork are time consuming and a waste of resources. Academic administrators face many difficulties in
coming out with the manually-done examination schedules in each semester [1–4]. The
difficulties are due to the large number of courses, lecturers, students, examination
venues, invigilators. In addition, academic administrators have to assign these so that
they satisfy hard and soft constraints. Hence, problems of examination timetabling can
be specified as problems in assigning a set of exams to a given number of timeslots and
exam venues to a set of constraints. Therefore, an automated timetabling system is

© Springer Nature Singapore Pte Ltd. 2019
B. W. Yap et al. (Eds.): SCDS 2018, CCIS 937, pp. 216–229, 2019.
https://doi.org/10.1007/978-981-13-3441-2_17

needed to replace the manual scheduling in producing feasible and high quality examination schedules. Exam scheduling is concerned with scheduling a set of examinations within a limited number of timeslots to ensure that certain constraints are satisfied [3, 4].

There are two kinds of constraints in examination scheduling; soft constraints and hard constraints. Hard constraints are those that must be satisfied, while soft constraints are not essential to a schedule but their violations should be minimized in order to increase the quality of a schedule [3, 4]. A common example of soft constraints is when exams are spread as evenly as possible in the schedule. Needless to say that it is not usually possible to have solutions as they do not violate some of the soft constraints because of the complexity of the problem. An examination scheduling is called feasible timetable when all required hard constraints are satisfied and all exams have been assigned to timeslots. The common hard constraints which must be satisfied are [3–7]:

i.   Student should not have to sit for more than one exam at the same time.
ii. The scheduled exams must not exceed the capacity of the examination venue.
iii. No invigilators should be required to be at two different examination venues at the same time.

Due to the importance of setting the fine examination timetables, this work focuses on developing an intelligent exam scheduling system. This system has been developed using the concept of greedy algorithm. The solution consists of scheduling a set of examinations according to respective timeslots and venues in order to overcome the constraints as much as possible. It is imperative to note that scheduling problems can be solved using artificial intelligent algorithms the choice of using which algorithm is crucial. The success or the failure of a scheduling system depends on the model software developed. Basically, a good software development model will remove mistakes found, and dictate the time which is required to complete a system. Therefore, this study employs the incremental software development model. In this model, the definition of requirement, design, implementation, and its testing were done in an iterative manner and overlapping; resulting in the completion of the software. This model was chosen because all the required data could be prepared before a schedule could be produced.

This work was motivated by the need to implement automatic exam scheduling system in order to carry out examinations scheduling process as no students or invigilators should be at more than one examination venue at the same time and the scheduled exams must not exceed the examination venue capacity. In addition, this system can be used by administrators to inform students about date and time of exams that occurs on the same day or on consecutive days.

A brief introduction to examination scheduling will be given in Sect. 2 and it will be followed with presentation of the literature reviews in which discusses previous studies and the gap that exists in the studied area. The project methodology and instruments applied in this study are described in Sect. 3. Section 4 describes and presents the details of proposed algorithm. Finally, Sect. 5 reports the conclusion and explanation on future direction of this research.

2 Related Works

Many studies that were conducted on the effects of automated timetabling system since 1996 stated that this system was able to reduce cost, time and effort in setting final exams and avoid conflicts and mistakes such as students having two exams or more at the same time [4–16]. The purpose of this section is to provide the literature related to this study.

2.1 Introduction to Scheduling

Scheduling concerns all activities with regard to creating a schedule. A schedule is a list of events organized (events are activities to be scheduled such as courses, examinations and lectures) and different hard constraint to be satisfied as they take place at a particular time. Therefore, a schedule shows who meet at which location and at what time. A schedule should satisfy a set of requirements and must meet the demands of all people involved concurrently as far as possible [11–16].

Saviniec and Constantino [12] argues that in many activities, construction of a schedule is a difficult task due to the broad range of events which must be scheduled and the large number of constraints which have to be taken into consideration. They also mentioned that manual solution in generating a schedule requires a significant amount of effort therefore automated methods in development of timetabling has attracted the attention of the scientific community for over 40 years [12]. According to Woumans et al. [17], a schedule is feasible when sufficient resources (such as people, rooms, and timeslots) are assigned for every event to take place. Needless to say is that the constraints in scheduling are known into soft constraints and hard constraints. Violations of soft constraints must be minimized to increase the quality of schedule and increase the satisfaction of stakeholders who were influenced by the schedule as much as possible, while hard constraints should be satisfied in all circumstances [16, 17].

2.2 Scheduling in Sectors

Babaei et al. concluded that the scheduling problem can be classified in many sectors including sports scheduling (e.g.: scheduling of matches between pairs of teams); transportation scheduling (e.g.: bus and train scheduling); healthcare scheduling (e.g.: surgeon and nurse scheduling) and educational scheduling (e.g.: university, course and examination scheduling) [3]. Recent research papers mentioned that a scheduling problem is a problem with four parameters including: a finite set of meetings, a finite set of resources, a finite set of constraints and a finite set of times. The problem is to allocate resources and times to the meetings in order to meet the constraints as well as possible [10–14]. Among types of scheduling, educational scheduling is one of the most important administrative activities which occur periodically in academic institutions as studies have revealed significant attention to educational scheduling [15–18]. The quality of the educational scheduling will benefit on different stakeholders including administrators, students and lecturers.

The objective of educational scheduling is to schedule the events including courses, examinations and lectures which take place at academic institutions so that both hard and soft constraints be managed well. The educational scheduling problems can be categorized into three main categorizes including: School scheduling (courses, meetings between a teacher and a class at universities or schools), University course scheduling (lectures in courses presented at a university) and examination scheduling (examinations or tests at universities or schools). This study focused on examination scheduling. Examination schedule is an important and time-consuming task for educational institutions since it occurs periodically and requires resources and people.

2.3 Overview of Algorithms Used in Developing Examination Scheduling

Some studies concluded that using algorithms of artificial intelligence can construct good schedules automatically as these algorithms begin with one or more initial solutions and involve search strategies in order to solve scheduling problems [7–9].

Muklason et al. [7] mentioned that the complexity of modern examination scheduling problems had incited a trend toward more general problem-solving algorithms of artificial intelligence like evolutionary algorithms, ant algorithms, tabu search, greedy and genetic algorithms. Problem-specific heuristics may be involved in the context of such algorithm to optimize the number of possible solutions processed. In general, preparing schedules through algorithms seems to be an attractive alternative to manual approach [7–10]. The aim of this section is to provide a brief discussion on some of these algorithms which is commonly used in optimization problems of scheduling and also, discuss how these algorithms can generate an automatic exam timetabling systems.

Graph Algorithm. Studies conducted by Woumans et al. [17] and Babaei et al. [3] have shown that complete schedules can be achieved by using graph algorithms and the basic graph coloring according to scheduling heuristics. Scheduling heuristics is a constructive algorithm that arranges the examinations by how difficult they are to be timetabled. The examinations are ordered by this algorithm and then events are sequentially assigned into valid time periods so that no events in the period are in clash with each other. In these algorithms, scheduling problems are usually indicated as graphs. Vertices represent the events and the edges indicate the presence conflicts between the events [3, 18]. In exam scheduling problems, vertices in a graph represent the exams and the edges between two vertices represent hard constraint between exams. For example, when students attend two events, an edge between the nodes indicates that there is a conflict. The graph problem of allocating colors to vertices is that no two adjacent vertices are colored by the same color. Each color corresponds to a period of time in the schedule.

Genetic Algorithm. Genetic algorithm is considered as evolutionary algorithm which have been inspired by evolutionary biology fields such as inheritance, mutation, selection, and crossover which is also known as recombination [8]. Pillay and Banzhaf [8] mentioned that this kind of algorithm is operated by genetic factors (such as crossover, selection and mutation) that influence the chromosomes in order to improve or enhance fitness in a population. The chromosomes are found in a fixed string or "helix" in which each position is called a gene and each gene has information of solution. By using selection operators such as roulette wheel, the best solution is usually selected to become parents. The crossover operations, in which they create one or more offspring from two existing parents, can be in various forms. They are one-point crossover, two-point crossover, cycle crossover and uniform crossover. In applying genetic algorithm to solve a problem, several restrictions such as population size, crossover rate, mutation rate and the number of generations should be considered. Pillay and Banzhaf [8] has employed genetic algorithm to solve examination time-tabling problem. The value of the required parameters was set empirically, for example, the length of the chromosomes was set as the number of examinations. The gene of the solution is represented by the timeslot for the examination.

Tabu Search. Tabu Search is a meta-heuristic, which can be considered for solving exam scheduling problems. This algorithm prevents cycling by keeping a list of pre-vious solutions or moves and explores solutions which are better than the currently-known best solution for solving scheduling problems [18–20]. According to Amaral and Pais [18], the solution procedure using tabu search for solving examination scheduling problems was divided into two phases. In the first phase, objects (exams) were assigned to timeslots while fulfilling a "pre-assignment" constraint. In the second phase, the students were divided into groups in order to reduce the number of conflicts. In both phases, tabu search is employed and various neighborhoods are considered. All moves are allowed in the first phase. However, in the second phase, the moves are limited to switch between two objects only whereby it satisfies the condition of at least one of the objects is involved in a conflict. A tabu list of moves was kept in both phases by this algorithm with the condition that it permitted the most promising tabu moves.

Greedy Algorithm. Greedy algorithm is appropriate to solve optimization problems and in order to do so, iterative methods are employed. This algorithm is applicable at any moment, according to a given data element selection. An element should have the best or optimal characteristics (e.g.: shortest path, minimum investment, the highest value, and maximum profit). According to Babaei et al. a greedy algorithm is a mathematical procedure that approach and solves a problem based on solutions of smaller instances. It forms a set of objects from the smallest possible element [3]. Greedy algorithm can be a valuable tool in solving examination scheduling problems. This algorithm finds a consistent set of values which are allocated to the variables respectively based on their priority on the best selection as to satisfy the predefined constraints. This was similar to the findings of another studies conducted by Leite et al. which stated that a scheduling problem is formulated by a number of variables (exams) to which values (time periods and venues) have to be assigned to fulfill a set of constraints [6].

2.4   Issues on Solutions to Examination Scheduling Problem

The overview of developing exam scheduling with some algorithms of artificial intelligent such as greedy algorithm, graph algorithm, genetic algorithm and tabu search have been mentioned in the previous sections. In graph algorithm, exam scheduling problems are represented as graphs where exams are represented as vertices and clashes between exams are represented by edges between the vertices. Genetic algorithms can be stated as a natural evolving process which manipulates solutions, which are coded as chromosomes, within the search space. The process utilizes the crossover and mutation operators. Genetic algorithm can be used to solve examination timetabling problem by setting the value of required parameters and employing a repair mechanisms to overcome the infeasibility of offspring. Another aspect of this algorithm is the use of mutation operator to generate the offspring solutions. It is derived from the uniform crossover operator.

The overall defining feature of tabu search is the keeping of a list of previous solutions or moves in order to avoid cycling. As Amaral and Pais [18] argued, in order to solve the exam scheduling problem by employing the tabu search, the solution procedure is classified into two phases. The first phase involves the allocation of exams into timeslots and simultaneously, satisfying the "reassignment" constraint. The second phase involves the grouping of exam candidates. This is to minimize the number of conflicts. In both phases, the algorithm keeps a tabu list of solutions and moves on the pretext that it permits the most promising tabu moves.

In this study, algorithm that has been chosen to tackle the examination scheduling is greedy algorithm. The choice or selection made by the greedy algorithm depends on the choices made, during that particular moment. It iteratively makes one choice after another in order to minimize the conflicts that may have arisen. Due to the time limitation and knowledge of requirements for an automated schedule construction, we employs greedy algorithm for solving examination scheduling problems. The uses of other algorithms increase the complexity. Complexity is a measure of the amount of time and space used by an algorithm in terms of an input of a given size. Complexity focus on how execution time increases with dataset to be processed. The basic problem in examination scheduling is due to number of clashes between courses. This is when; greedy algorithm is used to minimize the conflict between courses. Hence, by using this algorithm, the process of generating exam scheduling will be easier and faster. Needless to say that, the greedy algorithm always makes the choice that looks the best at the moment. This algorithm build up a solution piece by piece, always choosing the next piece that offers the most obvious and immediate benefit. Greedy algorithm provides optimal solution by making a sequence of the best choices available. These are advantages of the greedy algorithm and reasons that the authors of this paper have selected the greedy algorithm for the development of the automatic exam scheduling.

2.5   Software Development Models

Software development process or software development life cycle is a set of steps or activities to be conducted in the development of a software product. Perkusich et al. [20] have highlighted that the models of information, required data, behaviors and control flow are needed in producing software. In producing these models, a clear understanding of requirements and what is expected of system are required. Therefore, it is necessary to follow and select a formal process for the development of a software product in order to improve its quality and productivity and to avoid over budgeting. There are several software development models in software engineering that have described when and how to gather requirements and how to analyze those requirements as formalized in the requirements' definition. The following Table 1 is based on a study on comparison between six (6) models of software engineering including waterfall model, prototyping model, incremental development model, spiral development model, rapid application development, and extreme programming model [20–22].

Table 1. A comparison between software models.

Software models	Process
Waterfall model [21]	i. Used when requirements and technology are very well understood and sometimes it is hard for customer to express all requirements clearly ii. Used when definition of product is stable iii. Phases of specification and development are separated in this model
Prototyping model [22]	i. Used when requirements are not stable and must be clarified ii. This model helps developer or customer to understand requirements better iii. This process is iterated until customers & developer are satisfied and risks are minimized and process may continue forever
Incremental development model [22]	i. Used when staffing is not available for a complete implementation and early increments is implemented with fewer people ii. Used when requirements of projects are well known but requirements are evolved over time and the basic functionality of software are needed early iii. Used on projects which have great length development schedules
Spiral development model [22]	i. This model is similar to the incremental model, but has more emphases on risk analysis ii. Used when risk and costs evaluation is important iii. Used when users are not sure of their needs and requirements are complex
Rapid application development [21]	i. Customers and developers must be committed to the rapid-fire activities for success of projects ii. Used when requirements are well known and user involved during the development life cycle iii. Used when software systems should be designed in a short time
Extreme Programming model [22]	i. In this model, the key activity during a software project is coding and the communication between teammates is done with code ii. Used when requirements change rapidly

Studies conducted by [19, 22] have revealed that waterfall model is one of the oldest types of software process to have a linear framework and a development method that are sequential. Perkusich et al. [20] expressed that waterfall model completed a phase of software development. Then development moved forward to the next phase as it could not revert to the pervious phases of development. Prototyping model is an iterative framework and a prototype constructed during the requirements phase by developers. Then users or customers evaluate this prototype. Lei et al. [21] concluded that incremental development model is a combined linear iterative framework which each release in this process is a mini-waterfall as this model attempts for compensating the length of waterfall model projects by creating usable functionality earlier. Other study in incremental development model concluded when this model is used that developer plans to develop software product in two (2) or more increments and requirements of the project have been well defined but the basic functionality of software are needed early. Spiral development model is a combination of the waterfall model features and prototyping model features to combine elements of both designing and prototyping. Spiral development is an iterative process to be used for expensive, large, and complex models where requirements of the project are very difficult. Rapid Application Development (RAD) is an iterative framework and incremental software process model to stress a short development life cycle and this process involves construction of prototypes. Time constraints imposed on scope of a RAD project. Extreme programming model is one of the newest types of software process and customer involvement in the development team is possible. This model improves the efficiency of development process but doing this model is hard due to take a lot of discipline that must be done to each other [20–22].

With regard to what needed to be understood on the requirement of the system and the development process involved, this study employs incremental development model. One of the most crucial factors to determine the success or the failure of scheduling systems is the employment of an appropriate software development model. Basically, a good software development model will remove mistakes and decrees the time that completes the system. Despite the widespread use of artificial intelligence algorithms in providing the automated schedule systems, there is still deficiency in contribution of software development models to solve scheduling problems. For producing these models, a clear understanding of requirements and what is expected of system are required. Therefore, it is necessary to follow and select a formal process for development of a software product in order to improve the quality and productivity and avoid over budgeting. Hence, solving examination scheduling problems through the implementation of incremental development model with adaptation of greedy algorithm was designed and implemented in this study.

3 Research Methodology

In order to ensure that this research work was done in a systematic and orderly manner in terms of the approach and method, it employed the following steps in developing the scheduling system:

i. Allow the user to enter username and password to login and the system should verify username and password.
ii. Allow the user to import student registration data from a registration excel file

   iii. Allow the user to manage (import/add/delete/update) related data such as: Staff information, Examination venue information and Exam time slot

   iv. Allow the user to enter exams settings (number of exam days, start date for first exam)

   v. Assign date and time for each course: System must be able to check for any clash such as student should not have to sit for more than one exam in the same date and time and no invigilators should be required to be at two different examination venues at the same time.

   vi. Assign a suitable room for each course: The room should have enough capacity to accommodate the course even if there are other subject being scheduled there at the same date and time.

   vii. Assign the invigilator for each room: As staff might have to invigilate more than one exam, system must make sure that staff are not scheduled to be at two different rooms at the same time.

   viii. Print the exam schedule based on request from staff: System should allow user to print the exam schedule based on a number of suitable report that may be necessary depending of needs of academic department.

   ix. Email the exam schedule: System provides the capability for staff to specify the email address for students and lecturers and allow to staff to email exam schedule to them.

Incremental development model is used to analyze the scheduling system, solve all of its development problems, and improve the quality of software development. In this model, the definition of requirement, design, implementation, and testing is done in an iterative manner, overlapping, resulting in completion of incremental of software product. All the requirements implemented in the system are broken down in to five (5) use cases including Login Staff, Setup Parameter, Generate Exam Schedule, Print Schedule and Email Schedule. Under this model, the use cases of system are divided into two (2) increments. Use cases of Set up Parameter and Login Staff have the highest priority requirements and are included in the first increment. The use cases of Generate Exam Schedule, Print Schedule and Email Schedule have same priority and are included in the second increment as specified in the Fig. 1. In this model, requirements can be delivered with each increment. This is done so that the functionality of system is available earlier in the development process. Early increments help to draw out requirements for later increments.

The incremental development model was chosen because it was able to prepare all the required data before a schedule can be produced. Increment 1 covered the activity related to login and preparing data for producing exam scheduling such as importing student registration data from a registration excel file, importing examination venue information, staff information and exam time slot. Whereas increment 2 involved the analyses, design and tests for the critical part of the system that generated the exam schedule such as assigning date and time for each exam so that students should not have to sit for more than one exam on the same date and time. Besides that, assigning a suitable venue for each exam was also done to ensure that there was enough space to

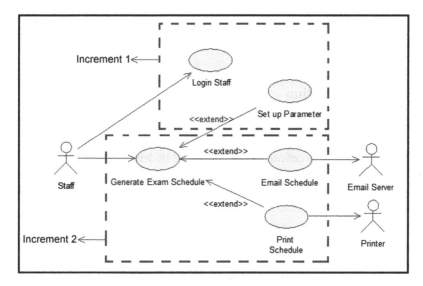

Fig. 1. Incremental development model

accommodate the students even though there were many exams which took place at the same date and time. Assigning invigilators for each venue should not be scheduled at two different venues at the same time. After that, the exam schedule was printed or emailed to them.

The life cycle of software development is described in Fig. 2. In Fig. 2, the software development process is divided into two (2) increments. Life cycle started by analyzing the requirements. The next step was the designing part of the software, preparing the preliminary design and conducting a review by clients. Then, the implementation phase started. After implementation was done, the next step which was

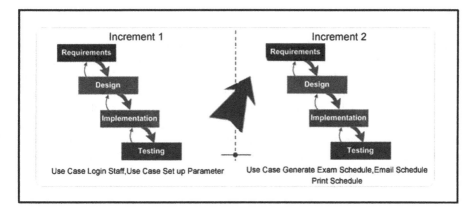

Fig. 2. Life cycle of software development in incremental model

testing started. By doing the testing, any error (bug) was defined and eliminated in the program and ensured that software worked as anticipated under all predictable conditions.

4 Proposed Algorithm

A set of exams $E = \{e_1, e_2 \ldots e_n\}$, and students who have enrolled for each exam are given in an Excel file. We compute the conflict for each pair of exams, and the size of the overlap, which can be defined as the number of students who are enrolled on both exams. The following notation and mathematical formal are used in our algorithm:

N: number of exams.
M: number of student.
K: number of student enrollment.
S: the size of exam venues in one period.
$C = [C_{mn}]$ NxN is the symmetrical matrix which states the conflicts of exams.
   C_{mn} is the number of students taking both exam m and exam n where $m \in \{1 \ldots N\}$ and $n \in \{1 \ldots N\}$.
   $G = 0.75 * S$ (0.75 is the percent of full size of exam venues, this percent is computed from result of recent papers)
   $P = K/G$ is the number of time period that can by achieve as 2 period in one day.

Our algorithm (input I: list exams)
  Begin
    While (solution is not complete) do
      Select the best element N in the
      Remaining input I;
      Put N next in the output;
      Remove N from the remaining input;
    End while
  End

Figure 3 shows steps of the examinations scheduling process through our algorithm. Our algorithm solves the optimization problems by finding the best selection at that particular moment. In exam scheduling problems, exams with greater conflicts have higher priority to be scheduled. Thus, this algorithm gets the list of courses. For each of the course, a list of the courses that are in conflict with other courses is available. Then, course with greater number of conflicts are selected. Date and timeslot and suitable venue for that course are specified. This algorithm sets invigilators to invigilate that course at that time and venue as invigilators are not assigned to more than one venue in specified timeslot.

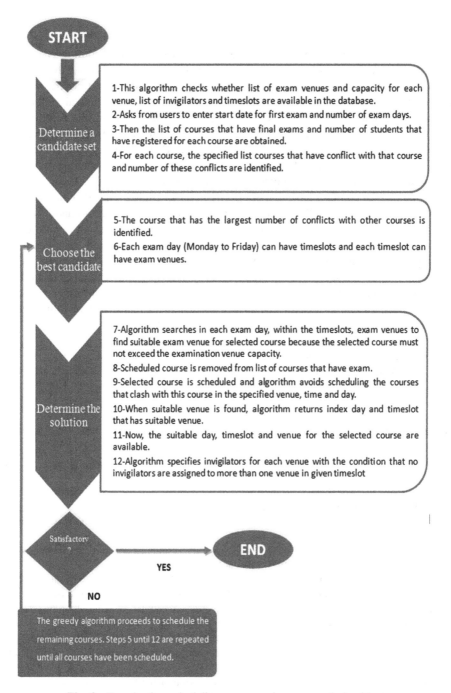

Fig. 3. Examination scheduling process using proposed algorithm

5 Conclusion

One of the most crucial factors to determine success or failure of scheduling systems is the employment of an appropriate software development model. Basically, a good software development model can remove any error, and orders the time required to complete a system. Despite the widespread use of artificial intelligence algorithms in providing the automated schedule systems, there is still deficiency in the contribution of software development models to solve scheduling problems. In producing these models, a clear understanding of requirements and what is expected of system are needed. Therefore, incremental software development model with adaptation of greedy algorithm was developed to overcome timetable scheduling problems. Exams with a greater number of conflicts have higher priority to be scheduled. The advantages of our algorithm is that it orders the exams based on the choice of the best candidate (the course with the most number of conflicts) and try to allocate each exam to an orderly timeslot and thus, satisfying all the constraints. Each scheduled course is removed from the list of courses and our algorithm proceeds to schedule the remaining courses. Our algorithm builds up a solution piece by piece, always chooses the next piece that offers the most obvious and immediate benefit. Making a comparison with other artificial intelligent algorithms in a comprehensive form will be a major part of future work available based on this study.

Acknowledgements. The authors are grateful to the Research Management Centre (RMC) UiTM for the support under the national Fundamental Research Grant Scheme (600-IRMI/FRGS 5/3).

References

1. Ayob, M., et al.: Intelligent examination timetabling software. Procedia-Soc. Behav. Sci. **18** (1), 600–608 (2011)
2. Alzaqebah, M., Abdullah, S.: Hybrid bee colony optimization for examination timetabling problems. Comput. Oper. Res. **54**, 142–154 (2015)
3. Babaei, H., Karimpour, J., Hadidi, A.: A survey of approaches for university course timetabling problem. Comput. Ind. Eng. **86**, 43–59 (2015)
4. Balakrishnan, N., Lucena, A., Wong, R.T.: Scheduling examinations to reduce second-order conflicts. Comput. Oper. Res. **19**(5), 353–361 (1992)
5. Elloumi, A., Kamoun, H., Jarboui, B., Dammak, A.: The classroom assignment problem: complexity, size reduction and heuristics. Appl. Soft Comput. **14**, 677–686 (2014)
6. Leite, N., Fernandes, C.M., Melício, F., Rosa, A.C.: A cellular memetic algorithm for the examination timetabling problem. Comput. Oper. Res. **94**, 118–138 (2018)
7. Muklason, A., Parkes, A.J., Özcan, E., McCollum, B., McMullan, P.: Fairness in examination timetabling: student preferences and extended formulations. Appl. Soft Comput. **55**, 302–318 (2017)
8. Pillay, N., Banzhaf, W.: An informed genetic algorithm for the examination timetabling problem. Appl. Soft Comput. **10**(2), 457–467 (2010)
9. Qarooni, D., Akbarzadeh-T, M.R.: Course timetabling using evolutionary operators. Appl. Soft Comput. **13**(5), 2504–2514 (2013)

10. Rahman, S.A., Bargiela, A., Burke, E.K., Özcan, E., McCollum, B., McMullan, P.: Adaptive linear combination of heuristic orderings in constructing examination timetables. Eur. J. Oper. Res. **232**(2), 287–297 (2014)
11. Saviniec, L., Santos, M.O., Costa, A.M.: Parallel local search algorithms for high school timetabling problems. Eur. J. Oper. Res. **265**(1), 81–98 (2018)
12. Saviniec, L., Constantino, A.: Effective local search algorithms for high school timetabling problems. Appl. Soft Comput. **60**, 363–373 (2017)
13. Sagir, M., Ozturk, Z.K.: Exam scheduling: mathematical modeling and parameter estimation with the analytic network process approach. Math. Comput. Model. **52**(5–6), 930–941 (2010)
14. Song, T., Liu, S., Tang, X., Peng, X., Chen, M.: An iterated local search algorithm for the University Course Timetabling Problem. Appl. Soft Comput. **68**, 597–608 (2018)
15. Turabieh, H., Abdullah, S.: An integrated hybrid approach to the examination timetabling problem. Omega **39**(6), 598–607 (2011)
16. Kahar, M.N.M., Kendall, G.: The examination timetabling problem at Universiti Malaysia Pahang: comparison of a constructive heuristic with an existing software solution. Eur. J. Oper. Res. **207**(2), 557–565 (2010)
17. Woumans, G., De Boeck, L., Beliën, J., Creemers, S.: A column generation approach for solving the examination-timetabling problem. Eur. J. Oper. Res. **253**(1), 178–194 (2016)
18. Amaral, P., Pais, T.C.: Compromise ratio with weighting functions in a Tabu Search multi-criteria approach to examination timetabling. Comput. Oper. Res. **72**, 160–174 (2016)
19. Koulinas, G.K., Anagnostopoulos, K.P.: A new tabu search-based hyper-heuristic algorithm for solving construction leveling problems with limited resource availabilities. Autom. Constr. **31**, 169–175 (2013)
20. Perkusich, M., Soares, G., Almeida, H., Perkusich, A.: A procedure to detect problems of processes in software development projects using Bayesian networks. Expert Syst. Appl. **42**(1), 437–450 (2015)
21. Lei, H., Ganjeizadeh, F., Jayachandran, P.K., Ozcan, P.A.: Statistical analysis of the effects of Scrum and Kanban on software development projects. Robot. Comput.-Integr. Manuf. **43**, 59–67 (2017)
22. Qureshi, M.R.J., Hussain, S.A.: An adaptive software development process model. Adv. Eng. Softw. **39**(8), 654–658 (2008)

Visualization of Frequently Changed Patterns Based on the Behaviour of Dung Beetles

Israel Edem Agbehadji[1], Richard Millham[1(✉)], Surendra Thakur[1],
Hongji Yang[2], and Hillar Addo[3]

[1] ICT and Society Research Group, Department of Information Technology,
Durban University of Technology, Durban, South Africa
israeldel2006@gmail.com,
{richardml, thakur}@dut.ac.za
[2] Department of Computer Science, University of Leicester, Leicester, UK
[3] School of Information Systems and Technology, Department of M.I.S.,
Lucas College, Accra, Ghana

Abstract. Nature serves as a source of motivation for the development of new approaches to solve real life problems such as minimizing the computation time on visualization of frequently changed patterns from datasets. An approach adopted is the use of evolutionary algorithm based on swarm intelligence. This evolutionary algorithm is a computational approach that is based on the characteristics of dung beetles in moving dung with limited computational power. The contribution of this paper is the mathematical formulation of the unique characteristics of dung beetles (that is, path integration with replusion and attraction of trace, dance during orientation and ball rolling on straight line) in creating imaginary homes after displacement of its food (dung) source. The mathematical formulation is translated into an algorithmic structure that search for the best possible path and display patterns using simple two dimensional view. The computational time and optimal value are the techniques to select the best visualization algorithm (between the proposed dung beetle algorithm and comparative algorithms –that is Bee and ACO). The analysis shows that dung beetle algorithm has mean computational time of 0.510, Bee has 2.189 and ACO for data visualization has 0.978. While, the mean optimal value for bung beetle is 0.000117, Bee algorithm is 2.46E−08 and ACO for data visualization is 6.73E−13. The results indicates that dung beetle algorithm uses minimum computation time for data visualization.

Keywords: Dung beetle · Data visualization · Bioinspired
Frequently changed patterns · Path integration

1 Introduction

Visualization is the process of displaying information using graphical representations [1] to aid understanding. Whereas, data visualization is representation of data in a systematic form with data attributes and variables for the unit of information. Text with numeric values can be put into a systematic format using a conventional approach such as bar charts, scatter diagram and maps [2]. The general purpose of a visualization

© Springer Nature Singapore Pte Ltd. 2019
B. W. Yap et al. (Eds.): SCDS 2018, CCIS 937, pp. 230–245, 2019.
https://doi.org/10.1007/978-981-13-3441-2_18

system is to transform numerical data of one kind into graphical format in which structures of interest in the data become perceptually apparent [3]. By representing data into the right kind of graphical array [3] humans can be able to identify patterns in dataset. These conventional approaches could be challenge in terms of computational time to visualize the data. This challenge serves as the motivation to find new ways to reduce computational time during data visualization. Our approach is inspired by the behavior of animals such as dung beetles. The significance of a bioinspired behaviour such as dung beetle behaviour for big data visualization is the ability to navigate and perform path integration with minimal computational power. The dung beetle behaviour when expressed as an algorithm can find best possible approach to visualize discrete data using minimal computational power that is suitable when data coming from different sources would have to be visualize quickly with less computational time. When there is less computational time required to visualise patterns characterize as moving with speed (referring to velocity characteristics of big data framework) then large volumes of data could be viewed with limited computational time using visual formats for easy understanding [1]. The advantage of visual data format is that it integrates the human creativity and general knowledge with the computational power of computers which makes the process of knowledge discovery an easier process [4, 5]. This paper proposes a new bio-inspired/metaheuristic algorithm, the Dung Beetle Algorithm (DBA), which is based on ball rolling, dance and path integration behavior of dung beetle. Mathematical expressions were formulated from the behaviour in terms of basic rules for systematic representation of discrete data points in two dimensions graph/linear chart. The basis for using linear graph is to identify the point at which data points convey [6]. The author of [6] has shown that if the values convey then the value on X-axis of a graph are continuous that create a graphical view on data. The remainder of this paper is organised as follows. Section 2 introduces related work on data visualization, description of dung beetle behaviour, the proposed dung beetle algorithm, evaluation of visualization technique and the experimental results. Section 3 presents the conclusion and future work.

2 Related Work

Conventional techniques for data visualization consider performance scalability and response time during visual analytics process [2]. Response time relates to the speed (that is velocity characteristics of big data framework) at which data points arrives and how frequently it changes when there is large volume of data [6]. Among techniques of visualization are dense pixel display, stacked display technique [7–9] and bioinspired approach includes flocking behavior of animals and cellular ant based on ant colony system [10]. The author of [7] has shown that the concept of dense pixel technique maps each dimension value both text and numeric data to a colored pixel and then group the pixels belonging to each dimension into adjacent areas using circle segments technique (that is, close to a center, all attributes close to each other enhance the visual comparison of values). Stacked display technique [8, 9] displays sequential actions in a hierarchical fashion. The hierarchical nature forms a stack of display to depict a visual format. The basic idea behind the stack display is to integrate one coordinate system into another, that is, two attributes form the outer coordinate system, and two other attributes are integrated into the outer coordinate system, and so on thereby forming multiple layers into one layer.

Currently, the animal behaviour/bioinspired approach for visualization include the use of cellular ant based on any colony system [10] and flocking behaviour of animals. Flocking behavior for data visualization [11] focused on simplified rules that models the dynamic behaviour of objects in n-dimensional space. The spatial clustering technique helps in grouping each dynamic behaviour or similar features of data as a cluster that is viewed in n-dimensional space on a grid. In order to assist users of the visual data to understand patterns a blob shape was used to represent group of spatial cluster. These blob shape represents data plotted on grids.

The authors of [10] have shown that the combined characteristics of ant and cellular automata can be used to represent datasets in visual clusters. The cellular ants used the concept of self-organization to autonomously detects data similarity patterns in multi-dimensional datasets and then determine the visual cues, such as position, color and shape size, of the visual objects. A cellular ant determines its visual cues autonomously, as it can move around or stay put, swap its position with a neighbor, and adapt a color or shape size where each color and shape size represents data objects. Data objects are denoted as individual ants placed within a fixed grid creates visual attributes through a continuous iterative process of pair-wise localized negotiations with neighboring ants in order to form a pattern that can be visualized on a data grid. When ants perform continuously pairwise localized negotiation, its swap the position of one ant with another ants which relates to swap of one color with another in a single cluster [11]. In this instance, the swap in positions relates to interchange between data values that are plotted on a grid for visualization by users. Generally, there is no direct predefine mapping rule that interconnects data values with visual cues to create the visual format for users [11]. Hence, the shape size scale adjustments are automatically adapted to data scale in an autonomous and self-organizing manner. In view of this, instead of mapping a data value to a specific shape size, each ant in ant colony system maps one of its data attributes onto its size by negotiating with its neighbors. During the shape size negotiation process, each ant compares randomly the similarity of its data value and circular radius size that is measured in screen pixels. It is possible that each ant can grow large or become small, therefore simplified rules from ant behaviour are expressed and applied to check how ants can grow in their neighboring environment. These rules are significant in determining the scalability of visualized data whereas the randomize process is significant in determining the adaptability of data value. The process of shape size scale negotiation may require extensive computational time in coordinating each ant into a cluster or single completed action.

It has been indicated in [3] that data visualization evaluation techniques gives an idea that leads to improvement on data visualization methods. Although there is lack of quantitative evidence of measuring the effectiveness of the data visualization techniques, the author of [3] approach to quantitatively measure the effectiveness of visualization techniques was by generating arbitrarily/artificial test dataset with similar characteristics (such as data type- float, integer, and string; way in which the values relate to each other-the distribution) to real dataset and vary the correlation coefficient of two dimensions, the mean and variance of some of the dimensions, the location, size and shape of clusters. Some generic characteristics of the data types includes nominal —data whose values have no inherent ordering; ordinal—data whose values are ordered, but for which no meaningful distance metric exists; and metric — data which has a meaningful distance metric between any two values. When some parameters (such as statistical parameters) that defines the data characteristics are varied on at a time within an experiment in a controlled manner, it is helps in evaluating different visualization techniques to find where the point data characteristics are perceived for the first time or point where characteristics are no longer perceived in order to build more realistic test data with multiple parameters to define the test data.

Another approach that was proposed by [3] is when the same test data is used in comparing different visualization techniques so as to determine the strengths and weaknesses of each technique. The limitation of these approaches is that the evaluation is based only on users experience and use of the visualization techniques. The author of [12] has shown that the effectiveness of visualization technique is the ability to enable the user to read, understand and interpret the data on display easily, accurately and quickly. Thus, effectiveness depends not only on the graphical design but also on the users' visual capabilities [12]. The authors of [13] define effectiveness as the capability of human to view data on display and interpret faster the results, convey distinctions in the display with fewer errors. Mostly, effectiveness is measured in terms of time to complete a task or quality of the tasks' solutions [14, 15].

Some visualization evaluation techniques include observation by users, the use of questionnaires and graphic designers to critique visualized results [16] and give an opinion. Although, these visualization evaluation techniques are significant, it is subjective and qualitative, thus a quantitative approach could provide an objective approach to measure visualization evaluation techniques.

The paper proposes a bioinspired computational model that requires less computational time in coordinating data points into a single action. This bioinspired computational model is referred to as dung beetle algorithm for visualization of data points on a data grid. The section describes the behaviour of dung beetles and the mathematical expressions that underpins the behaviour of the dung beetle algorithm.

2.1 Description of Dung Beetle Behavior

Background

Dung beetle is an animal with a very tiny brain (similar to a grain of rice) that feeds on the dung of herbivorous animals. The dung beetle are known to use minimal computational power for navigation and orientation using celestial polarization pattern [17]. These dung beetles are grouped into three namely; rollers, tunnelers, and dwellers. Rollers form a dung into a ball and it is rolled to a safe location. On the other hand, tunnelers land on a pile of dung and simply dig down to bury a dung. Whilst Dwellers stays on top of a dung pile to lay their eggs.

Given that there are different behaviour that categories each group of dung beetle, the study focus on the category of ball roller for data visualization purposes. During the feeding process, each beetle (ball Rollers) carries a dung in a form of ball roll from the source of food to a remote destination (referred as Home). An interesting behaviour of dung beetle is the use of the sun and celestial cues in the sky as a direction guide in carrying ball roll along a straight path from dung pile [18]. Given that celestial body always remain constant relative to the dung beetle, the beetle keeps moving on a straight line [17] until it reaches the final destination. In the process of moving patterns are drawn without the aid of a designer [19]. Additionally, they navigate by combining internal cues of direction and distance with external reference from its environment and then orient themselves using the celestial polarized pattern [17, 20]. However, if a source of light is removed completely, dung beetle stop moving and stay at a stable position (or unknown state) until the source of light is restored before it climbs on top of its dung ball to perform orientation (referred to as a dance) during which it locate the source of light and then begin to move toward its Home. Thus, beetles homed using an internal sense (derive from sensory sources including visual) of direction rather than external references [21].

Another interesting behaviour is that given a burrow (Home) and a forage (food), the dung beetle is able to move in search of forage by counting the number of steps, and when returning Home, the motion cues are used to integrate the path in order to reduce the distance in moving. The path integration technique is significant in reducing the time of moving Home. However, when forage is displaced to a new position or environment, dung beetle is unable to locate its Home using landmark information. This is because landmark navigation involves complex perceptual and learning processes which are not always available to animals [22]. Thus animals that uses landmark navigation technique require extensive computational time because each animal needs a memory of previous position to help it move to the current land mark. The challenge is that at each point information about landmark navigation needs to be stored and this may result in large storage space.

It has been indicated in [23] that animals in a new environment centre their exploration base on a reference point in order to path integrate. In this regard, every displacement of forage which leads to path integration from a reference point creates an imaginary home and this subsequently creates a stack of neighboring imaginary homes close to each other. In this context, these real or imaginary homes are circular holes (representing data grid) where ball roll (that is data values) are placed as pixels.

The path integration [24] is based on the assumption that movement of dung beetle from one position to another may be achieved by adding successive small change in position incrementally, and continuous updates of direction and distance from the initial point [21] using the motion cues. In other words, it allows beetles to calculate a route from initial point without making use of landmark information. Adding these successive small movements on a route creates a stack of moves in a hierarchical fashion. The basic steps of path integration process are the continuous estimation of self-motion cues to compute changes in location (distance) and orientation (head direction) [21].

Simplified behaviour of dung beetle
The authors of [19] have indicated that a guiding principle for visualization is the use of simplified rules to produce complex phenomena. The simple rules relates to basic rules which steers the dynamic behaviour of dung beetles may be characterized as follows:

Ball rolling: on a straight line.

The basic rules formulation on ball rolling is expressed as the distance d between two positions (x_i, x_{i+1}) on a plane. This is calculated using the straight line equation as:

$$d(x_i, x_{i+1}) = \sqrt{\sum_{i=1}^{n} (x_{i+1} - x_i)^2} \tag{1}$$

Where x_i represents the initial position and x_{i+1} the current position of dung beetle on a straight line, n is the number of discrete points.

Path integration: Sum sequential change in position in hierarchical fashion and continuously update direction and distance from the initial point to return home. During the path integration, the basic rule formulation on change in position is expressed as:

$$x_{t+1}^k = x_t^k + \beta_m (x_{i+1} - x_i)_t^k + \varepsilon \tag{2}$$

Where x_{t+1}^k represents the current position of a dung beetle, β_m represents motion cues. Since path integration is an incremental recursive process, error ε is introduced as random parameter in the formulation to account for cumulative error. Each frequent return to a home reset the path integrator to zero state, so that each trip starts with an error-free path integrator [21]. Thus, total path is expressed as sum of all paths, that is:

$$path = \left[\sum_{i=1}^{n} x_{t+1}^k \right] \tag{3}$$

Where current position is x_{t+1}^k and n represents the number of paths. In order to control the movement v between a 'real home' and 'imaginary home' to ensure the current position x_{t+1}^k converges to the 'real home' of a dung beetle during path integration the following expression was applied as follows:

$$v = v_o + path - (\mu_1 P + \mu_2 A) \tag{4}$$

Where v_o represents the initial movement, μ_1 is a factoring co-efficient of repulsion P between each dung beetle, μ_2 is a factoring co-efficient of attraction A between each dung beetle when a trace is detected by another dung beetle. Where P and A are expressed as in [25].

$$P = 1 - d(x_i, x_{i+1}) \theta / \left(d(x_i, x_{i+1})_{max} \pi \right) \tag{5}$$

$$A = \theta / \pi \tag{6}$$

Where P is the repulsion between each dung beetle, θ is the angle of dung beetle, $d(x_i, x_{i+1})$ is the distance between two dung beetles, $d(x_i, x_{i+1})_{max}$ is the maximum distance recorded between two dung beetles, π represents the ratio of circumference to a diameter.

i. Dance: combining internal cue of direction and distance with external reference from its environment and then orient themselves using the celestial polarized pattern. During the dance, the internal cue (I_q) of distance and direction is less then external reference point (E_r) (that is a random number). Thus, basic rule formulation on orientation (δ) after the dance is expressed as:

$$\delta = \left[I_q(d, M) \leq E_r\right] \tag{7}$$

$$\delta = \alpha * \left[E_r - I_q(d, M))\right] \tag{8}$$

Where α is a random parameter to control the dance, E_r is a specified point of reference, d represents the distance of internal cues, M represents the magnitude of direction expressed as a random number (between 0 and 1).

2.2 Dung Beetle Algorithm

In creating the visual pattern, the self-adapting basic rules that were formulated to depict the dynamic behaviour of dung beetle was applied to find optimal solution to create a visual pattern of data points on a grid. The algorithm on the basic rules formulation is expressed in Fig. 1 as follows:

```
Objective function f(x), x=(x₁,x₂,..xd)ᵀ
        Initialization of parameters;
        Population of dung beetle xᵢ(i=1,2,..,k);
        Choose a random "real Home"
WHILE ( t < stopping criteria not met)
  FOR i=1: k //for each dung beetle in the population
     Roll ball
     Perform a dance
     Integrate path
     Evaluate position within external reference point
     Compute movement v using equation (4)
     IF v1 <v2 //Compare v1 (current movement) and v2(previous movement)
        Replace with minimum v
     ENDIF
  END FOR
     Update external reference point Check stopping criteria
END WHILE
```

Fig. 1. Proposed *dung beetle algorithm*

2.3 Evaluation of Visualization Technique

In line with [14, 15] approach to measure effectiveness of visualization evaluation technique was in terms of computational time to complete a visualization task and the quality of the tasks' solutions was considered in terms of the optimal solution from the proposed bioinspired visualization algorithm. The comparative visualization algorithm are namely Bee algorithm and ACO for data visualization.

3   Experimental Results and Analysis

The algorithm for the proposed Dung Beetle-Based Algorithm (DBA) was implemented in MATLAB R2017B and tested on stock market dataset. The basic parameters for the dung beetle algorithm is defined as follows: error ε is 0.05 and β_m represents motion cues is set to 0.2. The basis for error parameter of 0.05 is to allow 95% accuracy of selecting the best path and 5% chances of choosing incorrect path which may lead to 'imaginary home'. The basis for 0.2 motion cue (or 20%) is due to the fact that other factors (e.g., hill and other impediments which can lead dung beetles to getting stuck in one place) in the environment (that accounts for 80%) may obscure the view of dung beetles in moving dungs from one location to another.

The experiment was conducted in two stages firstly, association rules generated from previous work (using bioinspired algorithms such as Kestrel-based search algorithm (KSA), ACO, PSO, BAT and WSA-MP) on stock market data with frequently changed numeric attributes and time dimension was used [26] with an initial modified closeness preference of support-confidence (MCPconf) value of 0.9 and user time preference of 0.7. The basis for using 0.9 value is to extract high confidence association rules between 90 to 100% and within time interval of 0 to 0.7. Secondly, dung beetle algorithm was applied to create graphical display of results on modified closeness preference of support-confidence (MCPconf) value. Although, this paper has could not discuss the association rules, the results of association rules from each algorithm from previous work [26] was displayed using the proposed dung beetle algorithm for data visualization and compared with data visualization algorithm such as Bee algorithm and ACO for data visualization. The results are presented in three parts: firstly, the use of dung beetle algorithm to visualize data mining results from bioinspired algorithms such as KSA, ACO, PSO, BAT and WSA-MP; secondly, the use of Bee algorithm to visualize data mining results from KSA, ACO, PSO, BAT and WSA-MP; and thirdly, the use of ACO for data visualization to view data mining results from KSA, ACO, PSO, BAT and WSA-MP.

The first part involves the use of dung beetle algorithm for visualization of association rule mining results from KSA, ACO, PSO, BAT and WSA-MP. Table 1 shows the MCPconf values that were generated from the association rules as follows:

Table 1. MCPconf values from KSA

Modified CPsc value (%)	90.3246	99.1485	94.5423	95.4177	96.2931	93.5961	95.4094	94.5341
Rule#	1	2	3	4	5	6	7	8

Modified CPsc value (%)	95.8549	91.6942	98.6783	98.6607	98.6607	99.0389	94.4377	92.7195
Rule#	9	10	11	12	13	14	15	16

It is observed from Table 1 that, 16 association rules were generated within the stipulated MCPconf value. The details on these rules can be cited in previous works.

The least MCPconf value was 90.3246% while the highest was 99.1485%. Based on the Table 1, the nature of the two dimension graphical display using dung beetle algorithm is shown in Fig. 2 of appendix 1. Figure 2 shows the display on the best cost for dung beetles in each iteration towards an optimal solution. The path descends gradually from the start of iteration, although there were steep slopes along the path the algorithm converges to an optimal value of 0.00011665 with elapsed time of 0.401061 s. Table 2 shows the MCPconf values that were generated using ACO to mining association rules are tabulated as follows:

Table 2. MCPconf values from ACO

Modified CPsc value (%)	92.9081	93.4948	95.3061	94.4317	95.3061	98.6503	99.0285
Rule#	1	2	3	4	5	6	7

Modified CPsc value (%)	94.4278	95.3022	94.4278	95.8196	91.6604	98.642
Rule#	8	9	10	11	12	13

It is observed from Table 2 that 13 association rules were generated within the MCPconf value of 0.9. The details on these rules can be cited in previous works. The least MCPconf value was 91.6604% while the highest was 99.0285%. Based on the Table 2, the nature of the graphical display using dung beetle algorithm is shown in Fig. 3 of appendix 1. Figure 3 shows the display on the best cost for dung beetles in each iteration towards an optimal solution. The path descends gradually from the start of iteration, maintained a steep slope, maintained a constant best cost between 40th and 60th iteration before converging to an optimal value of 7.0315e−05 at elapsed time of 0.485009 s. Table 3 shows the MCPconf values that were generated using PSO to mine association rules are tabulated as follows:

Table 3. MCPconf values from PSO

Modified CPsc value (%)	99.2603	90.5613	94.9438	90.5107	90.5103
Rule#	1	2	3	4	5

It is observed from Table 3 that 5 association rules were generated within the MCPconf value of 0.9. The details on these rules can be cited in previous works. The least MCPconf value was 90.5103% while the highest was 99.2603%. Based on the Table 3, the nature of the graphical display using dung beetle algorithm is shown in Fig. 4 of appendix 1. Figure 4 shows the display on the best cost for dung beetles in each iteration towards an optimal solution. The path descends gradually from the start of iteration to the 20th iteration, maintained a steep slope, the path also maintained a constant best cost (in terms of minimal value) before finally converging to an optimal value of 0.00016533 at elapse time of 0.493069 s. Table 4 shows the MCPconf values that were generated using BAT to mine association rules are tabulated as follows:

Table 4. MCPconf values from BAT

Modified CPsc value (%)	90.5716	99.2277	94.9603	90.5264	90.5260
Rule#	1	2	3	4	5

It is observed from Table 4, that 5 association rules were generated within the MCPconf value of 0.9. The details on these rules can be cited in previous works. The least MCPconf value was 90.5260% while the highest was 99.2277%. Based on the Table 4, the nature of the graphical display using dung beetle algorithm is shown in Fig. 5 of appendix 1. Figure 5 shows the display on the best cost for dung beetles in each iteration towards an optimal solution. The path descends gradually from the start of iteration, maintained a steep slope towards the 80th iteration, and maintained a constant best cost on the curve before converging to an optimal value of 0.00014318 at an elapse time is 0.589264 s. Table 5 shows the MCPconf values that were generated using WSA-MP to mine association rules are tabulated as follows:

Table 5. MCPconf values from WSA-MP

Modified CPsc value (%)	93.5951	95.4084	94.5331	95.925	91.7612	
Rule#	1	2	3	4	5	

Modified CPsc value (%)	98.7505	92.8651	98.6756	99.0538	95.3265	94.452
Rule#	6	7	8	9	10	11

It is observed from Table 5 that 11 association rules were generated within the MCPconf value of 0.9. The details on these rules can be cited in previous works. The least MCPconf value was 91.7612% while the highest was 99.0538%. Based on the Table 5, the nature of the graphical display using dung beetle algorithm is shown in Fig. 6 of appendix 1. Figure 6 shows the display on the best cost for dung beetles in each iteration towards an optimal solution. The path descends gradually from the start of iteration, maintained a constant best cost (in terms of minimal value) and converges to an optimal value of 9.1295e-05 with an elapse time of 0.582776 s.

Secondly, Bee algorithm for data visualization was used to visualize results of association rule that were mined using KSA, ACO, PSO, BAT and WSA-MP. The MCPconf values in Table 1 was used to avoid its repeating. The nature of the graphical display using Bee algorithm on KSA is shown in Fig. 7 of appendix 1. Figure 7 shows the display on the best cost for Bee algorithm in each iteration towards an optimal solution. The curve descends gradually from the start of iteration, maintained a constant best cost (in terms of minimal value) between the 60th to 70th iteration before converging to an optimal value of 1.0844e-08. Elapsed time is 2.167966 s. The MCPconf values in Table 2 was used to avoid its repeating, Using the Bee algorithm for visualization, the nature of the graphical display using Bee algorithm on ACO results is shown in Fig. 8 of appendix 1. Figure 8 shows the display on the best cost for Bee algorithm in each iteration towards an optimal solution. The curve descends gradually from the start of iteration and converges to an optimal value of 6.1772e-08 at an elapse time of 2.134924 s. The MCPconf values in Table 3 was used to avoid its repeating. Using the Bee algorithm for visualization, the nature of the graphical display using Bee algorithm on PSO is shown in Fig. 9 of appendix 1. Figure 9 shows the display on the best cost for Bee algorithm in each iteration towards an optimal solution. The curve descends gradually from the start of iteration and converges to an optimal value of 1.2743e-08. Elapsed time is 2.186376 s. The MCPconf values in Table 4 was used to avoid its repeating. Using the Bee algorithm for visualization, the nature of the graphical display using Bee algorithm on BAT is shown in Fig. 10 of appendix 1. Figure 10 shows the display on the best cost for Bee algorithm in each iteration towards an optimal solution. The curve descends gradually from the start of iteration, maintained a constant best cost (in terms of minimal value) after the 20th iteration to the 40th iteration until finally converging to an optimal value of 7.1857e-09. Elapsed time is 2.309688 s. The MCPconf values in Table 5 was used to avoid its repeating. Using the Bee algorithm for visualization, the nature of the graphical display using Bee algorithm on WSA-MP is shown in Fig. 11 of appendix 1. Figure 11 shows the display on the best cost for Bee algorithm in each iteration towards an optimal solution. The curve descends gradually from the start of iteration and converges to an optimal value of 1.8478e-08. Elapsed time is 2.150612 s.

Thirdly, ACO for data visualization was used to visualize the results on association rule that were mined from KSA, ACO, PSO, BAT and WSA-MP. The MCPconf values in Table 1 was used to avoid its repeating. The nature of the graphical display using ACO for data visualization on KSA is shown in Fig. 12 of appendix 1. Figure 12 shows the display on the best cost for ACO algorithm in each iteration towards an optimal solution. The nature of the curve is linear or related to a straight line however, the curve converged to an optimal value of 1.1458e-12 at an elapse time of 1.020023 s. The MCPconf values in Table 2 was used to avoid its repeating. Using the ACO for visualization, the nature of the graphical display using ACO for data visualization on ACO for mining results is shown in Fig. 13 of appendix 1. Figure 13 shows the display on the best cost for dung beetles in each iteration towards an optimal solution. The nature of the curve is linear but maintained a constant best cost towards the 100th iteration before converging to an optimal value of 1.2667e-12 as elapsed time of 1.042381 s. The MCPconf values in Table 3 was used to avoid its repeating. Using the ACO for visualization, the nature of the graphical display using ACO for data visualization on PSO mining results is shown in Fig. 14 of appendix 1. Figure 14 shows the display on the best cost for dung beetles in each iteration towards an optimal solution. The nature of the curve is linear however, the curve converged to an optimal value of 8.9363e-14 with an elapse time of 0.913326 s. The MCPconf values in Table 4 was used to avoid its repeating. Using the ACO for visualization, the nature of the graphical display using ACO for data visualization on BAT mining results is shown in Fig. 15 of appendix 1. Figure 15 shows the display on the best cost for dung beetles in each iteration towards an optimal solution. The nature of the curve is linear however, the curve converged to an optimal value of 9.2904e−14. Elapsed time is 0.956751 s. The MCPconf values in Table 5 was used to avoid its repeating. Using the ACO for visualization, the nature of the graphical display using ACO for data visualization on WSA-MP mining results is shown in Fig. 16 of appendix 1. Figure 16 shows the display on the best cost for dung beetles in each iteration towards an optimal solution. The nature of the curve is linear however, the curve converged to an optimal value of 7.6804e−13. Elapsed time is 0.958605 s. The nature of curves that were obtained from the bioinspired data visualization algorithms namely dung beetle algorithm, Bee algorithm and ACO for data visualization indicates that while dung beetle algorithm and bee algorithm maintained a curved path, ACO for data visualization is linear until it converge to best optimal value. The high best cost observed at the initial iteration contributed to the nature of graph in ACO for data visualization.

The experimental results that were obtained on the computational time (that is, elapse time) and optimum value (in terms of the best cost) is tabulated on Tables 6 and 7. The computation time is measured in seconds. Table 6 shows the tabulated results on the optimum value of data visualization algorithms namely the proposed Dung Beetle Algorithm (BDA), Bee algorithm and ACO for data visualization. While Table 7 shows the computational time required by the algorithm to output both optimum results and visualization of data mining results on data grid. The bioinspired data mining algorithm considered are KSA, ACO, PSO, BAT and WSA-MP.

Table 6. Summary of optimum values from bioinspired data visualization algorithms

Bioinspired data mining algorithms	Bioinspired data visualization algorithms		
	Proposed DBA (s)	Bee algorithm	ACO for data visualization
KSA	0.00011665	1.0844e−08	1.1458e−12
ACO	7.0315e−05	6.1772e−08	1.2667e−12
PSO	0.00016533	1.2743e−08	8.9363e−14
BAT	0.00014318	7.1857e−09	9.2904e−14
WSA-MP	9.1295e−05	1.8478e−08	7.6804e−13
Mean	0.000117	2.46E−08	6.73E−13

Table 6 illustrates the optimal value (in terms of best cost) required for each algorithm to compute and display the results in a graphical format. It is observed that ACO for data visualization has least optimum values among the bioinspired data visualization algorithms as evident from each bioinspired data mining algorithms. It is possible that the number of search agents in the ACO for data visualization may have contributed to the algorithm generating the least optimum values as many parameters are tuned in the search space to produce each best optimal value.

Table 7 illustrates the computational time (measured in seconds) required for each algorithm to compute and display results on a grid for users to view. The results shown on Table 7 indicates that the proposed DBA has the least computational time in each bioinspired data mining algorithm. The least computational time could be attributed to the parameters used in the algorithm. In order to find the mean computational time spent by each bioinspired data visualization algorithm, the mean computational time was computed over all five bioinspired data mining algorithm. The proposed DBA spent 0.510236 s while Bee algorithm spent 2.189913 s and ACO for data visualiza-tion spent 0.978217 s. The mean of the computational time shows that the ACO for

Table 7. Summary of computation time obtained from bioinspired data visualization algorithms.

Bioinspired data mining algorithms	Bioinspired data visualization algorithms		
	Proposed DBA	Bee algorithm	ACO for data visualization
KSA	0.401061	2.167966	1.020023
ACO	0.485009	2.134924	1.042381
PSO	0.493069	2.186376	0.913326
BAT	0.589264	2.309688	0.956751
WSA-MP	0.582776	2.150612	0.958605
Mean	0.510236	2.189913	0.978217

data visualization is as twice the mean computational time of dung beetle algorithm while the computational time for Bee algorithm approximately four times the computational time of dung beetle algorithm which indicates that the proposed DBA spent less computational time as compared with Bee algorithm and ACO for data visualization. The least on the mean of computational time in DBA could be attributed to the ability to attract and repulse other paths which could increase the computation time of the algorithm in converging to optimality.

4   Conclusion and Future Work

The aim of this paper is to propose a *Dung Beetle-Based Algorithm* (BDA) for data visualization. The computational time and optimal value were parameter applied to evaluate effectiveness and quality of the data visualization techniques. The analysis shows that dung beetle algorithm is effective at visualizing data mining results while the quality of the optimum solution could be improved. ACO for data visualization has a best optimum solution but the effectiveness could be enhance while Bee algorithm has a low level of effectiveness and quality of the optimum solutions. *The results from dung beetle algorithm confirmed the preposition that* dung beetle are known to use minimal computational power for navigation and orientation using celestial polarization pattern [17]. In future, the quality of optimal solution from dung beetle algorithm will be enhanced and the effectiveness can be tested further on different real world problem of data visualization.

Appendix 1

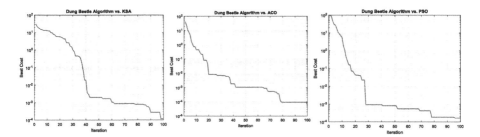

Fig. 2. Dung beetle display best cost on path traversed by KSA

Fig. 3. Dung beetle display best cost on path traversed by ACO

Fig. 4. Dung beetle display best cost on path traversed by PSO

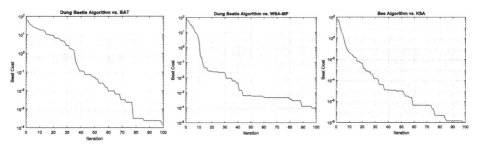

Fig. 5. Dung beetle display best cost on path traversed by BAT.

Fig. 6. Dung beetle display best cost on path traversed by WSA-MP.

Fig. 7. Bee algorithm display on best cost by KSA

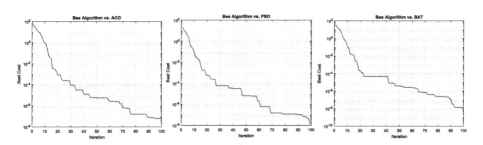

Fig. 8. Bee algorithm display on best cost by ACO

Fig. 9. Bee algorithm display on best cost by PSO

Fig. 10. Bee algorithm display on best cost by BAT

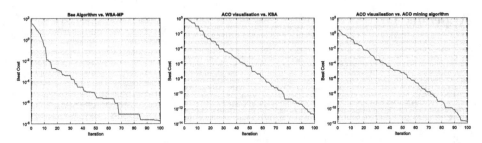

Fig. 11. Bee algorithm display on best cost by WSA-MP

Fig. 12. ACO algorithm display on best cost by KSA.

Fig. 13. ACO for visualization display best cost on by ACO from data mining phase

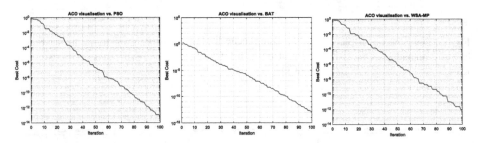

Fig. 14. ACO for visualization display best cost using results on ACO from data mining phase

Fig. 15. ACO for visualization display best cost on by BAT from data mining phase

Fig. 16. ACO for visualization display best cost using results on WSA-MP from data mining phase

References

1. Ward, M., Grinstein, G., Keim, D.: Interactive Data Visualization: Foundations, Techniques, and Application. A K Peters/CRC Press (2010)
2. Wang, L, Wang, G., Alexander, C.A.: Big data and visualization: methods, challenges and technology progress. Digital Technol. **1**(1), 33–38 (2015). http://pubs.sciepub.com/dt/1/1/7. Accessed 26 June 2018
3. Keim, D.A., Bergeron, R.D., Pickett, R.M.: Test Data Sets for Evaluating Data Visualization Techniques. (1994). https://pdfs.semanticscholar.org/7959/fd04a4f0717426ce8a6512596a0 de1b99d18.pdf
4. Choy, J., Chawla, V., Whitman, L.: Data visualization techniques: from basics to big data with SAS visual analytics. (2011). https://www.slideshare.net/AllAnalytics/data-visualization-techniques. Accessed 20 Apr 2018
5. Keim, D.: Designing pixel-oriented visualization techniques: theory and applications. IEEE Trans. Vis. Comput. Graph. **6**(1), 59–78 (2000)
6. Keim, D. A.: Information visualization and visual data mining. IEEE Trans. Vis. Comput. Graph. **8**(1) (2002)

7. Leung, C.K., Kononov, V.V., Pazdor, A.G.M., Jiang, F.: PyramidViz: visual analytics and big data visualization of frequent patterns. In: IEEE 14th International Conference on Dependable, Autonomic and Secure Computing, 14th International Conference on Pervasive Intelligence and Computing, 2nd International Conference on Big Data Intelligence and Computing and Cyber Science and Technology Congress (2016)

8. Moere, A.V., Clayden, Justin J., Dong, A.: Data clustering and visualization using cellular automata ants. In: Sattar, A., Kang, B.-h. (eds.) AI 2006. LNCS (LNAI), vol. 4304, pp. 826–836. Springer, Heidelberg (2006). https://doi.org/10.1007/11941439_87

9. Vande Moere, A., Lau, A.: In-formation flocking: an approach to data visualization using multi-agent formation behavior. In: Randall, M., Abbass, Hussein A., Wiles, J. (eds.) ACAL 2007. LNCS (LNAI), vol. 4828, pp. 292–304. Springer, Heidelberg (2007). https://doi.org/10.1007/978-3-540-76931-6_26

10. Marghescu, D.: Evaluating Multidimensional Visualization Techniques in Data Mining Tasks. (2008). http://www.doria.fi/bitstream/handle/10024/69974/MarghescuDorina.pdf?sequence=3&isAllowed=y. Accessed 02 Apr 2018

11. Card, S.K., Mackinlay, J.D., Shneiderman, B.: Readings in Information Visualization - Using Vision to Think, San Francisco. Morgan Kaufmann Publishers, CA (1999)

12. Dull, R.B., Tegarden, D.P.: A Comparison of Three Visual Representations of Complex Multidimensional Accounting Information". J. Inf. Syst. **13**(2), 117 (1999)

13. Risden, K., Czerwinski, M.P.: An initial examination of ease of use for 2D and 3D information visualizations of web content. Int. J. Hum.-Comput. Stud. **53**, 695–714 (2000)

14. Santos, B.S.: Evaluating Visualization techniques and tools: what are the main issues? (2008). http://www.dis.uniroma1.it/beliv08/pospap/santos.pdf

15. Wits University: Dung Beetles Follow the Milky Way: Insects Found to Use Stars for Orientation. ScienceDaily. (2013). https://www.sciencedaily.com/releases/2013/01/130124123203.htm. Accessed 20 Mar 2017

16. Dacke, M., Byrne, M.J., Baird, E., Scholtz, C.H., Warrant, E.J.: How dim is dim? Precision of the celestial compass in moonlight and sunlight. Philos. Trans. R. Soc. Lond. B Biol. Sci. **366**, 697–702 (2011)

17. Kuhn, T., Woolley, O.: Modeling and Simulating Social Systems with MATLAB. Lecture 4 – Cellular Automata. ETH Zürich (2013)

18. Dell'Amore, C.: Dung beetles navigate via the milkyway, first known in animal kingdom. News Watch, National Geographic Society (2013)

19. Etienne, A.S., Jeffery, K.J.: Path integration in mammals. Hippocampus **14**, 180–192 (2004)

20. Etienne, A.S., Maurer, R., Saucy, F.: Limitations in the assessment of path dependent information. Behavior **106**, 81–111 (1988)

21. Golani, I., Benjamini, Y., Eilam, D.: Stopping behavior: constraints on exploration in rats (Rattus norvegicus). Behav. Brain Res. **53**, 21–33 (1993)

22. Mittelstaedt, H., Mittelstaedt, M.-L.: Homing by path integration. In: Papi, F., Wallraff, H.G. (eds.) Avian navigation, pp. 290–297. Springer, New York (1982). https://doi.org/10.1007/978-3-642-68616-0_29

23. Agbehadji, I.E., Millham, R., Fong, S.J., Yang, H.: Kestrel-based search algorithm for association rule mining of frequently changed items with numeric and time dimension (under consideration) (2018)

24. Lu, C.-T., Sripada, L.N., Shekhar, S., Liu, R.: Transportation data visualisation and mining for emergency management. Int. J. Critical Infrastruct. **1**(2/3), 170–194 (2005)

25. Keim, D.A.: Visual exploration of large data sets'. Commun. ACM **44**, 38–44 (2001)

26. Mamduh, S.M., Kamarudin, K., Shakaff, A.Y.M., Zakaria, A., Abdullah, A.H.: Comparison of Braitenberg vehicles with bio-inspired algorithms for odor tracking in laminar flow. NSI J. Aust. J. Basic Appl. Sci. **8**(4), 6–15 (2014)

Applications of Machine Learning Techniques for Software Engineering Learning and Early Prediction of Students' Performance

Mohamed Alloghani[1,2(✉)], Dhiya Al-Jumeily[1], Thar Baker[1],
Abir Hussain[1], Jamila Mustafina[3], and Ahmed J. Aljaaf[1,4]

[1] Liverpool John Moores University, Liverpool L3 3AF, UK
M.AlLawghani@2014.ljmu.ac.uk,
{D.Aljumeily, t.baker, A.Hussain, A.J.Kaky}@ljmu.ac.uk,
[2] Abu Dhabi Health Services Company (SEHA), Abu Dhabi, UAE
mloghani@seha.ae
[3] Kazan Federal University, Kazan, Russia
dnmustafina@kpfu.ru
[4] Centre of Computer, University of Anbar, Ramadi, Iraq
a.j.aljaaf@uoanbar.edu.iq

Abstract. Educational data mining has been widely used to predict student performance and establish intervention strategies to improve that performance. Most studies have implemented machine learning algorithms for interventions but the use of data mining in appraising student performance in learning software is obscure. Furthermore, some of the studies that have explored the use of machine learning in predicting student performance in software learning have only used Random Forest, and as such, this study used the same dataset to implement 7 other algorithms and establish the most efficient. The study used two different sets of data and established that Neural Network was the most efficient with regards to the first dataset although Random Forest was the most efficient with regards to the second dataset. Both the NN graphics and RF tree diagram are presented, and the predictions from the two models also compared.

Keywords: Data mining · Random Forest · Performance prediction
Software engineering · Machine learning

1 Introduction

Machine learning refers to a computer program that makes deductions, draws influences, and makes conclusions based on experienced entrenched in classes of tasks. The program has a performance measure for each of the task and its basic intention is to improve the experience that it learns. Machine learning algorithms or computer programs that learn experiences are becoming popular, especially with the progression towards artificial intelligence. At the core of the development and increased likelihood of using machine learning or artificial intelligence in education is Industry 4.0 and its related concepts. That is, Industry 4.0 proposes and promises to instigate Education 4.0 which will promote and place education as a "smart factor."

© Springer Nature Singapore Pte Ltd. 2019
B. W. Yap et al. (Eds.): SCDS 2018, CCIS 937, pp. 246–258, 2019.
https://doi.org/10.1007/978-981-13-3441-2_19

The application of Industry 4.0 supersedes the conventional application of industrial revolution in higher education. In most cases, concepts and technologies aligned with Industry 4.0 are used in institutions of higher education to adopt different learning approaches including blackboard classes and distance learning modules. However, the influence of artificial intelligence in transforming workspace in the education sector is yet to be fully affected because stakeholders are undecided whether or not pursue the technologies due to insecurity perception. Nonetheless, it is certainly unanimous that Industry 4.0 will reduce the gap between humanity and social sciences.

2 Literature Review

Several studies have been conducted to predict student performance in the context of EDM. The objectives of such studies are to establish factors that influence student score and the recommended strategies for improving the final score based on the course and level of education. The studies [1, 10] explored modern approaches to predicting student performance using multi-agent data mining techniques and concluded that performance prediction with higher precision and accuracy is more beneficial to decision makers. The researchers used boosting techniques to improve the performance of the algorithms in determining the hidden patterns in the data. In specific, the study used adaptive boosting (AdaBoost) to improve binary classifiers although the researchers had to avoid multiclass target variables. Besides the AdaBoost algorithm, the researchers used Naïve Bayes and different variants of AdaBoost. That is, the researchers compared Naïve Bayes, AdaBoost M1, AdaBoost M2, Logit Boost, and SAMME. The argument for choosing these algorithms was that AdaBoost M1 and AdaBoost M2 suits binary and multiclass classification tasks while Logit Boost suits classification tasks involving binary attributes with poorly separated classes, and it relies on least squares boosting. Finally, the Stage wise Additive Modeling using Multiclass Exponential Loss Function (SAMME) was used because of its ability to return one weighted classifier compared to other boosting options [1]. The evaluation approach used in the study focused on High, Average, and Poor grade levels. Despite the declaration of the study to focus on the prediction of the performance of the students, the results were not compressive and not all the models were compared, and result interested. Hence, it is inconclusive that which of the models performed better in predicting the performance of the student.

Asif, Merceron, and Pathan [2] conducted a case study on prediction of student academic performance at degree level using multi-layer perceptron (MLN) and artificial neural network algorithms and concluded that ANN is more accurate the MLP. Furthermore, the study also used k-nearest neighbor using a different number of centroids and compared the performance of the model. The other model used in the study is Naïve Bayes classifier and decision tree based on the GINI index. The study established that the Naïve Bayes algorithm outperformed the other algorithms, and also noted a significant difference between decision tree with GINI and decision tree with information gain. The overall conclusion of the study suggested that graduation with a given degree was dependent on various aspects of the performance of the student. Of importance, is the fact that the paper considered the influence of socio-economic and other demographic factors on the performance of the student in their fourth year and subsequent graduation. Based on the findings and conclusion of the study, the graduation tendencies are dependent on scores and grades in the first and second years of study.

Mueen, Zafar and Manzoor [3] also conducted a study student performance modeling and prediction using data mining techniques. The study used students' academic records as well as their participation in other activities such as forum discussions. The study champions for the use of EDM to improve academic performance and researchers implemented Neural Network (NN), Naïve Bayes (NB), and decision tree (DT) algorithms. The study also established that Naïve Bayes was the best performing algorithm with over 86% performance prediction accuracy. The other evaluation techniques used in the study included accuracy, precision, and recall, and the main algorithms compared included Naïve Bayes, MLP, and C4.5. Regarding specificity, Naïve Bayes, MLP, and C4.5 had 89.1%, 83.2%, and 78.4% respectively. The C4.5 is a tree pruning algorithm and as such considered as a decision tree algorithm. However, there are other pruning algorithms including J48 and CHAID, which also have variants such as J48 Graft and Improved CHAID.

Based on the results from the other studies, it is evident that EDM is essential in predicting the performance of the student. As Devasia, Vinushree and Hegde [4] concluded, Naïve Bayes is more accurate compared to regression, decision tree, and neural networks, and the study relied on admission details, course prerequisites, subject details, attendance, and student marks to make the predictions. It can be concluded that Naïve Bayes theorem is the best performing algorithm in predicting the academic performance of the student. However, learning is wide and encompassing and the data on various aspects continue to grow, and data mining will also become applicable to assessing performance in other technical aspects of student performance.

3 Methodology

The data used in the study and the study approach including a detailed discussion of the algorithms used in the study are presented in the following subsections.

3.1 Data Source and Types

The dataset used in the study was a product of the Software Engineering Team Assessment and Prediction (SETAP) project and it consists of over 100 team activity measures as well as outcomes for 74 student teams. The study used the 0.7 version of the SETAP machine learning data, and it contains information and files collected over several semesters from software engineering classes at San Francisco State University. The data consists of distinct student activity measures, and each student was a member of either the local (same university) or global (different universities) team. The weekly student activity measures were aggregated for each team to create the team activity measure, and the evaluation of each of the student was based on the student's efficiency of handling software engineering processes and understanding of software engineering products. Hence, the outcome attribute consists of product and process. The data has five major milestones namely M1 (High-Level Requirements & Specs), M2 (Detailed Requirements & Specs), M3 (First Prototype), M4 (Beta Release), and M5 (Final Delivery). The data was collected over 7 semesters for the period spanning Fall 2012 and Fall 2017. The information was gathered for over 383 students corresponding to 18 class sections. The Team Activity Measure (TAM) collated data has 115 attributes and 2 class labels. The TAM consists of 59 local teams and over 15 global teams.

3.2 Study Approach

The study uses visual programming tools and conventional performance metrics to compare Decision Tree, Random Forest, Naïve Bayes, Neural Network, k-Nearest Neighbor (kNN), Logistic Regression, Support Vector Machine, and AdaBoost. The preprocessing techniques used in the study involved feature selection and the experiment focused on milestones 1 to 5 and their influence on final grades. That is, the final grades were set as the target variable while the rest of the attributes were treated as features.

The visual program for executing the analysis is as shown in Fig. 1 below.

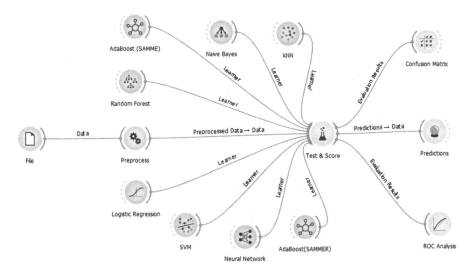

Fig. 1. The visual programming for assessing the algorithms used in predicting the performance of the students in software engineering learning

In Fig. 1, the Test & Score widget in the visual program compares the 8 algorithms based on area under the ROC curve, classification accuracy (CA), F-measure, precision, recall, and log loss. The study assumed that the efficiency of the software learning is equivalent to the efficiency of the algorithm in predicting the grade of the student. The visual program evaluates the 8 algorithms and establishes the best performing one, which is then used to predict software learning outcome among engineering students.

3.3   Algorithms

The mathematical information on the 8 algorithms is presented in the following subsection.

3.3.1   Random Forest Classifier

The RF classifier has been used in different fields including remote sensing, land classification, and diagnosis and prognosis of different maladies. A random forest classifier is closely related to decision tree in that the RF combines tree predictors such that each tree is dependent on the magnitude of a random vector. The algorithm assigns the random vector through independent sampling and it is assumed to be of the same distribution as the rest of the random vectors in the tree. As a convention, the generalization error associated with forest converges to a threshold when the number of trees in the forest becomes infinitely large. The generalization error is based on the following Eq. [8].

$$Err(\varphi_\iota) = EX, Y\{L(Y , \varphi_\iota(X))\} \tag{1}$$

In which, iota (ι) is the learning set that the random tree classifier (φ_ι) is created from, and the L is the loss function that result approximates the differences between the individual tree in the forest.

It is imperative to note that the algorithm uses bootstrapping to improve the performance of the individual trees in the forest. During implementation, the random forest grows trees searching for the best feature among a random subset of attributes. The process makes the algorithm diverse and thereby improving its outcome.

3.3.2   Neural Network

The neural network algorithms are based mathematical processing of information through emulation of the biological systems. The neural networks are the driving force behind multi-layer perceptron, deep learning, and the subsequent artificial intelligence. Arguably, the objective is not fully achieved although the artificial neural network has proven quite effective in different applications. Nonetheless, the study focused the NN algorithm with a neuron expressed as follows.

$$h_j(x) = \alpha\left(w_j + \sum\nolimits_{i=1}^{n} w_{ij}x_i\right) \tag{2}$$

In Eq. 2, h_j refers to the hidden layers, w_{ij} are the weight of the connection between the input and hidden layers, and α is the activation function and it can either be a sine function, a sigmoid function or a SoftMax function.

3.3.3   Support Vector Machine

The SVM algorithm is technically a linear classifier although with a requirement that the data points in the dataset are linearly separable. The general assumption of linear classifiers is that the output attribute can be expressed as a linear combination of predictors, and it is the linear combination of the input that forms the hyperplane. However, it is imperative to note that linear classifiers also model non-linear relationships between classifiers. That is, the linear techniques can be used to transform input variable that does not necessarily have linear relationships. The unique feature of the SVM as a linear classifier is that its hyperplanes are not always equivalent so that a good separation is realized when margin to the nearest training point on the hyperplane is the possible largest value. From a mathematical perspective, SVM s are maximum-margin models of the linear kind expressed using Eq. 2 below.

$$\phi(x) = \begin{cases} c_1 & if\ b + \sum_{j=1}^{p} x_j w_j > 0 \\ c_2 & \text{Otherwise} \end{cases} \tag{3}$$

In which x_j are the set of predictors or classification features, w_j the coefficients of the predictors, b the constant or intercept of the linear model. Assuming that the outcome or predictand is a binary attribute then, support vector machine learns patterns in the data and produce classes based on a primal optimization problem. In general, SVM, though linear in nature, extends to non-linear tasks through the projection of input attribute space in higher dimensional spaces based on kernel functions.

3.3.4 k-Nearest Neighbor

The nearest neighbor algorithm is memory based and does not require any model fitting. It assumes that the algorithm iterates through the data until it finds a number of attributes in the training sample with the shortest distance to the new sample. The minimum distance is inferred and compared to the output variable. In general, the kNN averages the output from k closest training subset data points based on the following computation.

$$\varphi(x) = \frac{1}{k} \cdot \sum_{(x_i, y_i) \in NN(x, L, k)} y_i \tag{4}$$

In Eq. 4, $N(x, L, k)$ refers to the k nearest neighbor of the predictor (x) in the learning set space (L). In a classification task, the output prediction is calculated as the dominating class among the k nearest neighbors using the following equation.

$$\varphi(x) = \arg \max_{c \in y} \sum_{(x_i, y_i) \in NN(x, L, k)} y_i \tag{5}$$

In which, the output class contains the target variable $(c \in y)$ and the nearest neighbor expression is retained. It should be noted that distance between the neighbor is metric, but the Euclidean distance was given preference in this study.

3.3.5 Naïve Bayes

The NB algorithm relies on the Bayes probability theorem. It provides a conditional probability of an event occurring in an experiment given the other or others have occurred. In the context of this study, suppose M is a characteristic that affects learning and completion of Milestone1 and N is the performance of the student in Milestone 2 then the Bayes conditional probability explaining the influence of this outcome on software learning computed using the following equation.

$$P(N/M) = \frac{P(M \cap N)}{P(N)} \tag{6}$$

For conditional probability to hold, the probability of M must exceed zero and $P(N/M)$ denotes the probability of M given N. the specific application and the subsequent interpretation are based on the fact that a student either scored an A or an F so that conditional probability in Eq. 6 should become $P(F/A)$.

3.3.6   Logistic Regression

It is one of the predictive machine learning techniques although it requires categorical target variables. Some applications are specific on the nature of the target variable with some studies insisting on binary variables as the predictand. However, logistic regression as a classifier can handle multi-class target variable and this is the case in this paper. The performance or grade awarded at the end of the learning contains grades from A to F and as such qualifies to be a multi-level categorical variable.

In classification application, logistic regression predicts the technical interlude between classes. It ideally predicts the probability that given inputs belong to the default class. That is, students who have completed the training and completed all milestones both individual and in teams should pass and have a proper understanding of the software and how it works. The logistic regression, therefore, predicts the probability that a student has passed based on their average performance. The technical interlude can be represented as follows.

$$P(x) = P(\gamma = 1|x) \tag{7}$$

In Eq. 7, the probability of milestone performance $P(x)$ suggests that the milestone belongs to the default class denoted by $\gamma = 1$ or the default successful training class. The gamma equals 1 expression refers to a student scoring an A. It is imperative to note that logistic regression is a linear machine learning technique although it is transformed using the logistic function.

3.3.7   Adaptive Boosting

The AdaBoost machine learning techniques have several algorithms but this study focused in SAMME and SAMME.R. The Stage-wise Additive Modeling using a Multi-class Exponential loss function (SAMME) is a multi-class AdaBoost algorithm that fits a classifier to a training set then compute the generalization error using an equation similar to Eq. 1. The SAMME.R is a variant of the SAMME and it uses a Lagrange optimization function to minimize the reserialization error. Furthermore, SAMME.R uses class probability estimates in its iterations and it converges more quickly than its counterpart [9].

4   Results and Discussions

The experimental results are presented sequentially, and the presentation is based on the two datasets. However, some of the preliminary statistics and facts about the two datasets are also presented.

4.1   Basic Statistics

The SETAP Product T8 consists of 42 A scores and 32 F scores. The 42 teams had different number of students all the aggregation led to the conclusion that all team members scored an A. Similar assumptions and conclusions were made about the teams that scored F. As for those teams that scored an A, total coding hours, sharing of unique commitment message, and personal meeting hours per week were attributes with the greatest influence. However, gender, semester, and team distribution also played an essential role in the effectiveness of the learning. In specific, teams that were led by male students had 81.1% chance of scoring A while teams lead by female students had 18.9% of passing. Regarding semester, teams completing and submitting the milestones during spring were more likely to score an A than those submitting during fall. The score statistic was similar for SETAP Product T9 dataset with 42 teams scoring an A and 32 teams scoring an F. The major contributing factors were slightly different although discrete variables such as gender, semester, and team distribution maintained their ranking order but not their magnitude of influence.

4.2   Experiment

The model comparison results for SETAP Product T8 data is summarized as follows. The metrics used to compare the models include area under the curve (AUC), classification accuracy (CA), F-measure, and Log Loss. It should be noted the precision and recall metrics are used to compute F1 (Table 1).

Table 1. The performance metrics of the 8 algorithms (average A and F classes) for SETAP product T8

Method	AUC	CA	F1	Precision	Recall	Log loss
kNN	0.641	0.593	0.596	0.602	0.593	2.193
SVM	0.535	0.533	0.525	0.600	0.533	0.693
SAMME.R	0.539	0.547	0.550	0.557	0.547	15.658
SAMME	0.539	0.547	0.550	0.557	0.547	0.767
Random Forest	0.569	0.553	0.546	0.542	0.553	0.933
Neural Network	0.659	0.587	0.591	0.608	0.587	1.280
Naive Bayes	0.591	0.553	0.555	0.593	0.553	3.747
Logistic Regression	0.643	0.620	0.624	0.634	0.620	3.052

Based on the scoring methods, especially with specific focus to model prediction efficiency and classification accuracy, it suffices to conclude that Neural Network outperformed the other models. In specific, Neural Network covered an area of 65.9% under the ROC curve similar to the ones in Figs. 2 and 3. kNN and logistic regression covered areas of 64.1% and 64.3% under the ROC curve, while both AdaBoost algorithms covered an area of 53.9% and were the least performing algorithms. The Random Forest that Petkovic et al. [5–7] used by four of the seven algorithms showing that other methods can be used to produce a more accurate prediction of software learning among engineering students.

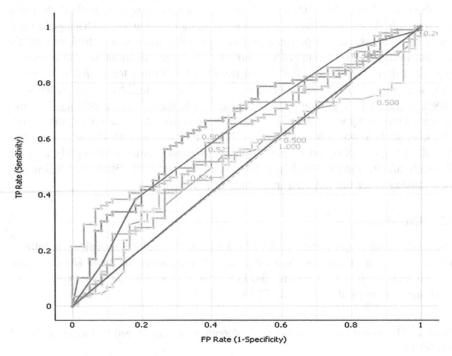

Fig. 2. ROC curve for the Grade A class as the target group

Figure 2 illustrates the ROC curve for Grade A as the target class shows that Naïve Bayes, Random Forest, Logistic Regression, SVM, Neural Network, and kNN had AUC of 0.524, 0.5, 0.537, 0.5, 0.485, 0.4 respectively. Logistic regression is the most efficient method for predicting grade A among the teams hence the most effective algorithm. Logistic regression had a classification accuracy of 62.2% and a classification error of 38.3%. The kNN algorithm also had a classification accuracy of 62.2% but it had a higher classification error (45%). Both SAMME and SAMME.R had classification accuracy and error of 57.8% and 50%. The SVM algorithm had the lowest classification accuracy of 38.9% while the neural network had a classification accuracy of 56.7% and a classification error of 38.3%. The performance of the models in predicting the grade F score can also be summarized and discussed as follows.

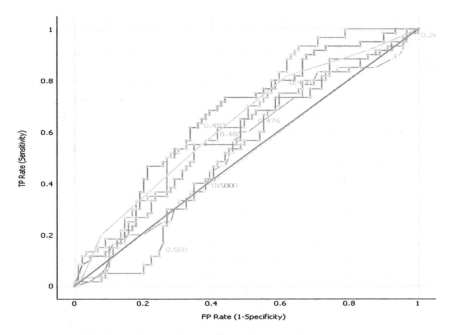

Fig. 3. ROC curve for the Grade F class as the target group

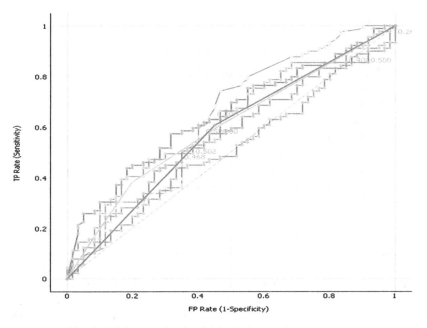

Fig. 4. ROC curve for the Grade A class as the target group

The above Fig. 3 depicts the ROC curve for Grade F as the target class shows that Naïve Bayes, Random Forest, Logistic Regression, SVM, Neural Network, and kNN had AUC of 0.476 0.5, 0.463, 0.5, 0.483, 0.4 respectively. Random Forest and SVM are the most efficient method for predicting grade F among the teams hence the most effective algorithm. Logistic regression had a classification accuracy of 61.7% and a classification error of 37.8%. The kNN algorithm also had a classification accuracy of 55% and a classification error of 37.8%. Both SAMME and SAMME.R had classification accuracy and error of 50% and 42.2%. The SVM algorithm had the highest classification accuracy (75%) while the neural network had a classification accuracy of 61.7% and a classification error of 43.3%.

Similarly, the model comparison results for SETAP Product T8 data is summarized as follows.

Based on the average performance metrics in Table 2, Random Forest was the most efficient in predicting student performance since its ROC curve covered the largest area (63.9%). Logistic regression, kNN, and Neural Network were three most efficient algorithms after Random Forest. The model finds should reflect what Petkovic et al. [5–7] established with regards to prediction of software leaning among engineering students. Regarding classification accuracy, Random Forest was the most accurate (62.7%), while logistic regression, SAMME, and SAMME.R had classification accuracy of 59.3%, 58%, and 58% respectively. More importantly, Random Forest has the least log loss value so that it minimizes errors associated with the prediction of the two performance classes.

Table 2. The performance metrics of the 8 algorithms (average A and F classes) for SETAP product T8

Method	AUC	CA	F1	Precision	Recall	Log loss
kNN	0.606	0.573	0.577	0.583	0.573	2.002
SVM	0.519	0.527	0.525	0.576	0.527	0.691
SAMME.R	0.575	0.580	0.584	0.591	0.580	14.506
SAMME	0.575	0.580	0.584	0.591	0.580	0.733
Random Forest	0.639	0.627	0.628	0.629	0.627	0.676
Neural Network	0.600	0.560	0.564	0.588	0.560	1.567
Naive Bayes	0.558	0.553	0.556	0.590	0.553	4.856
Logistic Regression	0.622	0.593	0.597	0.607	0.593	3.384

The above Fig. 4 shows the ROC curve for Grade A as the target class shows that Naïve Bayes, Random Forest, Logistic Regression, SVM, Neural Network, and kNN had AUC of 0.333, 0.451, 0.537, 0.5, 0.515, 0.4 respectively. Random Forest is the most efficient method for predicting grade A among the teams hence the most effective algorithm. Random forest had a classification accuracy of 67.8% and a classification error of 45%. The kNN algorithm also had a classification accuracy of 60% with a classification error of 46.7%. Both SAMME and SAMME.R had classification accuracy and error of 60% and 45%. The SVM algorithm had the lowest classification accuracy of 42.2% while the neural network had a classification accuracy of 52.2% and a classification error of 38.3%.

The performance of the models in predicting the grade F score can also be summarized and discussed as follows.

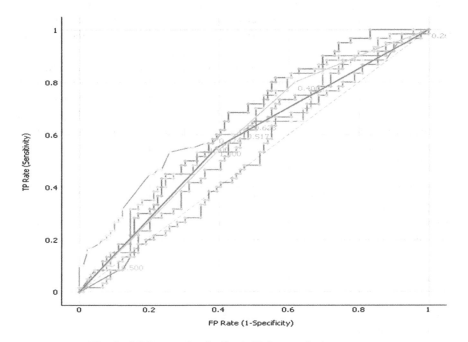

Fig. 5. ROC curve for the Grade F class as the target group

Figure 5 shows the ROC curve for Grade F as the target class shows that Naïve Bayes, Random Forest, Logistic Regression, SVM, Neural Network, and kNN had AUC of 0.311 0.493, 0.591, 0.5, 0.507, and 0.4 respectively. Logistic regression, SVM, and neural network are more efficient in predicting grade F among the teams than Random Forest, indicating the performance of the models also differ based on classes and the number of instances or observations. Logistic regression had a classification accuracy of 58.3% and a classification error of 40%. The kNN algorithm had a classification accuracy of 53.3% and a classification error of 40%. Both SAMME and SAMME.R had classification accuracy and error of 55% and 40%. The SVM algorithm had the highest classification accuracy (68.3%) while the neural network had a classification accuracy of 61.7% and a classification error of 47.8%.

5   Conclusion and Future Work

The SETAP project and the data gathered over its course have proven revolutionary in exploring student performance in learning software engineering. Even though EDM is a recognized concept and most institutions and instructors are using it to predict performance and develop intervention plans, its application in software learning appraisal and prediction remains obscure. The study demonstrated that machine learning algorithms can give different predictions depending on the dataset as well as the prevailing learning conditions. More importantly, the analysis established that Neural Network and Random Forest were the most efficient and accurate models for predicting the grades. Moving forward, the researcher should consider evaluating the two algorithms using different cross-validation folds, training set sizes, and a varying number of attributes. Of grave importance would be including such techniques in EDM platforms, and it would be prudent to implement the same study but using some of the proven EDM such as Interactive k-Means, Descent Gradient, Polynomial Classification, and Polynomial Regression.

Acknowledgment. We are grateful to the entire SETAP project team and we appreciate Professor D. Petkovic of San Francisco State University, Prof. Rainer Todtenhoefer of Fulda University, and Professor Shihong Huang of Florida Atlantic University for their role in the project and for sharing the data with UCI Machine Learning Repository.

References

1. Reddy, L., et al.: A modern approach student performance prediction using multi-agent data mining technique. i-Manager's J. Softw. Eng. **10**(1), 14–20 (2015)
2. Asif, R., Merceron, A., Pathan, M.: Predicting student academic performance at degree level: a case study. Int. J. Intell. Syst. Appl. **7**(1), 49–61 (2014)
3. Mueen, A., Zafar, B., Manzoor, U.: Modeling and predicting students' academic performance using data mining techniques. Int. J. Mod. Educ. Comput. Sci. **8**(11), 36–42 (2016)
4. Devasia, T., Vinushree, T., Hegde, V.: Prediction of students' performance using educational data mining. In: International Conference on Data Mining and Advanced Computing (SAPIENCE) (2016)
5. Petkovic, D., et al.: Using the random forest classifier to assess and predict student learning of software engineering teamwork. In: IEEE Frontiers in Education Conference (FIE) (2016)
6. Petkovic, D.: Work in progress: a machine learning approach for assessment and prediction of teamwork effectiveness in software engineering education. In: Frontiers in Education Conference Proceedings (2012)
7. Petkovic, D., et al.: Software engineering teamwork assessment and prediction using machine learning. In: Frontiers in Education Conference (IEEE), pp. 1–8 (2014)
8. Louppe, G.: Understanding random forests: from theory to practice. arXiv preprint (2014)
9. Zhu, J., Rosset, S., Zou, H., Hastie, T.: Multi-class AdaBoost. Ann Arbor **1001**, 1612 (2006)
10. Witten, I.: Data Mining: Practical Machine Learning Tools and Techniques. Morgan Kaufmann, Burlington (2016)

Data and Text Analytics

Opinion Mining for Skin Care Products on Twitter

Pakawan Pugsee[(⊠)], Vasinee Nussiri, and Wansiri Kittirungruang

Innovative Network and Software Engineering Technology Laboratory,
Department of Mathematics and Computer Science, Faculty of Science,
Chulalongkorn University, Bangkok, Thailand
pakawan.p@chula.ac.th

Abstract. Nowadays, the popularity in using skin care tends to increase and there are also a lot of exchanging opinions on online media, which directly affected to making decision on buying any products for customers. In this research, we want to find additional data for developing opinion analysis and separating emotional opinions about skin care messages. The methodology uses the data mining process, such as opinion mining with sentiment analysis through the machine learning algorithm for identifying the levels of positive and negative emotion in messages. Moreover, the skin care opinion mining application was developed based on the web application to display the results in the form of various representations. Furthermore, the performance of analytical methods is evaluated by the accuracy, precision, and recall rate, which are all more than 75%. Therefore, the automate analysis application can be employed as a helping tool for data analysis for the consumers, who are interested in skin care products, and for the entrepreneurs can know the customers' attitude of the products.

Keywords: Opinion mining · Skin care products · Naïve Bayes
Support vector machines

1 Introduction

Currently, skin care products are popular for the consumers and they are interested in buying skin care products, whether male or female. Moreover, there are many brands of skin care products divided into several types of facial and body care such as moisturizer, toner, cleaner, and mask. Therefore, many consumers take time to find information, for example, in terms of price, quality and brand for making the decision. A lot of useful information is in the form of Twitter's messages known as tweets which have been sent from the people who used skin care products because Twitter [1] is one of the online social media that the users can share their opinions and experiences. However, the consumers still must spend a lot of time for searching, reading, and understanding the large collection of tweets before buying skin care products.

As the mentioned above, this research analyzed and designed opinion mining methods, including implementing the web-based application for automatic analyzing tweets about skin care products. In addition, only the useful information that is positive, neutral, and negative messages for skin care products are represented by these text

B. W. Yap et al. (Eds.): SCDS 2018, CCIS 937, pp. 261–271, 2019.
https://doi.org/10.1007/978-981-13-3441-2_20

analysis methods. The consumers who are users of the application do not waste time reading and analyzing large amounts of data manually and they can decide to buy skin care products easier.

The details of this article will be described in the following sections. The background knowledge and related works are described in Sect. 2. The analysis and design methods are explained in Sect. 3, and the implementation is shown in Sect. 4. Section 5 demonstrates experimental results and the performance evaluation of this analysis. The conclusion is summarized in Sect. 6.

2 Background Knowledge and Related Works

Opinion mining with sentiment analysis combines the techniques of natural language processing based on machine learning, and text data mining with computational linguistics to analyze the opinions or attitudes of various article topics. The objective of the analysis is to evaluate the emotions and feelings of communication as the aspects of the product satisfactory [2–5]. There are some related researches as follows.

The article [6] is the opinion mining application to identify the comment messages about airline services, whether good or not on Twitter. The processes of opinion analysis are composed of two parts: the messages filtering to recognize only the subjective messages and the comments analysis to classify positive (good) or negative (not good). This application can analyze Twitter messages with the inputted keywords that the users want, such as the name of the airlines or the types of airline services. The application can help the customers to distinguish simply the services of these airlines are, and the airlines to know easily how to improve their services.

The research proposal [7] is the framework for the aspect classification of reviews about laptops from one of famous laptop review websites. Any paragraphs of the review pages of individual laptops are identified as the subjective or not. And then, the aspects of each subjective paragraph will be classified. Therefore, this framework can apply to the system for analyzing the laptop reviews as to help the customers make decisions before purchasing.

The paper [8] is the application development to classify any comments of the recipes from one of popular food community websites into positive or negative attitude. The sentiment analysis of food recipe satisfactory are divided into two parts: text comment processing of the natural language processing and the sentiment analysis of word concepts in the recipes comments. This application analyzes the sentiments of all recipes towards the user feedback of cooking with these recipes by using the interesting words according to the positive or the negative attitude. The output of the application is that the user like (positive) or not like (negative) the food recipes.

The research [9] is the satisfactory conclusion application for cosmetic product review comments to analyze the positive and negative attitude about various cosmetic products [10] by sentiment analysis. The application consists of four main parts: tagging parts of speech, checking words with the cosmetic sentiment lexicon, selecting sentiment words to create the classification model, and classifying product comments. The analysis methods use the machine learning technique called Naïve Bay Classifier to classify positive or negative comments. This classification application has high accuracy and precision on both positive and negative comments, but it is necessary to use positive and negative data in a similar proportion to train for learning.

As these researches mentioned above, the opinion mining with sentiment analysis are more useful for analyzing the opinion or the attitude of the consumers about the products. Although there are several applications which can classify sentiments of texts in different domains without the new training data process, the performance of the classification model varied according to the words in each domain. In addition, there are domain-specific words which affect the interpretation of real meaning. Therefore, our research further studied from the research [9], but this work focused on the comments about skin care products from Twitter by selecting text containing "#skincare" and categorizing these tweets according to sentiment levels into five groups: very positive, positive, moderate, negative, and very negative.

3   Analysis and Design Methods

3.1   Data Collection and Analysis

This research has compiled a commentary on the skin care products from Twitter known as a popular online social network, which there are many users and there is a variety of information about skin care products. Therefore, analyzing these messages can gather useful feedback on skin care products like comprehensive reviews of skin care products. Figure 1 displays the examples of tweets about skin care products.

[1] "RT @viviglowskincre: The lightening lotion and scrub doing its thing...#skincare #lighteninginabottle #review... https://t.co/76iclTflTI http..."
[2] "RT @viviglowskincre: Client's that share their updates, have my heart forever\xe d�◆\xed�◆\xed�◆\xed�◆\xed�◆\xed�◆#skincare #viviglowskincare #alln atural #allflawless https..."
[3] "RT @byalicexo: #ICYMI @Avon_UK milk & honey hand cream https://t.co /XmZwXnMnxG #bbloggers #beauty #skincare #milk #honey #sundayblogshare"

[4] "RT @viviglowskincre: Client's that share their updates, have my heart forever\xe d�◆\xed�◆\xed�◆\xed�◆\xed�◆\xed�◆#skincare #viviglowskincare #alln atural #allflawless https..."
[5] "The new Skincare Daily! [https://t.co/f2Kj8wLksv] This time with @BeautyReca p @KiehlsUK @Shelynx #skincare #natural"

Fig. 1. Examples of tweet data about skin care products

The style of the comment texts appeared on Twitter is comprised of Twitter account names and user comments. The characteristics of tweets also are short messages limited to 140 characters. Although tweets are shorter, compared to review comments in [9], there are too many special characters and the advertising messages which need to be removed. To evaluate the efficiency of our analysis and design methods, tweets with "#skincare" are collected to capture the essentials of comments by Twitter API.

3.2   Design Methods for Generating Classification Model

Our opinion mining with sentiment analysis use the natural language processing and the machine learning techniques to classify the sentiments of texts. Therefore, tweet data are transformed into providing data for generating classification models. Methods for generating classification model, as displayed in Fig. 2, are described as follows.

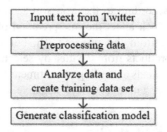

Fig. 2. Classification model generation for tweet data about skin care products

Step 1: Retrieve text from Twitter with "#skincare" and keep them as separate texts, as shown in Fig. 1.

Step 2: Preprocessing data to eliminate punctuation, symbols, number, and other special characters by using regular expressions, including changing all letters to lowercase as presented the result in Fig. 3.

[1] "the lightening lotion and scrub doing its thingskincare lighteninginabottle reviewh ttp"
[2] "clients that share their updates have my heart foreverskincareviviglowskincare all natural allflawless"
[3] "icymi avonuk milk honey hand creambbloggers beauty skincare milk honey sund ayblogshare"
[4] "clients that share their updates have my heart foreverskincareviviglowskincare all natural allflawless"
[5] "the new skincare dailythis time with beautyrecap kiehlsuk shelynx skincare natura l"

Fig. 3. Examples of tweet data about skin care products without non-letters

The NLP library of Rstudio 3.3.1 [11] has taken responsibility to identify word parts of speech (POS), such as nouns, verbs, adjectives, and adverbs. The featured study on potential words for sentiment identification of the article [12, 13] concluded that the feature selection is important for generating suitable classification model. Referring to the words in tweet data, adjectives, and adverbs are the most frequently used for describing the properties of products, and verbs can express the feeling. Therefore, non-content words, for example conjunction and preposition, also are removed and only content words are analyzed in the next step.

Step 3: Analysis of the texts for separating into 4 categories: unrelated, neutral, negative, and positive messages. To create training data, all collected tweets are recognized manually by three readers.

- Analyze to identify unrelated message, such as advertising and the sale announcements. Our research analyzed many tweet data and found that there are some words or phrases most frequently contained within the advertising or the sale announcement statements, i.e. "visit us", "order now", "sale", "free shipping", "preorder", "available", and "our". Therefore, all tweet data with these words or phrases are classified into unrelated messages.

- Analyze to classify non-expressive commentary and sensory feedback messages that are informative messages or neutral messages by the machine learning techniques. The example of neutral tweets is displayed in Fig. 4.

Neu	Face Moisturizer Clinique Moisture Surge Extended Thirst Relief
Neu	Purchase for yourself or a friend this fall Limited time only
Neu	Purify with YouLab SkinCare AgelessLiving Daily Cleanser

Fig. 4. Examples of neutral tweets about skin care products without non-letters

- Analyze to classify positive or negative messages by the machine learning techniques. The example of positive/negative tweets is shown in Fig. 5.

P	Loving the skincare and makeup from rodial skincare Have you tried it yet
N	White Mask is too oil I do not like it
P	I am so lucky to have found the perfect skincare in savyboheme
P	Make your feet flawless get a smooth skin and stop smelly feet with perfederm
N	testimonialthis is my year old son who gets quite bad eczema jeunesse luminesce skincare beauty

Fig. 5. Examples of positive/negative tweets about skin care products without non-letters

To generate a classification model, the training data set are created for providing data for the machine learning techniques.

Step 4: Use the machine learning library of Rstudio 3.3.1 [11] to create classification models for categorizing tweet data. According to the research [9], Naïve Bayes had higher performance than other techniques in their experiments, but they did not run on the support vector machines (SVMs). Therefore, our research chose Naïve Bayes and SVMs to compare the result efficiency. Consequently, there are 4 generated classification models: the neutral statement classification by Naïve Bayes or SVMs, and the positive/negative statements classification by Naïve Bayes or SVMs.

3.3 Design Methods for Analyzing Tweet Data

Methods of opinion mining with sentiment analysis for analyzing tweet data are separated into two main parts: preprocessing and classification as shown in Fig. 6. The first part (preprocessing) consists of searching to collect tweets using the key-word with preprocessing data and eliminating unrelated messages to provide the data set for classifying sentiments by the second part (classification). To analyze sentiments, there are two classification models by the machine learning techniques: neutral comments and positive or negative comments. In addition, the sentiment levels of positive and negative comment messages are detailed before representing the result.

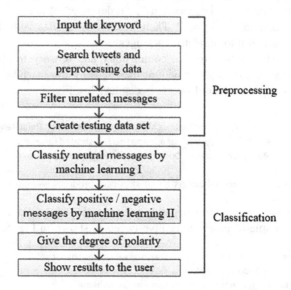

Fig. 6. Opinion mining with sentiment analysis for tweet data about skin care products

Step 1: The opinion mining web application starts by receiving the keyword from the users.

Step 2: Find the tweets containing the keyword and preprocessing data, as well as step 2 of design methods for generating classification model, to remove all non-letters and non-content words.

Step 3: Identify unrelated messages according to the words and the phrases most frequently found in advertising and sale announcement statements. Then, these tweets are deleted from the data set.

Step 4: Create the test data set.

Step 5: Classify information and neutral messages by the machine learning. These statements are kept for displaying the result and all statements with sentiment polarity are sent to the next step in analyzing.

Step 6: Classify positive and negative messages by the machine learning.

Step 7: Give the degree of polarity for messages from step 6 into 4 levels: very positive, positive, negative, very negative. The revised information of words' polarity from SentiWordNet [14] is the polarity lexicon for counting words with the positive and negative feelings in each message. Tweets are the short messages so if positive messages contain more than 3 positive words, they will be very positive, and if negative messages contain more than 3 negative words, they will be very negative.

These previous rules generated from calculating the number of positive and negative words found in messages for average value, minimum value, and maximum value. However, the double negative statements are still the problem because the grammar of the sentence is not considered.

Step 8:   Show the results of the opinion mining with sentiment analysis to the users.

4   Implementation

The web application implementing our opinion mining with sentiment analysis is developed and the best classification models from the experimental data are embedded in this opinion mining web application. The first result page of the web application when the user inputs the keyword "etude", known as one famous brand of cosmetic products, are shown in Fig. 7. Additionally, Figs. 7(a) and (b) are the enlarged texts of messages in the positive, and negative frames respectively.

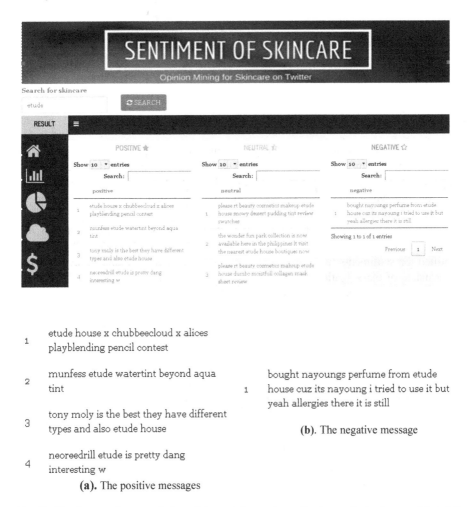

1	etude house x chubbeecloud x alices playblending pencil contest
2	munfess etude watertint beyond aqua tint
3	tony moly is the best they have different types and also etude house
4	neoreedrill etude is pretty dang interesting w

(a). The positive messages

| 1 | bought nayoungs perfume from etude house cuz its nayoung i tried to use it but yeah allergies there it is still |

(b). The negative message

Fig. 7.   The first result page of the opinion mining web application with the keyword "etude"

Figure 8 displays the bar graph of the number of messages in different sentiment levels in the second result page of the web application. The x-axis is five sentiment levels: very negative, negative, neutral, positive, and very positive, and the y-axis is the number of messages.

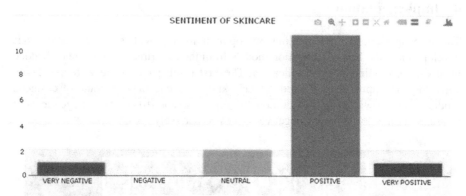

Fig. 8. The second result page of the opinion mining web application

5 Experimental Results and Evaluation

Our research experimented on messages about skin care products corrected from Twitter for opinion mining with sentiment analysis. The experimental data were 10,017 tweets with "#skincare", which were composed of 1,098 unrelated messages (advertising or sale announcement). Therefore, there were 8,919 messages performed to generate the classification models for analyzing messages about skin care products. These messages consisted of 3,215 information or neutral messages and 5,704 positive/negative messages (4,499 positive & 1,205 negative), which all manually identified the sentiments (neutral, positive, negative) by three readers. To evaluate the performance of classification, the accuracy, precision, and recall values [15] are calculated from a confusion matrix as shown in Tables 1 and 2.

Table 1. A confusion matrix

Predicted class	Actual class	
	Negative	Positive
Negative	TN	FN
Positive	FP	TP

Table 2. Performance rates

	Accuracy	Precision	Recall
Negative	(TP+TN)/(TP+TN+FP+FN)	TN/(TN+FN)	TN/(TN+FP)
Positive		TP/(TP+FP)	TP/(TP+FN)

The precision rate indicates the classification efficiency of individual class data, and the recall rate explains that the data of each class can be fully classified (without missing).

5.1   Classification of Neutral Messages

The first classification model is to identify messages into neutral statements or positive/negative statements. According to the research [9], Naïve Bayes and SVMs were selected for the machine learning part based on the 10-fold cross validation. The results of classifying the neutral messages by Naïve Bayes and SVMs are demonstrated in Tables 3 and 4 respectively. The performance of classification models by both machine learning techniques is also shown in Tables 5 and 6.

Table 3. A confusion matrix of neutral classification by Naïve Bayes.

Predicted class	Actual class	
	Neutral	Pos/Neg
Neutral	2,343	769
Pos/Neg	872	4,935
All	3,215	5,704

Table 4. A confusion matrix of neutral classification by SVMs.

Predicted class	Actual class	
	Neutral	Pos/Neg
Neutral	2,556	549
Pos/Neg	659	5,155
All	3,215	5,704

Table 5. The performance of neutral classification by Naïve Bayes.

	Accuracy	Precision	Recall
Neutral	0.82	0.75	0.73
Pos/Neg		0.85	0.87

Table 6. The performance of neutral classification by SVMs.

	Accuracy	Precision	Recall
Neutral	0.86	0.82	0.80
Pos/Neg		0.89	0.90

Tables 3 and 4 shows the neutral classification results of Naïve Bayes comparing to SVMs. There were 2,343 neutral messages and 4,935 positive/negative messages correctly classified by Naïve Bayes, while 1,641 messages were identified incorrectly. Another neutral classification model by SVMs recognized 2,556 neutral messages and 5,155 positive/negative messages precisely, but there were the number of incorrectly classified messages of 1,208 messages.

Referring to Tables 5 and 6, the overall performance of neutral classification by SVMs is higher than that of by Naïve Bayes. Moreover, all evaluated values of the SVMs classification are higher than 80%, while the precision and recall values of the Naïve Bayes classification of neutral statements are less than 80%. Although the precision and recall of neutral statements are less than those of positive/negative statements, both Naïve Bayes and SVMs neutral classification models are reasonably effective for identifying the statements without the sentiment polarity.

5.2 Classification of Positive/Negative Messages

The second classification model is to classify messages into positive or negative statements. The 10-fold cross validation were applied to generate the model like the first classification model. The results of classifying the polarity messages by Naïve Bayes and SVMs are expressed in Tables 7 and 8 respectively. Additionally, the performance of these polarity classification is displayed in Tables 9 and 10.

Table 7. A confusion matrix of sentiment classification by Naïve Bayes.

Predicted class	Actual class	
	Negative	Positive
Negative	945	255
Positive	260	4,244
All	1,205	4,499

Table 8. A confusion matrix of sentiment classification by SVMs.

Predicted class	Actual class	
	Negative	Positive
Negative	918	153
Positive	287	4,346
All	1,205	4,499

Table 9. The performance of sentiment classification by Naïve Bayes.

	Accuracy	Precision	Recall
Negative	0.91	0.79	0.78
Positive		0.94	0.94

Table 10. The performance of sentiment classification by SVM.

	Accuracy	Precision	Recall
Negative	0.92	0.86	0.76
Positive		0.94	0.97

According to Tables 7 and 8, the 945 negative messages with the 4,244 positive messages were correctly classified by Naïve Bayes, and the 918 negative messages with the 4,346 positive messages were appropriately identified by SVMs. On the other hand, there were the 260 negative messages and the 255 positive messages incorrectly classified by Naïve Bayes, including the 287 uncorrected positive messages and the 153 uncorrected negative messages by SVMs.

The performance of these two sentiment classification models as shown in Tables 9 and 10 can be concluded that the overall performance of sentiment classification by SVMs is higher a little bit than that of by Naïve Bayes. In addition, both of sentiment classification models can determine the positive statements better than the negative statements with all evaluated values of performance more than 90%. However, the recall values of both negative classifications are less than 80%. One reason is that the amount of negative statements is much less than the number of positive statements, so the model may not recognize the polarity of statements correctly.

Discussing both neutral and polarity classification, the results found that when the amount of one class is much less than the number of another class, SVMs classification has higher performance than Naïve Bayes classification. Moreover, the error analysis is caused by that the experimental data may not cover all words related to skin care products, such as slang terms. Furthermore, some ambiguous messages and ridiculous statements may not be clearly classified.

6 Conclusion

The web application implementing the proposed opinion mining for skin care products can analyze tweet data effectively. The data analysis for opinion mining with sentiment analysis consists of two main parts: preprocessing and classification. There are two classification models for identifying information or neutral statements and positive/negative statements. The analysis results are in the form of messages in 3 categories (neutral, negative, positive) and the bar graph of the number of messages in 5 sentiment levels (very negative, negative, neutral, positive, and very positive). The performance evaluation results found that most of evaluated values are more than 80%. Therefore, the developed opinion mining web application can help users easily analyze tweets about skin care products.

References

1. Twitter homepage. https://twitter.com. Accessed 14 Sept 2017
2. Fang, X., Zhan, J.: Sentiment analysis using product review data. J. Big. Data. **2**(5), 1–14 (2015). https://doi.org/10.1186/s40537-015-0015-2
3. Isah, H., Trundle, P., Neagu, D.: Social media analysis for product safety using text mining and sentiment analysis. In: 14th UK Workshop Proceedings on Computational Intelligence, pp. 1–7. IEEE, UK (2014). https://doi.org/10.1109/ukci.2014.6930158
4. Liu, B.: Sentiment Analysis and Opinion Mining. Morgan & Claypool, California (2012)
5. Cambria, E., Das, D., Bandyopadhyay, S., Feraco, A.: A Practical Guide to Sentiment Analysis (Socio-Affective Computing 5). Cham, UK (2017). https://doi.org/10.1007/978-3-319-55394-8
6. Pugsee, P., Chongvisuit, T., Na Nakorn, K.: Opinion mining on Twitter data for airline services. In: 5th International Workshop Proceedings on Computer Science and Engineering: Information Processing and Control Engineering, pp. 639–644 (2015). (in Russia)
7. Chatchaithanawat, T., Pugsee, P.: A framework for laptop review analysis. In: 2nd International Conference Proceedings on Advanced Informatics: Concepts, Theory and Applications, pp. 1–5. IEEE, Thailand (2015). https://doi.org/10.1109/icaicta.2015.7335358
8. Pugsee, P., Niyomvanich, M.: Sentiment analysis of food recipe comments. ECTI-CIT. **9**(2), 182–193 (2015)
9. Pugsee, P., Sombatsri, P., Juntiwakul, R.: Satisfactory analysis for cosmetic product review comments. In: 2017 International Conference Proceedings on Data Mining, Communications and Information Technology, pp. 1–6. ACM, Thailand (2017). https://doi.org/10.1145/3089871.3089890
10. MakeupAlley. http://www.makeupalley.com/product/
11. RStudio. https://www.rstudio.com
12. Shuai, H.H., et al.: Mining online social data for detecting social network mental disorders. In: 25th International Conference Proceedings on World Wide Web, pp. 275–285. ACM, Canada (2016). https://doi.org/10.1145/2872427.2882996
13. Qazi, A., Raj, R., Hardaker, G., Standing, C.: A systematic literature review on opinion types and sentiment analysis techniques: Tasks and challenges. Internet Res. **27**(3), 608–630 (2017). https://doi.org/10.1108/IntR-04-2016-0086
14. SentiWordNet. http://sentiwordnet.isti.cnr.it/
15. Data School. https://www.dataschool.io/simple-guide-to-confusion-matrix-terminology/

Tweet Hybrid Recommendation Based on Latent Dirichlet Allocation

Arisara Pornwattanavichai[✉],
Prawpan Brahmasakha Na Sakolnagara,
Pongsakorn Jirachanchaisiri, Janekhwan Kitsupapaisan,
and Saranya Maneeroj

Department of Mathematics and Computer Science, Faculty of Science,
Chulalongkorn University, Bangkok, Thailand
{Arisara.p, Prawpan.b, Pongsakorn.j,
Janekhwan.k}@math.sc.chula.ac.th,
Saranya.M@chula.ac.th

Abstract. Recommender system was created to recommend products to users that user may interest. The most recommender systems use two kinds of recommendation techniques which are collaborative filtering (CF) and content-based filtering (CBF). CF use combination of ratings from users in the system who are similar to target user to recommend. Users who are similar to the target user are called neighbors. Therefore, CF will give variety recommendations. CBF uses the past behavior of the target user to find a similar item to the target user's behavior to recommend. Nowadays, there are many data on social networks including tweet data in the Twitter. Thus, many researchers have studied recommender systems which based on tweet using latent Dirichlet allocation (LDA) to extract latent data from observed data. However, those researches use either CF or CBF with LDA only. However, disadvantages of CF are sparsity and cold-start problem. So, the system cannot efficiently recommend. For CBF, it cannot recommend a new product that users may be interested. Therefore, this research recommends tweets base on hybrid recommender system with LDA, which combines CF and CBF to solve disadvantages of CF and CBF. From experimental results, the proposed method outperforms in term of mean absolute error and coverage.

Keywords: Hybrid recommender system · Latent Dirichlet allocation
Tweet recommendation

1 Introduction

1.1 Recommender Systems

Recommender system (RS) [1, 2] is the system that created for suggesting items that an active user may interest. The suggestion of RS base on information of the active user that was given to the system in the past. There are two main techniques of RS which are content-based filtering (CBF) [1] and collaborative filtering (CF) [1].

© Springer Nature Singapore Pte Ltd. 2019
B. W. Yap et al. (Eds.): SCDS 2018, CCIS 937, pp. 272–285, 2019.
https://doi.org/10.1007/978-981-13-3441-2_21

CBF is the technique that suggests an item which is similar to items that the active user liked in the past. Furthermore, preference of the user will be extracted. There are some advantages of CBF. First, CBF does not need much information. Furthermore, CBF starts to recommend in the early step and can recommend a unique taste item for the active user.

However, CBF is also has a problem. Because CBF recommend only the item that has a similar type to the items that active user has rated in the past, an item that does not similar to them will be not recommended. For example, if the user has rated only hip-hop songs, it is impossible that the system will recommend a pop song to the active user. So, items that recommended to the active user are not diverse. This problem is called serendipitous problem.

Another main technique is CF; CF is the technique that can solve the serendipitous problem by recommending items of other users in the system that similar to the active user. The advantage of CF is a diversity of items. CF can recommend the item from many types depend on other users in the system. The limitation of CF is sparsity. Sparsity occurs when the information in the system is too sparse and do not enough to find the similar neighbors.

To solve the problem of CF and keep the advantages of CBF, the technique that is a combination of CBF and CF is introduced which is called a hybrid [1, 2].

In the recent years, RS is very popular and is applied in many fields such as film industry [3–5], music industry [6, 7], and social network [8–10]. One of the social networks that RS has an influence is Twitter.

1.2 Twitter

Twitter [11] is a social network which messages that communicate on Twitter are compact, simple and fast. The user in the system can write words for posting up to 240 words which this action is called "tweet". Twitter allows the user to receive messages from following users which the messages are called "tweet" too. Every interaction between user will appear in the timeline of each user. Moreover, Twitter allows repeating the tweet from the other user which this action is called "retweet." Nowadays, there are many tweet messages on user timeline. Sometimes, tweet messages do not match user preference. Thus, there are many researches in recommender system that focus on the tweet domain.

1.3 Latent Dirichlet Allocation (LDA)

Latent Dirichlet Allocation (LDA) [12] is a probabilistic generative model that can extract latent topic by using observed data. LDA is widely used in topic modeling. The basic idea of LDA for document generation is following:

1. Randomly choose a distribution over topics.
2. For each word in the document
   a. Randomly choose a topic from the distribution over topics from the first step.
   b. Randomly choose a word from the topic distribution over the vocabulary corresponding to step a.

From the generative process above, it can be represented as a graphical model in Fig. 1. In general, the input of LDA is documents-words co-occurrence matrix, and LDA returns θ and ϕ which are documents-topics distribution and topics-words distribution respectively. These two distributions are used for many applications including recommender system.

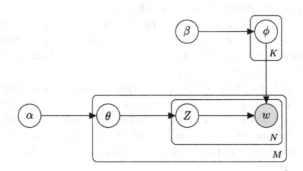

Fig. 1. Graphical model of LDA

Where each variable in the graphical model denotes:

- w denotes word which has N words in the corpus
- Z denotes latent topic of words
- θ denotes documents-topics distribution which has M documents
- ϕ denotes topics-words distribution which has K topics
- α and β are the prior distribution of θ and ϕ respectively

1.4   Twitter Recommendation with LDA

From limitation of CF and CBF and capability for extracting latent topic of LDA, there are many recommender system research which aims to apply LDA to either CF or CBF [13–15] on the tweet domain. Each research tries to embed user and item to document and item with a different assumption. After that, model parameters from LDA will be applied to either CF or CBF to make a recommendation. In this case, a tweet recommendation that applies LDA to CF or CBF will be introduced.

First, Improved Collaborative Filtering Algorithm using Topic Model [16] is CF-RS. This research is introduced to recommend top-N items to the active user. From Fig. 2, items act as documents and users act as words. Items are represented as a random mixture of latent topics; each topic is characterized by a distribution of users. The result from LDA is applied to find a distribution of user-topic and use it to find similarity between the target user and other users. k-users that most similar to the target user will be treated as user's neighbors. Rating of the target user on the target item is predicted using weight average on the rating of a neighbor on the target item where the weight is a similarity between the target user and neighbor.

Third, Recommendations Based on LDA Topic Model in Android Applications [17] is CBF-RS. This research studied how to recommend the application to the user

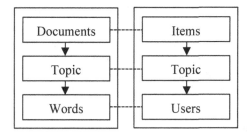

Fig. 2. An analogy between items and users

which the user would most prefer. First, bringing the application's description and the user's comment through LDA to find the probability distribution of the application's topics. Next, finding similarity between the applications that user had been used and the other application by comparing the probability distribution of the application's topics with KL-divergence. Finally, recommending the top-N most similar application to the target user.

Fourth, User interest prediction in Microblog using Recommendation Method [18] use LDA and matrix factorization to make CBF-RS. First, they find the user-topic distribution and the topic-tweet distribution using LDA. However, they want to improve the accuracy of this work, so they use matrix factorize on user-topic distribution to find the new user-topic distribution, which was more accurate than the normal user-topic distribution that received from LDA. Then, compared the new user-topic distribution and topic-tweet distribution that derived from LDA to find user-tweet preference matrix which it told how much the user had assigned a preference value to each tweet.

From the previous researches, many recommendation techniques apply LDA to either CF or CBF only. However, both CF and CBF have different advantages and disadvantages. CBF recommends overspecialized item and this item will be recommend repeatedly to a target user. Thus, CBF cannot recommend a variety of items. On the other hands, CF requires many data to find appropriate neighbors to make effective recommendations. If the amount of data is not enough, sparsity [2] and the cold-start [2, 19] problem will occur. Therefore, using only CF or CBF is not enough to make effective recommendations. From limitations of CF and CBF, we proposed improved tweet recommendation method by applying LDA on both CF and CBF to make effective recommendations.

2   The Proposed Method

Many recent works used LDA to extract latent data in Tweet recommendation works. However, the previous works used LDA with either CF or CBF. If we bring the advantage of CBF that does not require many data to reduce the cold-start problem and the advantage of CF that can recommend many categories. It may improve the efficiency of recommendation, compared with the previous works. From the above reasons, we begin this improvement recommendation research which can recommend interesting tweet to each user by using LDA on hybrid recommendation (hybrid is a kind of recommendation techniques which applied both CF and CBF together) on Twitter. The purpose of this research is to present the new research procedure which can recommend tweet by using LDA on a hybrid approach.

In this section, we first describe data preparation for our processes. Then, we present our CF part, CBF part and, prediction of user's preference for tweet steps.

2.1 Data Preparation

From data on this work, we extract 11,685 tweet messages of 3,436 Twitter users. Each user has an average rating of 16. We call this data as "Original Data". In original data, we create a user-tweet matrix and user-user matrix. The user-tweet matrix represents the relationship between all users and all tweets in binary form. If user u never tweet or retweet tweet message t, the value in position (u, t) in the user-tweet matrix is 0. Otherwise, the value is 1. The user-tweet matrix can be depicted in Fig. 3.

$$
\begin{array}{c}
\begin{array}{ccccccc} t_1 & t_2 & t_3 & \ldots & t_{t-2} & t_{t-1} & t_t \end{array} \\
\begin{array}{c} u_1 \\ u_2 \\ \vdots \\ u_{u-1} \\ u_u \end{array}
\begin{bmatrix}
1 & 1 & 1 & & 0 & 0 & 0 \\
0 & 0 & 0 & \cdots & 0 & 0 & 0 \\
\vdots & \vdots & & \ddots & & \vdots & \\
0 & 0 & 0 & \cdots & 0 & 0 & 0 \\
0 & 0 & 0 & & 0 & 0 & 0
\end{bmatrix}
\end{array}
$$

Fig. 3. The user-tweet matrix

After that, we create a user-user matrix. This matrix represents the relationship between all users in binary form. If user u does not follow user v. The value in position (u, v) in the user-user matrix is 0. Otherwise, the value is 1. The user-user matrix can be depicted in Fig. 4.

$$
\begin{array}{c}
\begin{array}{ccccccc} v_1 & v_2 & v_3 & \ldots & v_{v-2} & v_{v-1} & v_v \end{array} \\
\begin{array}{c} u_1 \\ u_2 \\ \vdots \\ u_{u-1} \\ u_u \end{array}
\begin{bmatrix}
1 & 0 & 0 & & 0 & 0 & 0 \\
0 & 1 & 0 & \cdots & 0 & 0 & 0 \\
\vdots & \vdots & & \ddots & & \vdots & \\
0 & 0 & 0 & \cdots & 0 & 1 & 0 \\
0 & 0 & 0 & & 0 & 0 & 1
\end{bmatrix}
\end{array}
$$

Fig. 4. The user-user matrix

2.2 CBF Part

In this part, we apply CBF to estimate user's preference on the tweet or pseudo-rating to fulfill user-tweet matrix by using LDA. First, we apply user-tweet matrix as input to find θ or user-topic distribution matrix. Each row and each column of θ represents each user and each topic respectively. Moreover, we find ϕ or topic-tweet distribution matrix which each row and each column represent each topic and each tweet respectively. θ and ϕ can be depicted as Figs. 5 and 6 respectively.

$$
\begin{array}{c}
\begin{array}{ccccc}
T_1 & T_2 & T_3 & \cdots & T_T
\end{array} \\
\begin{array}{c} u_1 \\ u_2 \\ \vdots \\ u_{u-1} \\ u_u \end{array}
\left[
\begin{array}{ccccc}
5 \times 10^{-3} & 5 \times 10^{-3} & 9.05 \times 10^{-1} & \cdots & 5 \times 10^{-3} \\
3.33 \times 10^{-3} & 3.33 \times 10^{-3} & 3.33 \times 10^{-3} & & 3.33 \times 10^{-3} \\
\vdots & & \vdots & \ddots & \\
2 \times 10^{-2} & 2 \times 10^{-2} & 2 \times 10^{-2} & \cdots & 2 \times 10^{-1} \\
7.69 \times 10^{-3} & 7.69 \times 10^{-3} & 7.69 \times 10^{-3} & & 7.69 \times 10^{-3}
\end{array}
\right]
\end{array}
$$

Fig. 5. The user-topic distribution matrix (θ)

$$
\begin{array}{c}
\begin{array}{ccccc}
t_1 & t_2 & t_3 & \cdots & t_t
\end{array} \\
\begin{array}{c} T_1 \\ T_2 \\ \vdots \\ T_{T-1} \\ T_T \end{array}
\left[
\begin{array}{ccccc}
1.12 \times 10^{-5} & 1.12 \times 10^{-5} & 1.12 \times 10^{-5} & \cdots & 1.12 \times 10^{-5} \\
1.2 \times 10^{-5} & 1.2 \times 10^{-5} & 1.2 \times 10^{-5} & & 1.2 \times 10^{-5} \\
\vdots & & \vdots & \ddots & \vdots \\
1.05 \times 10^{-5} & 1.05 \times 10^{-5} & 1.05 \times 10^{-5} & \cdots & 1.05 \times 10^{-5} \\
1.03 \times 10^{-5} & 1.03 \times 10^{-5} & 1.03 \times 10^{-5} & & 1.03 \times 10^{-5}
\end{array}
\right]
\end{array}
$$

Fig. 6. The topic-tweet distribution matrix (ϕ)

Then, we apply θ and ϕ to Eq. (1) which is a multiplication of θ and ϕ. The result is the full user-tweet matrix in Fig. 7 such that the u_i and t are row and column respectively.

$$
\begin{array}{c}
\begin{array}{ccccc}
t_1 & t_2 & t_3 & \cdots & t_t
\end{array} \\
\begin{array}{c} u_1 \\ u_2 \\ \vdots \\ u_{u-1} \\ u_u \end{array}
\left[
\begin{array}{ccccc}
2.97 \times 10^{-3} & 2.97 \times 10^{-3} & 1.98 \times 10^{-3} & \cdots & 1.69 \times 10^{-5} \\
2.09 \times 10^{-5} & 2.09 \times 10^{-5} & 1.73 \times 10^{-5} & & 1.41 \times 10^{-5} \\
\vdots & & \vdots & \ddots & \vdots \\
7.64 \times 10^{-5} & 7.64 \times 10^{-5} & 5.46 \times 10^{-5} & \cdots & 3.51 \times 10^{-5} \\
3.56 \times 10^{-5} & 3.56 \times 10^{-5} & 2.73 \times 10^{-5} & & 1.98 \times 10^{-3}
\end{array}
\right]
\end{array}
$$

Fig. 7. The user-tweet preference matrix

$$
u - t\ preference_{i,j} = \theta_{i1}\phi_{1j} + \theta_{i2}\phi_{2j} + \ldots + \theta_{iT}\phi_{Tj} \tag{1}
$$

Where each position in the matrix is $u - t\ preference_{i,j}$ that represents preference value of user i to tweet j.

As we can see, all processes in this part only consider about user's characteristic to all tweets in the system. Thus, this process is CBF.

2.3   CF Part

In this part, we apply user-user matrix (U-V matrix) to find the probability that a target user u will follow other users v in the system. From the idea, "if user u follows other users, it means that both users has the same interest or they are similar". Therefore, we apply the probability that a target user u will follow other users as the similarity between the user u and other users in the system. However, the user-user matrix is sparse. Thus, we apply GMF to the user-user matrix for prediction user-user similarity. Then, we find top 60 neighbors of the target user u by ranking top 60 maximum similarity in user-user similarity matrix. After that, we will get the list of users who are the top 60 neighbors of the user u and their similarity between them. The user-user matrix which is the output of GMF can be depicted as Fig. 8.

$$
\begin{array}{c c c c c c}
 & v_1 & v_2 & v_3 & \cdots & v_v \\
\begin{matrix} u_1 \\ u_2 \\ \vdots \\ u_{u-1} \\ u_u \end{matrix} &
\begin{bmatrix}
9.81 \times 10^{-8} & 1.17 \times 10^{-7} & 2.18 \times 10^{-8} & \cdots & 7.13 \times 10^{-5} \\
1.65 \times 10^{-7} & 1.81 \times 10^{-7} & 1.66 \times 10^{-7} & & 1.21 \times 10^{-2} \\
\vdots & & \vdots & \ddots & \vdots \\
1.54 \times 10^{-2} & 1.56 \times 10^{-2} & 1.58 \times 10^{-2} & \cdots & 1.31 \times 10^{-2} \\
1.28 \times 10^{-2} & 1.31 \times 10^{-2} & 8.66 \times 10^{-3} & \cdots & 9.52 \times 10^{-3}
\end{bmatrix}
\end{array}
$$

Fig. 8. The user-user matrix

Generalized Matrix Factorization. Generalized Matrix Factorization (GMF) [20] is a technique for predicting data based on matrix factorization and neural network. The previous work applies user-tweet matrix as the input of GMF, but in our work, we apply user-user matrix as the input of GMF. After that, we use those vectors to predict the relationship between the user and item. So, GMF is used to predict unknown data when the data is high sparsity.

In our method, we apply GMF to the user-user matrix to find the relationships between users. In the beginning, the prediction is started by splitting the dataset into a training set and test set.

Test Set. The test set was extracted from both original user-user matrix and user-item matrix which consider only Twitter users number 0 to 1,027.

We mainly focus on the test set as the output data in our work. So, the test set was used in both CF and CBF part. In the CBF part, we apply the user-tweet matrix to be the input of LDA. In CF part, we apply user-user matrix as a test set of GMF.

Training Set. Training set includes an only user-user matrix. Moreover, we only choose tweet users number 1,028 to 3,436. User-user matrix from the training set only used in GMF for learning optimal parameter such as weight and bias of GMF.

After learning phase of GMF, we use the test set for prediction and get results as the relationship between all users in the system. The process of GMF starts with P and Q which are a vector of user u and user v respectively.

First, a latent vector of user u and latent vector of user v are denoted as p_u (or $P^T v_u^U$) and q_v (or $Q^T v_v^I$) respectively. Next, we apply these two vectors to mapping function of the first neural CF layer by element-wise product of vector method as in Eq. (2). After we get a vector $p_u \odot q_v$ from Eq. (2), we project this vector to the output layer in Eq. (3). Finally, we will get the output as the rating value that user u will give to user v.

$$\emptyset_1(p_u, q_v) = p_u \odot q_v \tag{2}$$

$$\hat{y}_{u,v} = a_{out}\left(h^T(p_u \odot q_v)\right) \tag{3}$$

Where $\hat{y}_{(u,v)}$ denotes the rating value that user u will give to user v, h^T and a_{out} denote the activation function and weights of the output layer respectively, and $\odot$ element-wise product. In this work, we use sigmoid activation function as Eq. (4).

$$S(x) = \frac{1}{1+e^{-x}} = \frac{e^x}{e^x+1} \tag{4}$$

After we finish all process of GMF, we will get user-user similarity matrix without unknown data. Then, we rank top 60 maximum similarities between the target user and the other users to get a neighbor list which the list will use it in the next part.

2.4 Prediction of User's Preference for Tweets

In this step, we will focus on which tweets will the target user like most. We apply user-tweet preference matrix which from CBF and user-user similarity matrix which is the output of GMF from CF to calculate user preference together. First, we pick tweet t and find the pseudo-preference value that target user u will give to tweet t by user-tweet preference matrix from CBF part, denoted as $rating_{u,t}$. From CF part, we get top 60 neighbors of the target user u from both GMF and other users in the system who have ever tweet/retweet the target tweet (t). The reason why we choose 60 neighbors and get some neighbor from users who have ever interacted with the target tweet because there are a few neighbors from GMF who have ever interacted with the target tweet.

After that, we can get the similarity value between target user u and target user u's neighbor, denoted as sim_{u,v_i} from the user-user matrix and get the pseudo-preference value that user u's neighbor, v gives to tweet t by user-tweet matrix from LDA from CBF part, denoted as $rating_{v,t}$. When we have already got sim_{u,v_i} and $rating_{v_i,t_i}$, we multiply them together to get $sim_{u,v_i} \times rating_{v_i,t_i}$ and sum this value from all neighbors of $user\ u$. Then, we divide it by the summation of sim_{u,v_i} from all neighbors of user u. So, we have already got the value of CF part. Next, we multiply the value of CF part with 0.4 and sum it with $rating_{u,t}$ which is the value from CBF part that was multiplied with 0.6. After we got two values from both CF and CBF part, they are calculated as P_{ut}. Finally, we can get the predicted rating which $user\ u$ will give to tweet $t(P_{ut})$ in Eq. (5).

$$P_{ut} = 0.4\left(\frac{\sum_{i=1}^{N} sim_{u,v_i} \times rating_{v_i,t_t}}{\sum_{i=1}^{N} sim_{u,v_i}}\right) + 0.6\left(rating_{u,t}\right) \tag{5}$$

Where sim_{u,v_i} denotes the preference value the target user u has toward the neighbor v_i, and $rating_{u,t}$ denotes the pseudo-preference value that a user u gives to a tweet t.

Then, P_{ut} of all tweets from each user u would be ranking into a top-10 rank that is the top 10 tweets which the system will recommend to the target user u.

The reason of multiplication CF part with 0.4 and multiply CBF part with 0.6 is to focus on target user more than target user's neighbor.

As we can see, all processes in this step are finding the top-10 tweets to recommend target user by considering both user-tweet preference matrix and user-user matrix which is CBF and CF part respectively. Thus, this process is the hybrid procedure.

3   Experimental Results

Experimental results of our proposed model are presented by comparing with the other researches that use LDA with either CF or CBF. The research that uses only LDA with CF is Improved Collaborative Filtering Algorithm using Topic Model [16]. On the other hand, another research that uses only LDA with CBF is User Interest Prediction in Microblog using Recommendation Method [18].

3.1   Datasets

The Dataset that we use in our research consisted of 11,685 tweets provided by 3,436 users. We split 1,028 users and other 2,408 users to be a test set and a training set respectively. More details of the data set are shown in Table 1.

Table 1.   Information of the dataset

Number of users	1028
Number of tweets	11685
Number of rating	16312
Maximum number of tweet per user	341
Minimum number of tweet per user	1
Average number of tweet per user	16

3.2   Evaluation Metrics

To compare the efficiency, we choose these two matrices. First, mean absolute error (MAE) measure the prediction accuracy of the system. If the system has low MAE value, it means that research has high accuracy. Second, coverage measure the ability of the system to recommend items from the test set in percentage.

Mean Absolute Error (MAE). Mean Absolute Error (MAE) is commonly used to measure the prediction accuracy of the system. The MAE value is the mean of the errors between the predicted data from the system and the real data. If the research has a low MAE value, the results that obtained from the system will be very close to the actual data, and it means that method has a very high prediction accuracy. MAE can be computed as Eq. (6).

$$MAE(u_i) = \sum\nolimits_{i=1}^{n} \frac{|r_{u,i} - \hat{r}_{u,i}|}{n}. \qquad (6)$$

Where, $r_{u,i}$ is the real rating that a user u gives to an item i, $\hat{r}_{u,i}$ is the predict rating from the system rating that a user u would give to an item i, n is number of the data in the test set and $MAE(u_i)$ denotes the mean of the errors between the predicted data from the system and the real data.

Coverage. Coverage is a way to measure the extent of all items that a system can recommend based on the percentage of items in the test set that the system can retrieve. The equation that used to measure coverage is given in Eq. (7).

$$Prediction coverage = \frac{|I_p|}{|I|} * 100 \qquad (7)$$

Where, I denotes the set of available items in the test set, I_p denotes the set of items which a prediction can be made and prediction coverage is a percentage of items in the test set that the system can retrieve.

3.3   Experimental Results

The results of the proposed method, which is the result of the LDA combined with the Hybrid Recommendation (or a combination of CBF and CF) will be compared to the research that uses LDA with either CBF or CF. These three researches are implemented on the same dataset to avoid bias. The brief description of each research is in Table 2.

To compare MAE and coverage of these three researches, we compare them to the same dataset that we describe in Sect. 3.1. MAE and coverage of each research are shown in Table 3.

From Table 3, the research that got the lowest MAE value was Tweet Hybrid Recommendation based on Latent Dirichlet Allocation. Therefore, the proposed method has higher accuracy than the rest two researches. Meanwhile, coverage of the proposed method got a 100%, while [16] can predict only 11.27% (Fig. 9).

4   Discussion

From the accuracy in the previous shows that the proposed method which is hybrid RS with LDA has the best MAE and coverage. So, we will discuss the experimental results that are why the proposed method has the best accuracy by divided our discussion into two parts as CF with LDA and CBF with LDA.

Table 2. The brief description of each research

Research	Description
User interest prediction in Microblog using Recommendation Method	First, they find the user-topic distribution and the topic-tweet distribution using LDA. However, they want to improve the accuracy of this work, so they use matrix factorize on user-topic distribution to find the new user-topic distribution, which was more accurate than the normal user-topic distribution that received from LDA. Then, compared the new user-topic distribution and topic-tweet distribution that derived from LDA to find user-tweet preference matrix which it told how much the user had assigned a preference value to each tweet
Improved Collaborative Filtering Algorithm using Topic Model	The goal of this paper is to recommend top-N items to the active user. Items act as documents and users act as words, each topic is characterized by a distribution of users. The resulting from LDA is applied to find a distribution of user-topic and use it to find similarity between the active user and other users. K users that most similar to the active user will be treated as user's neighbors. Predicted rating of the active user on the target item is predicted using weight average on the rating of a neighbor on the target item where the similarity between the active user and neighbor act as a weight

Table 3. The MAE and Coverage Results

Method	MAE	Coverage
Tweet Hybrid Recommendation based on Latent Dirichlet Allocation (The proposed method)	**0.018**	**100%**
User interest prediction in Microblog using Recommendation Method (LDA+CBF)	0.260	100%
Improved Collaborative Filtering Algorithm using Topic Model (LDA +CF)	0.995	11.27%

4.1 User Interest Prediction in Microblog Using Recommendation Method (LDA+CBF)

MAE of the proposed method is lower than [18] because they do not apply user-tweet preference data from target user's neighbor. Thus, the recommendation does not include variety and cannot recommend some tweet that the target user may prefer. In contrast, the proposed method considers both target user's data and neighbor's data, doing so would increase prediction accuracy.

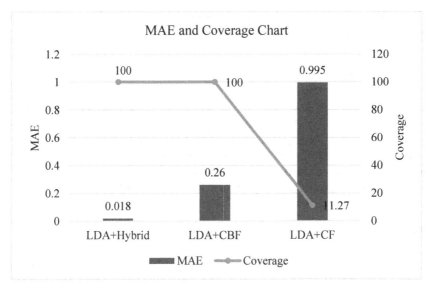

Fig. 9. Comparison of MAE and coverage

As a result, we can conclude that the proposed method has lower MAE than [18] because the proposed method applies data from target user's neighbor. While [18] only considers data from target user.

Both coverage values of the proposed method and [18] are 100% because they both apply Content-based filtering. It finds the rating that target user will give to a tweet by comparing between use-topic distribution and topic-tweet distribution. Thus, they can get all user-tweet preference data.

4.2   Improved Collaborative Filtering Algorithm Using Topic Model (LDA+CF)

MAE of [16] is higher than the proposed method. Since both two works have different ways to find target user's neighbor. [16] finds target user's neighbors by comparing the user-topic distribution of each user. If target user and other user have similar user-topic distribution, they will be neighbors. On the other hand, the proposed method finds target user's neighbor by considering user-user matrix as their relations and predict all sparse data in the user-user matrix by GMF. Moreover, the proposed method has an additional way to find target user's neighbors who interacted with target tweet by considering user-tweet matrix and get those users to be target user's neighbors. By doing so, the proposed method will get a better group of neighbors for the target user.

Coverage of [16] is less than the proposed method. Because [16] applies the real rating that user gives to tweet and the real rating is binary in prediction step. So, the rating in prediction equation can be 0. By doing so, the prediction rating can be sparse data. While the proposed method applies a rating that neighbor gives to tweet in prediction equation by using pseudo-value in full user-tweet rating matrix from LDA

(CBF part) which is not sparse data. So, the proposed method has higher efficiency in a number of prediction rating than [16].

5 Conclusions

This work proposes a new tweet recommendation method named Tweet Hybrid Recommendation based on Latent Dirichlet Allocation, which is a method, is used to recommend tweet for the target user by using LDA and Hybrid method. From the evaluation, we find that Tweet Hybrid Recommendation based on Latent Dirichlet Allocation has the lower MAE value and the higher coverage value than the current recommendation methods that apply LDA with either CF or CBF.

References

1. Adomavicius, G., Tuzhilin, A.: Toward the next generation of recommender systems: a survey of the state-of-the-art and possible extensions. IEEE Trans. Knowl. Data Eng. **17**(6), 734–749 (2005)
2. Guo, G.: Resolving data sparsity and cold start in recommender systems. In: Masthoff, J., Mobasher, B., Desmarais, M.C., Nkambou, R. (eds.) UMAP 2012. LNCS, vol. 7379, pp. 361–364. Springer, Heidelberg (2012). https://doi.org/10.1007/978-3-642-31454-4_36
3. Arora, G., Kumar, A., Sanjay-Devre, G., Ghumare, A.: Movie recommendation system based on users' similarity. IJCSMC **3**(4), 765–770 (2014)
4. Shreya, A., Pooja-Jain, A.: An improved approach for movie recommendation system. In: 2017 International Conference on I-SMAC (IoT in Social, Mobile, Analytics and Cloud) (I-SMAC) (2017)
5. Mirza, I., Suharjito, S.: Film recommendation systems using matrix factorization and collaborative filtering. In: November International Conference on Information Technology Systems and Innovation (ICITSI) 2014, Bandung, Bali (2014)
6. Kodama, Y., et al.: A music recommendation system. In: 2005 Digest of Technical Papers, International Conference on Consumer Electronics (ICCE) (2005)
7. Shakirova, E.: Collaborative filtering for music recommender system. In: 2017 IEEE Conference of Russian Young Researchers in Electrical and Electronic Engineering (EIConRus) (2017)
8. Nguyen, D.L., Le, T.M.: Recommendation system for Facebook public events based on probabilistic classification and re-ranking. In: 2016 Eighth International Conference on Knowledge and Systems Engineering (KSE) (2016)
9. Anandhan, A., Shuib, L., Akmar-Ismail, M., Ghulam, M.: Social media recommender systems: review and open research issues. IEEE Access **6**, 15608–15628 (2018)
10. Jonnalagedda, N., Gauch, S.: Personalized news recommendation using Twitter. In: 2013 IEEE/WIC/ACM International Joint Conferences on Web Intelligence (WI) and Intelligent Agent Technologies (IAT) (2013)
11. Kim, Y., Shim, K.: TWILITE: a recommendation system for twitter using a probabilistic model based on latent Dirichlet allocation. Inf. Syst. **42**, 59–77 (2013)
12. Blei, D.: Probabilistic topic models. Commun. ACM **55**(4), 77–84 (2012)

13. Chen, K., Chen, T., Zheng, G., Jin, O., Yao, E., Yu, Y.: Collaborative personalized tweet recommendation. In: SIGIR 2012 Proceedings of the 35th International ACM SIGIR Conference on Research and Development in Information Retrieval, pp. 42–48 (2012)
14. Chang, T.M., Hsiao, W.F.: LDA-based personalized document recommendation. In: PACIS 2013, p. 13 (2013)
15. Godin, F., Slavkovikj, V., De Neve, W., Schrauwen, B., Van de Walle, R.: Using topic models for Twitter hashtag recommendation. In: WWW 2013 Companion Proceedings of the 22nd International Conference on World Wide Web, pp. 593–596 (2013)
16. Na, L., Ying, L., Xiao-Jun, T., Hai-Wen, W., Peng, X., Ming-Xia, L.: Improved collaborative filtering algorithm using topic model. In: 17th International Conference on Parallel and Distributed Computing, Applications and Technologies (PDCAT), pp. 342–345 (2016)
17. Pan, T., Zhang, W., Wang, Z., Xu, L.: Recommendations based on LDA topic model in android applications. In: IEEE International Conference on Software Quality, Reliability and Security Companion (QRS-C), pp. 151–158 (2016)
18. Jiantao, Z., Ning, S.: User interest prediction in Microblog using recommendation method. In: IEEE 7th Joint International Information Technology and Artificial Intelligence Conference, pp. 367–370 (2014)
19. Hyung, J.: A new similarity measure for collaborative filtering to alleviate the new user cold-starting problem. Inf. Sci. **178**, 37–51 (2008)
20. He, X., Liao, L., Zhang, H., Nie, L., Hu, X., Chua, T-S.: Neural collaborative filtering. Paper Presented at the Proceedings of the 26th International Conference on World Wide Web, Perth (2017)

Assessing Structured Examination Question Using Automated Keyword Expansion Approach

Rayner Alfred[(✉)] and Kay Lie Chan

Knowledge Technology Research Unit, Faculty of Computing and Informatics, Universiti Malaysia Sabah, Jalan UMS, 88400 Kota Kinabalu, Sabah, Malaysia
ralfred@ums.edu.my, k-lie93@live.com

Abstract. Course assessment through written examination is the most common approach used to access student's learning curve in educational institutions today. In order to fulfill the learning objective, the examination question must be provided in accordance with the subject content learned by students. However, the process of preparing the examination questions is very challenging for most lecturers. The situation is getting more challenging when lecturers try to prepare reasonable and good quality questions that assess different capabilities and students' cognitive levels. Thus, the Bloom's Taxonomy has become a common reference for the learning and teaching process used as a guide for the production of exam questions. This paper proposes an automated assessment of structured examination questions using keywords expansion approach in order to determine the appropriate category based on Bloom taxonomy. This system focuses on applying the Revised Bloom's Taxonomy that fits well for computer science subject in order to categorize the level of difficulties for each examination question. A keyword expansion and WordNet have been integrated in this system in order to handle and find the nearest synonyms for the unknown keywords that exist in the examination question. Based on the test results obtained, the average percentage of correctly classified questions is 48.14% while the average percentage of misclassified questions is 51.86%. These results indicate that the results of evaluating examination papers manually are less accurate based on the results of evaluating examination papers generated using the proposed system.

Keywords: Revised Bloom's taxonomy · WordNet · Keyword expansion Synonyms

1 Introduction

Examination is the most common approach used by any higher education institutions for students' assessment. Question raised in the paper plays an important role in the efforts to test the students' overall cognitive level. Effective style of questioning is always an issue to help students attend to the desired learning outcome [1]. Furthermore, in order to make it effective, balancing between lower and higher-level question is a must.

© Springer Nature Singapore Pte Ltd. 2019
B. W. Yap et al. (Eds.): SCDS 2018, CCIS 937, pp. 286–298, 2019.
https://doi.org/10.1007/978-981-13-3441-2_22

Generating a good examination paper is a very difficult task because lecturer may have to consider many factors such as degree of difficulty, quantity of examination questions, and distribution of score. A common problem that exists is that academicians tend to prepare knowledge based category questions repeatedly throughout the whole question paper. These results in poor assessment of students' capability of grasping the knowledge learned. According to the Ministry of Higher Education (MOHE), a diploma level of examination question set should consist of 20%–30% cognitive domain, 45%–60% psychomotor and 15%–25% affective domain while for degree level is 40%–60% cognitive, 15%–45% psychomotor and 15%–25. In order to avoid this problem, a set of question papers that consists of different cognitive level of Bloom's Taxonomy should be prepared to assess the capability of the students in understanding and applying the knowledge learned.

Normally, academicians are able to categorize a question according to Bloom's cognitive level manually. However, not all academicians can identify the cognitive level of each question correctly due to different perspective [1]. Thus, this may lead to categorization of exam questions incorrectly and it also may fail to meet the standard of subject in examination. By manually categorizing the exam question according to Bloom's Taxonomy, it will take the educator's time and labor which could be spent on teaching efforts. This traditional approach could take a lot of instructors' hours of meetings and days of discussions to prepare exam sets for the semester. In order to standardize the assessment, this work proposes the assessment to be done automatically in the system. Thus, it can reduce time taken to categorize the difficulty level of the question and it also can lead to more consistent and reliable assessment result.

The core of this research work lies in its ability to identify and extract verbs known as keywords using natural language information retrieval processing and methods. In this work, the keyword of the exam question will be extracted and classified based on verb used in each question. Then, a keyword expansion approach will be used in order to identify the nearest synonyms for the unknown keyword found in the exam question. Basically, keyword expansion is the act of adding new keywords to current keyword list in the Bloom's Taxonomy.

In the current scenario, lecturers manually create examination questions, and the process of assessing the questions complexity is done separately. Therefore, the separate processes cause the lecturers to undergo two different workflows to complete an examination paper. In addition, lecturer must manually refer to Bloom's Cognitive Domain reference in order to assess the complexity level of the question items. These processes require dedicated efforts and time. Besides that, most of the present systems were designed to grade students on how well they have done on their examination only after they have answered all the questions in the exam that was assigned to them. There is no clear mechanism that is designed to define and standardize the level of difficulty for each exam question. Thus, it will lead to inconsistency of examination question assessment because different people will have different perceptions.

Nowadays, one of the big concerns for instructors is the process of creating a well-modified, challenging and high quality set of examination questions. An instructor reputation could easily be tarnished if the assessment given is flawed with ill-constructed questions [2]. Besides that, a poorly designed assessment question can fail the goal of examination and lead to unsatisfactory achievement of learning outcomes.

Apart from that, the existing system will affect the overall performance of assessment. For example, if the verb that exists in question but not matches the verb list in Bloom taxonomy, it will be considered as null entries.

2 Related Work

There are few existing systems that have been developed using Bloom taxonomy concepts in order to automate the process of examination questions. These systems include i-QuBES, automated exam question assessment based on summary, online test system based on Bloom's taxonomy and finally the learning management system (LMS).

The first system is called i-QuBES which is designed based on the requirements and guidelines of BHEPep UiTM Shah Alam in order to exploit the potential of course expertise in collecting items and question, hence effectively managing the collected questions [3]. The i-QuBES system allows users to automatically generate question paper in accordance to examination paper set specification, such as the content of the question, type of question, section of the question, the level of question, which are controlled by the faculty, as well as the margin setting of page cover of examination paper set. Then, I-QuBES system can be used to filter the examination paper based on a few parameters, such as course code for the examination paper, level of cognitive domain, current semester for the examination paper to be tested, percentage marks for each of the cognitive level, total marks needed for the examination paper, section required in the examination paper, question type, total mark per section and marks for the question type chosen. There are a few limitations found in i-QuBES. Currently, there is lack of error checking during item submission in i-QuBES. For example, if there is any submitted and approved question item that did not follow the predefined specifications or standards of UiTM' requirements, it will cause error in the entire examination paper set. Thus, it will also reflect contributor of the items. In i-QuBES, lecturers did not have the flexibility to create or design their own questions.

The next existing system is called an automated exam question assessment system (Summarization). In this system, there are five phases included such as, data collection, preprocessing, categorization, summarization and evaluation. In the first phase, this system collects the data from portable document file and analyzes in the preprocessing phase. Next, the system tokenizes the text documents and removes stop words. Then, the system uses a set based model algorithm to assess the examination question. One of the key features of the set-based model is the possibility of controlling the minimal frequency threshold of a termset [4]. Closed termset also was introduced in this model to further and sharpen the quality of the retrieved documents relevance to its query. Besides that, a summarization algorithm is used to generate a summary report of the drafted examination question according to the cognitive domain categories based on the verb found in the question. Thus, the accuracy of the classification will be calculated. Although there is benefits on the automated exam question assessment system (Summarization) system, but there are some limitations found in the system. For example, the system does not tolerate any spelling errors, which can hugely affect the classification accuracy. Besides that, if there is a verb that exists in question but not matches the verb list in Bloom taxonomy, the question will be considered as null entries and it will affect the overall performance of assessment. Thus, this system can be improved by adding keywords expansion method in order to handle the words that exist in question but not match the verb list in Bloom taxonomy. Thus, the question also will not consider as null entries and not affect the overall performance of assessment.

The next system is the online test system supporting Bloom's taxonomy automatic analysis system. In this system, teachers can edit, design and analyze individual question items and the whole exam sheet [5]. Beside that, students can attend examination and analyze their test results based on the Bloom's taxonomy. However, this system cannot handle words that are not listed in Bloom's Taxonomy. For example, if there is no keyword found in the examination question, the system will only categorize this question into 'No Keyword Item' category.

Finally, a LMS is a course management system that was designed to help lecturers to create an effective online learning environment [6]. This system provides functions such as registering courses online, course cataloging, bulletin system and information searching. However, Bloom's taxonomy is not incorporated into the LMS and this make it is difficult to analyze students' performance based on Bloom's taxonomy.

Thus, this paper proposes an Automated Keyword Expansion approach to assessing structured examination questions that will capture every word used for every single question stated in the exam papers and break it into words, phrases, symbols and other element through tokenization process. If the keywords are found in the question, the system will classify the level of difficulties of the question based on Bloom taxonomy. Then, it will summarize the content of the examination question and display percentages for each level. Each question will be identified and associated with the most relevant cognitive domain. Thus, the inconsistency of examination question assessment can be avoided since different people will have different perceptions. Besides that, WordNet also will be integrated in order to find the synonyms for the verb using in the examination question. WordNet is a large lexical database of English Language. In WordNet, nouns, verbs, adverbs and adjectives are grouped into sets of cognitive synonyms called synsets. In wordnet, synsets provide different semantic relationships such as synonymy (similar) and antonymy (opposite), hypernymy (superconcept)/hyponymy (subconcept), meronymy (part-of), holonymy (has-a) [7]. The main relation among the words in WordNet is synonymy. WordNet contains all the words' information, such as the pointer, concept, offset and so on. Pointer is the key to finding out the relationship between two words, contains the information of parent synset, children synset, the part of speech of concepts [8]. After found out the synonyms of the verb in the examination question, the system will map the keyword to the level or categories that the keyword belongs to.

3 Methodology

There are five phases that will be involved in this research work. These five phases include data collection, data preprocessing, identification of keyword, assessment of exam question, summarization and evaluation.

Data-collection is a technique that allows us to systematically collect information about our objects of study (people, objects, phenomena) and about the settings in which they occur. If the data collected were haphazardly, it will be difficult to answer research questions in a conclusive way. In this stage, data will be collect from portable document file (PDF) by convert into text document format. Then, this document will be analyzed in the preprocessing stage.

Data pre-processing is one of the methods in natural language processing that used to make the computer understand the structure or content of the text. Preprocessing involves the set of all documents are gathered and passed to the word extraction phases in which all words are extracted [9]. It will also make the text become more readable and easy to use for later process. Text preprocessing involves processes such as tokenization, stopwords removal, and stemming. Tokenization is a process where the task such as character sequence and a defined document unit, was chopping it up into pieces, called tokens, perhaps at the same time throwing away certain characters, such as punctuation. The stream of characters in a natural language text must be broken up into distinct meaningful units or tokens before any language processing beyond the character level can be performed. During this stage, the examination question will be converted into words, phrases, symbol or other meaningful elements. Besides that, all white spaces and a punctuations marks in the exam question will be removed except bracket and full stop. Then, the format of each question in the examination paper will also be identified based on the bracket and full stop found in the question. Stopwords removal is applied to the question in order to make the text more readable for later process. After the examination question has been tokenize into words and symbol, the system will removed all stopwords exist in the exam question. For example stop words include "the, as, of, and, or, to and etc. All the stopwords exist in the exam question needed to eliminate because it will reduce the size of indexing file [10]. Besides that, elimination of stopwords will also improve the overall efficiency and make effectiveness data. In this research work, after completed tokenization process, all the stopword in the text file will be removed. First, the system will read the text file that consists of tokens and it will convert the entire token into lowercase by using toLowerCase function. Then, it will compare the result produced in tokenization phase with stopword.txt in order to remove the stopword. If the word is a stopword and it exists in the stopwords.txt, the word will be eliminated in this phase. Stemming is process that provides mapping of different related morphological variants of words into their base or common form. There are various stemming approaches. Affix removal method is based on two principles, which is iterations and longest match. In this stage, affix removal method will be used in the system to remove the word that contain affixes and replaced those words using its root word. The main role of stemming is to remove various suffixes as result in the reduction of number of words, to have exactly matching stems, to minimize storage requirement and maximize the efficiency of IR Model (Vikram Singh and Balwinder Saini). For example, the words user, users and used, can be rooted to the word use. In this stage, all the word left after stopword removal stage will go through stemming process, which is reducing inflected or derived words to their word stem, base or root form.

In the identification of keywords phase, the keyword used in each question will be expanding for classifying each annotated question and level of difficulties based on the

Revised Bloom's taxonomy cognitive level. Besides that, English dictionary will be integrated in the system. For example, WordNet library was integrated in order to find the synonyms of keyword used in examination question.

There are two cases that need to be considering in this stages, which is when the keyword was found in the database and if the keyword not exist in the database.

1. Case 1: The keyword exist in the Bloom taxonomy level, the system will proceed to step 3.
2. Case 2: The keyword in the question does not exist in the database. So, it will find the nearest synonyms of the keyword through step 4.
3. In this stage, the system will compare each word in the exam question with the keyword list for Revised Bloom's Taxonomy that stored in database in order to identify the keyword in each exam question. For example, after data was cleaned through the data preprocessing phase, the words left will be stored in stemming's text file. Next, the system will compare every token in the stemming's text file with the Bloom's Taxonomy's keyword list that stored in database. If the token in the stemming's text file match the keyword list in the database, the system will extract the keyword and classify level of difficulties of the examination question based on keyword found.
4. However, if there is no matched keyword between token in the stemming's text file and keyword list in database, the system will handling this exception by integrate Wordnet in order to find the synonym of the keyword before extract and classify its difficulties level.

Therefore, the system will handle words that are not cover in Bloom Taxonomy. If there is unknown keyword that exists in the examination question, the system will using keyword expansion concept to find out the word in Wordnet database. Next, the verb used in the examination question will be replaced with its nearest synonyms that found in Wordnet database. After found out the synonyms of the verb in the examination question, the system will map the keyword to the level or categories that the keyword belong to.

In wordnet, s synonym set, or synset, is a group of synonyms. A synset, therefore, corresponds to an abstract concept. Formally, a synset is a set of one or more synonymous words that may be substituted for each other in context without changing the overall meaning of the sentence in which they are contained. The synonyms contained within a synset are called lemmas.

There are two steps in this procedure:

Use breadth-first searching (BFS) to find neighboring words around the query word. Theses neighboring words are related to each other through WordNet hypernymy-hyponymy relation. The maximal search depth is set to four in order to avoid an enormous search space. Using Eq. (1) to measure the similarity between the query word and the neighboring words found in step 1 [11], where c_i is a concept or a word, $depth(c_i)$ is the shortest distance from the root to node c_i, $len(c_1, c_2)$ is the path length from node c_1 to node c_2, and finally $lso(c_1, c_2)$ is the lowest super-ordinate of node c_1 and node c_2. One hundred words with the greatest values of simwp (c1, c2) are selected as candidate words for the next procedure.

$$sim_{wp}(c_1,c_2) = \frac{2 \times depth(lso(c_1,c_2))}{len(c_1,lso(c_1,c_2)+len(c_2,lso(c_1,c_2))+2 \times depth(lso(c_1,c_2))} \quad (1)$$

For example, to determine the semantic similarity between "transform" and "transfer" as shown in Fig. 1, it will finds the lowest super-ordinate (LSO) of "transform" and "transfer" in the hypernymy hyponymy semantic tree and "change" is the LSO with depth (change) = 1. Then, the len (transform, change), and len (transfer, change) can be obtained. In this example, the len (transform, change) = 1, and len (transfer, change) = 2. Thus, from Eq. (1), the semantic similarity of "transform" and "transfer" is equal to 0.4.

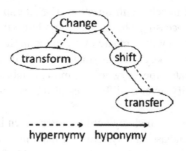

Fig. 1. Example of the hypernymy-hyponymy semantic structure of "transform" and "transfer"

After the keywords of the examination question were identified, the system will assess the examination question by identify the category of each examination question based on the Bloom's Taxonomy cognitive level. The percentage of each cognitive level used in each examination question will also be calculate and display. In the summarization and evaluation phase, the system will compute and summarize content of the examination paper. The total percentage for each cognitive domain level in Bloom Taxonomy that used in the exam question will be compute and display based on the marks given in the assessed question. Besides that, the assessment result that displayed by the system will also use to compare with the assessment of the examination question that manually produced. In this work, the subject that will be chosen to evaluate includes Information Retrieval, Database, and Theory of Computation. These subjects are chosen because it has been manually evaluated. In order to evaluate the system, comparisons between the result that has been evaluated using the system and the exam question that has been manually evaluated by lecturer will be make. Moreover, the percentages that match between the results evaluate by system and result that manually evaluated by lecturer will also be checked and summarize in order to evaluate and validate the correct cognitive level of the examination question.

4 Results and Discussion

In this paper, there are three examination papers are used (e.g., Database System, Information Retrieval and Theory of Computation).

In Table 1, it shows that for the Database System examination paper, there is around 52.63% of questions are correctly classified and 47.37% of wrongly classified question (Shown in Table 4). The percentage of correctly classified question is higher than the misclassified question. In short, the result generated using proposed system shows that *understanding* domain has the highest percentage compare to other cognitive level. This mean the database question set focus more on understanding, which will ask students to demonstrate understanding of facts and idea by organizing, comparing, translating, interpreting, giving descriptions, and stating main ideas.

Table 1. Comparison of terms found for databases system examination question.

Question	Keywords found manually	Keywords found automatically
Q1(a)	Determine (C5- Evaluating)	Name (C1- Remembering)
Q1(b)	Determine (C5- Evaluating)	Determine (C5- Evaluating)
Q1(c)	Determine (C5- Evaluating)	Determine (C5- Evaluating)
Q1(d)	Determine (C5- Evaluating)	Name (C1- Remembering)
Q2	Design (C6- Creating)	Design (C6- Creating)
Q3	Find (C1- Remembering)	Find (C1- Remembering)
Q4	Determine (C5- Evaluating)	Determine (C5- Evaluating)
Q5(a)	Describe (C2- Understanding)	Describe (C2- Understanding)
Q5(b)	Identify (C3- Applying)	Identify (C3- Applying)
Q6(a)	Describe (Understanding)	Explain (C2- Understanding)
Q6(b)(i)	Explain (C1- Remembering)	Explain (C2- Understanding)
Q6(b)(ii)	Explain (C1- Remembering)	Explain (C2- Understanding)
Q7(a)	Determine (C5- Evaluating)	Determine (C5- Evaluating)
Q7(b)	Determine (C5- Evaluating)	Determine (C5- Evaluating)
Q7(c)	Draw (C2- Understanding)	- (No Keyword)
Q8(a)	Explain (C2- Understanding)	Solve (C3- Applying)
Q8(b)	Explain (C2- Understanding)	Solve (C3- Applying)
Q8(c)	Explain (C2- Understanding)	Solve (C3- Applying)
Q8(d)	Explain (C2- Understanding)	Explain (C2- Understanding)

Tables 2 and 4 summarizes the percentage of correctly classify question found in Theory of Computation's question set is 38.46%, which is lower than the percentage of misclassify question, with 61.54%. This happen due to some of the manually evaluated question has no keyword found in the keyword list, so most of the lecturer will categorize that particular question based on their own level of perception. In general, this question set mainly focus on applying level since most of the keyword used in the examination question is under the keyword list in applying level. Therefore, this question set focus on the ability of student to solve problem in new situation by applying acquired knowledge, facts, techniques and rules in a different way.

Table 2. Comparison of terms found in Information retrieval examination question.

Question	Keywords found manually	Keywords found automatically
Q1(a)	Plot (C2- Understanding)	Recall (C1- Remembering)
Q1(b)	Compute (C1- Remembering)	- (No Keyword)
Q1(c)	Determine (C5- Evaluating)	Determine (C5- Evaluating)
Q1(d)	Which (C1- Remembering)	Measure (C5- Evaluating)
Q2(a)	Show (C3- Applying)	Relate (C1- Remembering)
Q2(b)	Show (C3- Applying)	Use (C3- Applying)
Q2(c)	Show (C3- Applying)	Select (C1- Remembering)
Q3(a)	Perform (C3- Applying)	Construct (C3- Applying)
Q3(b)	Compute (C1- Remembering)	Construct (C3- Applying)
Q3(c)	Determine (C5- Evaluating)	Determine (C5- Evaluating)
Q3(d)	Perform (C3- Applying)	Classify (C2- Understanding)
Q3(e)	Classify (C2- Understanding)	Classify (C2- Understanding)

Table 3 summarizes the results obtained for the Theory of Computation examination paper. In Table 4, the percentage of correctly classified question of this question set is 53.33%, which is 6.66% higher than misclassified question. In brief, the result generated using proposed system shows that remembering have the highest percentage which is 35% compare to other cognitive level in this question set. This mean the theory of computation question set focus more on remembering, which will test on how students will present and defend their opinion by making judgments about information, validity of ideas, or quality of work based on a set of criteria. Besides, the question under this cognitive level also exhibit memory of previously learned material by recalling facts, terms, basic concepts, and answers.

The graph shown in Fig. 2 indicates the percentage of correctly classify questions and misclassify questions in Database, Information Retrieval and Theory of Computation's question sets.

Based on this research work, there are three question sets that had been evaluated using both manually and proposed system. According to the evaluation, the percentage of correctly classify questions in Database and Theory of Computation question set is higher than misclassify percentage whereas the percentage of question that was correctly identified it's category in Information Retrieval question set is lower than misclassify question. The average percentage of correctly classify question is 48.14% which is lower than the average of misclassify question, 51.86%. This happened because not all academicians can identify the cognitive level in each question correctly due to different perspective and some them may not be aware of the learning taxonomies which suit in their disciplines. For example, if the keyword use in the examination question does not found in the keyword list of Revised Bloom's Taxonomy, then they will categorize that question into the cognitive level that they think it is

Table 3. Comparison of terms found in TOC examination question.

Question	Keywords found manually	Keywords found automatically
Q1(a)	Give (C2- Understanding)	Describe (C1- Remembering)
Q1(b)	Give (C2- Understanding)	- (No Keyword)
Q1(c)	Convert (C3- Applying)	- (No Keyword)
Q1(d)	Convert (C3- Applying)	- (No Keyword)
Q2(a)	Prove (C5- Evaluating)	Prove (C5- Evaluating)
Q2(b)	Prove (C5- Evaluating)	Prove (C5- Evaluating)
Q2(c)	Determine (C5- Evaluating)	Determine (C5- Evaluating)
Q2(d)	Find (C1- Remembering)	Find (C1- Remembering)
Q3(a)	List (C1- Remembering)	List (C1- Remembering)
Q3(b)	Build (C3- Applying)	Build (C3- Applying)
Q3(c)	Describe (C2- Understanding)	Describe (C1- Remembering)
Q4(a)	Build (C3- Applying)	Build (C3- Applying)
Q4(b)	Give (C2- Understanding)	- (No Keyword)
Q4(c)	Define (C1- Remembering)	Define (C1- Remembering)
Q4(d)	Describe (C2- Understanding)	Describe (C1- Remembering)

Table 4. Average percentage of correctly classify and misclassified question

Question sets	Database		Information retrieval		Theory of computation	
	Correctly classify	Misclassify	Correctly classify	Misclassify	Correctly classify	Misclassify
Percentage (100%)	52.63	47.37	38.46	61.54	53.33	46.67
Average % of correctly classified questions	$\frac{52.63 + 38.46 + 53.33}{3} = 48.14\%$					
Average % of misclassified questions	$\frac{47.37 + 61.54 + 46.67}{3} = 51.86\%$					

closer or most relevant to. Hence, this may lead to miss-categorization of keyword used in the exam questions. Besides, it may also fail to meet the standard of subject in examination because different people may have different level of perception and perspective.

Therefore, WordNet was integrated in this research work in order to find the nearest synonyms for the verb used in the examination question by using keyword expansion approach, if it does not match any verb in the Revised Bloom's Taxonomy keyword list. After found out the synonyms of the verb in the examination question, the system will map the synonym of the keyword to the most relevant cognitive level or categories that the keyword belongs to.

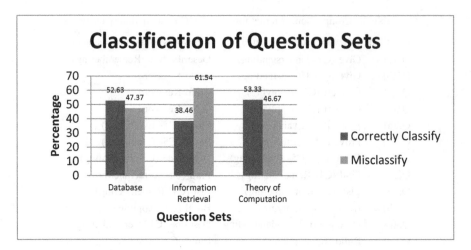

Fig. 2. Classification of question sets

Therefore, WordNet was integrated in this research work in order to find the nearest synonyms for the verb used in the examination question by using keyword expansion approach, if it does not match any verb in the Revised Bloom's Taxonomy keyword list. After found out the synonyms of the verb in the examination question, the system will map the synonym of the keyword to the most relevant cognitive level or categories that the keyword belongs to.

5   Conclusion

In general, there are five phases that included in this research work. These phases include data collection, data preprocessing, identification of keyword, assessment of exam question, summarization and evaluation. In this research work, an Automated Keyword Expansion Approach to Assessing Structured Examination Questions will capture every word used for every single question stated in the exam papers and break it into words, phrases, symbols and other element through tokenization process. If keyword is found in the question, the system will classify the level of difficulties of that question based on Revised's Bloom taxonomy. In addition, Wordnet was integrated in order to find the nearest synonyms of the keyword that was not listed in any cognitive level of the Bloom's Taxonomy categories. After found out the synonyms of the verb in the examination question, the system will map the keyword to the level or categories that the keyword belongs to. Then, the proposed system will summarize the content of the examination question and display percentages for each level. Each question will be identified and associated with the most relevant cognitive domain. Thus, the inconsistency of examination question assessment can be avoided since different people will have different perceptions. This research is also designed to help lecturer to prepare examination question set that fulfill the standard examination requirements of general institution based on Bloom's teaching and learning taxonomy in automated mode, with less or no human intervention for the assessment. Besides, this research implemented using Information Retrieval approach that is most current and intriguing trend in software engineering. It also has the ability to retrieve predetermined criteria efficiently and accurately. Next, this research work also intends to reduce the time taken to analyze and summarize drafted examination questions in order to produce more consistent and reliable assessment results. This research work mainly focus on the ability to implement a parser and tokenizer to extract entities from the drafted examination questions in English text, determine the format and mark given in the drafted question, remove all stop words, stem the tokens into its own root word, implement an assessment method to assess the drafted questions, as well as effectuate a summarization method to abridge the overall taxonomy of the drafted examination questions. By integrating Wordnet into this research work, the synonyms of verbs exist in the questions sets can be determine using keyword expansion method. There are few improvements that can be implemented in order to improve the accuracy and time taken used to compute the summarization of the examination questions sets. First, spell checker and language detection can be implemented to generate and produce more accurate summarization result of the question set. Next, other Bloom's Teaching and Learning Taxonomy domains such as affective domain and psychomotor domain can be integrated.

References

1. Yusof, N., Hui, C.J.: Determination of Bloom's cognitive level of question items using artificial neural network. In: 10th International Conference on Intelligent Systems Design and Applications, Cairo, pp. 866–870 (2010)
2. Ahmad, N.D., Adnan, W.A.W., Aziz, M.A., Yusof, M.Y.: Automating preparation of exam questions: exam question classification system (EQCS). In: 2011 International Conference on Research and Innovation, pp. 1–6 (2011)
3. Raus M.I.M., Janor, R.M., Sadjirin, R., Sahri, Z.: The development of i-QuBES for UiTM: from feasibility study to the design phase. In: 2014 IEEE 5th Control and System Graduate Research Colloquium, Shah Alam, Malaysia, pp. 96–101. UiTM(2014)
4. Pôssas, B., Ziviani, N., Meira Jr. W., Ribeiro-Neto, B.: Set-based model: a new approach for information retrieval. In: Proceedings of the 25th Annual International ACM SIGIR Conference on Research and Development in Information Retrieval (SIGIR 2002), pp. 230–237. ACM, New York (2002)
5. Chang, W.C., Chung, M.S.: Automatic applying Bloom's taxonomy to classify and analysis the cognition level of English question items. In: 2009 Joint Conferences on Pervasive Computing (JCPC), Tamsui, Taipei, pp. 727–734 (2009)
6. Salmah, F., Siti Hasnah, T., Asni, T.: Assessing perceptions of academic staff in using SmartUMS for teaching and learning. Int. J. E-Learn. Pract. (IJELP) 1(1), 60–67 (2014)
7. Krizhanovsky, A.A., Lin, F.: Related terms search based on WordNet/Wiktionary and its application in Ontology Matching. http://arxiv.org/abs/0907.2209. Accessed 10 Aug 2018
8. Li, H., Tian, Y., Ye, B., Cai, Q.: Comparison of current semantic similarity methods in WordNet. Paper presented at 2010 International Conference on Computer Application and System Modeling (ICCASM 2010), pp. 408–411 (2010)

9. Harshala, M.D., Chaitali, S.B., Minal, A.M., Minal, Y.P.: Language translator for deaf community. Int. Res. J. Eng. Technol. (IRJET) **3**(4), 848–852 (2016)
10. Vikram, S., Balwinder, S.: An effective tokenization algorithm for information retrieval systems. Int. J. Database Manag. Syst. (IJDMS) **6**(6), 13–24 (2014)
11. Quillian, M.: Semantic Memory. In: Minsky, M. (ed.) Semantic Information Processing, pp. 227–270. MIT Press, Cambridge (1968)

Improving Topical Social Media Sentiment Analysis by Correcting Unknown Words Automatically

Rayner Alfred$^{(\boxtimes)}$ and Rui Wen Teoh

Knowledge Technology Research Unit, Universiti Malaysia Sabah, Jalan UMS,
88400 Kota Kinabalu, Sabah, Malaysia
ralfred@ums.edu.my, ruiwen@hotmail.com

Abstract. In the digital world, social media has become one of the most popular communication mediums that allow users to share their views on various topics in their social network. For example, Twitter users are allowed to share their thoughts on various topic by sending tweets with a maximum length of 140 characters. Hence, social media driven information contains opinions and sentiments on various topics of interest which are extremely useful for companies to design marketing strategies. Sentiment Analysis is widely used to assist people to understand the massive amount of data available online and identify the polarity of the topical based social media opinions. However, social media platforms' users come from all over the world and have variation in terms of informal language and short notation used on social media platforms. Therefore, the identification on the polarity of topical social media has become more challenging and the accuracy on the polarity of topical social media opinions might be influenced. This paper investigates the effectiveness of applying different spelling correction algorithms, such as Levenshtein distance and Peter Norvig's algorithm for spelling correction of unknown words found in social media such as Twitter, before carrying out sentiment analysis. The evaluation of spelling correction algorithms on sentiment analysis is carried out by comparing the polarities of manually annotated tweets with the polarities obtained from the sentiment analysis algorithm. Based on the results obtained, there are slight improvements in term of percentage of matched polarity, where 1.6% improvement by using the Levenshtein distance-based algorithm and 2.0% improvement by using the Peter Norvig's algorithm.

Keywords: Sentiment analysis · Informal language · Spelling correction
Polarity

1 Introduction

Social media websites have become a world's largest simulated community where people used to express their opinions about certain events, products or services globally [1]. Millions or even billions of users are sharing their views on various aspects through popular and trendy websites such as Facebook, Twitter, Tumbler, Flicker, LinkedIn etc. [2].

© Springer Nature Singapore Pte Ltd. 2019
B. W. Yap et al. (Eds.): SCDS 2018, CCIS 937, pp. 299–308, 2019.
https://doi.org/10.1007/978-981-13-3441-2_23

However, social media platforms' users come from all over the world and have variation in terms of informal language and short notation used on social media platforms. In addition to that, social media postings are commonly prone to misspellings and may contain special characters that are harder to analyze as micro-blogging users tend to make spelling mistakes, use informal language and short notation when expressing their views. These misspellings may be formed from short form word, typing error or influenced by the dialect of the languages used. Due to these variations of texts formed and used on social media platform, the identification of topical social media polarity becomes more challenging due to the existence of those misspelled words. Meanwhile, the accuracy on the polarity of the topical based social media opinions in the current sentiment analysis system might be influenced as well.

The main aim in this research is to investigate the performance of several spelling correction algorithms that can be used to correct the unknown words due to misspellings or abbreviations before identifying the polarity of the topical based social media opinions. Hence, a framework that applies spelling correction module to handle informal language and short notation will be proposed in this paper. Then, an evaluation on the effects of applying spelling correction module in improving the polarity of the terms used on social media platforms will be conducted.

The rest of the paper follows, where Sect. 2 will highlight some related works on spelling correction and sentiment analysis algorithms. Section 3 will describe the experimental setup of this work. Section 4 discusses and analyses the results obtained. Section 5 will conclude the paper.

2   Related Work

2.1   Twitter Opinion Mining (TOM) Framework

In the proposed TOM framework, multiple techniques have been implemented that includes pre-processing steps and a hybrid scheme of classification that are applied for Twitter feed analysis and classification. The main aim of this research is to improve the accuracy of text classification and solve the data sparsity issues. The concept of the proposed algorithm is to pre-process the data and perform a different transformation in order to remove the slangs, grammatical mistakes and abbreviations before proceeding to the polarity classification.

TOM system tested the data obtained from the twitter streaming API as input items. Generally, the proposed system consists of three main modules. The first module is called data acquisition that obtains twitter feeds while the second module involves pre-processing of data and transforms the tweets from real values features or arbitrary components into data that can be used for the following polarity classification. Pre-processing module is the highlighted area for this research. The final module is the application of different classification techniques used to classify the tweets into different spectrums such as positive, negative or neutral.

The pre-processing steps consist of the removal of URLs, hash-tags, username and special characters; spelling correction using a dictionary; substitution of abbreviations and slangs with expansions, lemmatization and stop words removal. The proposed classification algorithm incorporated the hybrid scheme using an improved form of emoticon analysis [3], SentiWordNet analysis [4] and an enhanced polarity classifier using a list of positive or negative words [5].

2.2 Context Sensitive Spelling Corrector Framework

A context-sensitive spelling corrector has been introduced for sentiment analysis that applies hybrid approach of similarity measures to generate a candidate list of words and statistical language model (noisy channel) for choosing most likely spelling correction [1]. In the proposed framework, it consists of three major modules which are tokenization and error detection, generating candidates and language model.

The initial module of the framework is used to break up sentences into tokens or words and determine the typographical errors or focal words with a dictionary. It is required to break a sentence into small parts called tokens in order to retrieve sentence structure and its complete sense [6].

In order to generate a candidates list, Jaccard index [7] and Levenshtein [8] distance are used. Levenshtein distance is used as a measure of the similarity between two strings which are the source string and target string. The distance is the number of deletions, insertions or substitutions required to transform source string to target string [9]. Informally, the Levenshtein distance between two words is the minimum number of single character edits required to change one word into another. During the first phase, every dictionary and a focal word were expressed into uni-grams or bi-grams depending on the Levenshtein distance. Therefore, word was expressed into uni-gram if the Edit distance was greater than one. Otherwise, word was expressed as bi-grams. For the second phase, Jaccard index was used to calculate the similarity index between dictionary words and focal word in order to generate n candidates. The advantage of uni-grams is due to the high coverage with all similarity measures when Levenshtein distance is greater than one. Jaccard index is able to minimise the number of candidates by taking the top n measures while other similarity measures serve as base-line. The framework works by assuming the first letter of mistyped word is correct as it has been found that the first letter is usually typed correctly [10].

In language model module, a statistical language model is used to choose the best selection of the candidate words. A selection with the highest noisy channel probability is defined as the best in order to replace the focal word. According to Bigram Language Model (BLM), Eqs. (1) and (2) are used before and after BLM for a sentence of m words with w_f focal word, S_e is the sentence with typographical error, S_i is the sentence intended by writer and S is the intended sentence with highest likelihood.

$$S = \arg \max_{S_i} P(S_i|S_e) = \arg \max_{S_i} \frac{P(S_e|S_i)}{P(S_e)} = \arg \max_{S_i} P(S_e|S_i) \cdot P(S_i)$$

$$P(w_1, w_2, \ldots \ldots w_f, \ldots \ldots, w_m) = P(w_{f-1}w_f) = \frac{n(w_{f-1}w_f)}{N} \tag{1}$$

$$P(w_1, w_2, \ldots \ldots w_f, \ldots \ldots, w_m) = P(w_f w_{f+1}) = \frac{n(w_f w_{f+1})}{N}. \tag{2}$$

where $n(w_{f-1}w_f)$ and $n(w_fw_{f+1})$ are the number of times that grams appeared in the source text.

2.3   Lexical Normalisation of Twitter Data Work

Lexical normalisation involves the transformation of tokens into a canonical form consistent with the dictionary. These tokens are misspelled words or abbreviations due to character limit in Twitter. Each token is identified on a case by case basis before normalization techniques are used to correct the misspellings and make sense of the abbreviations and elisions frequently used in the Twitter text.

First, a token is identified by using a lexicon of 115 326 words. Tokens are included in the vocabulary (IV) if exact matching can be found with the lexicon of words while tokens that fall outside of these lexicon words are known as candidates for normalization and are further processed. However, Twitter text usually consists of hashtags with symbol "#" to indicate the keywords or topic for the tweet and "@" symbol that followed with user's Twitter username to refer to a user when replying or commenting the tweet. These tokens are parsed using a regular expression for the identification of special characters, punctuation and Twitter specific symbols. These special tokens will then be marked as "non-candidates ("NO")" and will not proceed for normalization. Once the candidates are identified, Levenshtein distance algorithm is used to treat misspellings different from standard spell checking scenario as it is not necessary to change misspelled word to correct word but to change a word that is not in our corpus into a spelling variant that we have seen in corpus which might not necessarily be correctly spelled. Hence, the algorithm for finding spelling equivalents should be in bi-directional as it could be needed in some cases. Then, Refined Soundex Technique is applied on the set of matches from Levenshtein distance. The aim is to refine the set and achieve results with approximate matches which are phonetically similar to the misspelling. The refined and phonetically similar set of words is known as "Phonetic Matches". Next, all possible terms having edit distances of less than or equal to 2 that consists of deletes, transposes, replaces and inserts from the query term, are generated and searched in the dictionary through the Peter Norvig's Algorithm. The achievement on accuracy for this algorithm is 80–90% which averaging at about 10 words per second [11]. Finally, the results obtained from Refined Soundex Technique and Peter Norvig's Algorithm will be compared. There will be no further spelling correction processing if only one result obtained from Refined Soundex Technique and it matches with the output from Peter Norvig's Algorithm. However, if there is more than one output obtained from Refined Soundex Technique, n-gram model which is a method used to check 'n' continuous words or sounds from a given sequence of text or speech is applied. The goal of this model is to predict the next word in a sequence. N-gram model also helps in analyzing the sentiment of text or document in sentiment analysis [12].

In summary, in Twitter Opinion Mining (TOM) framework, the basic pre-processing steps are able to clean and tokenize tweets. This simplified the continuous work for the identification of unknown words. In Context Sensitive Spelling Corrector framework, unknown words are transformed into known words using Levenshtein distance. However, the word changed might not fit the content of tweet text accurately. Hence, Lexical Normalization of Twitter Data work was introduced that combines few techniques such as Levenshtein distance, Refined Soundex Techniques, Peter Norvig's Algorithm and N-gram models in order to improve the accuracy of spelling correction on the unknown word by considering the content of the tweet text.

3 Methods

The main focus of this framework is to implement different spelling correction algorithms which can be used to transform misspellings or unknown words to known words based on the unknown words retrieved from the basic pre-processing module and identification of word module. The purpose of using different spelling correction algorithms is to investigate the performance of these spelling correction algorithms by comparing the accuracy of the correctly corrected words by each spelling correction algorithm. Then, the accuracy of identifying the polarity of topical social media with and without the application of spelling correction algorithm will be conducted.

The framework for this research is illustrated in Fig. 1. Each of these modules will be detailed in the following sections.

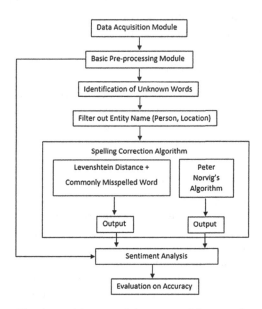

Fig. 1. Architecture of the proposed framework

3.1 Data Acquisition Module

The goal of data acquisition module is to extract or scrape Twitter tweets to Excel that consists of columns with tweet's text, retweet count and favorite count by using

REST API. However, APIs have their limitations as they provide only a small sample of all posted tweets. For instances, Twitter Streaming API enable real-time access to data available on OSN publicly but only approximately 1% of all tweets published on Twitter are accessible in real time. Meanwhile, the coverage of Twitter Search API depends on the combination of a search term's popularity and frequency. Therefore, exact numbers are not available and the data shown is usually underrepresentation compared to the total number of matching tweets as it is not possible to quantify this without resorting to complete except for commercially available Twitter datasets. Furthermore, Twitter Search API is unable to provide access to tweets with matching keywords that are older than approximately one week. In order to overcome these limitations, data collection has to be done continuously. The upper limit for the number of tweets that can be extracted by the API is around 100 tweets in one attempt. Therefore, few attempts are carried out in order to get more tweets. As our main focus for this research is on informal usage of English language and short notations, Twitter 4J library was configured to extract only English language tweets which act as the input for sentiment analysis or pre-processing module before the polarity classification.

3.2 Basic Pre-processing Module

The basic pre-processing module consists of removing URL, stop words, numbers, whitespace, punctuation, lemmatization and stemming words. This module involves pre-processing of data and transforms the tweets from real values features or arbitrary components into data that can be used for the following procedure.

3.3 Identification of Unknown Words

In order to get the unknown words from the corpus for spelling correction algorithm to process, an identification of unknown words process is done by comparing those words with the English words list available online. Those unfound words will be identified as unknown words which might due to slangs, misspellings or abbreviations.

3.4 Spelling Correction Algorithms

3.4.1 Levenshtein Distance

However, the language used by the user is very informal in most of the social media, as user tends to create their own words with spelling shortcuts, new words and abbreviations. Hence, spelling correction algorithm has to be applied in order to transform those unknown words into known words. An effective spelling correction algorithm able to transform unknown words into known words effectively and hence increase the accuracy in determining the polarity of topical based social media opinions as sentiment analysis does not involve informal words that are commonly used in social media such as lol and luv. The performance of different spelling correction algorithm in transforming the unknown words into known words is the main focus for this research in order to investigate methods used for spelling correction of unknown words found in social media into known words.

Levenshtein distance is used as a measure of the similarity between two strings which are the source string and target string. The distance is the number of deletions, insertions or substitutions required to transform source string to target string [9]. The Levenshtein distance between two strings W1 and W2 is given by is shown as below:

$$lev_{W1,W2}(m, n) = \begin{cases} \max(m, n) & \text{if } \min(m, n) = 0 \\ \min \begin{cases} lev_{W1,W2}(m-1, n-1)+1 \\ lev_{W1,W2}(m, n-1)+1 \\ lev_{W1,W2}(m-1, n-1)+1_{(W1 \neq W2)} \end{cases} & \text{otherwise} \end{cases} \quad (3)$$

where $m = |W1|$,
$n = |W2|$,
and $1_{(W1 \neq W2)}$ *is the indicator function and equal to zero,*
when $(W1_m = W2_n)$, *equal to* 1 *otherwise.*

Once the unknown words are identified, Levenshtein distance technique is used to find the matches from an English words list with a maximum edit distance of 2 for the unknown word. Levenshtein distance functions by taking two words and return how far apart they are. The algorithm is O(N * M) where N indicates the length of one word and M is the length of the other. However, comparing two words at a time is not sufficient but to search for the closest matching words from the word list which might be thousands or millions of words. Therefore, python program is used to work on that with the first argument is the misspelled word while the second argument is the maximum distance. As a result, a set of approximate matches with the distance is generated based on the textual similarity to the unknown words.

3.4.2 Commonly Misspelled Words
Next, commonly misspelled words list is used on the multiple outputs from the Levenshtein distance in order to remove all those unrelated corrected word suggestion and hence finalize the list of corrected word from the list of suggested correction of words. This words list is applied to replace those commonly misspelled unknown words into known words with the most appropriate corrected words from the multiple outputs of Levenshtein distance. This helps in determining a more accurate word to replace an unknown word.

3.4.3 Peter Norvig's Algorithm
Peter Norvig's Algorithm is also used to generate all possible terms with an edit distance of less than or equal to 2 that consists of deletes, transposes, replaces and inserts from the misspelled term and search in the dictionary (big.txt). This dictionary, big.txt contains about a million of words which is a concatenation of few public domain books from Project Gutenberg and lists of most frequent words from Wiktionary and the British National Corpus for the usage of Peter Norvig's Algorithm. By using this algorithm, only one best match closest to the misspelling will be displayed.

3.5   Sentiment Analysis

Sentiment Analysis is carried out to determine the polarity of topical based social media opinions after the replacement of known words into those tweets. The polarity can be differentiated into positive, negative or neutral.

Sentiment analysis is widely used in helping people to understand the massive amount of data available online by identifying the polarity of the topical based social media opinions. For instance, sentiment analysis over Twitter provides an efficient way to monitor opinions and views of publics towards their brands, business and directors. In the past, many sentiment analysis researches focus on product reviews like the sentiments such as positive, negative or neutral for products on Amazon.com. These sentiments used to be a convenient labelled data source which acts as quantitative indicators of the author's opinion for star ratings. Then, more general types of writing like blogs, news articles and web pages were created with the annotated datasets. Hence, sentiment analysis which provides a view regarding the sentiment expressed in those messages is one of the feedback mechanisms that mostly used in Twitter data analysis [13].

3.6   Evaluation Method

Then, an evaluation on the performance of different spelling correction algorithm is carried out to identify the accuracy of corrected words by each spelling correction algorithm. Those corrected words will replace those unknown words in tweets and the accuracy of corrected words will be annotated manually. If the corrected words match with sentence, then the corrected words are corrected correctly while the corrected words are considered as wrongly corrected if not match with the sentence.

Next, an evaluation on accuracy on the polarity of topical social media with and without the application of spelling correction algorithm is done by comparing the polarity results manually annotated with the polarity of sentiment analysis for uncorrected tweets, tweets with replacement of corrected words from Levenshtein distance and tweets with replacement of corrected words from Peter Norvig's Algorithm.

4   Results and Discussion

4.1   Evaluation of Corrected Words with Spelling Correction Algorithm

The total number of unknown words identifies is 595. For the evaluation on corrected words, the percentage of correctly corrected words for Levenshtein distance algorithm is 50.59% (301 words correctly corrected) while the percentage of correctly corrected words for Peter Norvig's algorithm is 59.66% (355 words correctly corrected). The percentages of the corrected words are not high as some words might not exist in the words list used and hence unable to be corrected. Even if the words are corrected, the words might not fit the tweet.

4.2 Evaluation of Sentiment Analysis

There are 489 tweets considered in this assessment in which 396 tweets have polarities which are correctly identified manually, 399 tweets have polarities which are correctly identified using the Levenshtein distance algorithm and finally 401 tweets have polarities which are correctly identified using the Peter Norvig's algorithm. In summary, for the evaluation on the polarities of topical social media, the percentage of matched polarity without the application of spelling correction algorithm is 80.98%. Meanwhile, with the application of spelling correction algorithms, the percentages of matched polarity are 81.60% and 82.00% respectively for Levenshtein distance and Peter Norvig's algorithms. Based on the results shown, the percentage of matched polarity increased with respect to the application of spelling correction algorithm. However, the increment on percentage matched polarity is not much with the application of spelling correction algorithms due to:

(i)   Corrected words are not correctly corrected.
> For example, in "obamacare *wisest* say begin time repeal amp replace", the wrongly corrected word, wisest is a positive word and hence determined as a neutral statement through sentiment analysis. But, it is supposed to be corrected as disaster that is a negative word.

(ii) Corrected words are not included in the word list for sentiment analysis.
> For example, in "pro life pro *family*", pro is not in the word list of sentiment analysis and hence this statement is determined as neutral.

(iii) Sentiment analysis unable to detect the sarcasm meaning of the sentence.
> For example, in "black democrat trump train", sentiment analysis unable to detect the hidden meaning of black democrat and determine this tweet as neutral. Yet, it is supposed to be negative statement.

(iv) Some words are dominated in the sentence with higher marks and therefore the polarity is influenced as polarity is calculated based on the sum of marks for words in a sentence.
> For example, in "chance *bite*", chance is dominated and determined as positive statement while it is supposed to be negative.

5   Conclusion

In Levenshtein distance, there are multiple outputs for each word. However, some of the outputs are not related to the tweet text of the unknown word. Therefore, commonly misspelled words list will be used to overcome the limitation of Levenshtein distance. For the remaining multiple outputs, few conditions are set in order to retrieve the best suit single output for each unknown word. However, the accuracy of the result is not high. For Peter Norvig's Algorithm, there are some of the unknown words are unable to be corrected if they do not exists in the dictionary, big.txt. Based on the results obtained in this paper, we can conclude that with the application of spelling correction algorithm, the percentage of matched polarity increases. This means that the accuracy of polarity increased with the application of spelling correction algorithms. Meanwhile, the limitation for sentiment analysis with the application of spelling correction algorithm is that the polarity of topical social media might be influenced if corrected words are not correctly corrected, corrected words are not included in the word list for sentiment analysis, sentiment analysis unable to detect the sarcasm meaning of the sentence and some words are dominated in the sentence with higher marks and therefore the polarity is influenced as polarity is calculated based on the sum of marks for words in a sentence. Future works for this research will includes the investigation of the context matching with the multiple outputs from Levenshtein Distance in order to overcome the current limitation of Levenshtein distance and increase the accuracy of corrected words. Meanwhile, few datasets will be extracted to investigate the accuracy of spelling correction module for the sentiment analysis module.

References

1. Fazal, M.K., Aurangzeb, K., Muhammad, Z.A., Shakeel, A.: Context-aware spelling corrector for sentiment analysis. MAGNT Res. Rep. **2**(5), 1–10 (2014). ISSN 1444-8939
2. Ayushi, D., Thish, G., Vasudeva, V.: Manwitter sentiment analysis: the good, the bad, and the neutral. In: Proceedings of the 9th International Workshop on Semantic Evaluation (SemEval 2015), Denver, Colorado, 4–5 June 2015, pp. 520–526. Association for Computational Linguistics (2015)
3. Read, J.: Using emoticons to reduce dependency in machine learning techniques for sentiment classification. In: Proceedings of the ACL Student Research Workshop (2005), pp 43–48 (2005)
4. Baccianella, S.A., Esuli, F.S.: SENTIWORDNET 3.0: an enhanced lexical resource for sentiment analysis and opinion mining. In: Proceedings of LREC (2010)
5. Liu, B., Li, S., Lee, W.S., Yu, P.S.: Text classification by labeling words. In: Proceedings of the National Conference on Artificial Intelligence, pp 425–430. AAAI Press/MIT Press, Menlo Park/Cambridge/London (2004)
6. Zubair, A.M., Aurangzeb, K., Shakeel, A., Fazal, M.K.: A review of feature extraction in sentiment analysis. J. Basic Appl. Sci. Res. **4**(3), 181–186 (2014)
7. Jaccard, P.: Distribution de la flore alpine dans le bassin des Dranses et dans quelques régions voisines. Bulletin de la Société Vaudoise des Sciences Naturelles **37**, 241–272 (1901)
8. Nerbonne, J., Heeringa, W., Kleiweg, P.: Edit distance and dialect proximity. In: Time Warps, String Edits and Macromolecules: The Theory and Practice of Sequence Comparison, 2nd edn, p. 15 (1999)
9. Gilleland, M.: Levenshtein distance in three flavors (2009). https://people.cs.pitt.edu/~kirk/cs1501/Pruhs/Spring2006/assignments/editdistance/Levenshtein%20Distance.htm. Accessed 10 Aug 2018
10. Yannakoudakis, E.J., Fawthrop, D.: The rules of spelling errors. Inf. Process. Manage. **19**(2), 87–99 (1983)
11. Bilal, A.: Lexical normalisation of Twitter data. http://www.aclweb.org/anthology/P11-1038. Accessed 10 Aug 2018
12. Abinash, T., Ankit, A., Santanu, K.R.: Classification of sentiment reviews using n-gram machine learning approach. Expert Syst. Appl. **57**, 117–126 (2016)
13. Bo, P., Lillian, L.: Opinion Mining and Sentiment Analysis. Found. Trends Inf. Retrieval **2** (1–2), 1–135 (2008)

Big Data Security in the Web-Based Cloud Storage System Using 3D-AES Block Cipher Cryptography Algorithm

Nur Afifah Nadzirah Adnan[✉] and Suriyani Ariffin

Faculty of Computer and Mathematical Sciences, Universiti Teknologi MARA,
40450 Shah Alam, Selangor, Malaysia
nurafifahnadzirahadnan@gmail.com,
suriyani@tmsk.uitm.edu.my

Abstract. Cloud storage is described as a place to store data on the net as opposed to on-premises arrays. It is well-known that cloud computing has many ability advantages and lots of organization applications and big data are migrating to public or hybrid cloud storage. However, from the consumers' attitude, cloud computing safety issues, particularly records protection and privacy safety problems, continue to be the number one inhibitor for adoption of cloud computing services. This paper describes the problem of building secure computational services for encrypted information in the cloud storage without decrypting the encrypted data. There are many distinct sorts of attacks and threats executed on cloud systems. Present day cloud storage service companies inclusive of Google Drive and Dropbox utilizes AES-256 encryption algorithm. Although, it is far nonetheless considered a secure algorithm to use presently, a brief look through history shows that each algorithm gets cracked subsequently. Therefore, it meets the yearning of computational encryption algorithmic aspiration model that could enhance the security of data for privacy, confidentiality, and availability of the users. The research method covers two principal levels, which are literature assessment and randomness tests on large number of data using NIST Statistical Test Suite which has been developed by National Institute of Standards and Technology (NIST). A studies assessment in this paper is made to decide if the research challenge has effectively able to mitigate common cloud storage carrier assaults. The outcomes from this paper affords insights to cutting-edge protection implementation and their vulnerabilities, as well as future enhancements that may be made to further solidify cloud storage solutions.

Keywords: Big data security · Cloud storage · Cloud security
3D-AES · Block cipher · Cryptography

1 Introduction

Big Data, in general is defined as a group of huge size of data sets with different types and due to its size, the data processing becomes hard when using traditional data processing algorithms and platforms. Lately, the number of data provisions such as social networks, sensor networks, high throughput instruments, satellite and streaming

© Springer Nature Singapore Pte Ltd. 2019
B. W. Yap et al. (Eds.): SCDS 2018, CCIS 937, pp. 309–321, 2019.
https://doi.org/10.1007/978-981-13-3441-2_24

machines has increased, and these environments produce huge size of data [11]. Nowadays, a big data as mentioned in [13], becomes the critical enterprises and governmental institutions application. Hence, there is an accelerating need for the challenges development of secure big data infrastructure that will support cloud storage and processing of big data in cloud computing environment.

Cloud storage is a service model in which data is maintained, managed and backed up remotely and made available to users over a network. Cloud computing is an innovation that uses the web and central remote servers to keep up information [10]. It enables consumers and businesses to utilize applications without establishment and access their own documents. This innovation permits for significantly more productive processing by concentrating stockpiling, memory, handling and transfer speed. The cloud computing model National Institute Standards and Technology (NIST) defined has three service models, which are Service (SaaS), Cloud Platform as a Service (PaaS) and Cloud Infrastructure as a Service (IaaS) [5].

While cost and convenience are two advantages of cloud computing, there are critical security worries that should be tended to while moving basic applications and delicate information to open and cloud storage [4]. Security concerns relate to risk areas, for example, outside information capacity, reliance on people in general web, absence of control, multi-occupancy and incorporation with inner security. Furthermore, privacy of data is also a main concern as client's own information might be scattered in different virtual data center instead of remain in the same physical area, indeed, even over the national fringes. Besides that, there are many distinct kinds of assaults and threats carried out to cloud systems. A number of them are viable simply due to the fact there is a cloud solution. Others are taken into consideration variations of commonplace attacks, with the distinction that they may be applied to the computational assets to be had to cloud solutions and cloud users. Man-in-the-cloud (MITC) is one of the common attacks currently occurring on cloud services [8]. MITC does not require any specific malicious code or exploit to be used within the preliminary contamination degree, thus making it very difficult to avoid.

Current cloud storage service providers such as Google Drive and Dropbox utilizes AES-256 encryption algorithm. Additionally, AES-256 is susceptible against brute force assault. Although, it is still considered a secure algorithm to use currently, a brief look through history shows that each algorithm gets broken eventually which is why it is imperative to constantly make new cryptographic algorithms to mitigate this ongoing issue.

Cryptography is the science or study of techniques of secret writing and message hiding [7]. While encryption is one specific element of cryptography in which one hides data or information by transforming it into an undecipherable code. Present day encryption calculations assume an essential part in the security affirmation of IT frameworks and correspondences as they can give secrecy, as well as the accompanying key elements of security which are authentication and integrity. The most broadly utilized symmetric-key cipher is AES, which was made to ensure government classified data. AES is an encryption standard adopted by the U.S. government and has been approved by the National Security Agency (NSA) for encryption of "top secret" information.

The 3D-AES block cipher is based on the AES block cipher which is a key-alternating block cipher, composed of rotation key function, minimum 3 iterations of round function and key mixing operations [9]. The technique for 3D-AES is utilized to generate symmetric keys by randomizing first key arrays three times which creates a superior key in every randomization. Accordingly, the last key will be more grounded than standard AES keys. This procedure is equipped for giving an abnormal state of instructive security of message secrecy, and originality traded between two parties and in addition decreasing the length of words.

Despite the fact that cloud computing provider vendors touted the security and reliability in their offerings, actual deployment of cloud computing offerings is not as secure and reliable as they declare. In 2009, the foremost cloud computing companies successively regarded several accidents. Amazon's simple storage service was interrupted twice in February and July 2009. In March 2009, safety vulnerabilities in Google medical doctors even caused serious leakage of user personal records. Google Gmail additionally regarded a worldwide failure as much as 4 h. As administrators' misuse main to lack of 45% user information, cloud storage vendor LinkUp had been pressured to close [5].

This paper analyzes existing challenges and issues involved in the cloud storage security concerns. These highlighted issues are grouped into architecture-related issues, attack vulnerabilities and cryptographic algorithm structures. The objective of this paper is to identify weak points in the cloud storage model. This paper presents a detailed and structured analysis for each vulnerability to highlight their root causes. Evaluation of the analysis will help cloud providers and security vendors to have a better understanding of the existing problems.

2 Review on Web-Based Cloud Storage

Cloud storage is gaining popularity lately. In employer settings, it is seen that the upward push in demand for statistics outsourcing, which assists within the strategic control of company statistics. It is also used as a middle technology in the back of many online services for personal programs. These days, it is easy to apply without spending a dime accounts for e mail, photograph album, report sharing and/or faraway get entry to, with storage size extra than 25 GB together with the cutting-edge wireless technology, customers can get right of entry to almost all of their documents and emails by using a mobile phone in any corner of the sector [6]. Figure 1 shows the standard architecture of cloud data storage service [12].

Data sharing is a crucial functionality in cloud storage. As an instance, bloggers can allow their friends view a subset of their non-public pictures. An employer can also grant her personnel get right of entry to a part of touchy records. The difficult problem is the way to effectively share encrypted statistics. Of route users can download the encrypted information from the garage, decrypt them, then send them to others for sharing, but it loses the value of cloud storage. Users must be able to delegate the get entry to rights of the sharing records to others in an effort to get right of entry to this information from the server without delay. However, locating an efficient and

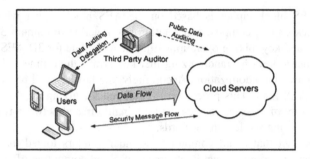

Fig. 1. Architecture of cloud data storage service

comfortable manner to proportion partial records in cloud storage is not always trivial. Figure 2 shows the challenges and issues related to cloud on-demand model [14].

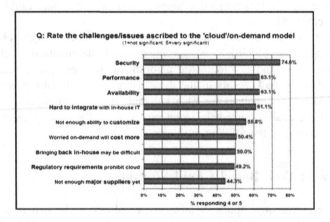

Fig. 2. Challenges and issues related to cloud on-demand model

As shown in Fig. 2, security is the top one concern. It is mentioned by the users of Cloud Computing whose worry about their businesses' information and critical IT resources in the Cloud Computing system which are vulnerable to be attacked. The second most concern issues are on performance and availability. The least concern of cloud computing users is there are not enough major suppliers yet [14].

The results from several research papers states that encryption of sensitive data information is crucial in protecting data integrity angst confidentiality. The most commonly used cryptography in cloud computing systems is AES algorithm because of the benefits it provides outweighs its overall weaknesses. Hence, an improvement to an already very stable algorithm such as 3D-AES provides a better security structure towards data protection. Table 1 below shows a brief summary of the comparison between AES and 3D-AES in terms of complexity, security, and performance from the results collected from different research papers. Since 3D-AES is an enhancement to AES, it is considerably more complex than AES as it involves more methods to accommodate a state that is represented in a 3D cube of $4 \times 4 \times 4$ bytes. This will inherently provide a higher level of security since additional steps are taken that adds more layers to the cipher architecture. However, this will also decrease its performance time slightly with the additional processing time required to encrypt or decrypt a higher bit count state.

Table 1. Comparison of AES and 3D-AES

	AES	3D-AES
Complexity	Implements four basic operations which are SubBytes, ShiftRows, MixColumns and AddRoundKey	Implements similar operations to AES. However, the state is represented in a 3D cube of 4x4x4 bytes
Security	Sufficient to protect classified information	Provides higher level of security due increased bit size
Performance	Decent performance	Decent performance

AES block cipher involves two main inputs, which are the plaintext to cipher considered as the state and also the cipher key. The state goes through four transformation processes which are subsequently known as SubBytes, ShiftRows, MixColumns and AddRoundKey. The SubBytes method utilizes the S-Box or substitution-box to substitute a byte from the state with the corresponding value in the S-Box. The ShiftRows process shifts or switch the array position of each bytes of the state. In MixColumns, the four numbers of one column are modulo multiplied in Rjindael's Galois Field by a given matrix. Lastly, the AddRoundKey function performs an XOR operation with the round key itself. These four main transformation steps are performing in repeated 10 rounds until completion. The MixColumns step along with the ShiftRows step is the primary source of diffusion in AES block cipher.

AES block cipher also has its own limitations and weaknesses. For example, the simplistic nature of the methods surrounding its architecture which involves only 4 basic operations can be both considered an advantage and a disadvantage. Additionally, every block is always encrypted in the same manner which means that the cipher can somewhat be easily implemented but also, be easily de-constructed or reverse engineered. Furthermore, through the years, it is widely known that old encryption methods will be cracked in due time which is why it is always important to figure out new cipher methods or improve upon already existing ones.

3   Review on 3D-AES Block Cipher

3D-AES block cipher is primarily based on the AES block cipher [2]. 3D-AES is a key-alternating block cipher which is composed of rotation key function that has minimum of three iterations of round functions, each with a key mixing operation. The three round functions in 3D-AES are nonlinear substitution function, permutation function and transposition function. Figure 3 shows the encryption and decryption process diagram of the 3D-AES block cipher in the form of 4×16 bytes [1].

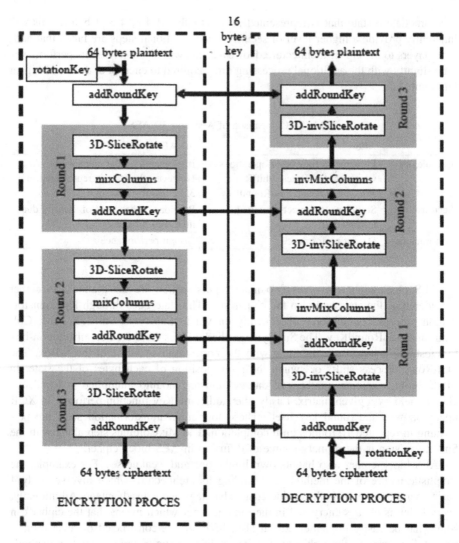

Fig. 3. Encryption and decryption of 3D-AES

3D-AES inherits the same basic operations of AES block cipher which are Sub-Bytes, ShiftRows, MixColumns and AddRoundKey. The only difference being that the state is represented in a 3D cube of $4 \times 4 \times 4$ bytes. Each slide of the Cube module implements a permutation process of rotating the x-axis, y-axis and z-axis, which is similar to the AddRoundKey operation in AES where the XOR operation is used. This key is known as the rotationKey. Every slice of the cube will be rotated at the 3D-SliceRotate function of the cube which is similar to the ShiftRows function in AES. Linear transformation then transposes the state of array much like MixColumns operation in AES. The three operations are repeated in three rounds. On the third round, where r = 3, the output cipher state is the ciphertext which operates on plaintext size of

16 × 4 bytes to produce a 64-byte output ciphertext. A 16-byte size secret key is required by the 3D-AES block cipher. Every operations in the 3D-AES block cipher are performed in the finite field of order 28, denoted by GF(28). Those extended structure increases the length of the processed block because of the use of several structure simultaneously. The block cipher of 3D-AES block cipher is managed to secure against a chosen plaintext attack and conventional non-related key attacks [1].

Encryption using 3D-AES algorithm on data that are stored on the cloud provides another degree of security on the overall architecture of the cloud. The design of 3D-AES was inspired by the AES encryption algorithm, in which text and key blocks are represented by a 2-dimensional state matrix of bytes. The main innovation of 3D-AES is the 4 × 4 × 4 3-dimensional state of bytes, that led to improvements in design, security and potential applications. By encrypting the data using a powerful algorithm such as 3D-AES, it can therefore mitigate data theft issues where the data is encrypted even in the event it is stolen through middle layer network attacks.

In [3] had mentioned that randomness test, avalanche effect and cryptanalysis are the measurement techniques which have been taken into consideration in the evaluation of the minimum security requirement of cryptographic block cipher algorithm. The 3D-AES already harnessed and analyzed using nine (9) different sets of data in evaluating the randomness of cryptographic algorithms as mentioned in [3]. However based on the analysis conducted towards all nine data categories using the NIST Statistical Test Suite, due to the high volume of data required (67240448 bits) during LDP and HDP testing data categories, the analysis cannot be recorded and analyzed. Hence, in this paper the LDP and HDP testing data categories will be conducted and tested in line with the need for big data security.

4 Experimental Design

The main characteristics that identify and differentiate one cryptographic algorithm from another are its ability to secure the protected data against attacks and its performance and complexity in doing so.

4.1 Design Flow

In this phase, a design of the proposed system will be design, coding, and implement in order to develop the system between AES and 3D-AES block ciphers only. Figure 4 shows the flow of this design phase.

As shown in Fig. 4, the first step of this phase is to develop the input sample data from the generator program. Once the sample data is implemented and tested, the output of the sample data is generated. The development of encryption and decryption function of 3D-AES block cipher is then follow and thus implement and test. Tested result from the developed functions is then verified and compared to identify the effectiveness level of the developed encryption and decryption functions of 3D-AES. Once the result is verified and compared, the next phase is entered to proceed with the security analysis of the proposed system.

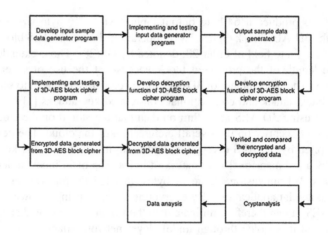

Fig. 4. Project design

4.2 Testing Data

The first categories of data with its purposes is Low Density Plaintext (LDP) Data Category. The LDP data category is formed based on low-density y-bit plaintext which is 516 bit plaintext. The blocks testing consists of $1 + 512 + 130816 = 131329$ blocks so 512 plaintext $\times 131329$ blocks $= 67240448$ bits as shown in Fig. 5.

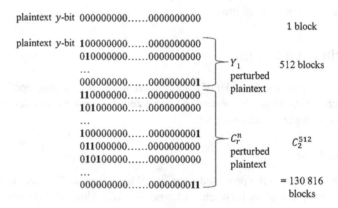

Fig. 5. Experiment testing on LDP data category

The second High Density Plaintext (HDP) Data Category. The HDP data category is formed based on high-density y-bit plaintext which is 516 bit plaintext. The blocks testing consists of $1 + 512 + 130816 = 131329$ blocks so 512 plaintext $\times$ 131329 blocks $= 67240448$ bits as shown in Fig. 6.

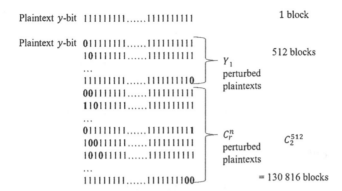

Fig. 6. Experiment testing on HDP data category

4.3 Experiment Architecture

The system consists of two main environments, which are the front-end web client and the back-end cloud storage server. The front-end client provides the user interface and interactions to communicate with the cloud storage server. The front-end client also consists of the web session storage provided by most modern websites today to storage necessary information related to the current user session. The back-end cloud storage server will store all the user's encrypted file and can only be accessed by the authorized user's credentials. Figure 7 shows the overall system architecture.

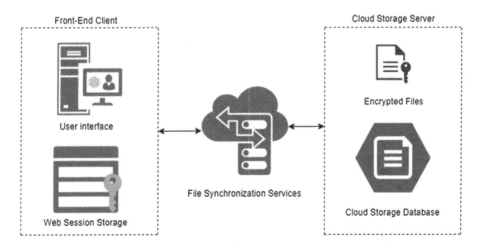

Fig. 7. Overall system architecture

Users are required to register and login to the system since each user are assigned with their own unique cipher key. The cipher key is stored in the web browser's session storage and is removed whenever the user logs out of the system. Whenever a user uploads a file, the file is read in binary format and undergoes the 3D-AES encryption process using the user's cipher key. The file's binary data is represented in a $4 \times 4 \times 4$ cube matrix array and goes through 3 rounds of 3D-SliceRotate, MixColumns and AddRoundKey methods for the diffusion process. The encrypted data will then go through the synchronization services to be stored in the cloud storage database. The reverse process is done whenever the user needs to download the file from the cloud storage database. The encrypted data is first downloaded onto the front-end client and the decryption process is made before presenting the user interface.

5   Implementation

Figure 8 shows the web architecture of the implementation of 3D-AES cryptography in a web-based file storage application. File sharing download and upload between the client and server occurs synchronously as most modern cloud storage solutions do. The symmetric key is both stored in the client session and the cloud storage. The key is unique to each users' application session and reset every time the user starts a new session in the application. When the file is being uploaded to the cloud server, the encryption process happens on the client side before transferring to the cloud server to protect the data contents. The file is then decrypted on cloud server side to be stored in the database. The process is vice versa with the download process.

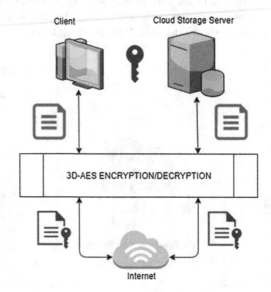

Fig. 8   Web architecture of the implementation of 3D-AES block cipher

6 Result Discussion

Based on the analysis conducted towards all nine data categories using the NIST Statistical Test Suite, the analysis results are shown in the following Table 2. Due to the high volume of data required (67240448 bits) during LDP and HDP testing data categories, the analysis cannot be recorded and analyzed.

Table 2. Randomness test report

NIST test suite	LDP	HDP
Frequency test	×	√
Block frequency test	×	√
Cumulative sums forward test	×	√
Runs test	×	√
Longest runs of one test	×	×
Rank test	×	×
DFT (spectral) test	×	×
Universal statistical test	×	×
Approximate entropy test	×	×
Random excursion test	×	×
Random excursion variant test	√	√
Serial test	×	×
Linear complexity test	√	√
Overlapping template matching	×	×
Non-overlapping template matching	×	×

Table 2 present and compare the randomness analysis result gathered between the seven out of nine types of data categories. If the rejected sequence is less than or equal ($\leq$) to the number of maximum rejection, then the result is passed with symbol √. If the rejected sequence is greater than ($\geq$) to the number of maximum rejection, then the result is failed with symbol ×. Conclusively, based on the results obtained, from 15 tests between two categories, the results on randomness test is passed only on test of Random Excursion Variant Test and Linear Complexity Test. The result reported may not be accurate due to very high number or bit during testing and the failure of hardware requirements.

From the literature, Fig. 9 shows a base chart comparison between AES cipher and 3D-AES cipher in terms of complexity, security and performance.

In terms of complexity, AES cipher may have the upper hand since the cipher architecture involves only 4 basic operations which are SubBytes, ShiftRows, Mix-Columns and AddRoundkey. On the other hand, 3D-AES utilizes the same 4 operations with additional methods to help with encrypting or decrypting the state that is represented in a 3D cube of 4 × 4 × 4 bytes. While AES is secure on its own, 3D-AES is providing a better level of security due to the fact that it utilizes a higher bit size. Besides that, both AES and 3D-AES cipher provides decent performance in terms

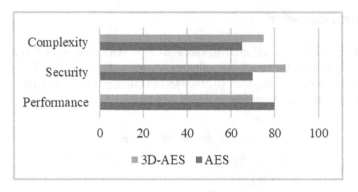

Fig. 9 Comparison between AES and 3D-AES

of encryption and decryption processing speed. However, AES cipher may be slight bit faster since it involves less processing steps compared to 3D-AES.

7 Conclusion

The cloud computing guarantees many opportunities whilst posing a unique safety and privacy challenges. The acknowledged problem with cloud computing is the issue of privacy and confidentiality of both the user and the computation of the data stored in the cloud storage. The solution to the problems was uniformly solved by sending the data encrypted to the cloud storage. Privacy is a primary concern in all of the challenges going through cloud computing. Many agencies and end-user customers are not at ease with the thought of storing their records on off-premise information centers or machines. End-users do not trust cloud services to save their personal facts and might favor to store the data locally on their devices at home. Many customers agree with that the records stored in cloud offerings may be exposed or stolen. While current cloud storage solutions provide a decent level of security in terms of protecting end-users' data, in practice the user information in cloud storage services are often exposed to the risk of unauthorized access. Ever though, the 3D-AES encryption claimed that can provides a higher degree layer of security, but the further randomness test with other technique need to be conducted again due to the failed randomness test in this paper.

Acknowledgment. This work is supported by the Fundamental Research Grant Scheme (FRGS) provided by the Ministry of Higher Education Malaysia, under the Grant Number FRGS/1/2015/ICT03/UiTM/02/6.

References

1. Ariffin, S., Hisan, N.A., Arshad, S., Bakar, S.H.: Square and boomerang attacks analysis of diffusion property of 3D-AES block cipher. In: 2016 12th International Conference on Natural Computation, Fuzzy Systems and Knowledge Discovery (ICNC-FSKD), Changsha, China, pp. 862–867. IEEE (2016)
2. Ariffin, S., Mahmod, R., Rahmat, R., Idris, N. A.: SMS encryption using 3D-AES block cipher on android message application. In: 2013 International Conference Advanced Computer Science Applications and Technologies (ACSAT), Kuching, Malaysia, pp. 310–314. IEEE (2013)
3. Ariffin, S., Yusof, N.A.M.: Randomness analysis on 3D-AES block cipher. In: 2017 13th International Conference on Natural Computation, Fuzzy Systems and Knowledge Discovery (ICNC-FSKD), Guilin, China, pp. 331–335. IEEE (2017)
4. Arockiam, L., Monikandan, S.: Data security and privacy in cloud storage using hybrid symmetric encryption algorithm. Int. J. Adv. Res. Comput. Commun. Eng. 2(8), 3064–3070 (2013)
5. Chen, D., Zhao, H.: Data security and privacy protection issues in cloud computing. In: International Conference on Computer Science and Electronics Engineering, Hangzhou, China, vol. 1, pp. 647–651. IEEE (2012)
6. Chu, C.K., Chow, S.S., Tzeng, W.G., Zhou, J., Deng, R.H.: Key-aggregate cryptosystem for scalable data sharing in cloud storage. IEEE Trans. Parallel Distrib. Syst. 25(2), 468–477 (2014)
7. Dictionary.com. http://www.dictionary.com/browse/cryptography. Accessed 26 Mar 2018
8. Galibus, T., Krasnoproshin, V.V., Albuquerque, R.D., Freitas, E.P.: Elements of Cloud Storage Security Concepts. Designs and Optimized Practices. Springer, Heidelberg (2016). https://doi.org/10.1007/978-3-319-44962-3
9. Kale, N.A., Natikar, S.B., Karande, S.M.: Secured mobile messaging for android application. Int. J. Adv. Res. Comput. Sci. Manag. Stud. 2(11), 304–311 (2014)
10. Kumar, A., Lee, B.G., Lee, H., Kumari, A.: Secure storage and access of data in cloud computing. In: 2012 International Conference ICT Convergence (ICTC), Jeju Island, South Korea, pp. 336–339. IEEE (2012)
11. Manogaran, G., Thota, C., Kumar, M.V.: MetaCloudDataStorage architecture for big data security in cloud computing. Procedia Comput. Sci. 87, 128–133 (2016)
12. Wang, C., Chow, S.S., Wang, Q., Ren, K., Lou, W.: Privacy-preserving public auditing for secure cloud storage. IEEE Trans. Comput. 62(2), 362–375 (2013)
13. Waziri, V.O., Alhassan, J.K., Ismaila, I., Dogonyaro, M.N.: Big data analytics and data security in the cloud via fully homomorphic encryption. Int. J. Comput. Control Quantum Inf. Eng. 9(3), 744–753 (2015)
14. Zhou, M., Zhang, R., Xie, W., Qian, W., Zhou, A.: Security and privacy in cloud computing: a survey. In: 2010 Sixth International Conference on Semantics Knowledge and Grid (SKG), pp. 105–112 (2010)

An Empirical Study of Classifier Behavior in Rattle Tool

Wahyu Wibowo[1($\boxtimes$)] and Shuzlina Abdul-Rahman[2]

[1] Institut Teknologi Sepuluh Nopember, 60111 Surabaya, Indonesia
wahyu_w@statistika.its.ac.id
[2] Research Initiative Group of Intelligent Systems,
Faculty of Computer & Mathematical Sciences, Universiti Teknologi MARA,
40450 Shah Alam, Selangor, Malaysia

Abstract. There are many factors that influence classifiers behavior in machine learning, and thus determining the best classifier is not an easy task. One way of tackling this problem is by experimenting the classifiers with several performance measures. In this paper, the behaviors of machine learning classifiers are experimented using the Rattle tool. Rattle tool is a graphical user interface (GUI) in R package used to carry out data mining modeling using classifiers namely, tree, boost, random forest, support vector machine, logit and neural net. This study was conducted using simulation and real data in which the behaviors of the classifiers are observed based on accuracy, ROC curve and modeling time. Based on the simulation data, there is grouping of the algorithms in terms of accuracy. The first are logit, neural net and support vector machine. The second are boost and random forest and the third is decision tree. Based on the real data, the highest accuracy based on the training data is boost algorithm and based on the testing data the highest accuracy is the neural net algorithm. Overall, the support vector machine and neural net classifier are the two best classifiers in both simulation and real data.

Keywords: Accuracy · Classifier · Empirical data · Machine learning

1 Introduction

There are many factors that influence classifiers behavior in machine learning and thus determining the best classifier is not an easy task. Classification is categorical supervised learning and the key point is to find the best model to predict categorical response variable based on a set of predictor variable. There are so many methods and algorithms to develop classification models from the simple to the complex model [1]. There is a good paper that evaluates hundreds of algorithms for classification [2]. Additionally, there are many software and packages to perform the classifier algorithm.

Rattle is an abbreviation for R Analytic Tool To Learn Easily. It is a popular graphical user interface (GUI) for data mining using R [3]. It provides many facilities to summarize the data, visualize, and model both supervised and unsupervised machine learning. Furthermore, Rattle provides the interactions with the GUI that can be extracted as R script such that it can be run independently of Rattle interface.

© Springer Nature Singapore Pte Ltd. 2019
B. W. Yap et al. (Eds.): SCDS 2018, CCIS 937, pp. 322–334, 2019.
https://doi.org/10.1007/978-981-13-3441-2_25

In terms of supervised machine learning, there are six classifiers model provided by Rattle. These are decision tree, boost, random forest, support vector machine, linear logit and neural net. However, it is hard to distinguish which classifier is better and can perform well. Therefore, this study attempts to experiment the behavior of those classifiers by applying both simulation and real datasets. One main issue is the performance of the model, in particular the accuracy and time processing.

The real data example is from an Indonesian Family Life Survey (IFLS) about working status of housewife, working or not working. This will be a binary response variable and the event is defined as housewife is working. It is interesting to look at the women working status as the role of women in the family is very important, not only taking care of the children, but also increasing family income through economic activities. Unfortunately, the indicator labor market shows that there is a gap productivity between women and men workforce. Labor force participation rate of women in Indonesia is around 50%, which is still far and below the participation of men, which is around 80%. The indicator also shows that the percentage of women part time worker is twice the percentage of men part time worker [4].

2 Classifier Brief Review

This section briefly reviews each classifier algorithm. For more detailed discussion on the subject and its application, readers can refer to the numerous resources for classifier algorithms as mentioned in [2, 5, 6].

Decision Tree. A decision tree model is one of the most common data mining models. It is popular because the resulting model is easy to understand. The algorithm uses a recursive partitioning approach. The method is also called as the Classification and Regression Tree (CART). This method is one of the classification methods or supervised learning. The decision tree uses a selective algorithm of binary recursive portioning. Decision tree method implementation is carried out with some stages i.e. determining training and testing data and construction of classification tree, pruning of a classification tree, determination of optimum classification tree. This algorithm is implemented in R by the library rpart [7].

Random Forest. Random forest is an ensemble of un-pruned decision trees and is used when we have large training datasets and particularly a very large number of input variables (hundreds or even thousands of input variables). The algorithm is efficient with respect to a large number of variables since it repeatedly subsets the variables available. A random forest model is typically made up of tens or hundreds of decision trees. This algorithm is implemented using the library randomForest [8].

Boost. The basic idea of boosting is to associate a weight with each observation in the dataset. A series of models are built, and the weights are increased (boosted) if a model incorrectly classifies the observation. The resulting series of decision trees form an ensemble model. The Adaptive option deploys the traditional adaptive boosting algorithm as implemented in the xgboost package [9].

Support Vector Machine. A Support Vector Machine (SVM) searches for the so called support vectors, which are data points that are found to lie at the edge of an area in space, which is a boundary from one class of points to another. In the terminology of SVM, we talk about the space between regions containing data points in different classes as being the margin between those classes. The support vectors are used to identify a hyperplane (when we are talking about many dimensions in the data, or a line if we are talking about only two dimensional data) that separates the classes. This algorithm is performed by the kernlab package [10].

Linear Logistic. It is a class of model regression between categorical response variable (y) with categorical, continuous, or mixed predictor variable (x). Logistic regression is used to find the correlation of dichotomous (nominal or ordinal scale by two categories) or polychotomous (nominal or ordinal scale with more than two categories) with one or more predictor variables that are continuous or categorical. The simplest model of logistic regression is binary logistic regression. This algorithm is implemented by the glm function [11].

Neural Net. Neural net is an information processing system that has characters such as the biological neural network, the human brain tissue. In neural networks, there is a term neuron or often called a unit, cell, or node. Each unit is connected to other units through layers with specific weights. The weight here represents the information used by the network to solve the problem. Each unit has an output called activation. Activation is a function of input received. A unit will send an activation signal to the other units on the next layer. This model is implemented by the nnet package [12].

Classifier Evaluation. The classifier performance will be evaluated by using accuracy and Receiving Operating Characteristic (ROC) Curve. Accuracy (Eq. 1) is computed from the confusion matrix as shown in Table 1.

$$Accuracy = \frac{n_{00} + n_{11}}{n_{00} + n_{01} + n_{10} + n_{11}} \tag{1}$$

Table 1. Confusion matrix

Actual Group		Predicted Group	
		1	0
Y	1	True Positive (n_{11})	False Positive (n_{10})
	0	False Negative (n_{01})	True Negative (n_{00})

The accuracy will be between 0 and 1. The greater the value of accuracy, the better is the model. The ROC curve is a curve created by plotting the true positive rate and the false positive rate. The area under this curve is the performance measurement of a binary classifier.

3   Data

This study experiments two sets of data i.e. the simulation and real data. Both sets are required to conduct the study such that the classifier behavior can be well understood. The following paragraphs explain the details about the data.

Simulation Data. The simulation data was generated using the logistic regression model. The five input variables was generated from the Normal distribution, i.e., $x_1 \sim$ Normal(1,1), $x_2 \sim$ Normal(2,1), $x_3 \sim$ Normal(3,1), $x_4 \sim$ Normal(2,1), $x_5 \sim$ Normal(1,1). Then, the coefficients correspond to the intercept and the predictors, beta1, beta2, beta3, beta4 and beta5 are determined. Intercept $= -1$; beta1 $= 0.5$; beta2 $= 1$; beta3 $= 3$; beta4 $= -2$; beta5 $= -3$.

Then, the linear predictor (*linpred*) and probability (*prob*) was calculated using the following formula,

$$linpred = -1 + 0.5x_1 + x_2 + 3x_3 - 2x_4 - 3x_5$$

$$prob = \frac{\exp(linpred)}{1 + \exp(linpred)}$$

Finally, the categorical target variable y, 0 or 1, was created by generating a series of number following Uniform (0,1). If this random number is less than prob, then y = 1, otherwise y = 0. These steps were replicated 10 times and each replicate would take 100000 observations.

Real Data. This is a secondary data from the survey of the Indonesian Family Life Survey (IFLS) wave 5 carried out in 2014 or referred to as IFLS-5 conducted by RAND Labor and Population. This data can be downloaded for free from https://www.rand. org/labor/FLS/IFLS/ifls5.html. The survey of family (Household Survey) was conducted in 13 out of 27 provinces in Indonesia. The provinces were DKI Jakarta, Jawa Barat, Jawa Timur, Kalimantan Selatan, Sulawesi Selatan, Sumatera Selatan, Nusa Tenggara Barat, Jawa Tengah, Yogyakarta, Bali, Sumatera Utara, Sumatera Barat dan Lampung. The location is presented in Fig. 1.

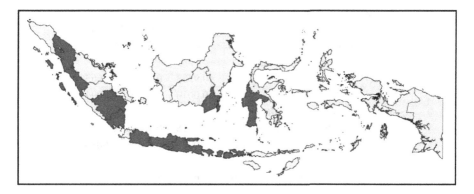

Fig. 1. Survey location of IFLS

The total number of respondents are 16,204 members of household interviewed and 4431 fulfilled the criteria of women and married. The data are then divided into two groups i.e. training and testing sets. The training set will be used to fit the model and will be validated using the testing set. The training set selected is 80% from the data and 20% as testing set. The variables are presented in Table 2.

Table 2. Research variables

Indicator	Description	Scale
Status of housewife (Y)	0: Not working 1: Working	Nominal
Last education (X_1)	0: No school 1: Graduated from elementary school 2: Graduated from junior high school 3: Graduated from senior high school 4: Graduated from college	Ordinal
Age (X_2)	-	Ratio
Household expenditure (X_3)	-	Ratio

4 Results

Simulation Data. The detailed results of each algorithm are presented in the Appendix. The summary is presented in Table 3. For the training data, random forest has the perfect accuracy while the lowest accuracy is the decision tree model. However, based on the testing data, the logit model has the highest accuracy. Based on the area

Table 3. Summary of the simulation study results

	Tree	Forest	Boost	SVM	Logit	Neural
Training Data Accuracy						
Mean	86.6600	100.0000	92.7100	91.4500	91.3900	91.4200
sd	0.3658	0.0000	0.0738	0.1080	0.0876	0.0919
Testing data accuracy						
Mean	86.3000	90.8100	90.8800	91.2500	91.4100	91.3800
sd	0.4137	0.2132	0.2044	0.1780	0.2601	0.2348
Area under curve training data						
Mean	0.8739	1.0000	0.9751	0.9533	0.9661	0.9663
sd	0.0058	0.0000	0.0003	0.0010	0.0004	0.0004
Area under curve testing data						
Mean	0.8689	0.9603	0.9628	0.9518	0.9660	0.9658
sd	0.0079	0.0017	0.0016	0.0023	0.0014	0.0014
Processing time (sec)						
Mean	4.7940	84.9000	3.8820	496.6200	2.2800	20.9750
sd	0.1940	5.4498	0.9242	11.9333	0.4474	1.1772

under curve measures, for the training data the highest accuracy is the random forest and the lowest is the decision tree model while for the testing data, the highest accuracy is the logit model and the lowest is the decision tree.

It is not surprising that the highest accuracy is the logit model because the simulation data is derived from the model. Thus, more details about the algorithm is needed. For this purpose, the ANOVA model would be applied by considering the classifier as the factor. By applying the (ANOVA) model, it is observed that the mean of accuracy is significantly different. Further comparison was made in which the results of the classifiers can be grouped into three. Furthermore, by multiple comparison among classifiers, the classifiers can be divided to three groups. The first are logit, neural and support vector machine. The second are boost and random forest and the third is the decision tree.

As an additional information, the processing time for model building is also presented. The results of the experiments have shown that the shortest processing time is the logit model and the longest processing time is the support vector machine. It needs to be noted that the processing time of the support vector machine is the highest among the classifiers. Certainly, processing time is a crucial issue especially in big data analytics (BDA).

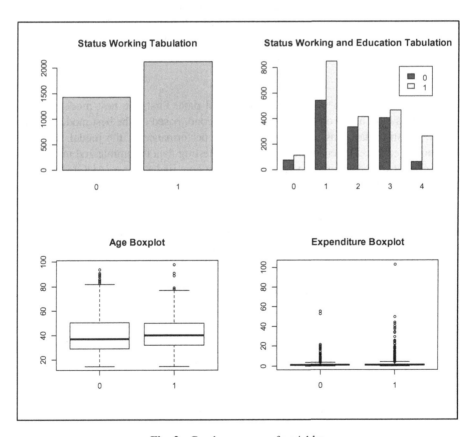

Fig. 2. Graph summary of variables

Real Data. The results presented are from the training set and the summary of variables as shown in Fig. 2. The percentage of the not-working group is 41% (1428) and that of the working group is 59% (2116). Based on the last education indicator, the frequency of the working group is higher than not-working group across the education level. However, the elementary and college education show a much different frequency between working and not-working group. In addition, for the education level no-school, junior and senior school the frequency is quite the same.

In addition, the distribution age of women for both working and not-working groups are quite the same, with several outliers. On the contrary, the distribution of expenditure is quite different. Expenditure distribution of the working group is more skewed than not-working group. Furthermore, Table 4 presents a numerically summary of age and expenditure for both groups. As can be seen, the average age between the working and not-working groups are not much different. In contrast, the average and standard deviation of household expenditures of the working group is greater than the household expenditures of the not-working group.

Table 4. Statistics summary

Status	Age		Expenditure	
	Mean	SD	Mean	SD
Not working	41	15	1.505.000	2.916.286
Working	42	12	1.885.000	4.242.965

Next, each algorithm was applied to the real data. First, the best model of each classifier was built based on the training data. Second, based on the best model of each classifier, testing data was used to evaluate the performance of the model. The performance of each classifier for both training and testing data is summarized in Table 5, which consist of the accuracy percentage and the area under curve (AUC). The ROC curve is presented in Appendix B.

As shown in Table 5, the classifier behavior of real data is different from the simulation data. The highest accuracy based on the training data is the boost algorithm, and the highest accuracy based on the testing data is the neural net algorithm. Then, using the area under curve criteria, the pattern is the same with the accuracy criteria.

Table 5. Classifier accuracy for real data

Criteria	Training data					
	Tree	Forest	Boost	SVM	Logit	Neural
Accuracy	64	71.5	77.5	64.7	59.4	64.7
AUC	0.6029	0.8276	0.8735	0.6671	0.5811	0.6612
	Testing data					
Accuracy	67.4	65.8	62.7	66.9	61.3	67.8
AUC	0.6236	0.6682	0.6399	0.6934	0.5789	0.6906

Additionally, using the real data, the logit model is no longer the highest accuracy algorithm in both training and testing data, otherwise it is the lowest one. For better understanding of the classifiers behavior, Table 6 presents the rank of the behavior. It is interesting to observe that the support vector machine and the neural net classifier are the two best classifiers in both simulation and real data. However, the main drawback of these two classifiers is that they are time consuming.

Table 6. Accuracy rank summary of classifier

Dataset	Rank Accuracy					
	Tree	Forest	Boost	SVM	Logit	Neural
Simulation	6	5	4	3	1	2
Real data	2	4	5	3	6	1

5   Conclusions

This study presents the empirical results on the behavior of different classifiers model based on the simulation and real data. The results have shown that it is not easy to conclude as to which is the best classifier algorithm. However, both the support vector machine and neural net algorithms are robust and performed well consistently in both simulation and real data. Even though a classifier may be superior in one situation, it would not guarantee that the same algorithm would also be superior in another situation. Instead of accuracy, the other issue to consider when employing classification or supervised machine learning is the size of the data. Data size is important because it will have implications on the processing time and computer memory usage. The researcher should be aware of the data size because some algorithms cannot work properly if the size is larger/too large and would require a big computer memory.

Acknowledgment. The authors are grateful to the Institut Teknologi Sepuluh Nopember that has supported this work partly through the Research Grant contract number 1192/PKS/ITS/2018 (1302/PKS/ITS/2018).

Appendix A. Summary of Results

Replication	Training data accuracy					
	Tree	Forest	Boost	SVM	Logit	Neural
1	86.9	100	92.8	91.5	91.4	91.5
2	87	100	92.7	91.6	91.5	91.5
3	86.7	100	92.7	91.3	91.3	91.3
4	87	100	92.6	91.3	91.4	91.4
5	86.3	100	92.7	91.5	91.4	91.5

(continued)

(*continued*)

Replication	Training data accuracy					
	Tree	Forest	Boost	SVM	Logit	Neural
6	86.8	100	92.7	91.4	91.3	91.3
7	85.8	100	92.8	91.5	91.5	91.5
8	86.6	100	92.7	91.4	91.3	91.4
9	86.7	100	92.6	91.4	91.3	91.3
10	86.8	100	92.8	91.6	91.5	91.5
Mean	**86.660**	**100.000**	**92.710**	**91.450**	**91.390**	**91.420**
sd	**0.366**	**0.000**	**0.074**	**0.108**	**0.088**	**0.092**

Replication	Testing data accuracy					
	Tree	Forest	Boost	SVM	Logit	Neural
1	86.4	90.6	90.8	91	91.2	91.1
2	86.2	90.6	90.6	91	91	91
3	86.3	91	91.2	91.5	91.7	91.7
4	86.6	91.1	91	91.4	91.8	91.7
5	86.2	90.7	90.7	91.1	91.3	91.3
6	86.2	90.6	90.7	91.2	91.3	91.4
7	85.3	90.9	91	91.4	91.5	91.5
8	86.3	90.6	90.7	91.2	91.2	91.2
9	86.8	90.9	91.1	91.4	91.7	91.5
10	86.7	91.1	91	91.3	91.4	91.4
Mean	**86.300**	**90.810**	**90.880**	**91.250**	**91.410**	**91.380**
sd	**0.414**	**0.213**	**0.204**	**0.178**	**0.260**	**0.235**

Replication	Area under curve training data					
	Tree	Forest	Boost	SVM	Logit	Neural
1	0.8788	1	0.9751	0.9524	0.9661	0.9664
2	0.8740	1	0.9751	0.953	0.9664	0.9666
3	0.8690	1	0.9748	0.952	0.9653	0.9655
4	0.8785	1	0.9747	0.9528	0.9658	0.966
5	0.8673	1	0.9755	0.9547	0.9664	0.9667
6	0.8820	1	0.9749	0.954	0.9657	0.9659
7	0.8636	1	0.9756	0.9538	0.9665	0.9667
8	0.8779	1	0.9752	0.9547	0.9665	0.9667
9	0.8742	1	0.9749	0.9521	0.9658	0.9661
10	0.8733	1	0.975	0.9531	0.9662	0.9664
Mean	0.8739	1	0.9751	0.9533	0.9661	0.9663
sd	0.0058	0	0.0003	0.0010	0.0004	0.0004

(*continued*)

(continued)

Replication	Area under curve testing data					
	Tree	Forest	Boost	SVM	Logit	Neural
Replication	Area under curve testing data					
	Tree	Forest	Boost	SVM	Logit	Neural
1	0.8697	0.9576	0.9615	0.9497	0.9647	0.9643
2	0.8615	0.9589	0.961	0.9483	0.9642	0.9639
3	0.8631	0.9623	0.9649	0.9548	0.9676	0.9673
4	0.8757	0.9625	0.9646	0.9544	0.968	0.9678
5	0.8597	0.9596	0.962	0.9529	0.9655	0.9654
6	0.8782	0.9597	0.9624	0.9512	0.9655	0.9654
7	0.857	0.9608	0.964	0.9529	0.9668	0.9665
8	0.873	0.9582	0.9603	0.9489	0.9642	0.964
9	0.8782	0.9611	0.9634	0.9512	0.9665	0.9662
10	0.8727	0.9621	0.9642	0.9534	0.9672	0.9669
Mean	**0.869**	**0.960**	**0.963**	**0.952**	**0.966**	**0.966**
sd	**0.008**	**0.002**	**0.002**	**0.002**	**0.001**	**0.001**
Replication	Processing time (sec)					
	Tree	Forest	Boost	SVM	Logit	Neural
1	4.51	76.8	5.39	504.6	3.2	19.37
2	4.71	81.6	3.22	494.4	2.49	21.41
3	5.14	89.4	3.96	510.6	2.18	19.95
4	4.96	92.4	3.25	513.6	2.9	21.09
5	4.8	90.6	4.69	483.6	2.12	22.9
6	4.55	79.8	3.11	481.8	1.92	21.28
7	4.74	90.6	4.82	496.2	1.98	21.69
8	4.74	83.4	4.58	496.8	1.91	21.74
9	4.99	84	2.79	504.6	1.93	19.06
10	4.8	80.4	3.01	480	2.17	21.26
Mean	**4.794**	**84.900**	**3.882**	**496.620**	**2.280**	**20.975**
sd	**0.194**	**5.450**	**0.924**	**11.933**	**0.447**	**1.177**

Appendix B. ROC Curve of Classifier Real Data

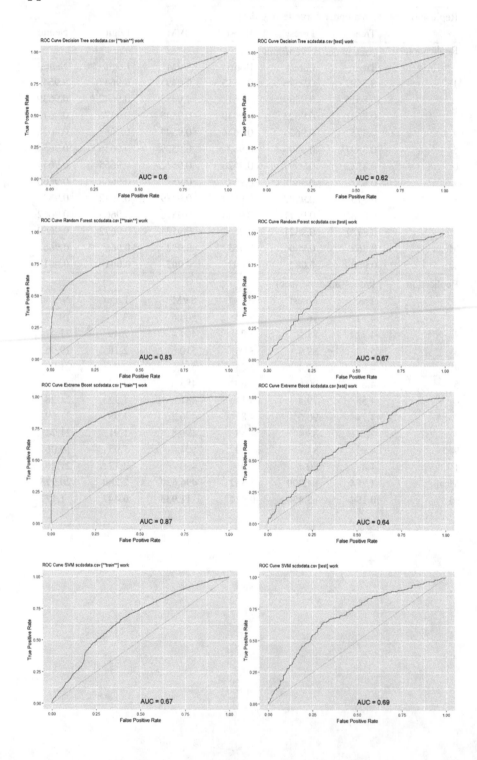

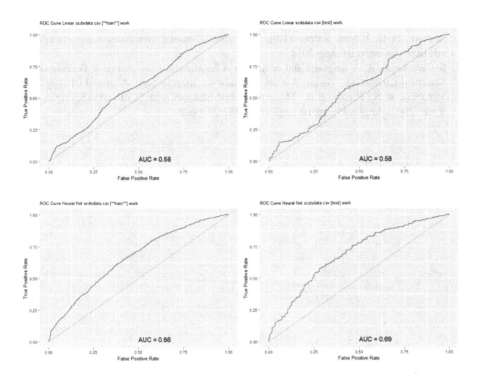

References

1. Hastie, T., Tibshirani, R., Friedman, J.: The Elements of Statistical Learning: Data Mining, Inference, and Prediction, 2nd edn. Springer, New York (2009). https://doi.org/10.1007/978-0-387-84858-7
2. Delgado, M.F., Cernadas, E., Barro, S., Amorim, D.: Do we need hundreds of classifiers to solve real world classification problems? J. Mach. Learn. Res. **15**, 3133–3181 (2014)
3. Williams, G.J.: Data Mining with Rattle and R: The Art of Excavating Data for Knowledge Discovery. Springer, New York (2011). https://doi.org/10.1007/978-1-4419-9890-3
4. Statistics Indonesia: Labor Market Indicators Indonesia, February 2017. https://www.bps.go.id/publication/2017/08/03/60626049b6ad3a897e96b8c0/indikator-pasar-tenaga-kerja-indonesia-februari-2017.html. Accessed 01 Aug 2018
5. Mutalib, S., Ali, A., Rahman, S.A., Mohamed, A.: An exploratory study in classification methods for patients' dataset. In: 2nd Conference on Data Mining and Optimization. IEEE (2009)
6. Ali, A.M., Angelov, P.: Anomalous behaviour detection based on heterogeneous data and data fusion. Soft. Comput. **22**(10), 3187–3201 (2018)
7. Therneau, T., Atkinson, B., Ripley, B.: rpart: recursive partitioning and regression trees. R package version 4.1–11. https://cran.r-project.org/web/packages/rpart/index.html. Accessed 01 Aug 2018
8. Liaw, A., Wiener, M.: Classification and regression by randomForest. R News **2**(3), 18–22 (2002)
9. Chen, T., He, T., Benesty, M., Khotilovich, V., Tang, Y.: xgboost: extreme gradient boosting. R package version 0.6.4.1. https://cran.r-project.org/web/packages/xgboost/index.html. Accessed 01 Aug 2018

10. Karatzoglou, A., Smola, A., Hornik, K., Zeileis, A.: kernlab - an S4 package for kernel methods in R. J. Stat. Softw. **11**(9), 1–20 (2004). https://www.jstatsoft.org/article/view/v011i09. Accessed 01 Aug 2018
11. R Core Team: R: A language and environment for statistical computing. R Foundation for Statistical Computing, Vienna, Austria. https://www.R-project.org. Accessed 01 Aug 2018
12. Venables, W.N., Ripley, B.D.: Modern Applied Statistics with S, 4th edn. Springer, New York (2002). https://doi.org/10.1007/978-0-387-21706-2

Data Visualization

Clutter-Reduction Technique of Parallel Coordinates Plot for Photovoltaic Solar Data

Muhaafidz Md Saufi[1(✉)], Zainura Idrus[1], Sharifah Aliman[2],
and Nur Atiqah Sia Abdullah[1]

[1] Faculty of Computer and Mathematical Sciences, Universiti Teknologi
MARA, Shah Alam, Selangor, Malaysia
muhaafidz@gmail.com, {zainura,atiqah}@tmsk.uitm.edu.my
[2] Advanced Analytic Engineering Center (AAEC),
Faculty of Computer and Mathematical Sciences,
Universiti Teknologi MARA, Shah Alam, Selangor, Malaysia
sharifahali@tmsk.uitm.edu.my

Abstract. Solar energy supplies pure environmental-friendly and limitless energy resource for human. Although the cost of solar panels has declined rapidly, technology gaps still exist for achieving cost-effective scalable deployment combined with storage technologies to provide reliable, dispatchable energy. However, it is difficult to analyze a solar data, in which data was added in every 10 min by the sensors in a short time. These data can be analyzed easier and faster with the help of data visualization. One of the popular data visualization methods for displaying massive quantity of data is parallel coordinates plot (PCP). The problem when using this method is this abundance of data can cause the polylines to overlap on each other and clutter the visualization. Thus, it is difficult to comprehend the relationship that exists between the parameters of solar data such as power rate produced by solar panel, duration of daylight in a day, and surrounding temperature. Furthermore, the density of overlapped data also cannot be determined. The solution is to implement clutter-reduction technique to parallel coordinate plot. Even though there are various clutter-reduction techniques available for visualization, they are not suitable for every situation of visualization. Thus this research studies a wide range of clutter-reduction techniques that has been implemented in visualization, identifies the common features available in clutter-reduction technique, produces a conceptual framework of clutter-reduction technique as well as proposes the suitable features to be added in parallel coordinates plot of solar energy data to reduce visual clutter.

Keywords: Conceptual framework · Clutter-reduction technique
Parallel coordinates · Solar energy · Visualization

1 Introduction

Solar energy is an environmental-friendly energy generated from light. This type of energy is generated by two different technologies namely photovoltaic (PV) and concentrated solar power (CSP). For continuous research in the area of solar energy,

© Springer Nature Singapore Pte Ltd. 2019
B. W. Yap et al. (Eds.): SCDS 2018, CCIS 937, pp. 337–349, 2019.
https://doi.org/10.1007/978-981-13-3441-2_26

data on solar environment has been collected from various types of sensors. These data are continuously streaming into database every 10 min [1], thus ended up with huge amount of data. The huge amount of data is necessary for producing high quality of analysis result. During analysis, data are plotted via visualization method to assist researchers in extracting knowledge hidden behind these data. The data need to be visualized in order to extract the relationship between solar data attributes (i.e. Solar Radiation, Wind Speed, Gust Speed, Ambient Temperature, Relative Humidity and Module Temperature) as well as electricity produced by solar system [2].

One of visualization techniques that is used to visualize solar energy dataset is parallel coordinates plot. This is due to the fact that parallel coordinates plot is suitable for visualizing not only huge dataset but also streaming data which continuously added into the database. Moreover, parallel coordinates plot is a visualization method for multivariate data which can be used to analyze the many properties of a multivariate dataset. This visualization method consists of polyline which describes multivariate items that intersects with parallel axes that represent variables of data. Parallel coordinates plot is one of the popular visualization technique for huge dataset. The strength of parallel coordinates plot lies in its capability to give relationship overview in a single graph for speed understanding [3, 4].

However, the relationship and frequency of data polylines at particular spot are difficult to extract due to huge data. They cause the polylines to overlap on each other thus, clutter the visualization. A high amount of overlapping lines will hinder the analysis process such as extracting meaningful pattern [5, 6]. In such a case, relationships between parameters of solar energy cannot be seen visually. Not only data relationship, data density around the highly overlapped polylines areas also could not be identified. The solution to such issues is to implements clutter-reduction techniques to the visualization.

Clutter-reduction technique can simplify the view of parallel coordinates plot. Even though there are various clutter-reduction techniques available to help view cluttered parallel coordinates plot, not all of them are suitable in every situation of visualization. In order to choose the right technique, we need to understand each of the features available in the clutter-reduction techniques of parallel coordinates plot.

Thus, this paper will review 10 of the parallel coordinates plot with clutter-reduction techniques that have been published recently. The difference between these techniques in term of features for enhancing the parallel coordinates plot method will be identified. Finally, this research produce a conceptual framework for such clustering techniques, so most suitable features of clutter-reduction techniques will be implemented to solar data parallel coordinates plot visualization.

This paper is organized into a few topics, which are Introduction, Literature Review, Method, and Conclusion. These topics will cover the studies of a wide range of clutter-reduction techniques that has been implemented in visualization, it also identifies the common features available in clutter-reduction technique, produces a conceptual framework of clutter-reduction technique as well as proposes the suitable features to be added in parallel coordinates plot of solar energy data to reduce visual clutter.

2   Literature Review

This section will discuss the literature review of the following topics; Solar Energy, Photovoltaic Energy, Data Visualization, Parallel Coordinates Plot as well as Clutter-Reduction Technique for Parallel Coordinates Plot.

2.1   Solar Energy

Solar energy supplies a pure environmental-friendly and limitless energy resource for human [7]. The energy in sunlight can be converted into electricity, heat, or fuel. Although the costs of solar panels have declined rapidly, technology gaps still exist to achieve cost-effective scalable deployment combined with storage technologies to provide reliable energy [8]. This type of electricity source can be generated by two different technologies namely photovoltaic (PV) and concentrated solar power (CSP). This research will focus on PV technology, since the solar data collected for this research is done by this system.

2.2   Photovoltaic (PV) Technology

Photovoltaic (PV) technology does the conversion of energy from sun to electricity without harming the environment [9]. Therefore, it is classified as green energy.

There are two main components of PV namely PC panel and PV inverter in the process of energy conversion from sun to the public grid network. A PV panel consists of a number of PV cells which directly convert light energy into electricity by the photovoltaic effect. On the other hand, PV inverter is a power electronic component to convert the power from PV panels to AC power and injecting into the public grid.

The researchers are focusing on finding the efficient and effective method to generate maximum electricity output from the solar panel. In order to do that, performance of current solar generator system must be known. However, with the huge amount of data frequently acquired from the sensor, it is hard to capture the meaning behind these data. This can be solved with the help of data visualization.

2.3   Data Visualization

Data visualization can be defined as the use of computer-supported, interactive, visual representation of data to boost cognition, or the extraction and use of knowledge [10]. Data visualization is a procedure to help represent the complex data in an effective way. Large-scale data is often supported with graphic visualizations to help better understand the data and results [11]. The visualization helps provide insights that cannot be matched by traditional approaches [10]. Data visualization must be equipped with visual analytic features if the size of data is huge. Some of the common visual analytics techniques are filter, sort, zoom, brush, bind and range [12].

There are many data visualization techniques has been developed to efficiently reduce the mental workload and enlarge user's perception of the data [13]. Different visualization techniques should be selected depending on the objective. For example,

Parallel Coordinates Plot is suitable for visualized multidimensional information or dataset.

2.4 Parallel Coordinates Plot (PCP)

Several visualization methods for multi-dimensional data have been proposed in recent years such as scatterplot matrices (SPLOM), Multi-dimensional scaling (MDS) and parallel coordinates plot [14]. Parallel coordinates plot has become a standard for multidimensional data analysis and has been widely used for many researches [15]. This is because parallel coordinates plot is good for presenting overviews of the overall data, raw data set, and for showing relationships among the dimensions. This visualization method consists of polyline which describes multivariate items that intersects with parallel axes that represent variables of data. The design of 2D parallel axes allows the simultaneous display of multiple dimensions, and thus, high-dimensional datasets are visualized in a single image [16]. Figure 1 shows an example of traditional parallel coordinates plot in color.

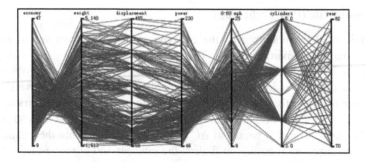

Fig. 1. Traditional parallel coordinates plot [14].

Parallel coordinates plot is suitable for visualizing a huge set of data like solar energy data, which are continuously added into the database frequently. However, parallel coordinates plot has several issues when it is applied to large datasets, such as line occlusion, line ambiguity, and hidden information [17]. The abundance of data causes the polylines to overlap from each other and disrupt the visualization. Making it arduous to extract data relationship and density from the parallel coordinates plot [3]. Thus this cluttered data and their frequency need to be highlighted. The next session will discuss about the clutter-reduction technique for parallel coordinates.

2.5 Clutter-Reduction Technique for Parallel Coordinates Plot

With huge amount of plotted data displayed together, excessive edge crossings make the display visually cluttered and thus difficult to explore [18]. A clutter-reduction technique is a solution to reduce the visual clutter in parallel coordinates. This technique is a method that render a fewer polylines with the aim of better highlight structures in the data. There are many ways to reduce visual clutter such as by enhancing the visual aspect, allowing user interactions to manipulate the visualization view, as well as implementing clutter-reduction based algorithm in parallel coordinates. By enhancing the visual such as applying colors allows instant recognition of similarities or differences of the large data items and expressed attributes relationship [19].

Based on the study of clutter-reduction techniques in the Method section, there are three types of clutter-reduction based algorithm, which are clustering, bundling and axis reordering algorithm. Some of the clutter-reduction techniques implements more than one of these algorithms.

Clustering algorithm is a technique where polylines are curved to a point of cluster group making them more distinguishable [17]. The Fig. 2 shows the visualization of parallel coordinates after implementing clustering algorithm. These techniques can be classified into four categories, which are partitioning methods, hierarchical methods, density-based methods and grid based methods [21].

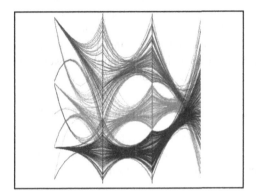

Fig. 2. Parallel coordinates plot with clustering algorithm [20].

Bundling techniques provide a visual simplification of a graph drawing or a set of trail, by spatially grouping graph edges or trails. This algorithm converts the cluster group of polylines into a stripe line. Thus, it simplifies the structure of visualization and become easier to extract the meaning or understanding in term of assessing relations that are encoded by the paths or polylines [22]. Figure 3 shows the visualization of parallel coordinates after implementing bundling algorithm.

The visual clutter also can be reduced by reordering the vertical axes. The axes of the dimension in parallel coordinates plot can be positioned in accordance to some effective rules such as similarity of dimensions to achieve good visual structures and patterns. The axes can be arranged either manually by the viewer or by using axis reordering algorithms that automatically arrange the vertical axis to a minimal number of visual clutters. Some of the popular algorithms that reorder the axes in parallel coordinates plot are Pearson's Correlation Coefficient (PCC) and Nonlinear Correlation Coefficient (NCC) [23].

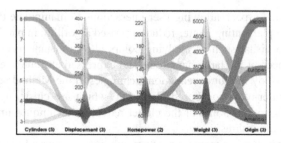

Fig. 3. Parallel coordinates plot with bundling algorithm [15].

3 Method

There are four steps that has been taken to identify the suitable features that should be implemented in clutter-reduction technique for parallel coordinates plot of solar data. These steps are, studying clutter-reduction techniques of parallel coordinates, extracting the common features available in clutter-reduction techniques, producing the conceptual framework of clutter-reduction technique as well as proposing the features of clutter-reduction technique that are suitable for solar data.

3.1 Study of Clutter-Reduction Techniques for Parallel Coordinates Plot

Since there are so many clutter-reduction techniques to overcome the clutter in parallel coordinates plot, the 10 latest techniques are chosen to be studied. All the chosen clutter reduction-techniques are applicable to traditional parallel coordinates plot.

3.2 Extract the Common Features of Clutter-Reduction Techniques

Based on the study of a few techniques, several features has be listed and compared in order to improve the readability of parallel coordinates plot. The Table 1 shows the comparison of the clutter-reduction techniques and the features that have been studied on this paper.

There are 12 features that can be extracted from all the studied clutter-reduction technique. These techniques may have more than one of these features. These features can be divided into three categories, which are visual, interaction and clutter-reduction algorithm.

3.3 Conceptual Framework of Cluttered-Reduction Technique for Parallel Coordinates Plot

After conducting the study on clutter-reduction techniques for parallel coordinates plot, a conceptual framework of the common features existed in these techniques has been produced. Figure 5 shows the conceptual framework of the features in clutter-reduction techniques for parallel coordinates plot.

Table 1. List of clustering techniques and its attributes.

Technique	Visual			Interaction					Algorithm			
	Colour transparency	Colour by cluster group	Highlight the selection	Brushing	Scaling/ zooming	Manual reordering	Adjustable parameter	Drill-down	Automatic reordering	Polyline reduction/ compression	Cluster	Bundling
[24] RBPCP	Yes	Yes	Yes	Yes	Yes	No	Yes	No	Yes	No	–	Yes
[15] Bundling with density based clustering	Yes	Yes	Yes	Yes	No	Yes	No	No	No	Yes	Density	Yes
[17] Rodrigo's bundling	No	Yes	No	No	No	No	Yes	No	No	Yes	Density	Yes
[25] NPCP	Yes	Yes	No	Yes	Yes	No	Yes	Yes	Yes	No	Hierarchical	Yes
[26] Cupid	Yes	Yes	Yes	Yes	No	Yes	Yes	Yes	Yes	Yes	Hierarchical	Yes
[27] Navigation information visualization of PCP	Yes	No	Yes	Yes	Yes	Yes	No	No	No	Yes	–	No
[14] Cluster-aware arrangement	No	No	Yes	No	No	No	No	No	Yes	No	Hierarchical	No
[28] Orientation-enhanced PCP	Yes	No	Yes	Yes	No	Yes	Yes	Yes	No	No	Hierarchical	No
[29] DSPCP	Yes	Yes	Yes	Yes	No	Yes	No	No	No	No	Density and Partition	No
[30] Progressive parallel coordinates	Yes	No	Yes	No	No	No	No	No	Yes	Yes	Hierarchy	No

Based on Fig. 4, the features of clutter-reduction technique for parallel coordinates plot can be categorized into three types, which are color features, user interaction and clutter-reduction based algorithm.

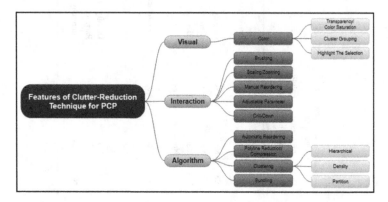

Fig. 4. Conceptual framework of the features in cluttered-reduction techniques for parallel coordinates plot.

The first feature is visual. Based on the studied technique, the main visual aspect is color usage at polyline. There are three ways of using color at the polylines. The first one is using different color to differentiate between different cluster groups of polylines. The different colored cluster group helps to easily differentiate between each group and see the pattern of the data went through the each parallel axes. Thus, the relationship between each colored stripe can be seen clearly. The second way of using color is by using semi-transparent color on polylines. The color of polylines becomes clearer and saturated as the semi-transparent polylines overlapped between each other. The highest density of the polylines area will display the highest color saturation. The techniques like Oriented-Enhanced Parallel Coordinates Plot [28] use the saturation to represent the density of the polylines at the edge crossing polylines. The color of other stripes will be look washed out or more grayish. The third way is by highlighting the selected cluster group. The color of unselected cluster group will turn grayish or transparent when one or more of cluster groups are selected. This helps to see the pattern of selected group clearer without being interrupted by the display of other polylines. There are some techniques such as Edge-bundling using density-based clustering [15] and DSPCP [29] use the saturation of the color to highlight the area or stripe which is selected by the viewer.

The next feature is interactivity in parallel coordinates. Each technique allows the viewer to manipulate the view of the parallel coordinates in many ways. Some of the common interactions are brushing, scaling/zooming, reordering, as well as modify the parameter. Brushing is a selection tool that enables the viewer to select a range of polylines. This can be done by dragging and clicking the mouse pointer around intended area. The tools will change the color of the selected polylines in more saturated color and makes the other polylines colors appear washed out or grayish. Some of the clutter-reduction techniques makes the view expands the selected polylines after making the selection. Scaling enable zooming in the parallel coordinates for the purpose of viewing more information of the particular area of polylines in detail. Reordering allows viewers to change the arrangement of the vertical axes and/or the order of the cluster groups, so they can reveal the hidden meaning behind each of the arrangement. The ability of changing the parameter of the plot such as the ratio of the unit of the parallel axes helps the viewer to modify the presentation of the visualization into a more comprehensive version. Drill-down feature allows users to select a specific polyline instead of cluster group to see more detail about the selected polyline.

There are several types of clutter reduction algorithm found in the study, which are automatic axes reordering algorithm, polyline reduction algorithm, clustering algorithm and bundling algorithm. Most of the studied clutter-reduction techniques use more than one type of algorithms.

The first algorithm is axis reordering. Axis reordering is a technique that basically changes the ordering of axis to achieve the minimal number of visual clutter. This arrangement can be either done manually by the viewer or automatically by using algorithm such as Pearson's Correlation Coefficient (PCC). Some of the techniques that implement this algorithm are Two-Axes Reordering [23] and Cluster-Aware Arrangement [14].

The next type of algorithm is polylines reduction/compression. Some of bundling techniques use polyline reduction algorithm to render a group of polylines or cluster group into a single stripe line, for example, Bundling Technique with Density Based Clustering [15] and Rodrigo's Bundling [17]. This polyline reduction algorithm simplifies the view of visualization. Polyline compression algorithm compresses the volume of data, which reduces the number of polylines to minimize the workload of the CPU, thus the rendering time becomes significantly faster. For example, Progressive Parallel Coordinates can achieve similar degree of pattern detection as with the standard approach by only using 37% of all data [30]. However, this algorithm lacks the support of data that changes frequently. This is because the reduction techniques need to recalculate the number of polylines every time which requires high resources of computer processor.

The next type of algorithm is clustering. Many clustering algorithm has been made. In this paper, only three types of clustering algorithm that have been studied, which are hierarchical, density and partition. The basic idea of hierarchical clustering algorithms is to construct the hierarchical relationship among data in order to cluster. Suppose that each data point stands for an individual cluster in the beginning, the most neighboring two clusters are merged into a new cluster until there is only one cluster left. The main advantages of hierarchical clustering are its suitability for data sets with arbitrary shape and attribute of arbitrary type, the hierarchical relationship among clusters are easily detected, and has relatively high scalability in general. The downside is the time complexity is high and it is necessary to preset a number of clusters. The next algorithm is density cluster. The basic idea of density clustering algorithms is that the data which is in the region with high density of the data space is considered to belong in the same cluster. The advantage of density based clustering is high efficiency of clustering process and suitable for data with arbitrary shape. However, this algorithm produces low quality clustering results when the density of data space is not even, a lot of memory is needed when the data volume is big, and the clustering results are highly sensitive to the parameters. The last clustering algorithm is partition clustering. The basic idea of partition clustering algorithms is to regard the center of data points as the center of the corresponding cluster. The main advantages of this algorithm are low in time complexity and high computing efficiency in general. One of the partition clustering, K-mean, is well known for its simplicity and feasibility [31]. This technique is based on distance matrix. Euclidean distance is used as a distance criterion. The algorithm starts with k initial seeds of clustering. All n data are then compared with each seed by means of the Euclidean distance and are assigned to the closest cluster seed [32]. However, the partition based clustering is not suitable for non-convex data, relatively sensitive to the outliers, easily drawn into local optimal, the number of clusters needed to be preset, and the clustering results are sensitive to the number of clusters.

The last algorithm is bundling, or also known as edge bundling. This algorithm clusters the data in every dimension and sets these clusters in relation to each other by bundling the lines between two axes. The bundles are then rendered using polygonal stripes. The advantage of stripe rendering is that this method is responsive even for very large amount of data. This is because instead of rendering line in each dimension independently, this method renders a bundle of lines as one polygonal stripe. This makes the rendering time independent to the number of observation points. The downside of edge bundling is the loss of visual correspondence to classic parallel coordinates plot [15]. This method will not allow the viewer to see particular information of a polyline because it is already combined with a group of polylines and displayed as a stripe.

3.4 Proposed Cluttered-Reduction Technique for Parallel Coordinates Plot of Solar Data

The current solar data has been taken from Green Energy Research Centre (GERC) at UiTM Shah Alam, Selangor. These data have been already visualized with Parallel Coordinates Plot by the researcher from this organization. The proposed cluttered-reduction technique will be implemented in current parallel coordinates visualization to improve some of the aspects. The improvements that are going to be done include the ability to see the relationship between the polylines and to see the density of the particular area of the plot. The features that are suitable for visualizing solar data in parallel coordinates plot are identified. Figure 5 shows the features that will be added in proposed cluttered-reduction technique for visualizing solar energy data by using parallel coordinates plot.

The proposed techniques will cover all these categories of features, which are color, interaction and cluttered-reduction algorithms. All the interaction and color features adds advantage to the parallel coordinates to the viewer, so there is no problem for implementing the most of color and interaction features. The color feature helps the analysts to differentiate the density of data around highly overlapped polylines areas, which is one of the main problem of visualizing a huge size of solar dataset in parallel coordinates plot.

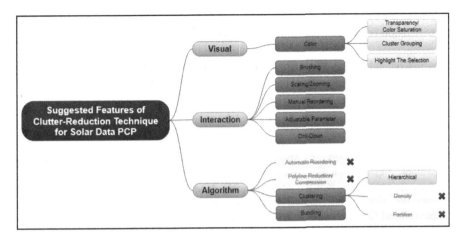

Fig. 5. Proposed cluttered reduction technique for solar energy data.

The next problem to solve is to make the relationship in solar data easier to comprehended and identified. The solution is by implementing some clutter-reduction based algorithms to simplify the presentation of visualization. However, not all algorithms are suitable for solar energy data.

First, it is worth noting that in the photovoltaic system of solar panel, the data are frequently added into database every 10 min [1]. This means that the algorithm must be suitable for data streaming. Thus, polyline compression algorithm cannot be used for this situation. Next is to choose a clustering algorithm that is suitable for solar data. Since the main focus of this research is to solve the relationship issue, hierarchy based clustering gives an advantage among the three types of clustering. Bundling algorithm will also be implemented in solar data, so the users can have more insights and knowledge over the data directly from the overview [17]. Since bundling algorithm has already been implemented, automatic reordering is unnecessary since the reason of reordering the axis is to reach the minimal number of visual clutter. Bundling algorithm has already solved the visual clutter issue.

4 Conclusion

Parallel coordinates plot alone will not help in comprehending the data easily. This proposed technique will enhance the speed and accuracy in extracting the meaning behind the solar energy data. The relationship between the data can be seen more clearly and the density of overlapped area of polylines can be identified by implementing the proposed clutter-reduction technique. This proposed technique is not only suitable for solar data, but it also is suitable to be applied at parallel coordinates plot for other streaming data that are updated in real time.

The conceptual framework in this paper can be a guideline in choosing the suitable parallel coordinates plot, not only limited to proposed technique, for their dataset.

There is still room especially in term of visual that can be explored to enhance the comprehension of parallel coordinates plot other than color aspects.

Acknowledgement. The authors would like to thank Faculty of Computer and Mathematical Sciences, as well as Universiti Teknologi MARA for facilities and financial support.

References

1. De Giorgi, M., Congedo, P., Malvoni, M.: Photovoltaic power forecasting using statistical methods: impact of weather data. IET Sci. Meas. Technol. **8**, 90–97 (2014)
2. Idrus, Z., Abdullah, N.A.S., Zainuddin, H., Ja'afar, A.D.M.: Software application for analyzing photovoltaic module panel temperature in relation to climate factors. In: International Conference on Soft Computing in Data Science, pp. 197–208 (2017)
3. Johansson, J., Forsell, C.: Evaluation of parallel coordinates: overview, categorization and guidelines for future research. IEEE Trans. Vis. Comput. Graph. **22**, 579–588 (2016)
4. Idrus, Z., Bakri, M., Noordin, F., Lokman, A.M., Aliman, S.: Visual analytics of happiness index in parallel coordinate graph. In: International Conference on Kansei Engineering & Emotion Research, pp. 891–898 (2018)
5. Steinparz, S., Aßmair, R., Bauer, A., Feiner, J.: InfoVis—parallel coordinates. Graz University of Technolog (2010)
6. Heinrich, J.: Visualization techniques for parallel coordinates (2013)
7. Sharma, A., Sharma, M.: Power & energy optimization in solar photovoltaic and concentrated solar power systems. In: 2017 IEEE PES Asia-Pacific Power and Energy Engineering Conference (APPEEC), pp. 1–6 (2017)
8. Lewis, N.S.: Research opportunities to advance solar energy utilization. Science **351**, aad1920 (2016)
9. Ho, C.N.M., Andico, R., Mudiyanselage, R.G.A.: Solar photovoltaic power in Manitoba. In: 2017 IEEE Electrical Power and Energy Conference (EPEC), pp. 1–6 (2017)
10. Dilla, W.N., Raschke, R.L.: Data visualization for fraud detection: practice implications and a call for future research. Int. J. Account. Inf. Syst. **16**, 1–22 (2015)
11. Schuh, M.A., Banda, J.M., Wylie, T., McInerney, P., Pillai, K.G., Angryk, R.A.: On visualization techniques for solar data mining. Astron. Comput. **10**, 32–42 (2015)
12. Idrus, Z., Zainuddin, H., Ja'afar, A.D.M.: Visual analytics: designing flexible filtering in parallel coordinate graph. J. Fundam. Appl. Sci. **9**, 23–32 (2017)
13. Chen, X., Jin, R.: Statistical modeling for visualization evaluation through data fusion. Appl. Ergon. **65**, 551–561 (2017)
14. Zhou, Z., Ye, Z., Yu, J., Chen, W.: Cluster-aware arrangement of the parallel coordinate plots. J. Vis. Lang. Comput. **46**, 43–52 (2017)
15. Palmas, G., Bachynskyi, M., Oulasvirta, A., Seidel, H.P., Weinkauf, T.: An edge-bundling layout for interactive parallel coordinates. In: 2014 IEEE Pacific Visualization Symposium (PacificVis), pp. 57–64 (2014)
16. Zhou, H., Xu, P., Ming, Z., Qu, H.: Parallel coordinates with data labels. In: Proceedings of the 7th International Symposium on Visual Information Communication and Interaction, p. 49 (2014)
17. Lima, R.S.D.A.D., Dos Santos, C.G.R., Meiguins, B.S.: A visual representation of clusters characteristics using edge bundling for parallel coordinates. In: 2017 21st International Conference Information Visualisation (IV), pp. 90–95 (2017)

18. Cui, W., Zhou, H., Qu, H., Wong, P.C., Li, X.: Geometry-based edge clustering for graph visualization. IEEE Trans. Vis. Comput. Graph. **14**, 1277–1284 (2008)
19. Khalid, N.E.A., Yusoff, M., Kamaru-Zaman, E.A., Kamsani, I.I.: Multidimensional data medical dataset using interactive visualization star coordinate technique. Procedia Comput. Sci. **42**, 247–254 (2014)
20. McDonnell, K.T., Mueller, K.: Illustrative parallel coordinates. In: Computer Graphics Forum, pp. 1031–1038 (2008)
21. Adhau, S.P., Moharil, R.M., Adhau, P.G.: K-means clustering technique applied to availability of micro hydro power. Sustain. Energy Technol. Assessments. **8**, 191–201 (2014)
22. Lhuillier, A., Hurter, C., Telea, A.: State of the art in edge and trail bundling techniques. In: Computer Graphics Forum, pp. 619–645 (2017)
23. Lu, L.F., Huang, M.L., Zhang, J.: Two axes re-ordering methods in parallel coordinates plots. J. Vis. Lang. Comput. **33**, 3–12 (2016)
24. Xie, W., Wei, Y., Ma, H., Du, X.: RBPCP: visualization on multi-set high-dimensional data. In: 2017 IEEE 2nd International Conference on Big Data Analysis (ICBDA), pp. 16–20 (2017)
25. Wang, J., Liu, X., Shen, H.-W., Lin, G.: Multi-resolution climate ensemble parameter analysis with nested parallel coordinates plots. IEEE Trans. Vis. Comput. Graph. **23**, 81–90 (2017)
26. Beham, M., Herzner, W., Gröller, M.E., Kehrer, J.: Cupid: cluster-based exploration of geometry generators with parallel coordinates and radial trees. IEEE Trans. Vis. Comput. Graph. **20**, 1693–1702 (2014)
27. Qingyun, L., Shu, G., Xiufeng, C., Liangchen, C.: Research of the security situation visual analysis for multidimensional inland navigation based on parallel coordinates (2015)
28. Raidou, R.G., Eisemann, M., Breeuwer, M., Eisemann, E., Vilanova, A.: Orientation-enhanced parallel coordinate plots. IEEE Trans. Vis. Comput. Graph. **22**, 589–598 (2016)
29. Nguyen, H., Rosen, P.: DSPCP: a data scalable approach for identifying relationships in parallel coordinates. IEEE Trans. Vis. Comput. Graph. **24**, 1301–1315 (2018)
30. Rosenbaum, R., Zhi, J., Hamann, B.: Progressive parallel coordinates. In: 2012 IEEE Pacific Visualization Symposium (PacificVis), pp. 25–32 (2012)
31. Tayfur, S., Alver, N., Abdi, S., Saatci, S., Ghiami, A.: Characterization of concrete matrix/steel fiber de-bonding in an SFRC beam: principal component analysis and k-mean algorithm for clustering AE data. Eng. Fract. Mech. **194**, 73–85 (2018)
32. Ay, M., Kisi, O.: Modelling of chemical oxygen demand by using ANNs, ANFIS and k-means clustering techniques. J. Hydrol. **511**, 279–289 (2014)

Data Visualization of Violent Crime Hotspots in Malaysia

Namelya Binti Anuar[1] and Bee Wah Yap[1,2(✉)]

[1] Centre for Statistical and Decision Science Studies, Faculty of Computer and Mathematical Sciences, Universiti Teknologi MARA, 40450 Shah Alam, Selangor, Malaysia
namelyaanuar@gmail.com, beewah@tmsk.uitm.edu.my
[2] Advanced Analytics Engineering Centre, Faculty of Computer and Mathematical Sciences, Universiti Teknologi MARA, 40450 Shah Alam, Selangor, Malaysia

Abstract. Crime is a critical issue that has gained significant attention in many countries including Malaysia. The Malaysian government has invested in a system known as the Geographical Information System (GIS) to map the crime hotspots in high prospect zones. However, the occurrences of violent crimes continue to increase at an alarming rate despite the implementation of the system. In order to combat crimes in a more effective manner in recent years, crime mapping has been proposed to identify crime hotspots in the country. This study applies crime mapping to identify crime hotspots in Malaysia. Data on crime for 14 states in Malaysia from 2007–2016 were obtained, with permission, from the Royal Malaysia Police or known as Police DiRaja Malaysia (PDRM) in Bahasa Malaysia. Data visualization was carried out using Tableau to gain more insights on the patterns and behaviours from violent crime data. The results show that Selangor has the highest number of violent crimes, followed by Kuala Lumpur and Johor. Perlis has the lowest number of violent crimes. Gang robbery is the highest in all 14 states. Interestingly, violent crimes being the highest in Selangor which also has the highest youth population. There is also a strong significant positive correlation between number of violent crime and youth population.

Keywords: Data visualization · Violent crime · Crime mapping
Hotspots

1 Introduction

Crime is a critical issue that has gained significant attention from many countries all over the world. Malaysia is no exception to the continuous increase in crime rates and this issue has become a key concern for policymakers to address [1–4]. According to a local newspaper (NSTP) report published on 7 May 2016, crime rates in Malaysia experienced a 4.6% increase in 2016. Mainstream media channels such as television, newspaper, and social media platforms have provided extensive coverage of criminal activities in Malaysia. The common criminal offences are rape, burglary, assault, and murder [5]. This serious issue needs to be tackled as it does not only cause loss of

© Springer Nature Singapore Pte Ltd. 2019
B. W. Yap et al. (Eds.): SCDS 2018, CCIS 937, pp. 350–363, 2019.
https://doi.org/10.1007/978-981-13-3441-2_27

properties or lives but also has a great impact on the economy and a negative psychological effect on victims. The serious crime situation also affects public confidence in the police [1].

Muhammad Amin [3] reported that the highest number of violent crimes was in 2009, between the years from 2004 to 2013. The Royal Malaysia Police (RMP) or also known as Police DiRaja Malaysia (PDRM) in Bahasa Malaysia, reported that although the number of violent crimes started fluctuating from the year 2009, the Overseas Security Advisory Council [6] (OSAC) noted that the overall crime rate is high for Malaysia. The three violent crimes, which were recorded to be highest are robbery without firearm, gang robbery without firearm, and also assault and battery. Selangor recorded the highest index crime rate and is followed by Kuala Lumpur and Johor Bahru, while Kelantan, Perlis, and Terengganu recorded the lowest index crime rates [3, 7].

PDRM has classified crimes into two categories, which are violent and property crimes in the index crime statistics. The definition of index crime statistics is *"the crime that is reported with sufficient regularity and with sufficient significance to be meaningful as an index to the crime situation"* [7]. Violent crimes include crimes of violence such as, murder, attempted murder, gang robbery with firearm, gang robbery without firearm, robbery with firearm, robbery without firearm, rape, and voluntarily causing hurt. Meanwhile, property crime includes offences involving the loss of property whereby there is no use of violence. The types of crimes in this category are housebreaking and theft during the daytime, housebreaking and theft at night, theft of lorries and van, theft of motor cars, theft of motorcycles and scooters, snatch theft and other forms of theft.

According to the OSAC [8], PDRM is a national police force that is well-trained and equipped. However, PDRM is sometimes limited in its effectiveness in the investigations of crimes. Thus, the achievements of combating crimes are slow, which highlight the criticality of this problem. In order to combat crimes in a more effective manner in recent years, crime mapping has been proposed to identify the crime hotspots. [9] has strongly emphasised the value of using a combination of different types of information to determine and predict crime patterns by analysing variables such as time, location, and types of crimes [10]. [11] emphasised that empirical studies on crimes in Malaysia are relatively few. From the current literature, it was found that the most recent study on crimes is by Zakaria and Rahman [1], which focuses on crime mapping for property crimes only in Malaysia.

The utilisation of the latest technology to address crimes is widely used in other countries such as in London and United States [12]. However, in Malaysia, the perspective towards using technology in criminal analyses has been minimal. Salleh *et al.* [13] have pointed out that insufficient knowledge in crime mapping using GIS has caused crime mapping to be under-utilised in solving crimes. Zainol *et al.* [10] have also concluded that the use of GIS for crime control in Malaysia is still relatively new. Crime mapping system will not only allow users to view information on crime patterns in their neighbourhood but also perform analysis on the web.

Murray *et al.* [14] reported that crime patterns can be analysed and explained using GIS because it offers a useful medium to highlight criminal activities data for a better understanding of the factors associated with crime rates and it could be used to predict potential crime hotspots. The integration of GIS remote sensing technology can benefit the nation to reduce the crime rates in Malaysia. There is also a possibility for the use of this system to discourage the public from committing criminal offences due to GIS remote sensing technology [13]. Interactive data visualization is very useful as it allows users to analyse large amount of data (both spatial and temporal) and users can select as well as filter any attributes during the analysis process [15–18]. Thus, this study analyses the crime data in Malaysia to identify crime hotspots using Tableau, an easy to use GIS software. The objective of the paper is to perform data visualization and crime-mapping based on violent crime data in Malaysia.

2   Related Literature

2.1   Crime Mapping

Mapping is a technique, which is widely employed in spatial analysis. The objective of mapping is to determine the relationship between exposure and the related cases [1]. In this study, mapping is used in the context of crime mapping. Crime mapping refers to a process that helps in the identification of crime patterns and is highlighted as a crucial task in police enforcement [12]. In the past decades, police officers have utilised the traditional pin-up map method to identify areas which have a high level of crimes. They also write reports to identify crime patterns. However, this conventional pin-up method is time-consuming, inefficient, and requires a large amount of manpower.

The London Metropolitan Police Department (LMPD) created the crime mapping method in the 1820s, which was then popularised by large police departments in the United States [12]. Van Schaaik & Van Der Kemp [19] have pointed out that crime mapping is recognised as a technique to analyse crimes and has been increasingly implemented in law enforcement. Many enforcement authorities such as the Federal Bureau Investigation (FBI), Central Intelligence Agency (CIA), and the US Marshall have employed crime mapping to analyse and investigate the current crime situation of a country. Based on crime mapping, the identification of high and low crime areas can be done. Thus, the authorities are able to identify high-risk areas which are susceptible to crimes.

Crime mapping is also a well-known technique that is capable to forecast crime patterns in the future. The information from past data can assist authorities to create preventive measures to decrease the level of crimes in high-risk areas. Asmai et al. [20] have retrieved Communities and Crime dataset from UCI Machine Learning Repository and conducted crime mapping by utilising Apriori association rule mining. However, the study showcased a disadvantage of using Apriori association rule mining, which does not specify and visualise which location has high crime rates. Another weakness is that it does not use a real dataset from the local authority, and thus, the results may not be precise and cannot be generalised. Hence, GIS system has been proposed to solve this problem since it can store an infinite amount of data and map it accurately.

2.2   Geographical Information System (GIS)

GIS is defined as "a set of a computer-based system for capturing, managing, integrating, manipulating, analysing, and displaying data which is spatially referenced to Earth" [21]. In simple terms, GIS does not only electronically display and store data in a large database but also enables many layers of information to be superimposed in order to obtain and analyse information about a specific location [22]. GIS is a universal system as it is widely used in small, medium, and large police departments globally [12]. Information which can be superimposed into GIS includes types of crime, time of crime, and geographic coordinates of crime which allows many police administrators to analyse crime patterns anywhere at any time [23]. Nelson *et al.* [9] have also emphasised the value of using a combination of different types of information in identifying the patterns of violent crimes in the city centre by analysing a range of variables recorded by the police, relating to where and when violent crimes occurs in the city centre. The different categories of information, whether relating to the type or function of place or temporality, all need to be referenced to specific locations. Without this degree of precision in geo-referencing, a more detailed understanding of violent crimes and disorders is impossible. In addition, they mentioned that GIS often lack location details (specific place where the crime is recorded as occurring and includes street, car park, public house, nightclub or shop) which could assist in exploring the various factors involved in violent crimes. While the spatial definition of the crime data is of paramount importance in the use of crime pattern analysis, the availability of information relating to time-specific functions can be of equal importance as well. The recording of the time of occurrence of violent crimes is probably the most reliable and consistent information.

Chainey & Ratcliffe [24] stressed that GIS and crime mapping should be implemented together in order to design a powerful tool for crime mapping and crime prevention. Several studies have been conducted to examine the effectiveness of GIS. Abdullah *et al.* [25] have used both GIS and Artificial Neural Network (ANN) to conduct crime mapping. They reported that the combination between GIS and Royal Malaysian Police's PRS system have inserted automation and have become an important enabler to the crime mapping database. However, they did not thoroughly compare the two techniques and did not explain the procedures of ANN. Thus, the role played by GIS in relation to ANN was not thoroughly explained.

Salleh *et al.* [13] conducted a study to examine the potential use of GIS and remote sensing system to determine the hotspots crime areas/crime hotspots based on historical data of crimes in Malaysia from the year 2007 to 2009, and has successfully identified the hotspots for burglaries in Malaysia. However, they have strongly recommended field validations, and various groups and types of crimes to be investigated especially crimes that are closely related with the criminal minds such as vandalism, rapist, murder and domestic violence.

3 Method

GIS is a powerful software tool that allows an individual to create anything from a simple point map to a three-dimensional visualization of spatial or temporal data [26–29]. Furthermore, GIS allows the analyst to view the data behind the geographic features, combine various features, manipulate the data, and perform statistical functions. There are many different types of GIS programmes which include desktop packages (e.g., ArcView®, MapInfo®, GeoMedia®, Atlas GIS®, Maptitude®, QGIS®, ArcInfo®, Tableau, Intergraph® and arcGIS®). This study unitizes Tableau to perform data visualizations of violent crime data in Malaysia. Trend charts, bar charts and crime mapping were developed using Tableau.

3.1 Data Description

This study used secondary data on the number of violent crimes in Malaysia provided by the Royal Malaysia Police (RMP) or known as Police DiRaja Malaysia (PDRM) in Bahasa Malaysia. Table 1 lists the variables of this study. This paper analysed only the violent crimes data for 14 states in Malaysia from the year 2007 to 2016.

Table 1. Description of variables

Variable name	Description		Unit	Source
CRIME	Total number of violent crimes per year for: 1. Murder 2. Rape 3. Assault 4. Gang Robberies		Number	PDRM
POP	The number of population is the total number of people from the age of 15–24 living in each state		Number ('000)	DOSM
UN	Number of unemployed people as a percentage of the labour force		Percent	DOSM
STATE	Fourteen (14) states in Malaysia:			PDRM
	1. Johor	8. Perlis		
	2. Kedah	9. Perak		
	3. Kelantan	10. Pulau Pinang		
	4. Kuala Lumpur	11. Sabah		
	5. Melaka	12. Sarawak		
	6. Negeri Sembilan	13. Selangor		
	7. Pahang	14. Terengganu		

Figure 1 shows a sample of crime data in Malaysia from PDRM that consists of the number of violent and property crimes for every state in Malaysia.

JENAYAH INDEK SELURUH MALAYSIA :
Mengikut Tarikh Siasatan Dari 1/01/2016 Hingga 31/12/2016

KESALAHAN	JOHOR	KEDAH	KELANTAN	KUALA LUMPUR	MELAKA	NEGERI SEMBILAN	PAHANG	PERAK	PERLIS	PULAU PINANG	SABAH	SARAWAK	SELANGOR	TERENGGANU	Jumlah
JENAYAH KEKERASAN :															
BUNUH	70	17	10	41	13	17	15	42		28	60	27	105	11	456
ROGOL	274	165	144	93	60	107	134	96	31	63	193	138	305	81	1,886
SAMUN BERKAWAN BERS/API	10	2	1	13	2	2		8		2	3	15	7		65
SAMUN BERKAWAN TANPA BERS/API	1,308	461	71	2,272	610	474	234	539	17	406	118	281	4,028	88	10,907
SAMUN BERSENJATAPI	3	2	1	4		2	1	1		1		2		1	18
SAMUN TANPA S/API	447	194	25	710	276	223	58	197	9	224	60	76	905	59	3,463
MENCEDERAKAN	708	398	291	643	193	250	209	412	52	312	213	414	1,260	167	5,531
JUMLAH KEKERASAN	2,820	1,239	543	3,776	1,154	1,004	651	1,295	109	1,036	647	953	6,610	407	22,326
JENAYAH HARTABENDA :															
CURI	2,073	1,082	613	3,595	519	1,015	627	955	192	1,010	1,648	1,330	4,793	447	19,894
CURI MOTOKAR	1,443	497	614	2,104	170	177	254	386	20	449	213	748	3,309	203	10,607
CURI MOTOSIKAL	4,686	3,135	1,945	3,864	1,246	1,053	1,399	2,112	228	2,401	850	2,006	8,890	949	34,754
CURI VAN/LORI/7BERAT	400	111	90	495	25	116	103	118	4	110	136	174	1,140	28	3,050
CURI RAGUT	44	99	61	1,288	6	6	29	60	17	191	96	75	983	8	2,963
PECAH RUMAH DAN CURI	1,475	1,287	682	1,867	544	1,023	719	915	85	917	1,757	1,540	5,497	452	18,760
JUMLAH HARTABENDA	10,121	6,201	4,005	13,213	2,510	3,390	3,126	4,546	546	5,078	4,720	5,873	24,612	2,087	90,028
JUMLAH JENAYAH INDEKS	12,941	7,440	4,548	16,989	3,664	4,474	3,772	5,841	655	6,116	5,367	6,826	31,222	2,494	112,354
JUMLAH KECURIAN KENDERAAN	6,529	3,733	2,649	6,463	1,441	1,346	1,756	2,616	252	2,960	1,219	2,928	13,339	1,160	48,411
JUMLAH JENAYAH JALANAN	1,799	754	157	4,370	892	703	921	796	43	821	274	432	5,916	155	17,333

Fig. 1. Sample of crime dataset from PDRM

3.2 Spatial Analysis of Kernel Density Estimation Using Geographical Information System (GIS)

Crime mapping using kernel density estimation method was employed to identify the crime hotspots in Malaysia. There are many crime-mapping techniques that can be utilised for identifying crime hotspots. However, this study focuses only on Kernel Density Estimation (KDE) as KDE is known as a heat map and is regarded as the most suitable common hotspot mapping technique for crime data visualizations [24, 29–31]. Furthermore, KDE has become a popular technique for mapping crime hotspots due to its growing availability in many GIS software, its perceived good accuracy of hotspot identification, and the visual look of the resulting map in comparison to other techniques [29, 30]. According to [31], KDE function is expressed as:

$$f(x) = \frac{1}{nh^2} \sum\nolimits_{i=1}^{n} k\left(\frac{d_i}{h}\right)$$

(1)

Where,
$f(x) =$ Density value at location (x).
$n =$ Number of incidents.
$h =$ Bandwidth.
$d_i =$ Geographical distance between incident i and location (x).
$k =$ Density function, known as the kernel.

3.3 Correlation

Correlation is a measure of strength and direction of the linear relationship between two continuous variables. Spearman correlation coefficients (r) values ranges from −1 to +1 where the sign indicates whether there is a positive correlation or a negative correlation [32]. The Spearman correlation for pairs of values of (x, y) is computed as follows:

$$r = \frac{n \sum xy - \sum x \sum y}{\sqrt{[n \sum x^2 - \sum (x^2)][n \sum y^2 - \sum (y^2)]}} \tag{2}$$

Where,

r =   correlation coefficient
n =   number of pairs of scores
$\sum xy$ =   Sum of the products of paired scores
$\sum x$ =   Sum of x scores
$\sum y$ =   Sum of y scores
$\sum x^2$ =   Sum of squared x scores
$\sum y^2$ =   Sum of squared y scores

The strength of relationship between the two variables is low if the value falls in the range of 0.1 to 0.29, medium if in the range 0.30 to 0.49 and large (or very strong) if r is more than 0.5 [33]. The null hypothesis is Ho: There is no significant correlation between x and y and the test statistic is $t = r/s_r$, where $s_r = \sqrt{\frac{1-r^2}{n-2}}$ [34].The null hypothesis is rejected if $t > t_{\alpha/2,\ n-2}$ where α the significance level is set at 5%. Alternatively, the null hypothesis will be rejected if the p-value for the test statistic is less than 5%. Since the data is not-normal, Spearman rank correlation $r_s = 1 - \frac{6 \sum_{i=1}^{n} d_i^2}{n(n^2-1)}$ was used instead, where d_i is the difference in ranks for pairs of observations.

4   Results and Discussions

4.1   Malaysia Violent Crime Hotspot Visualization

Data visualization for Malaysia Violent Crimes from the period of 2007 to 2016 for 14 states in Malaysia are shown in Figs. 2 to 10. We first illustrate crime mapping using Tableau, which is shown in Fig. 2.

Fig. 2. Hot-spots crime mapping (Color figure online)

Figure 2 illustrates the crime map for the number of violent crimes for the 14 states for ten years (2007–2016) using Tableau. The colour indicator ranges from lighter to darker colour where darker colour indicates higher intensity of violent crimes. The map shows that Selangor, Johor and Kuala Lumpur have darker colours, which indicate that the number of violent crimes is high in these states.

Figure 3 shows the chart for the total number of violent crimes (2007–2016) for each state. It can be seen that Selangor has the highest number of violent crimes (89,538 cases), followed by Kuala Lumpur (58,600 cases).

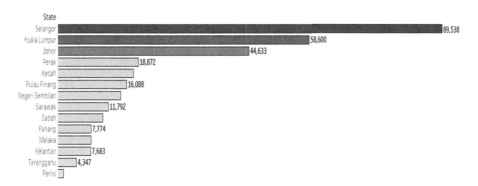

Fig. 3. Total number of violent crimes for each state (2007–2016)

Figure 4 displays clustered bar chart for the total number of violent crimes for each crime category in each state. There are five categories of violent crimes, which are assault (blue colour), gang robberies (orange colour) murder (red colour), rape (light blue colour) and robbery (green colour). The bar chart shows that gang robbery is the highest violent crime for most of the states.

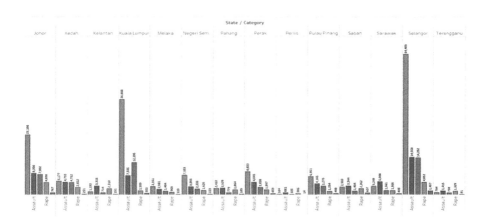

Fig. 4. Clustered bar chart for violent crime category for each state (Color figure online)

Figure 5 shows the dashboard that combines Figs. 2, 3 and 4. The figure displays the map and several charts. The dashboard is interactive as it allows filtering of states and year. The dashboard also shows the total number of violent crimes for each state. Hence, to make a comparison of selected year and state, both the variables can be selected under filter. We can click on the year or state which we want to view. For example, by clicking only Selangor state, and 2016, the dashboard will change from displaying all states to only Selangor and year 2016 only. This technique of data

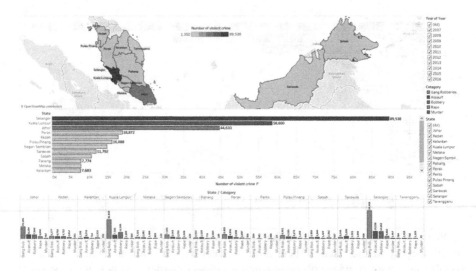

Fig. 5. Visualization dashboard

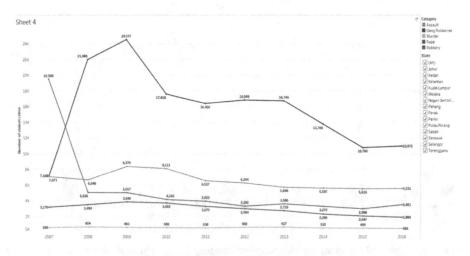

Fig. 6. Violent crimes filtered by states.

visualization using Tableau is very effective in displaying the trend of crimes in each state in Malaysia (Fig. 6).

As Selangor has the highest number of violent crimes in Malaysia, Fig. 7 illustrates the clustered bar charts for each category of violent crimes in every district in Selangor. Due to the availability data by districts given by PDRM, Fig. 7 displays the data for 2016. The chart shows that Petaling Jaya has the highest number of violent crimes in Selangor and gang robberies recorded the highest number in all five districts.

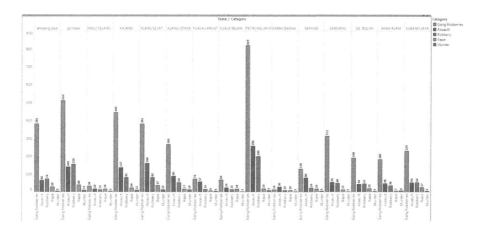

Fig. 7. Clustered bar chart for violent crime category for each district in Selangor (2016)

Figure 8 shows the chart for total violent crimes and youth populations for each state. The chart indicates that Selangor has the highest youth population in Malaysia and the highest number of violent crimes.

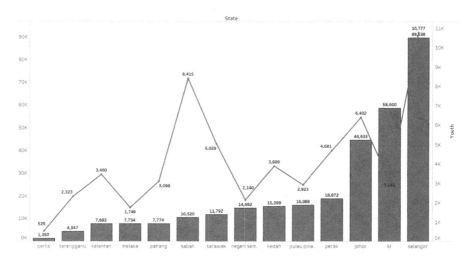

Fig. 8. Chart for total violent crimes and youth population

Figure 9 illustrates a scatter plot for crime and youth population for each states in Malaysia for the year of 2016 only. Figure 9 indicates that there are 3 outliers in the chart which are Selangor, Kuala Lumpur and Sabah.

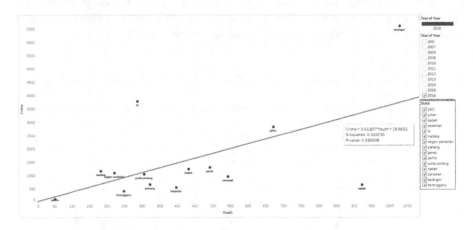

Fig. 9. Scatter plot for crime and youth population (2016)

Figure 10 displays the scatter plot for crime and youth populations and unemployment rates for each year from 2007 to 2016. The scatter plot indicates there indicates that there exists a positive correlation between crime and youth population. However, the scatter plot for crime and unemployment does not indicate a linear relationship between crime and unemployment. The correlation results in Table 2 show that crime has significant positive correlation with youth population. Meanwhile, there is no significant correlation between crime and unemployment.

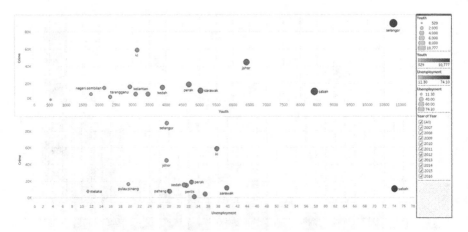

Fig. 10. Scatter plot for crime with youth population and unemployment

Table 2. Summary statistics and Spearman correlations

Year	2007	2008	2009	2010	2011	2012	2013	2014	2015	2016
Crime										
Min	90	129	153	146	142	158	155	126	142	109
Max	11321	11706	11338	9488	8141	8296	8653	7402	6583	6610
Mean	2511	2702	3026	2438	2190	2139	2098	1816	1557	1594
Skewness	2.15	2.08	1.59	1.84	1.73	1.89	2.05	2.12	2.33	2.22
POP'(000)										
Min	47	50	53	55	55	55	55	55	53	51
Max	1129	1137	1130	1101	1071	1047	1051	1045	1038	1029
Mean	396	403	408	410	415	419	427	431	433	436
Skewness	1.54	1.52	1.48	1.39	1.27	1.12	1.14	1.09	1.05	1.00
r_s	0.69**	0.7**	0.7**	0.7**	0.64*	0.60*	0.52	0.53	0.57*	0.39
UN(%)										
Min	2	1	2	1	1	1	1	1	1	1
Max	7	7	8	8	7	8	7	7	7	9
Mean	3.19	3.26	3.64	3.24	3.14	3.14	3.2	3.14	3.24	3.53
Skewness	2.34	2.40	2.24	2.15	1.41	1.57	3.28	1.42	1.37	1.97
r_s	−.095	.011	.055	−.134	−.022	0.86	−.01	.16	−.05	−.044

**p-value < 0.01; *p-value < 0.05; r_s is Spearman rank correlation

5   Conclusion

Data visualizations using GIS tools are very useful to gain more insights about the patterns and behaviourisme of data. The officials at PDRM found the analysis of the crime data very useful as it can give them greater insights on the trend of crimes and hotpsots in various districts and states in Malaysia. Further analysis can be done to identify the crime hotspot districts in Selangor, Johor and Kuala Lumpur. The interactive filtering provided in Tableau allows interactive visualization and selection of variables, which aid in giving more informative presentations during meetings or in reports. Crime mapping helps in decisions such as on police interventions. Increasing police patrols at hotspot areas can effectively reduce the number of crimes in these areas. The presence of police units can make the community live with less fear of being robbed or attacked. In future analysis, panel modeling will be conducted to investigate the association between the number of violent crimes with youth population, unemployment rate and Gross Domestic Product (GDP).

Acknowledgement. We would like to thank the Polis DiRaja Malaysia (PDRM) for the permission to use the crime data for academic purpose, we are also grateful to the Research Management Centre (RMC) UiTM for the financial support under the university Research Entity Initiatives Grant (600-RMI/DANA 5/3/REI (16/2015)).

References

1. Zakaria, S., Rahman, N.A.: The mapping of spatial patterns of property crime in Malaysia: normal mixture model approach. J. Bus. Soc. Dev. **4**(1), 1–11 (2016)
2. Ishak, S.: Perceptions of people on police efficiency and crime prevention in urban areas in Malaysia. Econ. World **4**(5), 243–248 (2016). https://doi.org/10.17265/2328-7144/2016.05.005
3. Muhammad Amin, B., Mohammad Rahim, K., Geshina Ayu, M.S.: A trend analysis of violent crimes in Malaysia. Health **5**(2), 41–56 (2014)
4. Performance Management and Delivery Unit (PEMANDU). GTP Annual Report 2010 (2010). https://www.pemandu.gov.my/assets/publications/annual-reports/GTP_2010_EN.pdf
5. Habibullah, M.S., Baharom, A.H., Muhamad, S.: Crime and police personnel in Malaysia: an empirical investigation. Taylor's Bus. Rev. (TBR) **4**(2), 1–17 (2014)
6. Overseas Security Advisory Council. Malaysia 2015 Crime and Safety Report (2015). https://www.osac.gov/pages/ContentReportDetails.aspx?cid=17215
7. Sidhu, A.S.: The rise of crime in Malaysia: an academic and statistical analysis. J. Kuala Lumpur R. Malays. Police Coll. **4**, 1–28 (2005)
8. Overseas Security Advisory Council. Malaysia 2016 Crime and Safety Report (2016). https://www.osac.gov/pages/ContentReportDetails.aspx?cid=19182
9. Nelson, A.L., Bromley, R.D., Thomas, C.J.: Identifying micro-spatial and temporal patterns of violent crime and disorder in the British city centre. Appl. Geogr. **21**(3), 249–274 (2001)
10. Zainol, R., Yunus, F., Nordin, N.A., Maidin, S.L.: Empowering Community Neighborhood Watch with Crime Monitoring System using Web-Based GIS, 1–10 (2011)
11. Foon Tang, C.: An exploration of dynamic relationship between tourist arrivals, inflation, unemployment and crime rates in Malaysia. Int. J. Soc. Econ. **38**(1), 50–69 (2011)
12. Levine, N.: Crime mapping and the crimestat program. Geogr. Anal. **38**(1), 41–56 (2006). https://doi.org/10.1111/j.0016-7363.2005.00673
13. Salleh, S.A., Mansor, N.S., Yusoff, Z., Nasir, R.A.: The crime ecology: ambient temperature vs. spatial setting of crime (Burglary). Procedia - Soc. Behav. Sci. **42**, 212–222 (2012)
14. Murray, A.T., McGuffog, I., Western, J.S., Mullins, P.: Exploratory spatial data analysis techniques for examining urban crime. Br. J. Criminol. **41**(2), 309–329 (2001). https://doi.org/10.1093/bjc/41.2.309
15. Bakri, M., Abidin, Siti Z.Z., Shargabi, A.: Incremental filtering visualization of JobStreet Malaysia ICT jobs. In: Mohamed, A., Berry, Michael W., Yap, B.W. (eds.) SCDS 2017. CCIS, vol. 788, pp. 188–196. Springer, Singapore (2017). https://doi.org/10.1007/978-981-10-7242-0_16
16. Idrus, Z., Abdullah, N.A.S., Zainuddin, H., Ja'afar, A.D.M.: Software application for analyzing photovoltaic module panel temperature in relation to climate factors. In: Mohamed, A., Berry, Michael W., Yap, B.W. (eds.) SCDS 2017. CCIS, vol. 788, pp. 197–208. Springer, Singapore (2017). https://doi.org/10.1007/978-981-10-7242-0_17
17. Abdullah, N.A.S., Wahid, N.W.A., Idrus, Z.: Budget visual: malaysia budget visualization. In: Mohamed, A., Berry, Michael W., Yap, B.W. (eds.) SCDS 2017. CCIS, vol. 788, pp. 209–218. Springer, Singapore (2017). https://doi.org/10.1007/978-981-10-7242-0_18
18. Rosli, N.A., Mohamed, A., Khan, R.: Visualisation enhancement of HoloCatT matrix. In: Badioze Zaman, H., Robinson, P., Petrou, M., Olivier, P., Schröder, H., Shih, Timothy K. (eds.) IVIC 2009. LNCS, vol. 5857, pp. 675–685. Springer, Heidelberg (2009). https://doi.org/10.1007/978-3-642-05036-7_64

19. Van Schaaik, J.G., Van Der Kemp, J.J.: Real crimes on virtual maps: the application of geography and GIS in criminology. In: Scholten, H.J., van de Velde, R., van Manen, N. (eds.) Geospatial Technology and the Role of Location in Science, pp. 217–237. Springer, Heidelberg (2009). https://doi.org/10.1007/978-90-481-2620-0_12

20. Asmai, S.A., Roslin, N.I.A., Abdullah, R.W., Ahmad, S.: Predictive crime mapping model using association rule mining for crime analysis. Age 12, 21 (2014)

21. Boba, R.: Introductory Guide to Crime Analysis and Mapping, 74 (2001). http://www.ncjrs.gov/App/abstractdb/AbstractDBDetails.aspx?id=194685

22. Peddle, D.R., Ferguson, D.T.: Optimisation of multisource data analysis: an example using evidential reasoning for GIS data classification. Comput. Geosci. 28(1), 45–52 (2002)

23. Markovic, J., Stone, C.: Crime Mapping and the Policing of Democratic Societies. Vera Institute of Justice, New York (2002)

24. Chainey, S., Ratcliffe, J.: GIS and Crime Mapping. Wiley, Wiley (2013)

25. Abdullah, M.A., Abdullah, S.N.H.S., Nordin, M.J.: Smart City Security: Predicting the Next Location of Crime Using Geographical Information System With Machine Learning. Asia Geospatial Forum Malaysia Asia Geospatial Forum, September 2013, pp. 24–26 (2013)

26. Dunham, R.G., Alpert, G.P.: Critical Issues in Policing: Contemporary readings. Waveland Press, Long Grove (2015)

27. Johnson, C.P.: Crime Mapping and Analysis Using GIS. In: Conference on Geomatics in Electronic Governance, Geomatics 2000, pp. 1–5, January 2000

28. Bailey, T.C., Gatrell, A.C.: Interactive Spatial Data Analysis, vol. 413. Longman Scientific & Technical, Essex (1995)

29. Chainey, S., Reid, S., Stuart, N.: When is a hotspot a hotspot? A procedure for creating statistically robust hotspot maps of crime, pp. 21–36. Taylor & Francis, London (2002)

30. Eck, J., Chainey, S., Cameron, J., Wilson, R.: Mapping crime: understanding hotspots (2005)

31. Williamson, D., et al.: Tools in the spatial analysis of crime. Mapp. Anal. Crime Data: Lessons Res. Pract. 187 (2001)

32. Pallant, J.: SPSS Survival Manual. McGraw-Hill Education, New York City (2013)

33. Cohen, L., Manion, L., Morrison, K.: Research Methods in Education. Routledge, Abingdon (2013)

34. Triola, M.F., Franklin, L.A.: Business Statistics. Addison-Wesley, Publishing Company, Inc., Abingdon (1994)

Malaysia Election Data Visualization Using Hexagon Tile Grid Map

Nur Atiqah Sia Abdullah[(⊠)], Muhammad Nadzmi Mohamed Idzham,
Sharifah Aliman, and Zainura Idrus

Faculty of Computer and Mathematical Sciences, Universiti Teknologi MARA,
40450 Shah Alam, Selangor, Malaysia
atiqah@tmsk.uitm.edu.my

Abstract. Data visualization is an alternative representation to analyze complex data. It eases the viewers to identify the trends and patterns. Based on the previous literature, some countries such as United States, United Kingdom, Australia, and India have used data visualization to represent their election data. However, Malaysia election data was reported in a static format includes graphs and tables, which are difficult for Malaysia citizen to understand the overall distribution of the parliament seats according to the political parties. Therefore, this paper proposed a hexagon tile grid map visualization technique to visualize the Malaysia 2018 General Election more dynamically. This technique is chosen as the hexagon offers a more flexible arrangement of the tiles and able to maintain the border of the geographic map. Besides, it allows the users to explore the data interactively, which covers all the parliaments in Malaysia, together with the winning party, its candidate, and demographical data. The result shows that the hexagon tile grid map technique can represent the whole election result effectively.

Keywords: Visualization · Malaysia 2018 election · Hexagon tile grid
Map visualization

1 Introduction

Data visualization is the art of making people understand data by converting them into visuals [1]. There are a lot of ways to visualize data and each has their own advantages and disadvantages. Visual make the process of understanding a data much faster than text [2]. Most of the human brains make use of the visual processing because our brains are active towards bright colors [3]. It is much slower to read information rather than visualizing it. Therefore, with the help of visuals, human can understand the complex message of science [3].

Data visualization can be used to represent data in various domains including emotions [4], social network [5], election data [6], budget [7] and etc. For the political domains, the most significant user is the political figures and the public audience themselves. Data visualization could show the magnitude of passive voters from the voting-eligible adults in the 2016 Presidential election [6]. Other than that, political

© Springer Nature Singapore Pte Ltd. 2019
B. W. Yap et al. (Eds.): SCDS 2018, CCIS 937, pp. 364–373, 2019.
https://doi.org/10.1007/978-981-13-3441-2_28

figures could also target the public which does not know who to vote for from the visualization [8].

In Malaysia, most of the data are represented using tabular format [9], simple bar charts [10], and infographic [11]. These data include election data, population statistics, budget data, economic, financial statistics, gross domestic product, and etc. For instance, election data consist of multiple information including state, district, name of candidate, political parties, population, demographic data, and etc. It can be presented better using visualization. Therefore, most of the countries, like US [12], UK [13], Australia [14], and India [15] have presented their election data using interactive data visualization techniques.

This study aims to visualize the Malaysia General Election 2018 in a more dynamic approach. It will display the election result based on 222 parliaments in 14 states. This study will help the citizen to view the information at the first glance. It is also imperative for them to understand the election result through data visualization.

2 Reviews on Election Data Visualization

Data visualization is the art of making people understand data by converting the data into visuals [1]. Visual make the process of understanding a data much faster than text [2]. Data visualization is being used in multiple industries include the domains of politics, business and research. Since the study focuses on the election data and map visualization, the literature reviews are mostly reviewed previous studies in election related representations, which include United States 2016 Election [12], United Kingdom 2017 General Election Data [13], Australia 2016 Election [14], and India 2014 Election [15].

US 2016 Election Data Visualization [12] uses bar chart and map data visualization technique, as shown in Fig. 1.

Fig. 1. US 2016 election data visualization

Bar chart communicates the most basic things of all election data, which is the Presidential votes and tally points. It shows the most important information for any election result such as the political stand for each of the political candidate. The simple color map visualization presents more granular data to reflect the results of Presidential vote. The map could be toggled from Presidential result to other representation such as the Senate, House and Governors result. The map also can be toggled from the state view to the county view. Moreover, even though the representation changes (Presidential, Senate, House or Governors), the visual shows the same layout and map types instead of using a different kind of representation for each of the categories.

United Kingdom uses a simple representation of the election data by showing the number of seats won, the actual number of votes and the percentage of votes domination by the political parties in UK. Then, the visual shows the dominance of the political parties by showing the number of seats as dotted square in the waffle chart and stacked bar chart [13], as shown in Fig. 2.

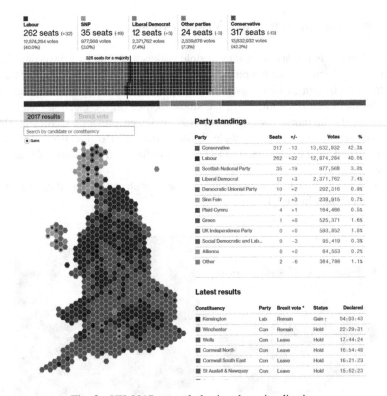

Fig. 2. UK 2017 general election data visualization.

A more detailed representation of the election data is shown by using the hexagon tile grid map and tables that present the status of each party and the political candidates. The hexagon tile grid map shows a semi-accurate representation of UK geographic map and each of the tiles represents the UK parliaments. The map is interactive, thus the viewer can click on the hexagon tile, the table of party standing and status figures will show the list of parties and political candidates' status of that particular parliament. Moreover, when viewer hover over the hexagon tiles, the visual will pop up a figure showing the list of political candidates together with the party that they represents and the percentage of seats won by that candidate in that particular parliament.

Figure 3 shows Australia election data visualization [14]. Google presented the data visualization for Australia 2016 general election using Google Interactive Election Map. The map shows a choropleth representation of the election data based on Australia geographical map. The choropleth map is divided into sections according to the states in Australia. Each state is represented by different color that represents the political parties that had won the election on that particular state. For example, blue state means that Coalition had won that particular state. The map can be zoomed and panned. It is also interactive because the viewer can click on one of the states and a more detailed description of that particular state's political condition will be displayed in the detail sections at the left side of the visual. The section shows the overall result of the election by a stacked bar chart and a simple table of description. The stacked bar chart shows the overall result of the election by the percentage of seats won by the political parties. The simple table shows the political party name, the election candidate name and its actual winning seat number with the percentages.

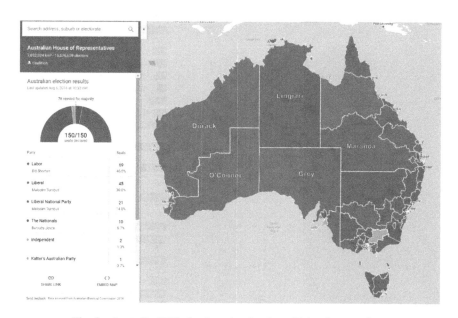

Fig. 3. Australia 2016 election visualization. (Color figure online)

India 2014 Election [15] uses data visualization for the election data, which a collaboration between Network18 and Microsoft India. The upper part shows a simple representation of the election data by presenting a stacked bar chart that shows the number of seats won by the political parties as a colored bar. It is easier for the viewers to understand because it shows literally which party is dominating the election seats and indirectly tells which party is winning. The map section presents a choropleth map that highlight the States of India according to the color of the party. The map is interactive because when the viewer hover the mouse across the states, it will pop up a dialog message showing the name of the election candidate, name of party, name of the state and total votes won on that particular state. Moreover, when the viewer clicks on one state, a table will pop up on the top-right corner of the map showing the name of the election candidates, their party color, their party name and their total votes for that particular state [15] (see Fig. 4).

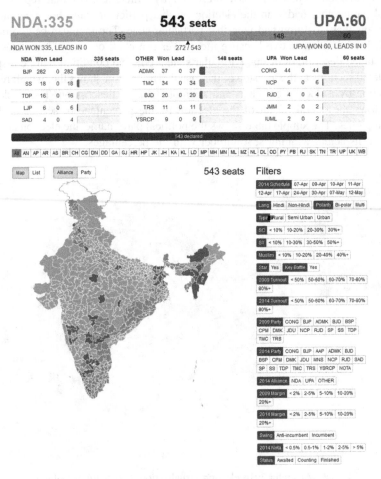

Fig. 4. India 2014 data visualization. (Color figure online)

From the literature, the following comparison table shows the summary about the data visualization techniques used in each election representation map (see Table 1):

Table 1. Comparison of election visualization techniques.

Country	Types of visualization techniques
US 2016 Election	Choropleth map, Stacked Bar Chart, Tabular Chart
UK 2017 Election	Waffle Chart, Stacked Bar Chart, Choropleth map, Diamond Tile Grid Map, Tabular Chart
Australia 2016 Election	Stacked Bar Chart, Tabular Chart, Choropleth Map
India 2014 Election	Stacked Bar Chart, Tabular Chart, Choropleth Map, Circular Tile Grid Map

Two simple and descriptive type of map data visualization for election data are choropleth map and tile grid map. This is because the election data concerns about the sensitivity of geographic and values of the data. Choropleth map concerns about the geographical sensitive data but not the actual value of the data. However, tile grid map concerns about the value sensitive data but not the geographical data.

From the reviews of election visualization techniques, this study is more suitable to implement the tile grid map because there are 222 parliaments in Malaysia, which each tile can represent different parliament seat. The tile grid map can represents fixed size of tiles and helps the viewer to interpret the map easier as the number of the parliaments is fixed. The study uses a combination of map and bar chart to show the multiple points of views to the viewer using the election data.

3   Hexagon Tile Grid Map Representation

After the reviews, the hexagon tile grid visualization technique is chosen for visualizing the Malaysia election data because the hexagon shape offers more flexible arrangement of the tiles and able to maintain the border of the geographic map. This study uses a combination of HTML, Cascading Stylesheet (CSS), Javascript (JS) and Data Driven Document (D3.js) together with D3.js hexagon plugin - hexbin. The HTML and CSS were used to setup the foundation of the User Interface (UI) of the system while JS and D3.js were used to implement the algorithm flow of the system such as creating and populating the hexagon based on the coordinate data stored in JSON file. The hexbin plugin of D3.js is used to create the hexagon tile for a better coordination. All the outputs in the HTML document is in Simple Vector Graphic (SVG) format produced by D3.js.

3.1   Prepare the Data

The first step in this study is to prepare the data. There are four main data files, which are namely "setting.json", "parliament.json", "election.json" and "demography.json". Data in "setting.json" file includes settings for the SVG elements, settings for hexagon (which is the hexagon radius), the settings for tooltip functionality and lists of colors used in the system including political party color and colors for each state. Most of these settings are used to create the system user interface.

Data in "parliament.json" file include settings for each hexagon that represents each parliament by states. The data includes the state name list of parliaments in the state. For each parliament, it consists of the parliament code, name and the coordinate of the hexagon. The parliament code represents the code that will be used as a key to find the election data related to the parliament in "election.json" file. The hexagon coordinate is x and y coordinates that populate a hexagon that is related to the particular parliament.

Data in "election.json" consists of the actual election data that related to the parliaments. The data include a list of states names and election result for the parliaments. Each result consists of the parliament code, total voters, votes for each political party and the information about the winning party and candidate.

Data in "demographic.json" consists of the demographic information for both state and its parliaments. The demographic data for the states consist of the gender distribution in the state. Besides, it contains the ethnic or race distribution in that parliament. These external files are then called using d3.json() function.

3.2   Plot Hexagon Tile Grid Map

This study implements the pointy-top hexagon and the offset coordinate system that uses the classical 2-dimensional coordinate, x-axis and y-axis. Hexbin plugin is used to implement this offset coordinate system and requires a list of coordinates for the hexagon. From the coordinates, hexbin will create a hexagon path and place the hexagon on the specified coordinates. Furthermore, hexbin will also automatically place a partially overlapping hexagon side by side. Therefore, there will be no partially overlapped hexagon in the visualization. The process of populating the hexagon is retrieving the parliament coordinate data from the "parliament.json". The width and height of the SVG element are initialized based on the setting value retrieved from "setting.json" data file. The hexbin variable initializes the hexbin plugin by setting up the hexagon radius value that retrieved from "setting.json" data file.

3.3   Set State and Tile Color

For each hexagon tile in the map, it is colored to differentiate the states in Malaysia. The initial color codes are stored in the "setting.json" file. However, when the user clicks on the state, it will cause the selected state to change the color of each hexagon to certain color in order to differentiate the wining party of the parliaments in the state. In this study, there are four different colors to differentiate the main political parties in Malaysia. For instance, light blue represents The Alliance of Hope (Pakatan Harapan/PH), dark blue represents The National Front (Barisan Nasional/BN), green represents Malaysian Islamic Party (Parti Islam Se-Malaysia/PAS), and grey color for other parties.

3.4   Set State Labels

Then it follows by setting up all the state labels with names. The labeling process is implemented after all the hexagon tiles are plotted into the map. The text in the label is based on the state label, which is stored in "parliament.json". The initialization of label style such as the font-weight, text-shadow, fill-text, cursor and pointer-event are set.

3.5 Set Event Listeners

The following step is to complete the event listeners for this visualization. The "mouse over" event will be triggered when the viewer hover the pointer over the hexagon tile. Then a tooltip will pop up to show the parliament code and parliament name. The next step is to create "on click" event listener. The event listener for the first level allows the viewer to click on the state, and then a popup board is displayed showing the demography of that state. The demographic information in this level contains the total population of the state and gender distribution. Then it sets up for the transition of zooming of the map so that it focuses on the selected state only. The zoom container is initialized that allows the zoom mechanic of the system.

For the "on click" event listener in the second level, two pie charts that contain election result and ethnic distribution will be displayed in the same popup board. The election result shows the total votes and candidates' names. The ethnic distribution shows the main races in Malaysia, which are Malay, Chinese, Indian, Sabahan, Sarawakian, and others. Finally, the Jason file is integrated in D3.js. It is needed to visualize the hexagon tile grid diagram. The d3.json function is used to load a file and returns its contents as Jason data object.

4   Results and Discussion

This study has created map visualization for Malaysia 2018 Election. Figure 5 shows Malaysia map in hexagonal coordinated format. Each state is labeled by its name and different color. The states are a group of hexagons that represents the parliaments.

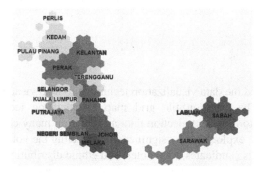

Fig. 5. Malaysia 2018 election visualization. (Color figure online)

The map also can be toggled from the state view to the parliament view. Thus, the viewer can click on the hexagon tile, a pie chart will show the involved parties and political candidates together with the party that they represent and the number of votes won by that candidate in that particular parliament. Besides, the hexagon will change its color to the winning party. Moreover, when the viewer hovers over the hexagon tile, the visual will pop up the parliament code and name. A bar chart is used to communicate the most basic things of the election data, which is the ethnic distribution for each parliament as displayed in Fig. 6.

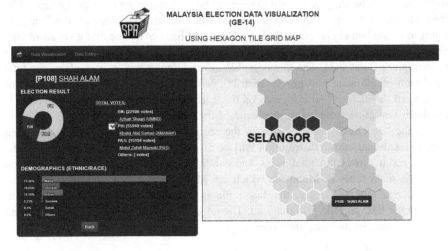

Fig. 6. Election result and ethnic distribution. (Color figure online)

This simple color map visualization presents more granular data to reflect the results of Malaysia 2018 General Election. It eases the exploration and interpretation of election data by providing a quick overview of winning parties in the particular state, the winning candidates, distribution of votes, and distribution of ethnic. It helps the associated agencies indirectly to analyze the voting pattern based on the demographic distribution.

5   Conclusion

This study has applied the data visualization technique to help visualize Malaysia 2018 General Election. The hexagon tile grid map visualization technique shows the potential to be used to represent election data as shown in many countries. It helps to promote creative data exploration by significantly reflecting the voting pattern between the political parties, its candidates, total votes, and ethnic distribution. The hexagon tile grid map visualization helps Malaysian to view the election result more interactively. The map can be toggled from the state view to the parliament view. Thus, the viewer can click on the hexagon tile to view the political parties, its candidates together with the number of votes won by that candidate in that particular parliament. Therefore, with the help of visuals, the viewer can interpret easily the election result in Malaysia.

Acknowledgments. The authors would like to thank Faculty of Computer and Mathematical Sciences, Universiti Teknologi MARA for sponsoring this paper.

References

1. Ephrati, A.: Buyers Beware: Data Visualization is Not Data Analytics (2017). https://www.sisense.com/blog/buyers-beware-data-visualization-not-data-analytics/
2. Gillett, R.: Why We're More Likely To Remember Content With Images and Video (Infographic) (2014). https://www.fastcompany.com/3035856/why-were-more-likely-to-remember-content-with-images-and-video-infogr
3. Balm, J.: The power of pictures. How we can use images to promote and communicate science (2014). http://blogs.biomedcentral.com/bmcblog/2014/08/11/the-power-of-pictures-how-we-can-use-images-to-promote-and-communicate-science/
4. Montanez, A. (2016). https://blogs.scientificamerican.com/sa-visual/data-visualization-and-feelings/
5. Desale, D. (2015). https://www.kdnuggets.com/2015/06/top-30-social-network-analysis-visualization-tools.html
6. Krum, R.: Landslide for the "Did Not Vote" Candidate in the 2016 Election! (2017). http://coolinfographics.com/blog/tag/politics
7. Abdullah, N.A.S., Wahid, N.W.A., Idrus, Z.: Budget visual: malaysia budget visualization. In: Mohamed, A., Berry, M.W., Yap, B.W. (eds.) SCDS 2017. CCIS, vol. 788, pp. 209–218. Springer, Singapore (2017). https://doi.org/10.1007/978-981-10-7242-0_18
8. Su-lyn, B.: How Malaysian politicians use big data to profile you (2017). http://www.themalaymailonline.com/malaysia/article/how-malaysian-politicians-use-big-data-to-profile-you#BYKLuqkk0vepBkUs.97
9. Pepinsky, T.: Ethnic politics and the challenge of PKR (2013). https://cpianalysis.org/2013/04/29/ethnic-politics-and-the-challenge-of-pkr/
10. Nehru, V.: Understanding Malaysia's Pivotal General Election (2013). http://carnegieendowment.org/2013/04/10/understanding-malaysia-s-pivotal-general-election#chances
11. Zairi, M.: Politik Pulau Pinang: Imbasan Keputusan Pilihanraya Umum 2008 & 2004 (2011). http://notakanan.blogspot.my/2011/08/politik-pulau-pinang-imbasan-keputusan.html
12. Lilley, C.: The 2016 US Election: Beautifully Clear Data Visualization (2016). http://www.datalabsagency.com/articles/2016-us-election-beautifully-clear-data-visualization/
13. U.K. Election (2017). https://www.bloomberg.com/graphics/2017-uk-election/
14. Australian House of Representatives (2016). https://ausvotes.withgoogle.com/?center=-26.539285,131.314157
15. India 2014 Election Data Visualization (2014). http://blog.gramener.com/1755/design-of-the-2014-election-results-page

A Computerized Tool Based on Cellular Automata and Modified Game of Life for Urban Growth Region Analysis

Siti Z. Z. Abidin[1]($\boxtimes$), Nur Azmina Mohamad Zamani[2]($\boxtimes$), and Sharifah Aliman[1]

[1] Advanced Analytics Engineering Centre, Faculty of Computer and Mathematical Sciences, Universiti Teknologi MARA, 40450 Shah Alam, Selangor, Malaysia
{zaleha,sharifahali}@tmsk.uitm.edu.my
[2] Faculty of Computer and Mathematical Sciences, Universiti Teknologi MARA Perak Branch, Tapah Campus, 35400 Tapah Road, Perak, Malaysia
azmina@uitm.edu.my

Abstract. There are many factors that can affect the urban growth and it has great implications towards socio-economic for the related areas. Usually, the urban planning and monitoring are performed and administered by the local authorities for improvement and development purposes. This research focuses on analyzing the urban growth of Klang Valley in Malaysia (a developing country), where this is the most rapid growth area in the country. This area is divided into ten districts with different management and development plans. This work proposes a computing tool that applies cellular automata and modified game of life techniques to perform detailed analysis on urban expansion of Klang Valley area based on temporal imagery datasets. As a case study, satellite images were taken from different years where the prediction can be observed within fifteen years duration. The cellular automata technique is used for extracting high details of aerial images based on every pixel, while the modified game of life is for analyzing urban expansion. Based on the analysis, the pattern of the growth in any selected region in the area can be identified and the urban planners for each district can work together, discuss and make decision for monitoring, changes and development of Klang Valley.

Keywords: Cellular automata · Computerized tool · Game of life
Satellite images · Urban growth analysis

1 Introduction

Malaysia, as a developing country, continues to transform non-urban areas into urban. The needs to monitor and make decision for the development are significant. The area which experienced the most urban growth is in Klang Valley, the selected area analyzed in this study. It covers the area of ten districts with each administered by local authorities. Urban growth uncertainly becomes the origin of socio-economic and environmental issues. Consequently, the issues lead to degeneration quality of life of

© Springer Nature Singapore Pte Ltd. 2019
B. W. Yap et al. (Eds.): SCDS 2018, CCIS 937, pp. 374–386, 2019.
https://doi.org/10.1007/978-981-13-3441-2_29

the urban dwellers in which, by the importance rights, obligatory to be avoided [1]. Thus, detection and prediction of urban growth is necessary and the necessity to have computerized tools to solve the issues and avoid incoming difficulties effectively. By analyzing the growth pattern, urban planners for each district can have significant information for making any decision regarding any changes or development of the related areas. Each area might have different case from others due to its governing regulation.

This work is a continuation of the previous methods on computerized tools [2–4]. The main improvements are on proposing new techniques and focusing the analysis not only the whole area, but also dividing the area into several regions based on the urban sprawl patterns. In order to get the detailed analysis on the imagery datasets, different region has different calculated weight based on interpolation levels. Thus, the results show the degree of accuracy has increased which give more benefits for urban planners to monitor the urban expansion.

This paper is divided into five Sections: Sect. 2 discusses on the related work while Sect. 3 describes the design of computerized tool that integrates cellular automata and modified game of life techniques. Next, Sect. 4 presents the results and analysis before the concluding remarks in Sect. 5.

2 Related Work

Change in landscape has been proven to have relationship with environmental degradation. The same goes to socio-economic because if the change in landscape has the relationship to environmental degradation, it also has the same relationship to socio-economic due to the complementary factors. For example, in Selangor, Malaysia, about ten years ago, there is approximately 70% of natural land such as agriculture field has been transformed to built-up land which probably brings huge impact towards natural ecosystem [5]. The result obtained from grid-based method which highlights spatial changes structurally. The estimation is based on fixed size grid to estimate the proportion category of an area. Urban growth pattern is closely related to urban sprawl. There are few types of elementary urban sprawl which are low-density (radial), ribbon and leapfrog sprawl [6] as shown in Fig. 1.

Systematic design usually produces good model of the target area and landscape. By modeling, options can be generated to meet the urban planner development needs with alternatives. The generated growth patterns are considered as historical data that also act as the source of future measures to be analyzed and predicted [7].

Several urban growth models have been proposed on analyzing pattern and scenario of several places; spa-tially-explicit logistic regression model for an African city, Kampala [1]. Another location uses SLEUTH model by calibration to show the growth coefficients for geographical constraints of mountain slopes in China. In this model, the index and spatial extent of coefficient are adjusted constantly to match the urban areas with its real form [8]. Besides in China, SLEUTH model is also applied to simulate future urban growth of Isfahan Metropolitan area from the year 2010 to 2050 in Iran [9]. Cellular automata (CA) has also been combined with Landscape Expansion Index (LEI) method for the urban growth simulation. This LEI-CA model was also used to

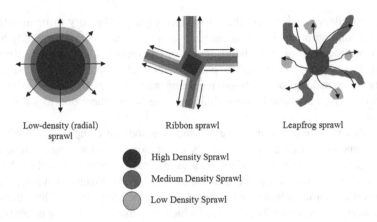

Low-density (radial) sprawl   Ribbon sprawl   Leapfrog sprawl

High Density Sprawl

Medium Density Sprawl

Low Density Sprawl

Fig. 1. Types of urban sprawl [6]

analyze the urban expansion in Dongguan, southern China [10]. Furthermore, an integrated Markov Chains-Cellular Automata (MC-CA) urban growth model is used to predict the growth of the megacity in Mumbai, India for the years 2020 to 2030 [11].

From the preliminary studies, most urban growth model applies cellular automata. Hence, this work combines cellular automata and modified game of life techniques for urban growth analysis.

3 Method for Computing Tool

In order to develop the urban growth system, an engineering method is applied to produce efficiency of system performance and structure. The components involved are system design, data collection and pre-processing and the application of modified game of life technique.

3.1 System Design Overview

This work uses spiral method that allows systematic design and implementation. During the development phase, there are four core stages. The first stage is requirement specification. This is a planning process where the cellular automata and modified game of life are explored to apply during the implementation part. Moreover, the flow of the system is designed for implementation purpose. In the second stage, prototype and implementation are involved based on the system flow by using a programming language. After the system is designed and implemented, testing is performed for the produced output. This test is necessary to ensure that the accuracy, effectiveness and efficiency of the whole system are acceptable. Finally, the results are observed and analyzed in accordance to the system objectives. The final results will produce the percentage of the process accuracy. The system design overview is shown in Fig. 2.

Among the whole process, getting the datasets and performing data pre-processing are the most important parts in the design.

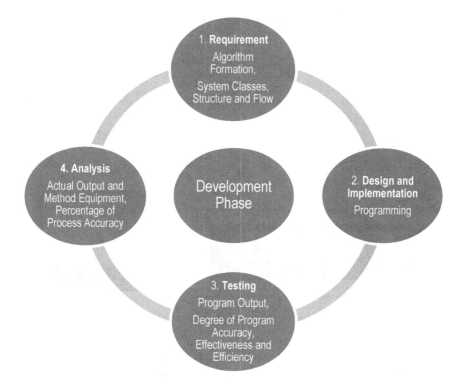

Fig. 2. System design overview

3.2 Data Collection and Pre-processing

Pre-processing is the first step which scans input images to extract meaningful information and obtain the images of growth patterns. From the collected data which is the satellite images (originally black and white), pixels, regions and transformation patterns of the images are identified by using cellular automata technique. Cellular automata have a finite amount of discrete spatial and temporal cells where each cell has its own state. This state can evolve according to its transition rules. In addition, digital images contain a set of cells called pixels.

Comparisons will be made towards each consecutive image to mainly achieve growth pattern between years. If there are three input images which are 1994, 1996 and 2000, the comparison will process 1994 with 1996 and 1996 with 2000. Therefore, if there is N total number of input images, the total number of growth pattern will be N − 1. Since each image is in binary form and two images are involved, comparison has to address four types of cases as shown in Table 1.

Based on Table 1, the pattern growth has different color for different cases. These colors are used to distinguish the regions with different states. Moreover, each of the color has its own index. Figure 3 shows an example of the growth pattern image for the year 1996 and 2000.

Table 1. The types of cases for image comparisons.

Image	State			
	Case 1	Case 2	Case 3	Case 4
Old image	Urban ☐	Non-urban ■	Urban ☐	Non-urban ■
New image	Urban ☐	Urban ☐	Non-urban ■	Non-urban ■
Pattern growth	Urban ■	Transformed ☐	Reverse transformed ☐	Non-urban ☐

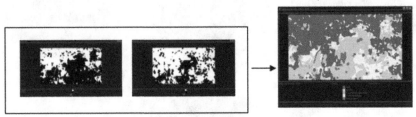

Fig. 3. An example of urban growth image (Color figure online)

From Fig. 3, it can be observed that some parts of the region has a transition from non-urban (black) to urban (white) and the transition, which is the growth pattern, is represented in colors. Red represents no change in the urban growth for the urban area. Green denotes no change in urban growth for the non-urban area. Yellow shows the change in urban growth, while grey represents otherwise. With the distinct color representation, users can identify and observe significant information quickly.

3.3   Technique: Cellular Automata and Modified Game of Life

Cellular Automata consists of cell, states, neighbourhood and transition rules. Game of life is a subset of cellular automata with the concept of living in real life. It is governed by several rules which are birth, survival and death. This concept is applied for analyzing and predicting the urban growth patterns. For this work, the living entity is the urban area which has growth expansion and survivability. In our case, death is impossible as urban areas will never become non-urban in which the Game of Life is modified by eliminating the death rule. Thus, cell survivability relies under the condition of its eight neighbouring cells which is known as Moore neighbourhood [12]. After required pixels have been detected, analysis and prediction are performed. The Game of Life rules are summarized as follows:

1. Birth: A cell (the center cell) will birth from dead state (non-existence state) if there is exactly three alive neighbours.

2. Survival: A cell remains alive when there are two or three neighbours alive.

3. Death: A cell will die if there are more than three alive due to overcrowding, or less than two neighbours because of loneliness.

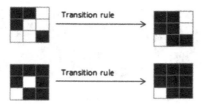

In this research, the Game of life is modified by eliminating Rule 3 (Death) because an urban area will continue to develop in most cases especially when it is applied to a developing area.

3.4 Region Detection

Region detection process is important to understand and show the rate of growth pattern by looking at the region dimension. By combining the cellular automata and modified game of life techniques, all similar states of neighbouring pixels will be clustered in the same region. However, the states which are already in urban condition will not be counted because urban region is meaningless for further processing. Figure 4 shows the region selection, labelled as G, where the selection is based on sprawl patterns.

At this point, region id, region color, total pixels and all coordinates in a region are gathered for later changes in the states. The region id may change over the time according to the urban expansion. Based on the growth patterns, the selected potential pixels are calculated by referring to all connected transformed regions. The transformed regions have its own growth factor to be classified for further processing. Thus, previous growth patterns are used to determine the transformation. Figure 5 depicts the change of growth from the potential pixels.

Information of all the detected regions are kept as a group of coordinates in a text file as shown in Fig. 6. The file can be considered as a temporary storage for processing purposes. The values of coordinates may vary according to the growth patterns.

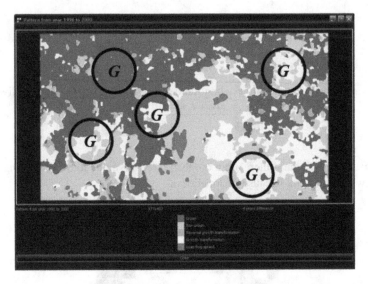

Fig. 4. Sprawl-based region selection

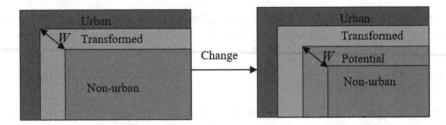

Fig. 5. Change of non-urban pixel to potential pixel

Fig. 6. Coordinates of regions

In Fig. 6, each region's information starts with the region id, region color, total pixels and all coordinates in a region. Each coordinate is separated by the symbol "!" as the delimiter for tokenization process, and it is represented in the form of "[x, y]". Each group of coordinates is within "[" and "]". From these data, the coordinates are displayed in form of different colors for the related regions involved.

4   Results and Analysis

This section presents the user interface of the proposed computerized tool and the output of the system. The use of colors and graphical representations are for user-friendly purposes. On top of map-based visualization, the system also provides media player concept so that the changes in urban expansion can be animated for better analysis.

4.1   User Interface

User interface is one of the important elements in a system design. Several icons are provided in the user interface for convenience and easiness. Figure 7 illustrates a few basic icons provided by the system to initiate the system.

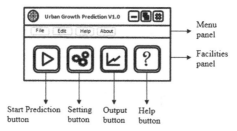

Fig. 7. Main system interface

There are four buttons in the main interface; *Start Prediction button. Setting button, Output button*, and *Help button*. The *Start Prediction button* is for starting a process, while the *Setting button* is to change colors. The *Output button* displays the analyzed images and system output. The *Help button* is to list the user guide.

Once the *Start Prediction button* is chosen, a new panel interface will appear to get the input data from data files. Figure 8 shows different panels that involve in this stage.

Figure 8(a) illustrates the panel with the selection for users to upload at least two image files (with different years) at a time. This allows the system to have at least two datasets for before and after conditions of the urban growth. After uploading the necessary files, users can click *Next* button to start the data processing as shown in Fig. 8(b). When the process interface appears, user can start the analysis and prediction. Preprocessing will be initialized first, followed by growth detection and lastly, urban prediction. The system also provides the concept of media player to allow users to observe the growth transformation through animation. Therefore, components such as screen label, play, pause, and stop button are provided in the output interface.

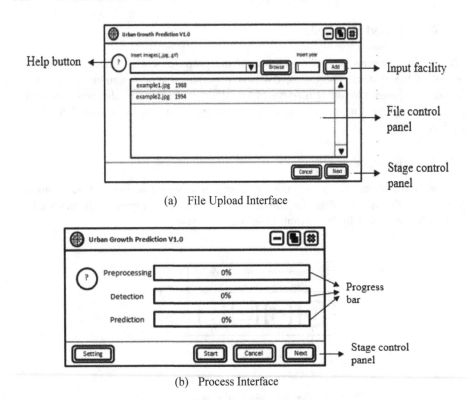

(a) File Upload Interface

(b) Process Interface

Fig. 8. Interface for selecting *Start Prediction Button*

4.2 Outcome

Every growth pattern will be processed to be in either urban or non-urban condition. Figure 9 denotes the significant key colors for representing all possible cases on the output map. There are three basic colors during the pre-processing process, which are red for urban pixel, green for non-urban, and if there is any transformation occurs to a pixel, that pixel will be represented as yellow. Other colors are added for the analysis (detection and prediction) phases to consider other cases. For example, the urban pixel is selected as potential pixel, it will be recolored to potential color as blue.

All state of pixels will also be recolored in gradient including the potential pixel to illustrate their change in time and the density of region. The indication in respect to time is stated in Table 2. The main purpose is to obtain more detailed information and better accuracy in the analysis.

In order to get the total growth, a growth factor is needed to calculate the affected regions. Hence, growth factor is produced by calculating the total number of affected pixels (transformed) and divides by the total of all pixels in the regions with similar growth pattern. This is summarized into the following formula:

Cases	Colors		Change
1	Urban		
2	Transformed		Urban
3	Leap frog sprawl		
5	Growth		
6	Potential		Non-urban
7	Non-urban		
8	Reverse transformed		

Fig. 9. Key colors of growth pattern (Color figure online)

Table 2. Indication of color gradient to time phase of pattern image.

State	Darker	Lighter
Urban	Newer	Older
Non-urban	Undetermined	Undetermined
Transformed	Older	Newer
Reverse transformed	Older	Newer
Leap frog sprawl	Older	Newer
Potential	Higher growth possibility	Low growth possibility

$$\textit{Growth Factor} = \frac{\text{Total neighbourhod pixels in a particular urban region}}{\text{Total of all pixels in all similar growth pattern urban regions}}.$$

After the growth factor was obtained, it is then multiplied by the total number of pixels in the transformed region. The formula is as follows:

$$\textit{Total Growth} = \text{Total pixels of transformed region} * \text{Growth Factor}$$

In addition, the result of the growth prediction will be less accurate if the distance between previous year's growth pattern and current year's growth pattern is far. After all processes are performed, the output result will be in a series of images illustrating the growth change patterns associated with the related years. This is shown in Fig. 10.

From the images, the similarity percentage will be calculated to show the correctness of the system as compared to the ground truth measurements. In order to get the similarity percentage, the difference between predicted images and real images are divided by the real image.

Processes   Result

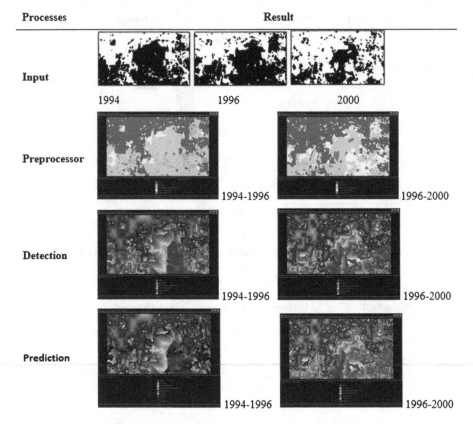

Fig. 10. Series of images of growth pattern analysis

Similarity percentage = (|Predicted Image−Real Image|)/Real Image

Besides static views of the growth pattern image, the change of colors can also be observed as the animation is produced. If the input size is big, the image will be resized to smaller scale. The output interface compresses all the important results to ease the user to analyze prediction. Therefore, Fig. 11 shows the output interface comprising animation panel, graph and time axis.

The animation will show the growth of the areas throughout the fifteen years duration. Besides displaying the change of colors, the populated graph is also being shown. Therefore, by having multiple ways of displaying the output results, the analysis can be performed and displayed in a more detailed and accurate way.

As a summary, static images of growth pattern using the three basic colors is to show the main transformation of the regions involved whereas by adding gradient colors, a more detailed cases can be observed. From the static output images, the results are enhanced to be visualized in a form of animation to show the growth change automatically throughout the selected years.

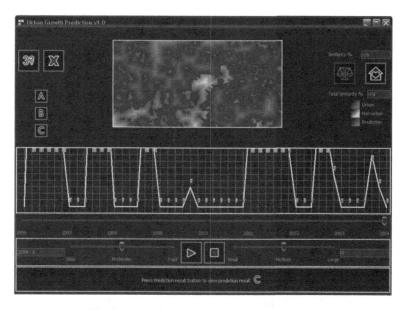

Fig. 11. Animation panel, graph and time axis.

5   Discussion and Conclusion

In this paper, a computerize tool for urban growth analysis and prediction is presented. Even though, a few tools have been proposed, this tool integrates cellular automata and modified game of life to analyze every pixel in the imagery datasets. In addition, the whole study area is divided into several regions with different growth patterns are identified and assigned different weight values. The division, which is based on the urban sprawl pattern, allows unique and complex analyses on the growth rate. These details differences allow more accurate interpolation level for predicting potential changes that might occur for the incoming years. Even though, there are many factors that can affect the urban growth, this approach allows users to analyze the overall urban areas before they can concentrate on looking into details of specific influential factors that cause a change to particular area. In general, this tool can assist all the local authorities to work together to perform systematic planning. Moreover, this algorithm has been embedded into a software tool. The prediction accuracy has also improved that provide the range of 75% to 95% as compared to previous (work) maximum accuracy rate of 93%. Since one region is divided into many regions, the analysis of pixels is performed in more detail which produced a better accuracy.

Acknowledgement. The authors would like to thank Universiti Teknologi MARA (UiTM) and Ministry of Education, Malaysia (600-RMI/DANA 5/3/REI (16/2015)) for the financial support. Our appreciation also goes to Mr. Mohd Ridzwan Zulkifli for his contribution on the programming.

References

1. Vermeiren, K., Van Rompaey, A., Loopmans, M., Serwajja, E., Mukwaya, P.: Urban growth of Kampala Uganda: pattern analysis and scenario development. Landscape and Urban Planning **106**, 199–206 (2012)
2. Abidin, S.Z., Jamaluddin, M.F., Abiden, M.Z.: Introducing an intelligent computerized tool to detect and predict urban growth pattern. WSEAS Trans. Comput. **9**(6), 604–613 (2010)
3. Ab Ghani, N.L., Abidin, S.Z., Abiden, M.Z.Z.: Generating transition rules of cellular automata for urban growth prediction. Int. J. Geol. **5**(2), 41–47 (2011)
4. Ghani, N.L.A., Abidin, S.Z.Z.: A modified landscape expansion index algorithm for urban growth classification using satellite remote sensing image. Adv. Sci. Lett. **24**(3), 1843–1846 (2018)
5. Abdullah, S.A., Nakagoshi, N.: Changes in landscape spatial pattern in the highly developing state of Selangor, Peninsular Malaysia. Landsc. Urban Plan. **77**, 263–275 (2006)
6. Sudhira, H.S., Ramachandra, T.V., Wytzisk, A., Jeganathan, C.: Framework for Integration of Agent-based and Cellular Automata Models for Dynamic Geospatial Simulations. Indian Institute of Science, Bangalore (2005)
7. Xian, G., Crane, M., Steinwand, D.: Dynamic modeling of tampa bay urban development using parallel computing. Compt. Geosci. **31**, 920–928 (2005)
8. Xie, Y., Ma, A., Wang, H.: Lanzhou urban growth prediction based on cellular automata. Paper Supported by National Basic Research Program of China (2009)
9. Bihamta, N., Soffianian, A., Fakheran, S., Gholamalifard, M.: Using the SLEUTH urban growth model to simulate future urban expansion of the Isfahan metropolitan area, Iran. J. Indian Soc. Remote. Sens. **43**(2), 407–414 (2015)
10. Liu, X., Ma, L., Li, X., Ai, B., Li, S., He, Z.: Simulating urban growth by integrating landscape expansion index (LEI) and cellular automata. Int. J. Geogr. Inf. Sci. **28**(1), 148–163 (2014)
11. Moghadam, H.S., Helbich, M.: Spatiotemporal urbanization processes in the megacity of Mumbai, India: a Markov chains-cellular automata urban growth model. Appl. Geogr. **40**, 140–149 (2013)
12. Moore, P.W.: Zoning and Neighbourhood Change: the Annex in Toronto, 1900–1970. Can. Geogr./Le Géographe Can. **26**(1), 21–36 (1982)

Staff Employment Platform (StEP) Using Job Profiling Analytics

Ezzatul Akmal Kamaru Zaman[✉],
Ahmad Farhan Ahmad Kamal, Azlinah Mohamed, Azlin Ahmad,
and Raja Aisyah Zahira Raja Mohd Zamri

Faculty of Computer and Mathematical Sciences, Universiti Teknologi MARA,
Shah Alam, Selangor, Malaysia
{ezzatul,azlinah,azlin}@tmsk.uitm.edu.my

Abstract. Staff Employment Platform (StEP) is a web-based application which employed machine learning engine to monitor Human Resource Management in hiring and talent managing. Instead of using the conventional method of hiring, StEP engine is built using decision tree classification technique to select the most significant skillsets for each job position intelligently, together with classifying the best position. The engine will then rank and predict competent candidate for the selected position with specific criteria. With the ranking method, the weightage of the profile skillset, qualification level and year of experience are summed up. Subsequently, this sum will be resulting in the competency percentage which is calculated by using a Capacity Utilization Rate formula. The proposed formula is designed and tested specifically for this problem. With the accuracy of 63.5% of Decision Tree classification, the integration of machine learning engine and ranking methods using Capacity Utilization Rate in StEP provides a feature to assist the company recruiters in optimizing candidates ranking and review the most competent candidates.

Keywords: Classification · Data analytics and visualization · Data science
Decision tree · Human resources management · SAS Viya · User profiling

1 Introduction

In recent years, job searching applications have brought much ease for job seekers. However, Human Resources (HR) officials face a challenging task in recruiting the most suitable job candidate(s). It is crucial for Human Resources Management (HRM) to hire the right employee because the success of any business depends on the quality of their employees. To achieve the company's goal, HRM needs to find job candidates that fit with the vacant position's qualifications, and it is not an easy task [1]. Besides that, the company's candidate selection strategy model is often changing for every company [2]. Competent talents are vital to business in this borderless global environment [3]. Even for a competent recruiter or interviewer, choosing the right candidate(s) is challenging [4]. In this era of Big Data and advancement in computer technology, the hiring process can be made to be easier and more efficient.

© Springer Nature Singapore Pte Ltd. 2019
B. W. Yap et al. (Eds.): SCDS 2018, CCIS 937, pp. 387–401, 2019.
https://doi.org/10.1007/978-981-13-3441-2_30

Based on leading social career website, LinkedIn, in the first quarter of 2017, more than 26,000 jobs were offered in Malaysia, where an estimate of 1029 jobs was related to computer sciences field. In April 2017, about 125 job offers were specifically for the data science field. According to the Malaysia Digital Economy Corporation (MDEC) Data Science Competency Checklist 2017, Malaysia targets to produce about16,000 data professionals by the year 2020 including 2,000 trained data scientists.

HR would have to be precise about what criteria they need to evaluate in hiring even though they are not actually working in the field. This can be done by doing a thorough analysis, converted into an analytical trend, or chart from the previous hiring. Hence, this will significantly assist HR in the decision making of job candidates recruitment [5].

In the era of Big Data Analytics, the three main job positions most companies are seeking recently are Data Engineer, Data Analyst and Data Scientist. This study aims to identify the employment criteria the three job position in Data Science by using data analytics and user profiling. We proposed and evaluated a Staff Employment system (StEP) that analyzes the user profiles to select the most suitable candidate(s) for the three data science job position. This system can assist Human Resource Management in finding the best-qualified candidate(s) to be called for interview and to recruit them if they are suitable for the job position. The data is extracted from social career websites. User profiling is being used to determine the pattern of interest and trends where different gender, age and social class have a different interest in a particular market [6]. By incorporating online user profiling in StEP platform, HRM can cost in job advertising and time in finding and recruiting candidates. An employee recruiting system can make it easier for recruiters to match candidates' profiles with the needed skills and qualification for the respective job position [7].

To recruit future job candidates, HRM may have to evaluate user profiles from social career websites like LinkedIn and Jobstreet (in Malaysia). StEP directly use data from these websites and run user profiling to get the required information. This information is then passed to the StEP' classification engine for prediction of the suitability of the candidates based on the criteria required. Based on the user profiles, StEP particularly uses the design of the social website, such as LinkedIn, to evaluate the significance of the user's **skills**, **education or qualification** and **experience** as the three employment criteria.

2 Related Machine Learning Studies

Classification techniques are often used to ease the decision-making process. It is a supervised learning technique to enable class prediction. Classification techniques such as decision tree can identify the essential attributes of a target variable such as Job position, credit risk or churn. Data mining can be used to extract data from the Human Resource databases to transform it into more meaningful and useful information for solving the problem in talent management [8]. Kurniawan et al. used social media dataset and applied Naïve Bayes, Decision Tree and Support Vector Machine (SVM) technique to predict Twitter traffic of word in a real-time pattern. As the result, SVM has the highest classification accuracy for untargeted word, however, Decision tree scores the highest classification accuracy for the targeted words features [9]. Classification has also been used in classifying the action of online shopping consumer. Decision tree (J48) has the second highest accuracy while the highest accuracy belongs to Decision Table classification algorithm [10]. Xiaowei used Decision Tree classification technique to obtain information about the customer on marketing on the Internet [11]. Sarda et al. also use decision tree in finding the most appropriate candidates for the job [12].

According to [13], decision tree also has the balance classification criteria result than other classification technique such as Naïve Bayes, Neural Network, Support Vector Machine. Hence, the result is more reliable and stable in term of classification accuracy and efficiency [14].

Meanwhile, ranking is a method to organize or arrange the result in the order from highest rank to lowest rank (or importance). Luukka and Collan uses the fuzzy method to do ranking in Human Resource selection where the solution is ranked by the weightage assigned for each of it. The best solution is one with the highest weightage. As the result, ranking technique can assist Human Resource Management (selection) in finding the ideal solution (most qualified candidates) for the organization [15]. There also exists a research on Decision Support System (DSS) to be applied in recruiting new employee for the company vacant position. The goal is to decide the best candidates from the calculated weight criteria and criteria itself [16].

In terms of managing interpersonal competition in making decision for a group, Multi Criteria Decision Making(MCDM) is the methods been used to solve it [17]. Recommender system is often being used to assist the user by providing choices of relevant items according to their interest to support the decision making [18].

3   Methods

3.1   Phase I: Data Acquisition by Web Scraping

In this paper, we focus on data science-related jobs, specifically Data Scientists, Data Engineers and Data Analysts. We scraped the profiles of those who are currently in those positions from LinkedIn. We have also specified the users' locations as Malaysia, Singapore, India, Thailand, Vietnam or China. To extract the data from LinkedIn, we performed web scraping using BeautifulSoup in Python. BeautifulSoup is capable of retrieving specific data and then save in any format.

Since the data is highly difficult to be extracted thru online streaming, we saved the offline copy of the data and thoroughly scrapped the details that we need from each page. This way, we can scrape data more cleanly and have control over data saving. The data was saved in CSV format. The raw data extracted were user's name, location, qualification level, skills with endorsements and working experiences measured in years. These are all features available on LinkedIn. A total of 152, 159 and 144 profiles of Data Analyst, Data Engineer and Data Scientist correspondingly have been scrapped. This raw data is saved in. CSV and a sample is shown in Fig. 1 below where each file has a various number of profiles per one run of the Python coding. It also contains some missing values such as profiles without education, experience or skills details. After data extraction, the data was kept in a structured form.

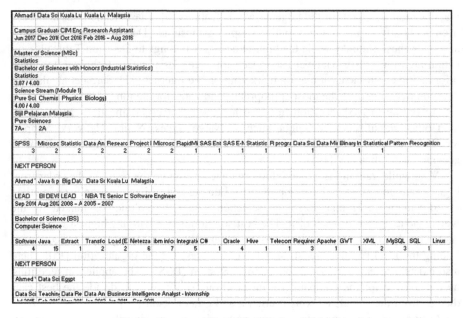

Fig. 1. Sample of data collected from LinkedIn

3.2   Phase 2: Data Preparation and Pre-processing

Data Pre-processing

The raw data is merged and carefully put into three tables containing the dataset for each job position; Data Scientist, Data Engineer and Data Analyst. From all of the datasets, each of the profiles has a various number of skillset, and some of the skillsets does not apply to the data science field, making it hard to implement in the system for determining which skillset is the most important to the data science field. To solve this problem, a sample of 20 per cent of the total profiles was taken randomly using SAS Viya 'Sampling' feature to identify which skills appeared the most in each of the profiles, such as data analysis, Big Data, Java and more. This process is called features identification.

In this phase, the data itself must be consistent, where situations like if a data scientist lists down his 'Carpenter' skills in his profile, the word Carpenter' has to be removed. Therefore, pruning of features must be done towards the skills stated for each user in the dataset. This is to get a reliable set of features for classification phase later. We upload the data into SAS Viya to produce two graphs to prune the skills feature by removing any skills with ≤ 5 number of profiles. Figure 2 shows the sampled dataset while Figs. 3 and 4 present the data samples before and after the pruning process. The profiles with missing values are removed hence the data is now cleaned and ready for further processing.

#	Name	Position	Location	Experiences (Years)	Education Level	Analytics	Azure	Big data
1	Ali Seyed Shirkhorsh	Sr. Data Scientist	Kuala Lumpur, Malaysia	5.25	Ph.D.			
2	Amin Jula	Senior Data Scientist / Train	Kuala Lumpur, Malaysia	9.67	Ph.D.			
3	Bilal Farooq	Head of Data Science	Selangor, Malaysia	14.82	Master	54		
4	Charles Martin	Data Scientist & Machine Le	San Francisco, United State	16	Ph.D.	36		9
5	Matteo Testi	Senior Data Science | Deep L	Rome, Italy	4.67	Master		14	
6	Muhammad Nazmi	Aspiring data scientist with	Kelantan, Malaysia	1.33	Bachelor's degree	2		
7	Nabilla Farhani	Data Scientist Business Frau	Kuala Lumpur, Malaysia	7.33	Bachelor's degree	2		
8	Poo Kuan Hoong	Data Scientist	Kuala Lumpur, Malaysia	19.33	Ph.D.			
9	Shahram Sabzevari	Data Scientist | Full Stack De	Kuala Lumpur, Malaysia	17.92	Master			
10	Wing Yuen Loon	Data Science & Innovation	Kuala Lumpur, Malaysia	29	Master	37		
11	Vincent Granville	Pioneering Data Scientist	Seattle, United States of Am	22.17	Ph.D.	99		9
12	Wayne Vovil	Chief Data Scientist / Hadoo	Vietnam	18	Certificate	33		9
13	Ronak Talreja	Data Scientist at The Data Te	Mumbai, India	4.92	Bachelor's Degree	20		
14	Daniel Tyszka Junio	Data Scientist at Hariken	Curitiba, Brazil	7.67	Bachelor's Degree	3	2	
15	Rishabh Malhotra	Data Scientist	Pune, India	1.67	Bachelor's Degree			
16	Sweekar Tanugula	Senior Data Scientist at GE H	Bengaluru, India	12	Bachelor's Degree	16		
17	Subhajit Gupta	Data Scientist at Emirates N	United Arab Emirates	8.92	Master	22		1
18	Khadir LAMRANI	Data Scientist -Senior-	Marrakech, Morocco	6.33	Master			
19	Neil Eklund	Chief Data Scientist at Schlu	San Francisco, United State	24	Ph.D.	49		
20	Sayali Sonawane	Data Scientist by profession	Maharashtra, India	3.92	Master			
Count				20		12	2	1
Total				234.92		373	16	33
AVG				11.746		31.0833	8	33

Fig. 2. Sample of cleaned dataset

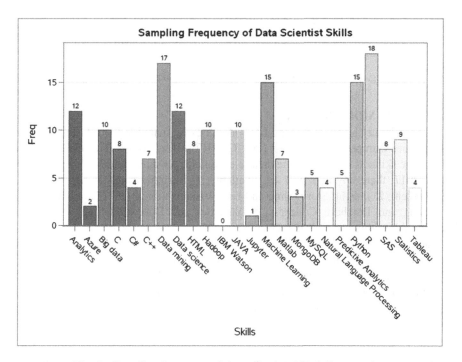

Fig. 3. Sampling frequency of data scientist skills before pruning

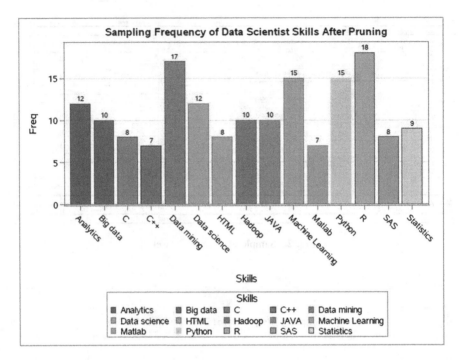

Fig. 4. Sampling frequency of data scientist skills after pruning

Mapping with MDEC Skillsets

Next, we validate the skills that we have identifies by mapping them to the MDEC's Data Science Competency Checklist (DSCC) 2017 skillset groups. This evaluation can confirm the skillsets required in the data science field. As shown in Fig. 5, according to DSCC 2017, there are nine skill sets available; 1. Business Analysis, Approach and Management; 2. Insight, Storytelling and Data Visualization; 3. Programming; 4. Data Wrangling and Database Concepts; 5. Statistics and Data modelling; 6. Machine Learning Algorithms; and 7. Big Data.

Each of the profiles' skillset has endorsement values. The feature is available in every profile of LinkedIn to represent the validation by others for the job candidate's skill as shown in Fig. 6. For this project, we use the endorsement value to determine the competency of the job candidate. This acts as the profile scoring method. This can help us to pinpoint the accurateness of the skillsets that the job candidates claimed they have.

Feature Generation

To properly determine the scores, we have taken the average endorsements from profiles that have endorsements more than 0. Figure 7 shows the average found for Data Scientist skills. To better visualize the scoreboard, the values are summed, and the skills are combined under its main skill group. Data Mining, Excel, R, SAS and statistics skills all belong under 'Statistics and Data Modelling' skill set as shown in Fig. 5. Profiles with endorsement value more than the average will be marked 1 where

Skillsets	MDEC	DS	DE	DA
Business Analysis, Approach and Management	Excel	Exce l	Exce l	Exce l
	Others	Analysis	Analysis	Analysis
Insight, Storytelling and data visualisation	SAS	SAS		
	Others	Analytics		Analytics
Programming	C	C		
	C++	C++		C++
	Java	JAVA	JAVA	JAVA
	Matlab	Matlab		
	Python	Python	Python	Python
	R	R	R	R
	Others	HTML		
Data Wrangling and database concepts	ETL		ETL	
	MongoDB		MongoDB	
	MySQL	MySQL	MySQL	MySQL
	Others	Data Mining	Data Mining	Data Mining
Statistics and data modelling	Data Mining	Data Mining		Data Mining
	Excel	Excel		Excel
	R	R		R
	SAS	SAS		
	SPSS			SPSS
	Others	Statistics		Statistics
Machine learning algorithm	Others	Data mining		
		Data science		
		Machine Learning		
Big Data	Hadoop	Hadoop	Hadoop	
	MongoDB		MongoDB	
	Others	Big data	Big data	
		Data science		

Fig. 5. Skillsets mapped with DSCC skillsets group

Fig. 6. Endorsement feature in LinkedIn

it means the job candidate is 'Highly skilled'. Profiles with endorsement value below than the average will be marked 0, 'Less skilled'. This binary value is called Skill Level feature that is another feature engineered and generated to enhance classification model. Hence, after data cleaning process is done, the sample sizes are 132, 98 and 99 respectively for Data Analyst, Data Engineer and Data Scientist.

3.3 Phase 3: Predictive Modelling and Ranking

In this phase, we performed two models that are predictive modelling and ranking to gain better accuracy in classifying the best position and ranking the most competent job candidates. The ranking is based on the scoring of job skills where a job candidate with the highest competency percentage is considered most eligible to hold the job position.

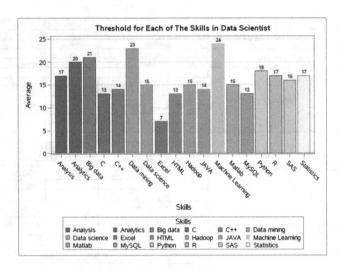

Fig. 7. Bar chart for data scientist skills

First, we calculate the weightage values using Feature Ranking to rank of the skills' score value. Subsequently, predictive modeling is employed where it is done by using classification model adapting decision tree to determine the best job position. Then ranking of job competency is done using Capacity Utilization Rate model. The calculations are explained as follows.

Feature Ranking Process
Each of the skillset group is being identified as the feature of the sample dataset where it comprises a various number of skills. These skills have the value of zero and one indicating the absence or presence of the skill respectively. Each of the skills scores will be summed as the total score for a particular skill set group. The weightage will be determined by the ranking of the skills that are low-rank value for low scores and high-rank value for a higher score. We use decision tree classification to determine the weightage. The skill with the highest importance value is given the highest weightage value. SAS Viya was used to build the decision tree and to determine the weightage for each skill.

We also ranked the qualification level and years of experience. For the qualification level, any job candidate with a professional certificate in data science will most likely be readily accepted in the industry, thus it is weighted as 3. Whereas a postgraduate is weighted 2 and a bachelor's degree graduate is given rank (or weight) of 1. Meanwhile, years of experience of more than 8 years is weighted 3, more than 3 years but less and equal to 8 years is weighted 2 and lastly, less or equal to 3 years is weighted 1.

Predictive Modeling Using Decision Tree
Classification engine is again being used to classify the three data science job position for a candidate. The target variable has three classes: Data Analyst, Data Engineer and Data Scientist. Meanwhile, the input features are the qualification, years of experience, weightage of the seven skillsets group that are 1. Business Analysis, Approach and

Management; 2. Insight, Storytelling and Data Visualization; 3. Programming; 4. Data Wrangling and Database Concepts; 5. Statistics and Data Modelling; 6. Machine Learning Algorithms; and 7. Big Data. This weightage is obtained in feature ranking process above.

Ranking Using Capacity Utilization Rate (CUR)
Then, the ranking is determined by calculating the job candidates' competency regarding their skills, combined with qualification level and years of experience. The job candidates' scores are summed up and calculated using a specific formula that can represent the job candidates' competency percentage. The competency percentage is calculated by using a Capacity Utilization Rate formula as shown in Fig. 8. This formula is adapted and designed specifically for this problem at which the formula is formerly known to be used in industrial and economic purposes.

$$\frac{7(1st\ skillset) + 6(2nd\ skillset) + 5(3rd\ skillset) + \cdots + 1(7th\ skillset)}{7(1st\ skillset\ \max value) + 6(2nd\ skillset\ \max value) + \cdots + 1(7th\ skillset\ \max value)}$$

Fig. 8. Capacity utilization rate

4   Results and Discussion

4.1   Weightage Using Feature Ranking Results

As discussed in 3., the weightage gained from summing the number of people with the skills. It is applied to the skillset groups using feature ranking. Since SAS Visual Analytics uses feature ranking as a measure of decision tree level, an importance rate table is gained, and the weightage is set as per the tree level. The highest importance rate for this data set is Machine Learning Algorithm skillset as shown in Table 1. This will make the weightage for that particular skill is ranked at highest that is 6 followed Big Data is 5, Statistics is 4, Programming is 3, Data Wrangling is 2, and subsequently, Business analysis and, Insight and Data Visualization skillset in which both resulted to 1.

Table 1. Classification weightage for all positions

Variable	Importance
Machine_learning_algorithm	31.7244
Big_Data	28.1628
Statistics_and_data_modelling	7.3953
Programming	3.3391
Data_Wrangling_and_databas_concepts	1.5428
Business_Analysis_Approach_and_Management	0.0000
Insight_Storytelling_and_data_visualization	0.0000

4.2   Classification Results and Discussion

In order to classify into class target that is Data Analyst, Data Engineer and Data Scientist, the data is being fed into SAS Visual Analytics to process the data for the classification engine. Then the tree graph of Decision Tree is produced as represented in Fig. 9. Decision Tree shows the accuracy result that is 63.5%. Figure 10 shows the confusion matrix of Decision Tree engine. Low accuracy of the result may be produced due to the imbalanced cleaned dataset where the sample dataset comprises of a higher number of Data Analyst that is 132 as compared to Data Engineer and Data Scientist with 99 and 98 samples respectively. Not only that, other parameter setting for example different percentage of training and testing set should be considered in order to increase the accuracy result as in this research, 70% training set is used to 30% is used for testing set.

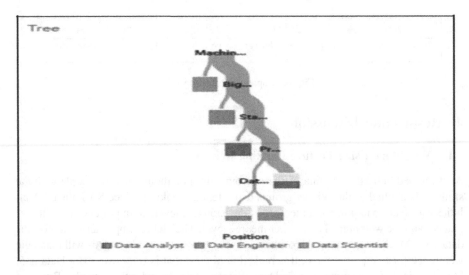

Fig. 9. Decision tree from classification model

4.3   Ranking Using CUR Results

After data position has been determined using classification model, the dataset is summed up for the job candidates' score ranking. Table 2 shows the total of the score for each of the job candidate. Table 3 states the Capacity Utilization Rate calculation and its percentage for each of the job candidates.

After calculating the Capacity Utilization Rate, the percentages are calculated and sorted to determine the best job candidate in the ranking using CUR model. Table 4 represents the ranking of most recommended Data Scientists in Asia. The percentage represents the job candidates' competency for Data Scientist.

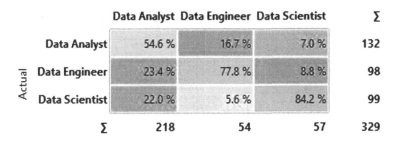

Fig. 10. Confusion matrix of decision tree

Table 2. Sample of data scientist skill score ranking results

#	Name	Exp Weig	QL Weigh	Programm	Machine l	Statistics	Business A	Data Wrar	Big Data	Insight, St	TOTAL
1	Ahmad Hakii	1	2	0	0	0	0	0	0	0	3
2	Ahmad Tarm	3	1	1	0	0	0	0	0	0	11
3	Ali Seyed Shi	2	2	2	0	0	0	1	0	0	21
4	Alireza Hoom	1	2	1	1	3	2	0	1	0	41
5	Amin Jula	3	2	5	2	1	1	1	0	0	64
6	Amir Rafieiar	3	2	1	0	0	0	0	0	0	12
7	Asif Muhamn	3	1	0	1	2	1	2	0	2	32
8	Asiya Bhat	2	1	0	0	0	0	0	0	0	3
9	Aswadi A Rah	3	2	0	0	0	0	0	0	0	5
10	Azizi Aziz	3	2	0	0	0	0	0	0	0	5
11	Bharat Bhush	3	2	0	0	0	0	0	0	0	5
12	Bilal Farooq	3	2	1	1	4	1	2	0	2	50
13	Brian Ho	3	2	1	0	0	1	0	0	0	16
14	Buddhika Sar	3	2	0	0	0	0	0	0	0	5

Table 3. Total score ranking and capacity utilization rate result

#	Name	TOTAL SCORE	TOTAL MAX	C.U.R	%
1	Ahmad Hakii	3	115	0.026087	2.61
2	Ahmad Tarm	11	115	0.095652	9.57
3	Ali Seyed Shi	21	115	0.182609	18.26
4	Alireza Hoom	41	115	0.356522	35.65
5	Amin Jula	64	115	0.556522	55.65
6	Amir Rafieiar	12	115	0.104348	10.43
7	Asif Muhamn	32	115	0.278261	27.83
8	Asiya Bhat	3	115	0.026087	2.61
9	Aswadi A Rah	5	115	0.043478	4.35
10	Azizi Aziz	5	115	0.043478	4.35
11	Bharat Bhush	5	115	0.043478	4.35
12	Bilal Farooq	50	115	0.434783	43.48
13	Brian Ho	16	115	0.13913	13.91
14	Buddhika Sar	5	115	0.043478	4.35
15	Caleb Foong	10	115	0.086957	8.70
16	Canh Tran	25	115	0.217391	21.74

Table 4. Ranking of job candidates

#	Name	Country	Experiences (Years)	Qualification Level	TOTAL SCORE	%
73	Sayali Son	India	3.92	Post Graduate	93	80.87
86	Wayne Vd	Vietnam	18	Certificate	67	58.26
29	Eugene Ya	Singapore	18.5	Post Graduate	66	57.39
59	Omar Sale	India	5.83	Bachelors Degree	65	56.52
5	Amin Jula	Malaysia	9.67	Post Graduate	64	55.65
82	Vala Ali R	Malaysia	15.67	Post Graduate	63	54.78
96	Xavier Co	Singapore	18	Post Graduate	62	53.91
57	Ng Kean C	Malaysia	4	Bachelors Degree	55	47.83
69	Ronak Tal	India	4.92	Bachelors Degree	55	47.83
56	Ng Kean C	Malaysia	3.92	Bachelors Degree	53	46.09
81	Sweekar T	India	12	Bachelors Degree	52	45.22
12	Bilal Faro	Malaysia	14.82	Post Graduate	50	43.48
74	Shahram S	Malaysia	17.92	Post Graduate	50	43.48
17	Chee Bing	Malaysia	4.25	Bachelors Degree	48	41.74
35	Jenna Yan	Malaysia	8.33	Bachelors Degree	48	41.74
92	Weimin W	Singapore	4	Post Graduate	48	41.74
83	Vincent F	Singapore	7.83	Post Graduate	47	40.87

4.4   Data Visualization

Viewing the outcome in tables are very hard to understand, especially to the untrained eye. This is where data visualization comes in handy. In this project, SAS Visual Analytics is used again to produce visualization to see a better result of performing machine learning and analytics upon the data.

Figure 11 represents the number of Data Scientists based on their skillsets. This graph uses the same data from Table 1 to produce the weightage for the analytics calculation. It is found that most of the Data Scientists have programming skills with 51 of them having the skills.

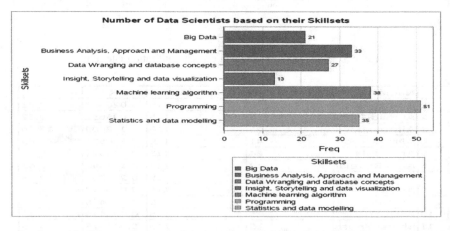

Fig. 11.   Number of data scientists based on their skillsets

4.5 Staff Employment Platform (StEP)

The Staff Employment Platform (StEP) is a web-based job candidate searching platform. For this project, this webpage is used to display the top 10 most suitable job candidates in positions, Data Scientist, Data Engineer and Data Analyst, for the company. From the list, company recruiters can search for the job position that they require and view the job candidates recommended for the position.

StEP provides a feature where the company recruiters can view the job candidates' profile to see their details. Figure 12 shows the list of top 10 most recommended job candidates for Data Scientist which is the result of our complex analytics. Furthermore, through these listings, recruiters are also able to view the job candidates' competency according to their job position and display the skills that the candidate has.

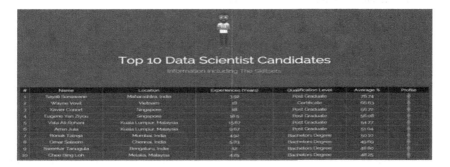

Fig. 12. Top 10 data scientists as job candidates

5 Conclusion

Finding the most suitable employee for a company is a daunting task for the Human Resource Department. Human Resources (HR) have to comb through a lot of information on social-career websites to find the best job candidate to recruit. Staff Employment Platform (StEP) uses SAS Viya in Machine Learning and Visual Analytics to perform job profiling and ranks the competent candidate for data science job positions. Job profiling is better when it is combined with analytics and machine learning, in this case, Classification by using Decision Tree. SAS Viya performs very well in visualizing data and produce clear and understandable charts and graphs as depicted in the sections above. The result is enhanced by using Capacity Utilization Rate formula which is adapted specifically for this problem to do the ranking of competence candidates. As a conclusion, we were able to propose a platform to find the three important criteria needed in the data science field, which are skills, qualification level and years of experience. From job profiles of Data Scientists, Data Engineers and Data Analysts, we were able to perform job profiling and gain thorough analysis of their skills and other important criteria.

Acknowledgement. The authors would like to thank Ministry of Education Malaysia for funding this research project through a Research University Grant; Bestari Perdana 2018 Grant, project titled "Modified Clustering Algorithm for Analysing and Visualizing the Structured and Unstructured Data" (600-RMI/PERDANA 513 BESTARI(059/2018)). Also appreciation goes to the Research Management Center (RMC) of UiTM for providing an excellent research environment in completing this research work. Thanks to Prof Yap Bee Wah for her time in reviewing and validating the result of this paper.

References

1. Mohammed, M.A., Anad, M.M.: Data warehouse for human resource by Ministry of Higher Education and Scientific Research. In: 2014 International Conference on Computer, Communications, and Control Technology (I4CT), pp. 176–181 (2014)
2. Shehu, M.A., Saeed, F.: An adaptive personnel selection model for recruitment using domain-driven data mining. J. Theor. Appl. Inf. Technol. 91(1), 117 (2016)
3. Tajuddin, D., Ali, R., Kamaruddin, B.H.: Using talent strategy as a hedging strategy to manage banking talent risks in Malaysia. Int. Bus. Manag. 9(4), 372–376 (2015)
4. Saat, N.M., Singh, D.: Assessing suitability of candidates for selection using candidates' profiling report. In: Proceedings of the 2011 International Conference on Electrical Engineering and Informatics (2011)
5. Charlwood, A., Stuart, M., Kirkpatrick, I., Lawrence, M.T.: Why HR is set to fail the big data challenge. LSE Bus. Rev. (2016)
6. Farseev, A., Nie, L., Akbari, M., Chua, T.S.: Harvesting multiple sources for user profile learning: a big data study. In: Proceedings of the 5th ACM on International Conference on Multimedia Retrieval, pp. 235–242. ACM, Shanghai (2015)
7. Ahmed, F., Anannya, M., Rahman, T., Khan, R.T.: Automated CV processing along with psychometric analysis in job recruiting process. In: 2015 International Conference on Electrical Engineering and Information Communication Technology (ICEEICT) (2015)
8. Yasodha, S., Prakash, P.S.: Data mining classification technique for talent management using SVM. In: International Conference on Computing, Electronics and Electrical Technologies (ICCEET), pp. 959–963. IEEE (2012)
9. Kurniawan, D.A., Wibirama, S., Setiawan, N.A.: Real-time traffic classification with twitter data mining. In: 2016 8th International Conference on Information Technology and Electrical Engineering (ICITEE), pp. 1–5. IEEE (2016)
10. Ahmeda, R.A.E.D., Shehaba, M.E., Morsya, S., Mekawiea, N.: Performance study of classification algorithms for consumer online shopping attitudes and behavior using data mining. Paper Presented at the 2015 Fifth International Conference on Communication Systems and Network Technologies (2015)
11. Xiaowei, L.: Application of decision tree classification method based on information entropy to web marketing. Paper Presented at the 2014 Sixth International Conference on Measuring Technology and Mechatronics Automation (2014)
12. Sarda, V., Sakaria, P., Nair, S.: Relevance ranking algorithm for job portals. Int. J. Curr. Eng. Technol. 4(5), 3157–3160 (2014)
13. Kotsiantis, S.B., Zaharakis, I., Pintelas, P.: Supervised machine learning: a review of classification techniques. Emerg. Artif. Intell. Appl. Comput. Eng. 160, 3–24 (2007)
14. Mohamed, W.N.H.W., Salleh, M.N.M., Omar, A.H.: A comparative study of Reduced Error Pruning method in decision tree algorithms. Paper Presented at the 2012 IEEE International Conference on Control System, Computing and Engineering (2012)

15. Luukka, P., Collan, M.: Fuzzy scorecards, FHOWA, and a new fuzzy similarity based ranking method for selection of human resources. Paper Presented at the 2013 IEEE International Conference on Systems, Man, and Cybernetics (2013)
16. Khairina, D.M., Asrian, M.R., Hatta, H.R.: Decision support system for new employee recruitment using weighted product method. Paper Presented at the 2016 3rd International Conference on Information Technology, Computer, and Electrical Engineering (ICITACEE) (2016)
17. Rosanty, E.S., Dahlan, H.M., Hussin, A.R.C.: Multi-criteria decision making for group decision support system. Paper Presented at the 2012 International Conference on Information Retrieval & Knowledge Management (2012)
18. Najafabadi, M.K., Mohamed, A.H., Mahrin, M.N.R.: A survey on data mining techniques in recommender systems. Soft Comput. (2017)

Author Index

Printed in the United States
By Bookmasters